[is__]
[bub_]

WOLVERINE BY BENJAMIN PERCY VOL. 1. Contains material originally published in magazine form as WOLVERINE (2020) #1-5. First printing 2020. ISBN 978-1-302-92182-8. Published by MARVEL WORLDWIDE, INC., a subsidiary of MARVEL ENTERTAINMENT, LLC. OFFICE OF PUBLICATION: 1290 Avenue of the Americas, New York, NY 10104. © 2020 MARVEL No similarity between any of the names, characters, persons, and/ or institutions in this magazine with those of any living or dead person or institution is intended, and any such similarity which may exist is purely coincidental. Printed in the U.S.A. KEVIN FEIGE, Chief Creative Officer; DAN BUCKLEY, President, Marvel Entertainment; JOHN NEE, Publisher; JOE QUESADA, EVP & Creative Director; TOM BREVOORT, SVP of Publishing; DAVID BOGART, Associate Publisher & SVP of Talent Affairs; Publishing & Partnership; DAVID GABRIEL, VP of Print & Digital Publishing; JEFF YOUNGQUIST, VP of Production & Special Projects; DAN CARR, Executive Director of Publishing Technology; ALEX MORALES, Director of Publishing Operations; DAN EDINGTON, Managing Editor; RICKEY PURDIN, Director of Talent Relations; SUSAN CRESPI, Production Manager; STAN LEE, Chairman Emeritus. For information regarding advertising in Marvel Comics or on Marvel.com, please contact Vit DeBellis, Custom Solutions & Integrated Advertising Manager, at vdebellis@marvel.com. For Marvel subscription inquiries, please call 888-511-5480. Manufactured between 9/25/2020 and 10/27/2020 by FRY COMMUNICATIONS, MECHANICSBURG, PA, USA.

10 9 8 7 6 5 4 3 2 1

Vol. 1

WOLVERINE

Writer:	Benjamin Percy
Artists:	Adam Kubert (#1A, #2-3) &
	Viktor Bogdanovic (#1B, #4-5)
Color Artists:	Frank Martin (#1A, #2-3) &
	Matthew Wilson (#1B, #4-5)
Letterer:	VC's Cory Petit
Cover Art:	Adam Kubert &
	Frank Martin
Head of X:	Jonathan Hickman
Design:	Tom Muller
Assistant Editors:	Chris Robinson &
	Lauren Amaro
Editor:	Jordan D. White
Collection Editor:	Jennifer Grünwald
Assistant Managing Editor:	Maia Loy
Assistant Managing Editor:	Lisa Montalbano
Editor, Special Projects:	Mark D. Beazley
VP Production & Special Projects:	Jeff Youngquist
SVP Print, Sales & Marketing:	David Gabriel
Editor in Chief:	C.B. Cebulski

[dawn_of_x]

[best__]
[there_]

[is__]
[bub_]

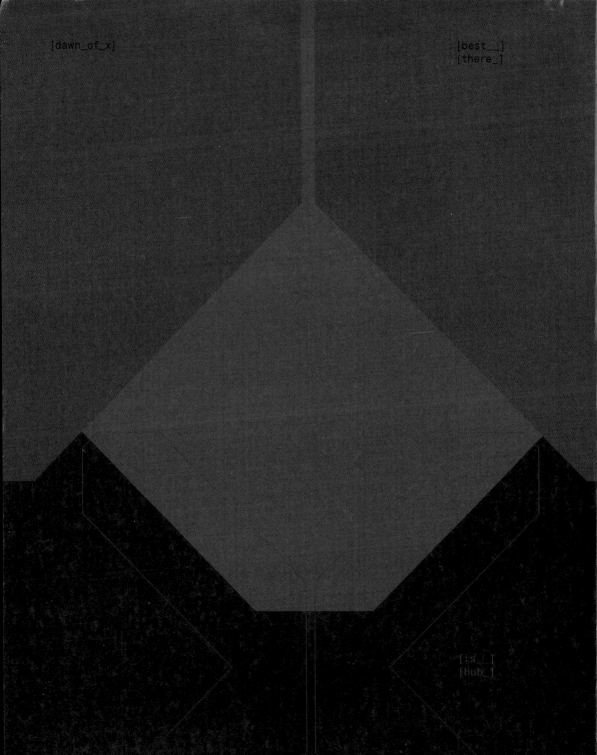

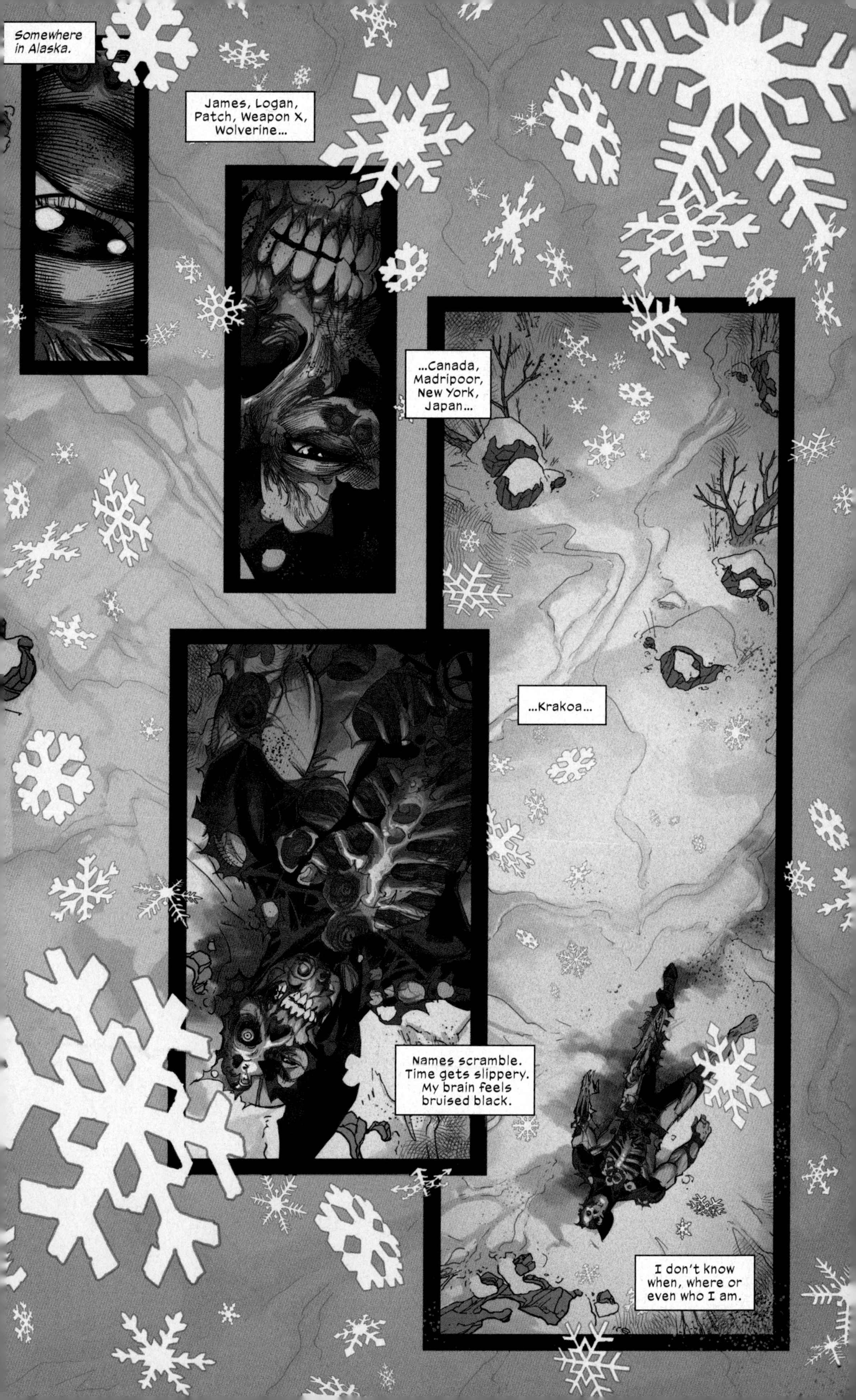
Somewhere in Alaska.
James, Logan, Patch, Weapon X, Wolverine...
...Canada, Madripoor, New York, Japan...
...Krakoa...
Names scramble. Time gets slippery. My brain feels bruised black.
I don't know when, where or even who I am.

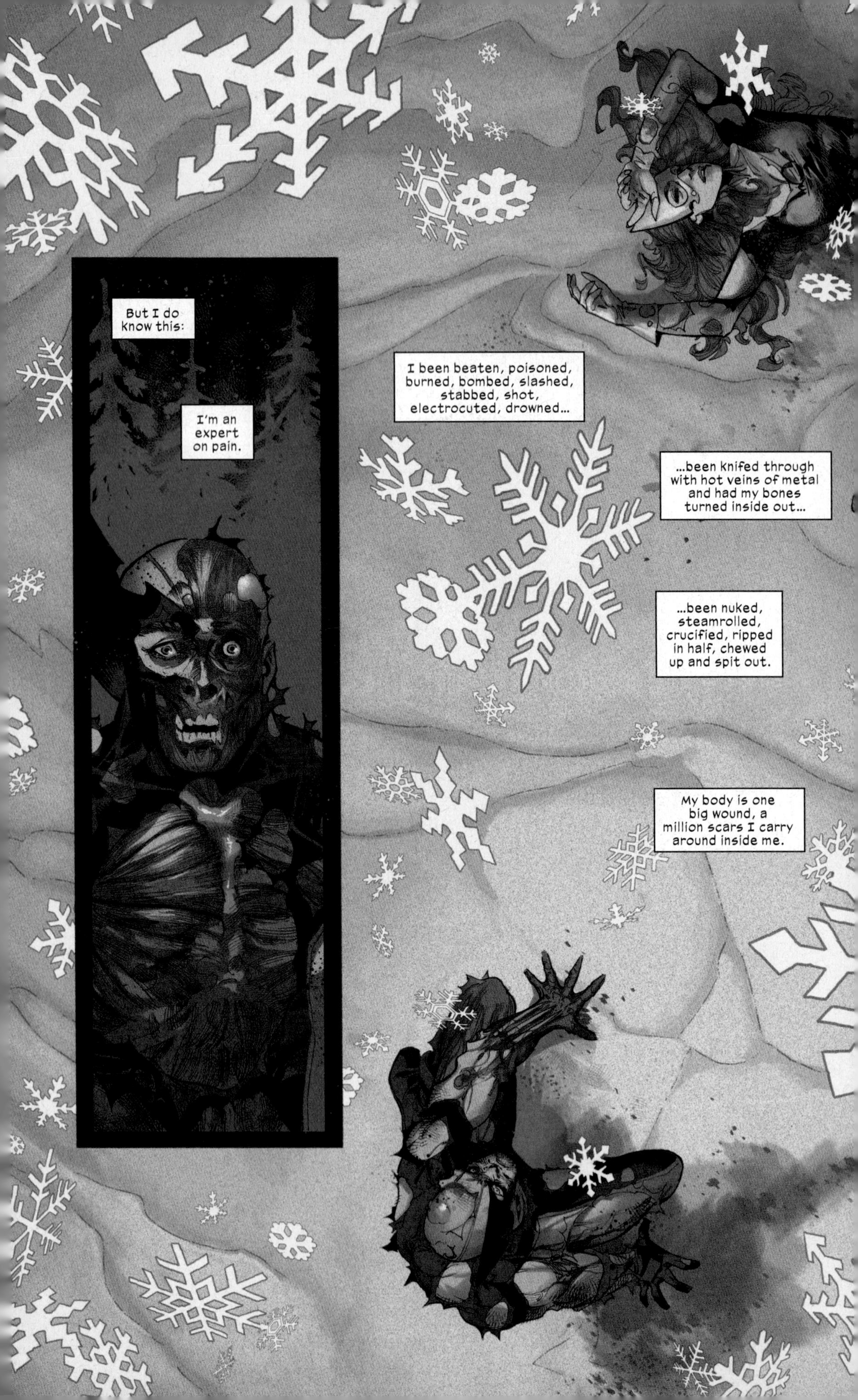

But I do know this:
I'm an expert on pain.
I been beaten, poisoned, burned, bombed, slashed, stabbed, shot, electrocuted, drowned...
...been knifed through with hot veins of metal and had my bones turned inside out...
...been nuked, steamrolled, crucified, ripped in half, chewed up and spit out.
My body is one big wound, a million scars I carry around inside me.

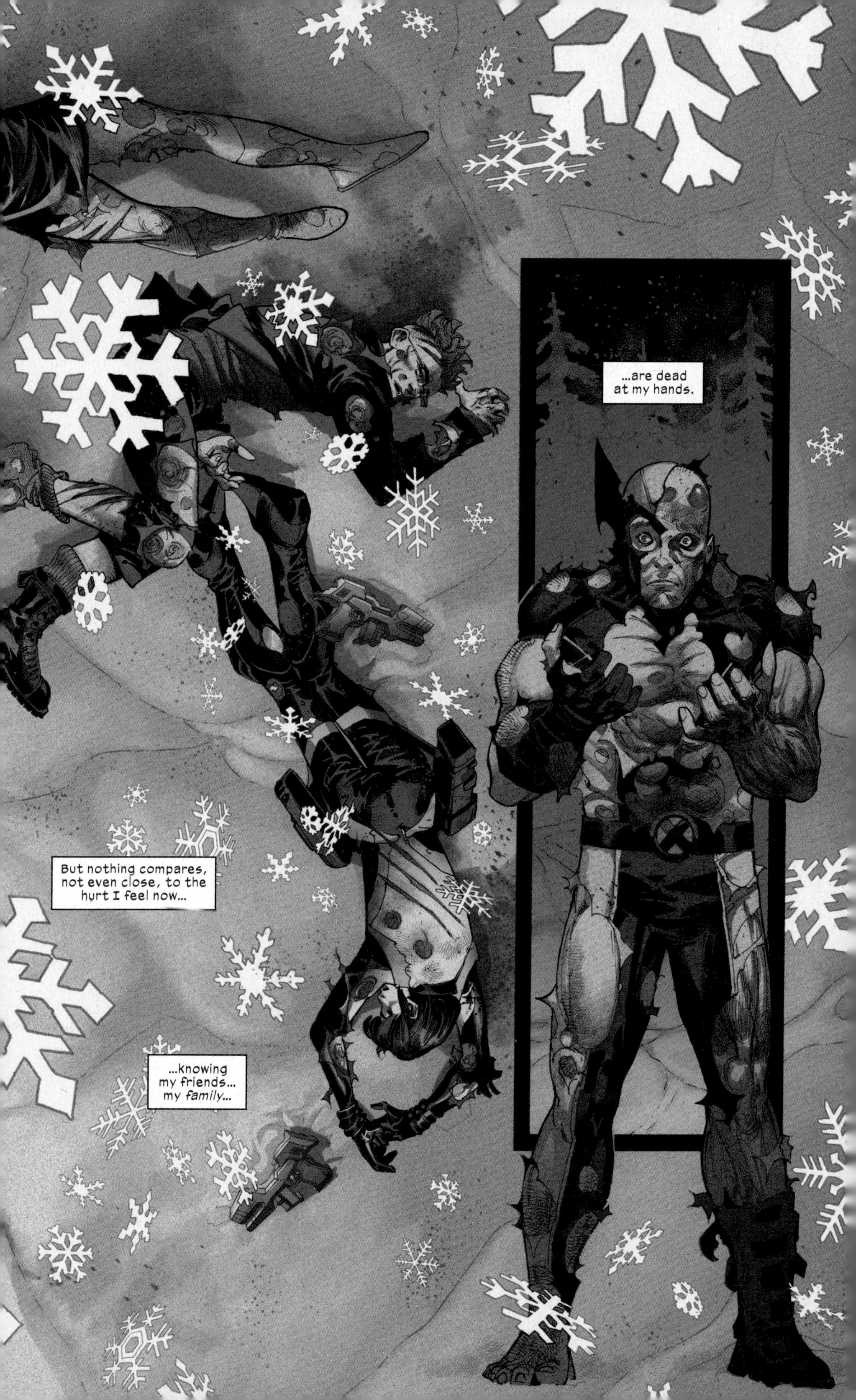
But nothing compares, not even close, to the hurt I feel now...
...knowing my friends... my *family*...
...are dead at my hands.

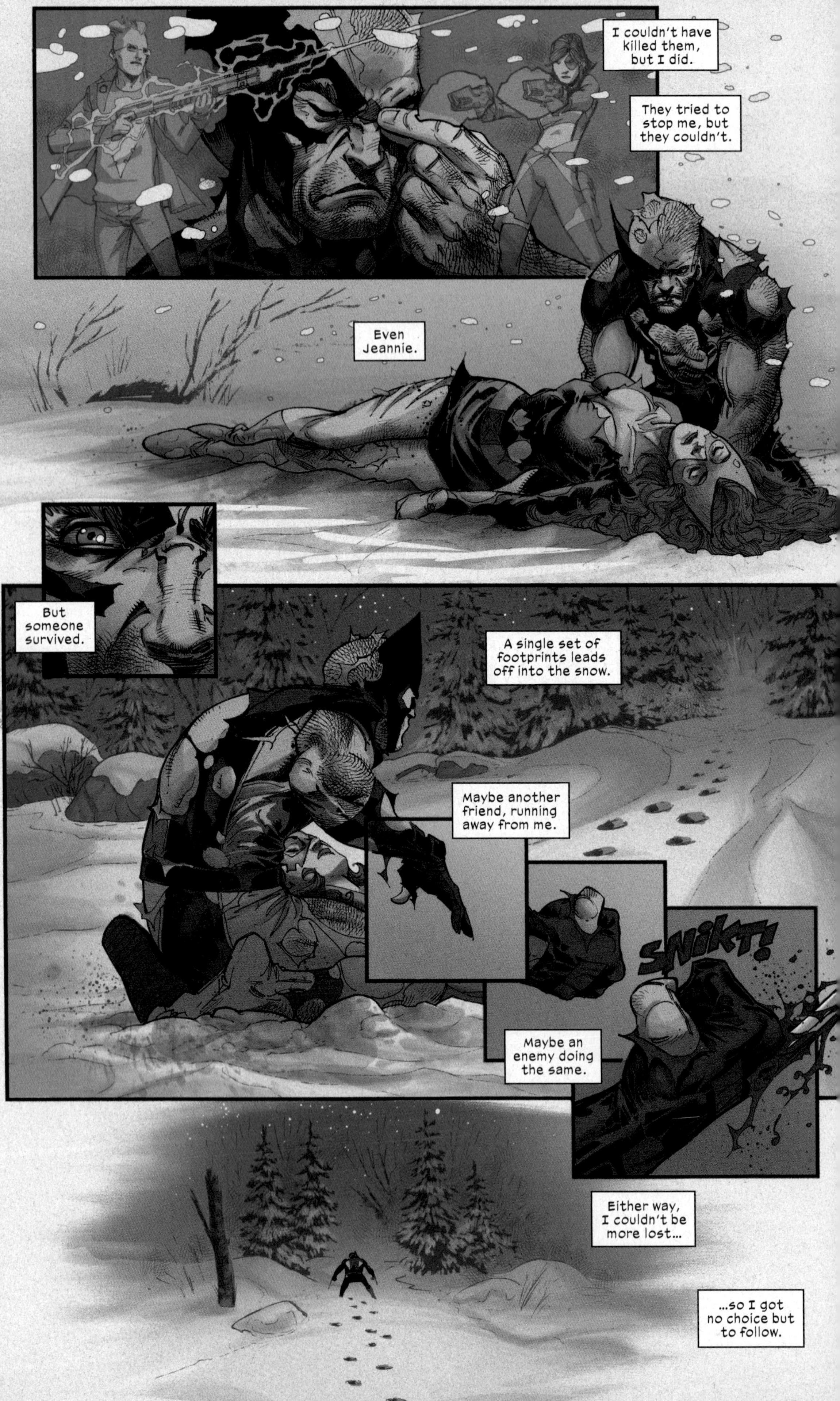
I couldn't have killed them, but I did.
They tried to stop me, but they couldn't.
Even Jeannie.
But someone survived.
A single set of footprints leads off into the snow.
Maybe another friend, running away from me.
SNIKT!
Maybe an enemy doing the same.
Either way, I couldn't be more lost...
...so I got no choice but to follow.

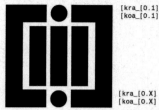

[kra_[0.1]
[koa_[0.1]

[kra_[0.X]
[koa_[0.X]

IF YOU REALLY WANT TO TANGLE WITH SOMEONE

Mutants around the world are flocking to the island-nation of Krakoa for safety, security and to be part of the first mutant society -- *even* Wolverine.

Yet, in spite of the wealth and opportunity ahead, Wolverine remains poised for the worst...

Wolverine

Marvel Girl

Kate Pryde

Sage

Domino

Kid Omega

Gateway

Beast

[kra_[0.7]...]
[koa_[0.7]...]

[A.dam_MAN_[tium]

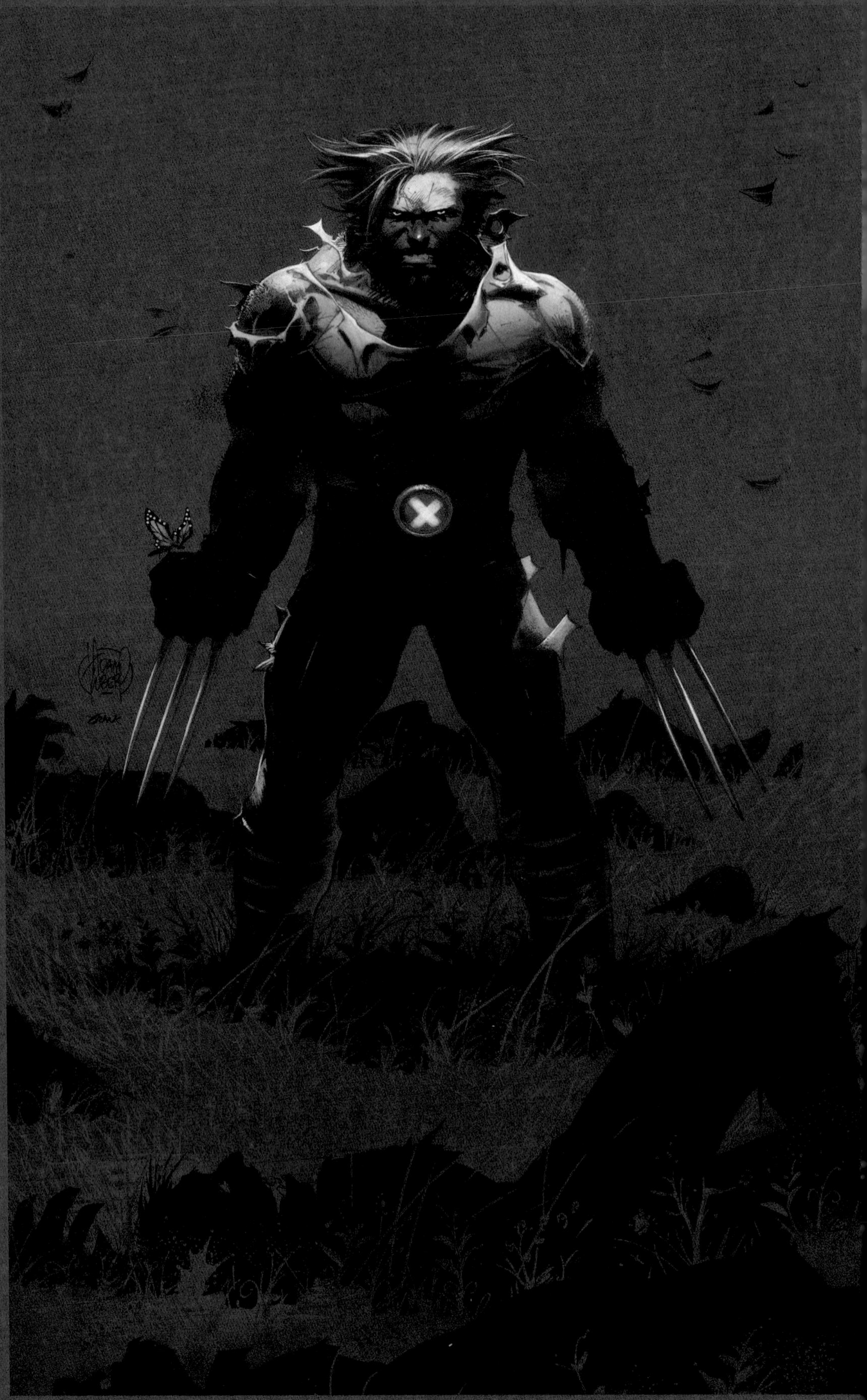

The Flower Cartel

[dawn_of_x]

[best__]
[there_]

[is__]
[bub_]

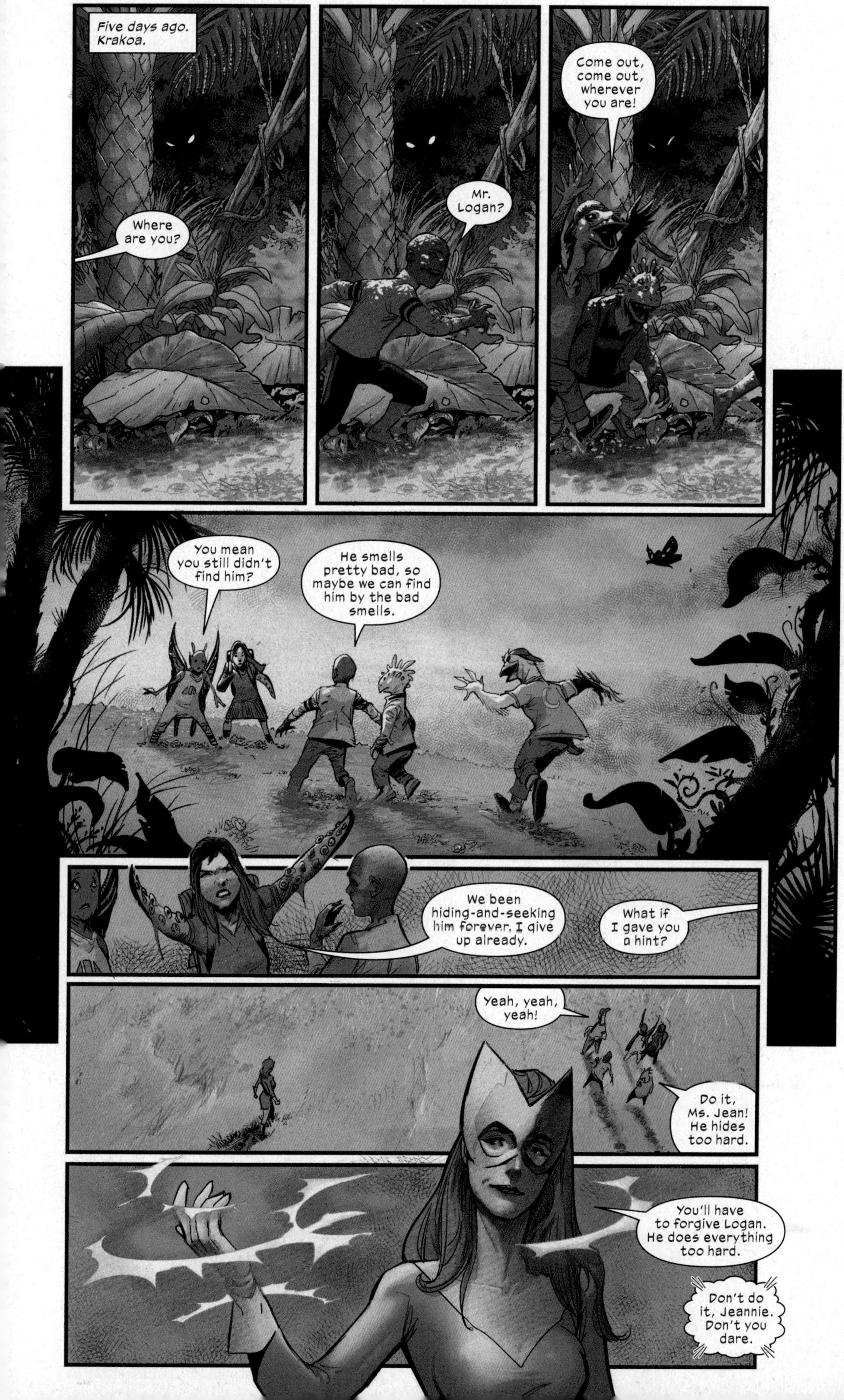
Five days ago. Krakoa.
Where are you?
Mr. Logan?
Come out, come out, wherever you are!
You mean you still didn't find him?
He smells pretty bad, so maybe we can find him by the bad smells.
We been hiding-and-seeking him forever. I give up already.
What if I gave you a hint?
Yeah, yeah, yeah!
Do it, Ms. Jean! He hides too hard.
You'll have to forgive Logan. He does everything too hard.
Don't do it, Jeannie. Don't you dare.

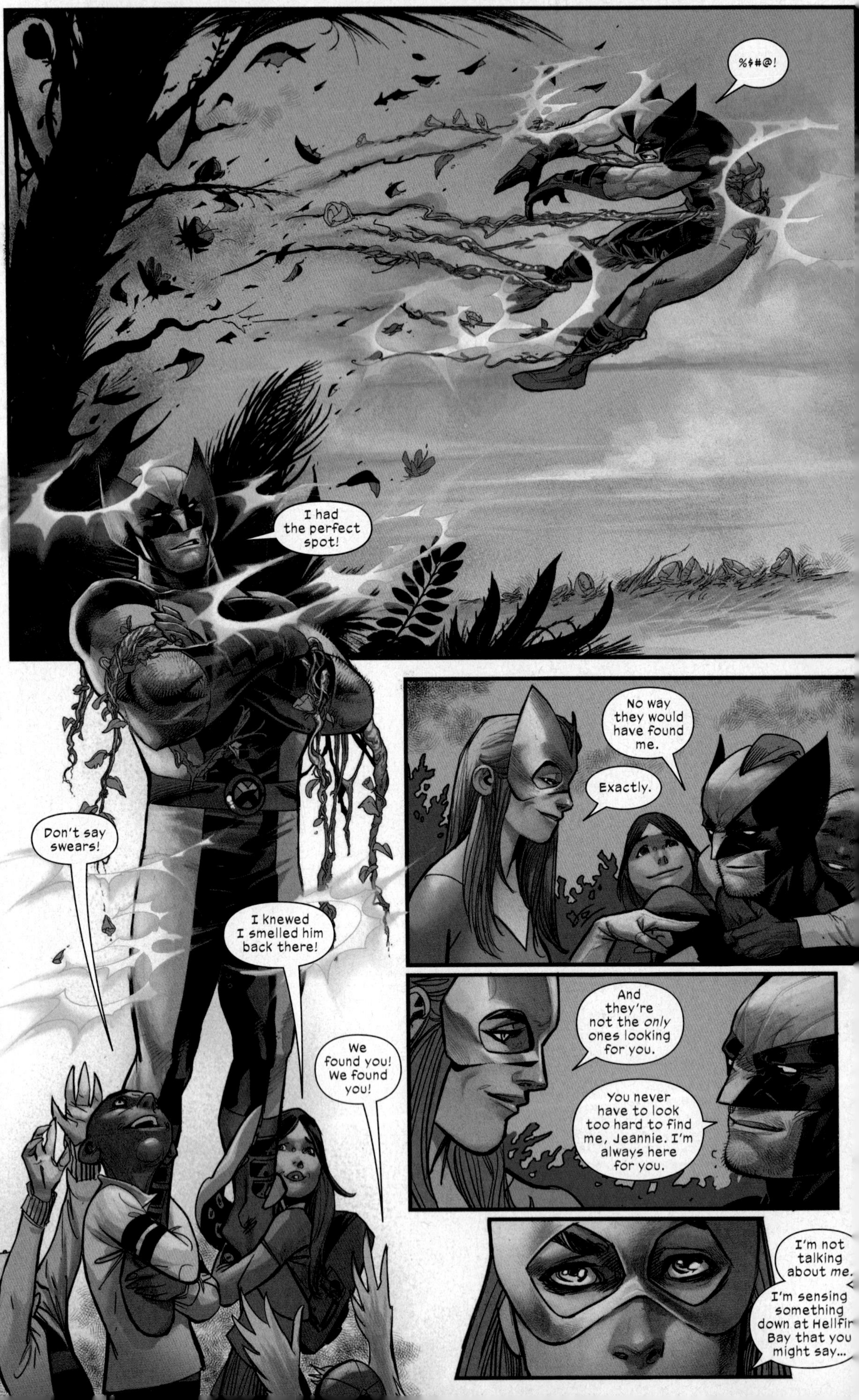
%$#@!
I had the perfect spot!
Don't say swears!
I knewed I smelled him back there!
We found you! We found you!
No way they would have found me.
Exactly.
And they're not the *only* ones looking for you.
You never have to look too hard to find me, Jeannie. I'm always here for you.
I'm not talking about *me*.
I'm sensing something down at Hellfir Bay that you might say...

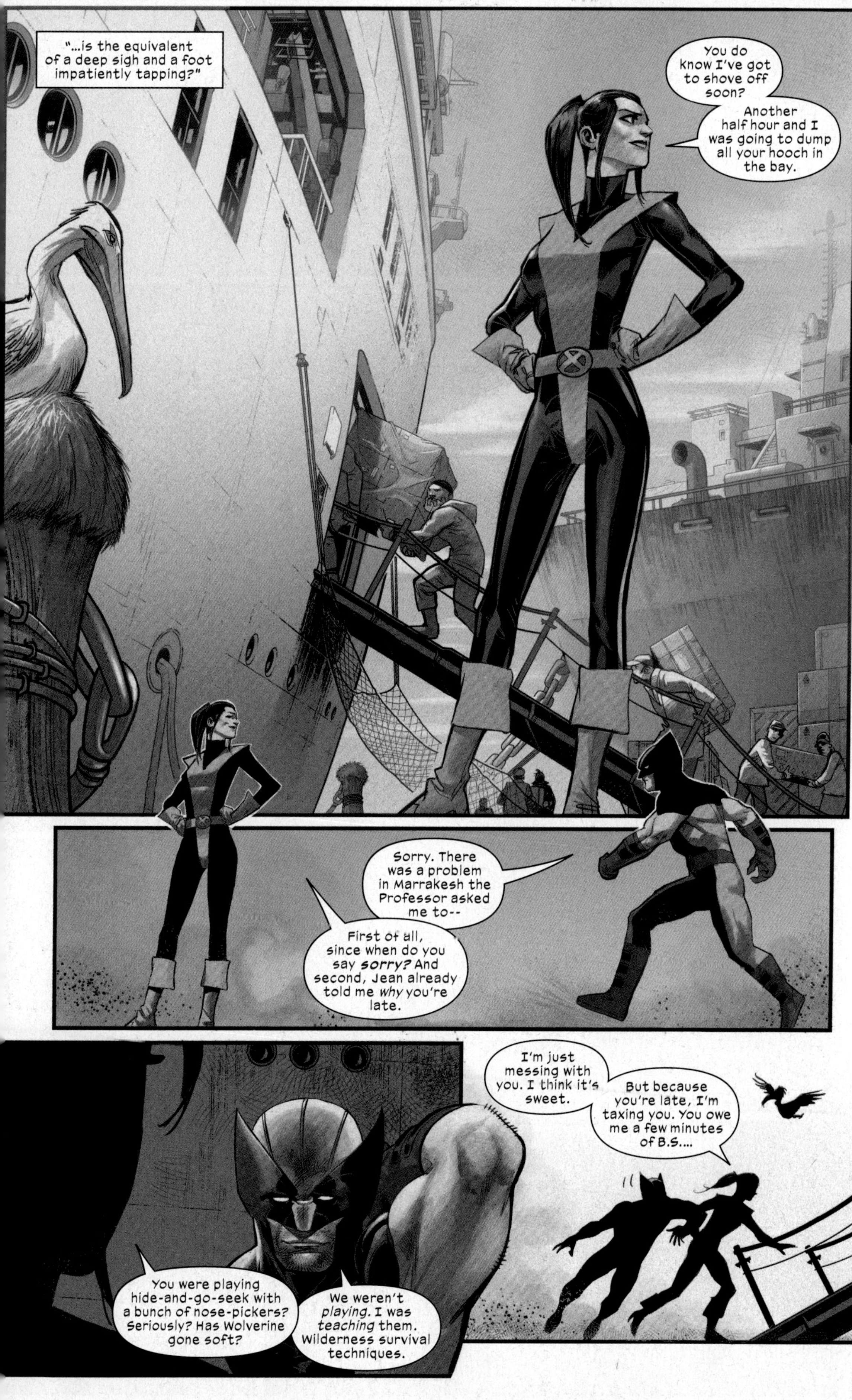
"...is the equivalent of a deep sigh and a foot impatiently tapping?"
You do know I've got to shove off soon?
Another half hour and I was going to dump all your hooch in the bay.
Sorry. There was a problem in Marrakesh the Professor asked me to--
First of all, since when do you say *sorry?* And second, Jean already told me *why* you're late.
I'm just messing with you. I think it's sweet.
But because you're late, I'm taxing you. You owe me a few minutes of B.S....
You were playing hide-and-go-seek with a bunch of nose-pickers? Seriously? Has Wolverine gone soft?
We weren't *playing.* I was *teaching* them. Wilderness survival techniques.

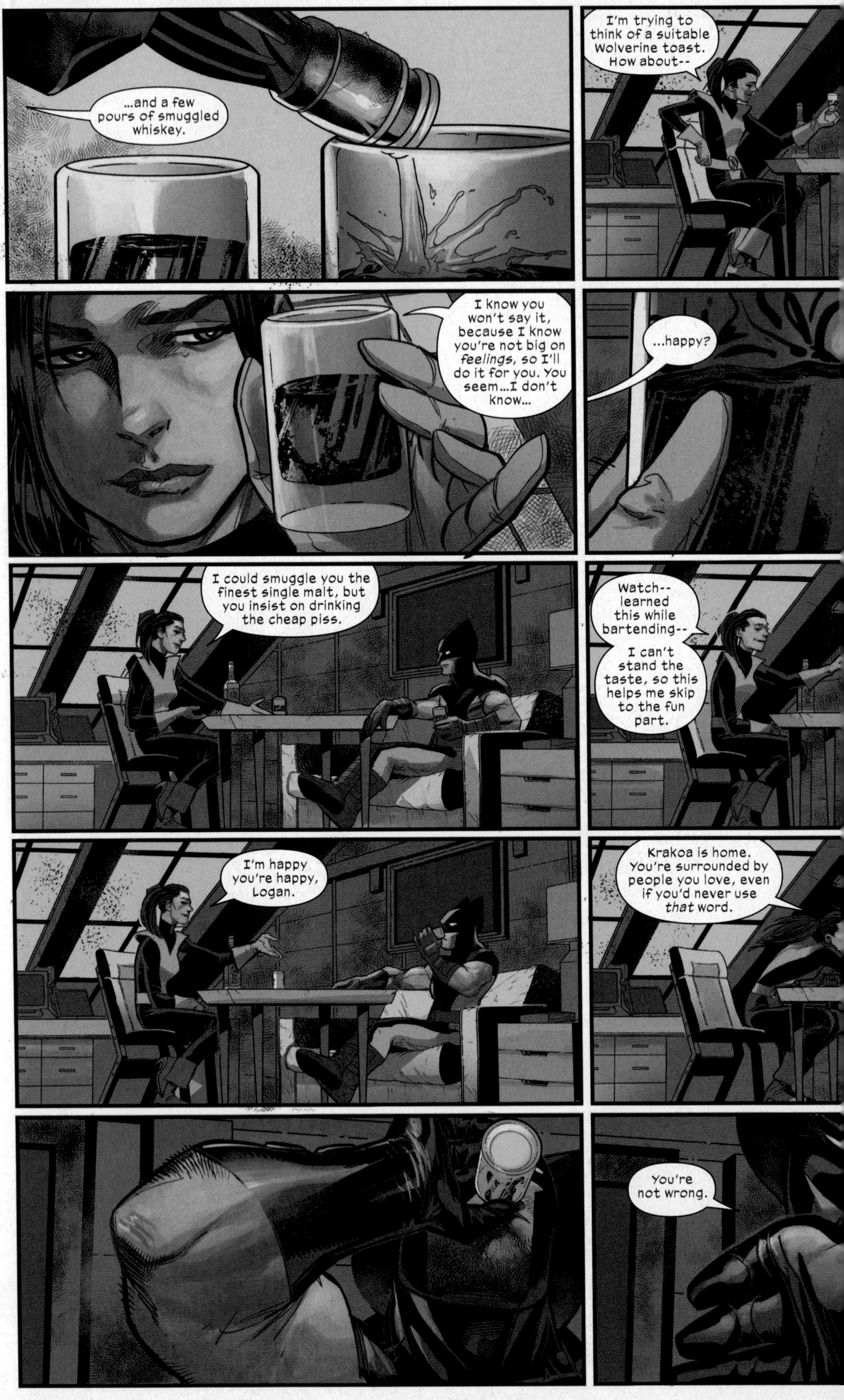
...and a few pours of smuggled whiskey.
I'm trying to think of a suitable Wolverine toast. How about--
I know you won't say it, because I know you're not big on *feelings*, so I'll do it for you. You seem...I don't know...
...happy?
I could smuggle you the finest single malt, but you insist on drinking the cheap piss.
Watch-- learned this while bartending--
I can't stand the taste, so this helps me skip to the fun part.
I'm happy you're happy, Logan.
Krakoa is home. You're surrounded by people you love, even if you'd never use *that* word.
You're not wrong.

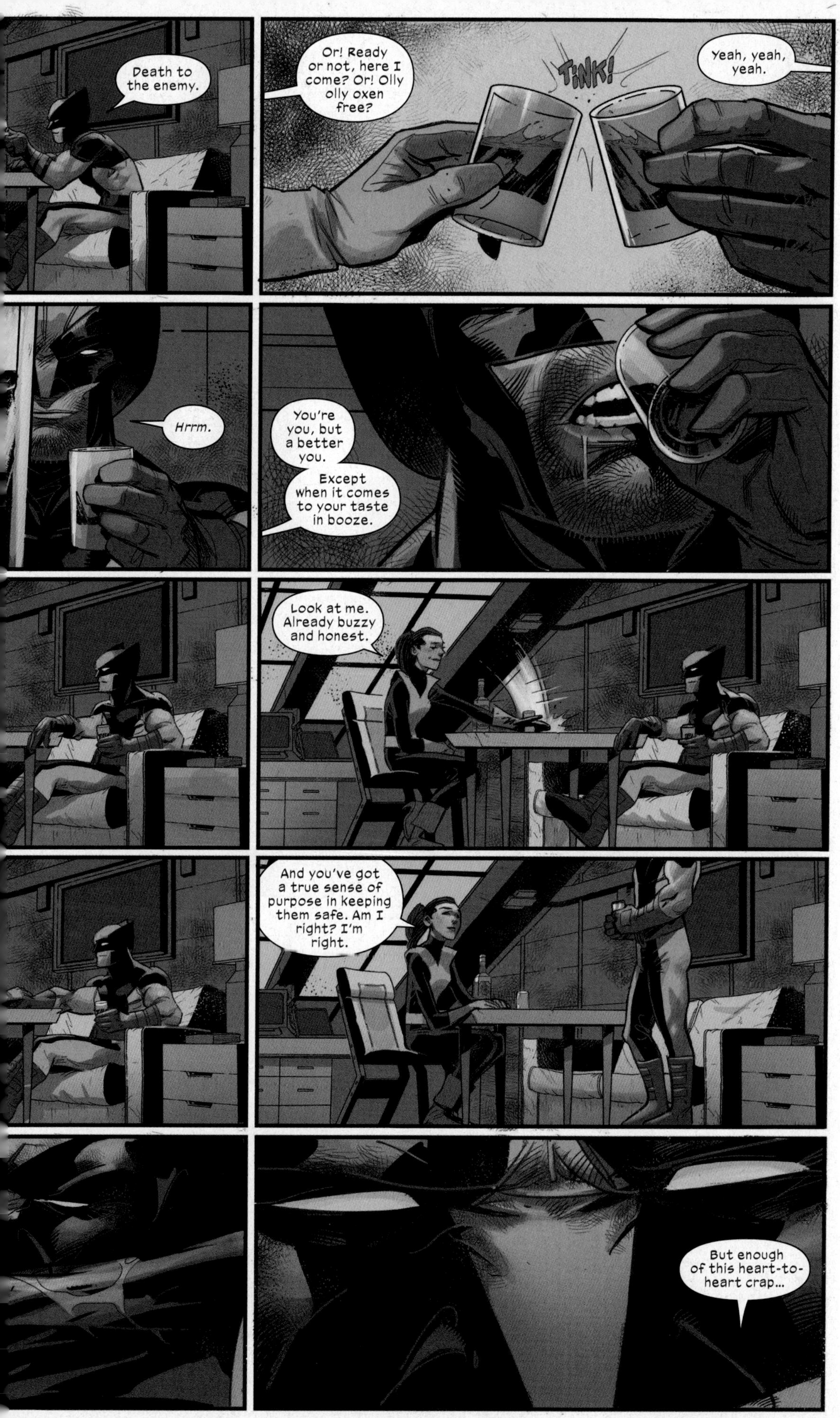
Death to the enemy.
Or! Ready or not, here I come? Or! Olly olly oxen free?
TINK!
Yeah, yeah, yeah.
Hrrm.
You're you, but a better you.
Except when it comes to your taste in booze.
Look at me. Already buzzy and honest.
And you've got a true sense of purpose in keeping them safe. Am I right? I'm right.
But enough of this heart-to-heart crap...

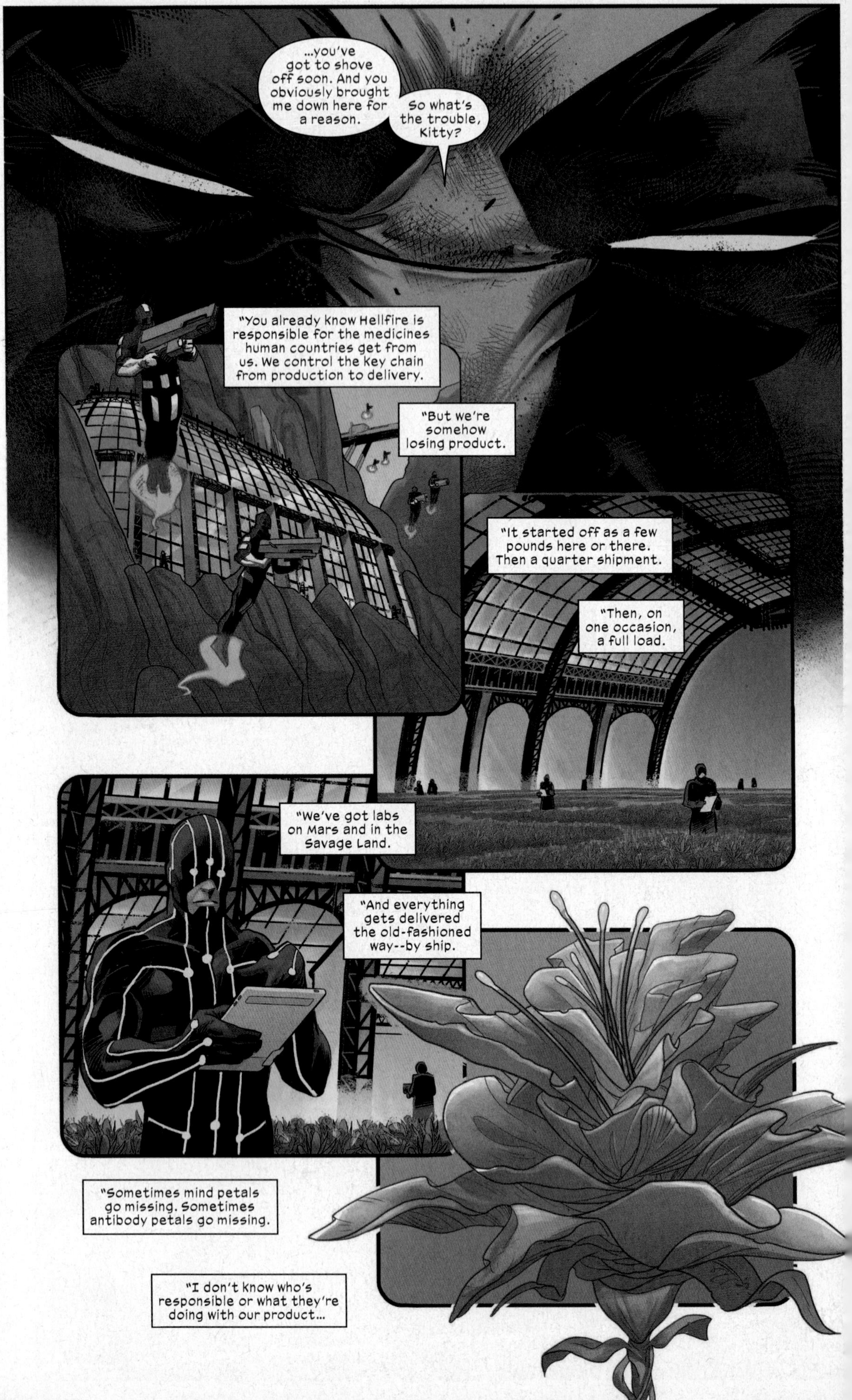
...you've got to shove off soon. And you obviously brought me down here for a reason.
So what's the trouble, Kitty?
"You already know Hellfire is responsible for the medicines human countries get from us. We control the key chain from production to delivery.
"But we're somehow losing product.
"It started off as a few pounds here or there. Then a quarter shipment.
"Then, on one occasion, a full load.
"We've got labs on Mars and in the Savage Land.
"And everything gets delivered the old-fashioned way--by ship.
"Sometimes mind petals go missing. Sometimes antibody petals go missing.
"I don't know who's responsible or what they're doing with our product...

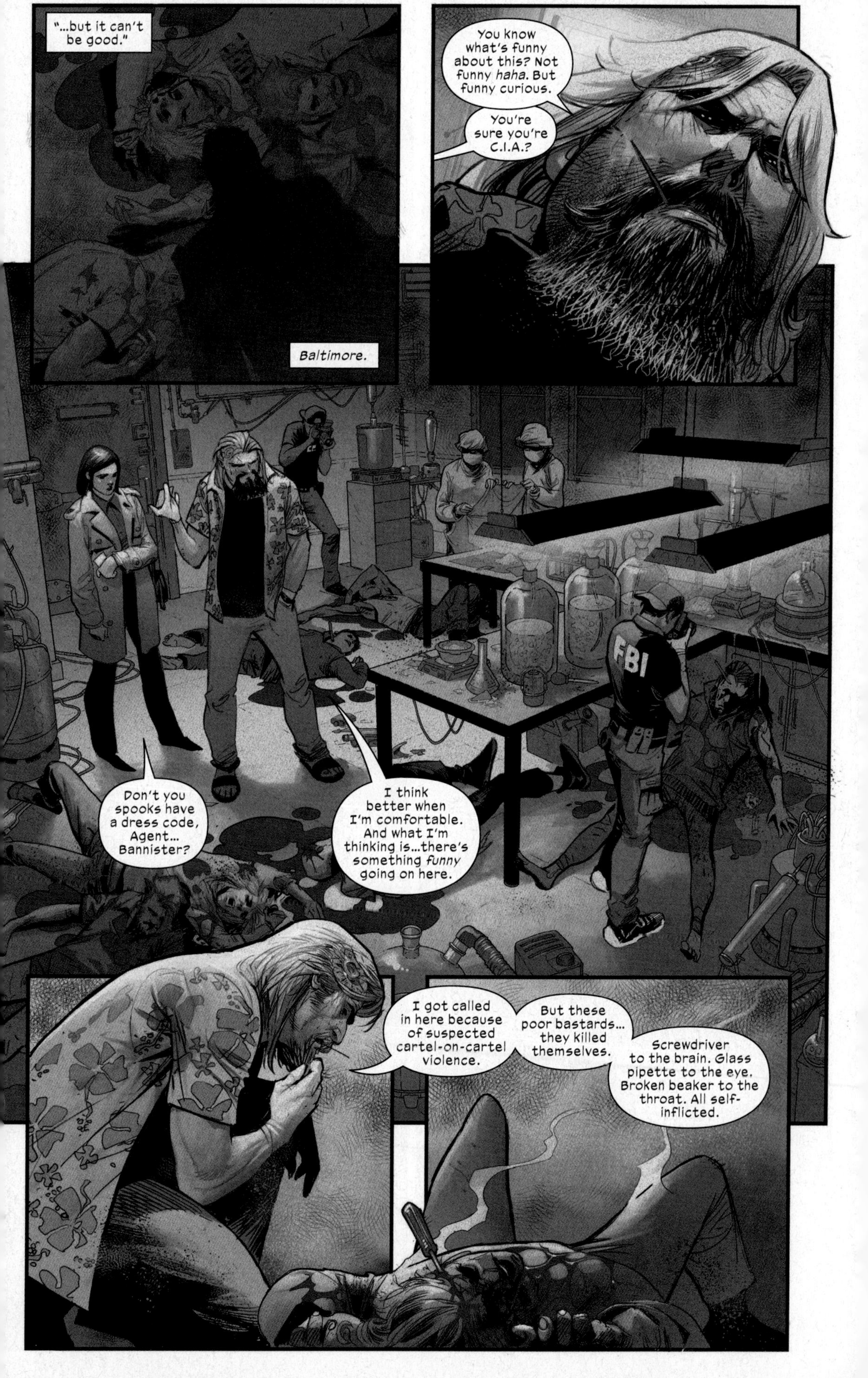
"...but it can't be good."
Baltimore.
You know what's funny about this? Not funny *haha*. But funny curious.
You're sure you're C.I.A.?
Don't you spooks have a dress code, Agent... Bannister?
I think better when I'm comfortable. And what I'm thinking is...there's something *funny* going on here.
FBI
FBI
I got called in here because of suspected cartel-on-cartel violence.
But these poor bastards... they killed themselves.
Screwdriver to the brain. Glass pipette to the eye. Broken beaker to the throat. All self-inflicted.

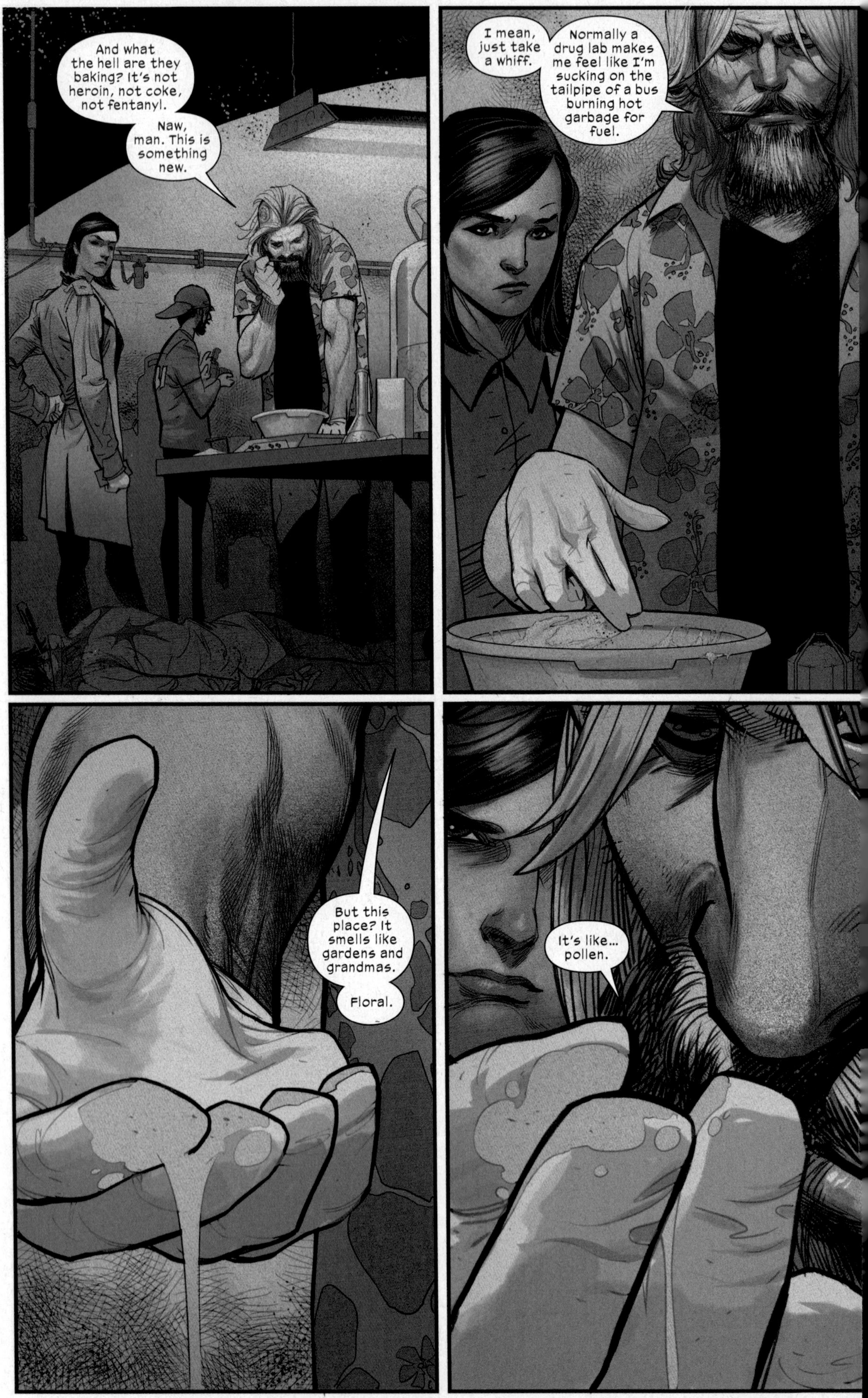
And what the hell are they baking? It's not heroin, not coke, not fentanyl.
Naw, man. This is something new.
I mean, just take a whiff.
Normally a drug lab makes me feel like I'm sucking on the tailpipe of a bus burning hot garbage for fuel.
But this place? It smells like gardens and grandmas.
Floral.
It's like... pollen.

POLLEN

Pollen has become an epidemic-level street drug in a short space of time. There are many versions available worldwide, but the only consistent source and product comes from the so-called Flower Cartel, which is believed to be involved in a violent campaign to wipe out any competition and interference.

Jeff Bannister is a senior narcotics agent notable for his decorated history in the Sinaloa and Chihuahua states of Mexico as well as his undercover work in Colombia and Venezuela. He is divorced, but after his daughter was diagnosed with leukemia two years ago, he requested and was granted a stateside transfer.

Ever since he began investigating pollen, he has been reporting to multiple superiors, one of whom he suspects heads a shadow group within the agency devoted to mutant surveillance.

When he proposed to arrange a covert operation—with a team posing as members of the narcotics trade eager to do business with the Flower Cartel—he did not run into the usual tangle of red tape and debriefings but instead received an immediate green light and seemingly unlimited resources.

Bannister's orders are unclear. On the one hand, his superiors seem to wholeheartedly endorse his proposal to crack down on the Flower Cartel.

On the other hand, he has taken several calls from the FBI, FBN, DEA, FDA and even the State Department. They all cite dissatisfaction with the manufacture, regulation and distribution of Krakoan pharmaceuticals. They have (so far unproven) suspicions that a mounting black market may tie back to the Hellfire Trading Company.

They have asked him to consider -- if the situation permits, of course -- keeping channels open.

Because collaborating with the drug traffickers will allow for a campaign of espionage, subversion, sabotage and -- possibly -- profit.

The Flower Cartel has since proposed a meeting.

The location: deep country Alaska.

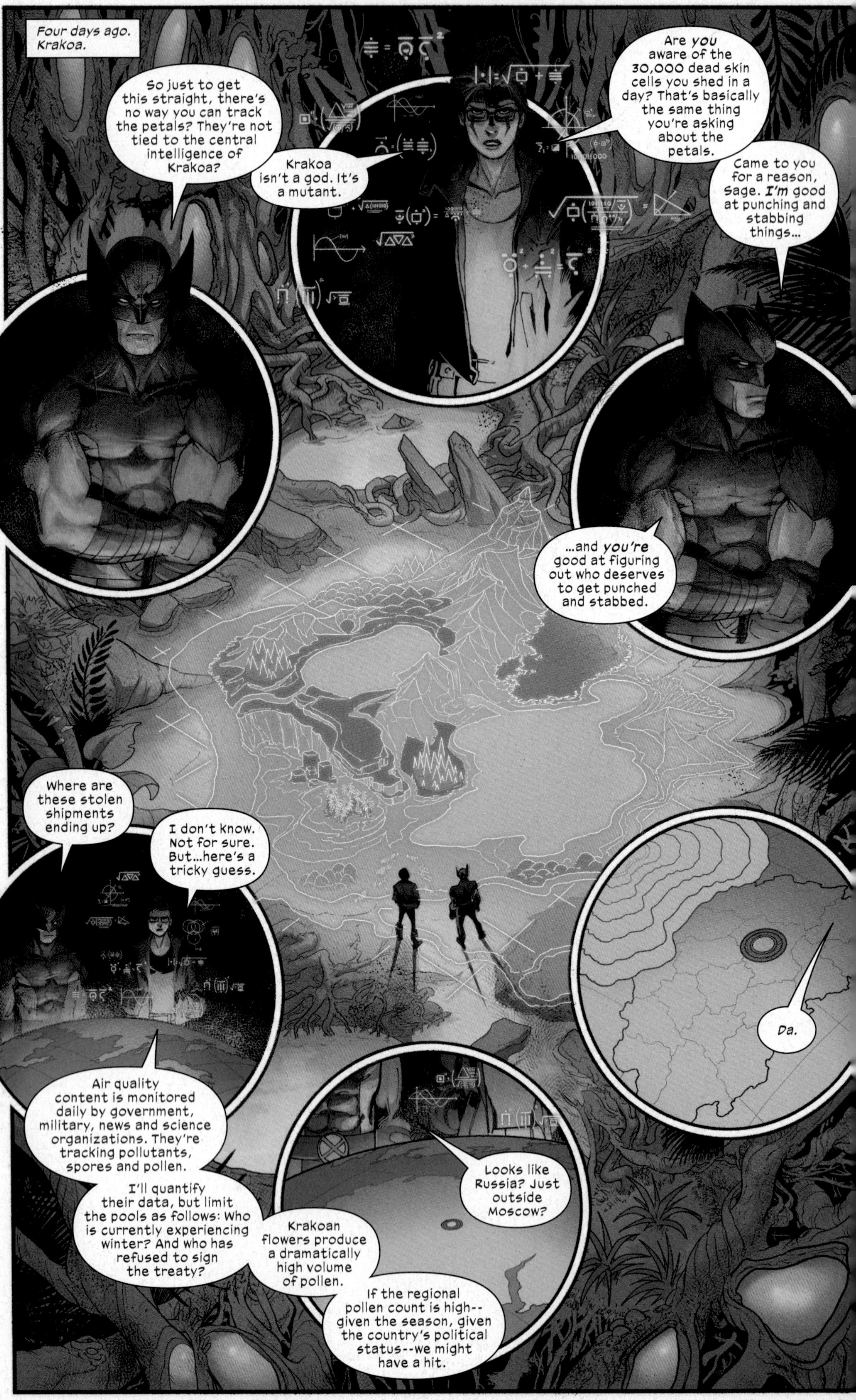
Four days ago. Krakoa.
So just to get this straight, there's no way you can track the petals? They're not tied to the central intelligence of Krakoa?
Krakoa isn't a god. It's a mutant.
Are *you* aware of the 30,000 dead skin cells you shed in a day? That's basically the same thing you're asking about the petals.
Came to you for a reason, Sage. *I'm* good at punching and stabbing things...
...and *you're* good at figuring out who deserves to get punched and stabbed.
Where are these stolen shipments ending up?
I don't know. Not for sure. But...here's a tricky guess.
Air quality content is monitored daily by government, military, news and science organizations. They're tracking pollutants, spores and pollen.
I'll quantify their data, but limit the pools as follows: Who is currently experiencing winter? And who has refused to sign the treaty?
Krakoan flowers produce a dramatically high volume of pollen.
If the regional pollen count is high--given the season, given the country's political status--we might have a hit.
Looks like Russia? Just outside Moscow?
Da.

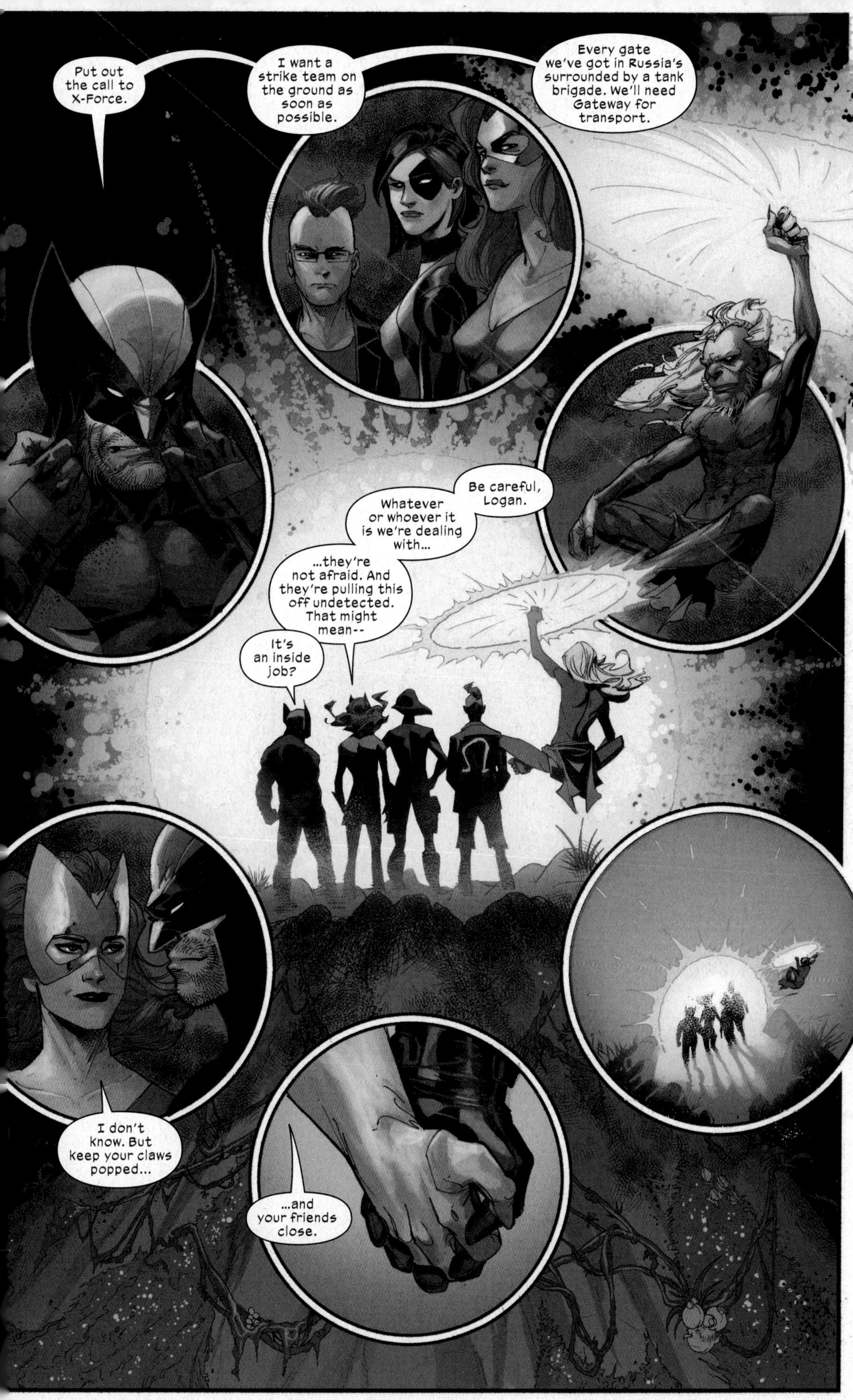
Put out the call to X-Force.
I want a strike team on the ground as soon as possible.
Every gate we've got in Russia's surrounded by a tank brigade. We'll need Gateway for transport.
Be careful, Logan.
Whatever or whoever it is we're dealing with...
...they're not afraid. And they're pulling this off undetected. That might mean--
It's an inside job?
I don't know. But keep your claws popped...
...and your friends close.

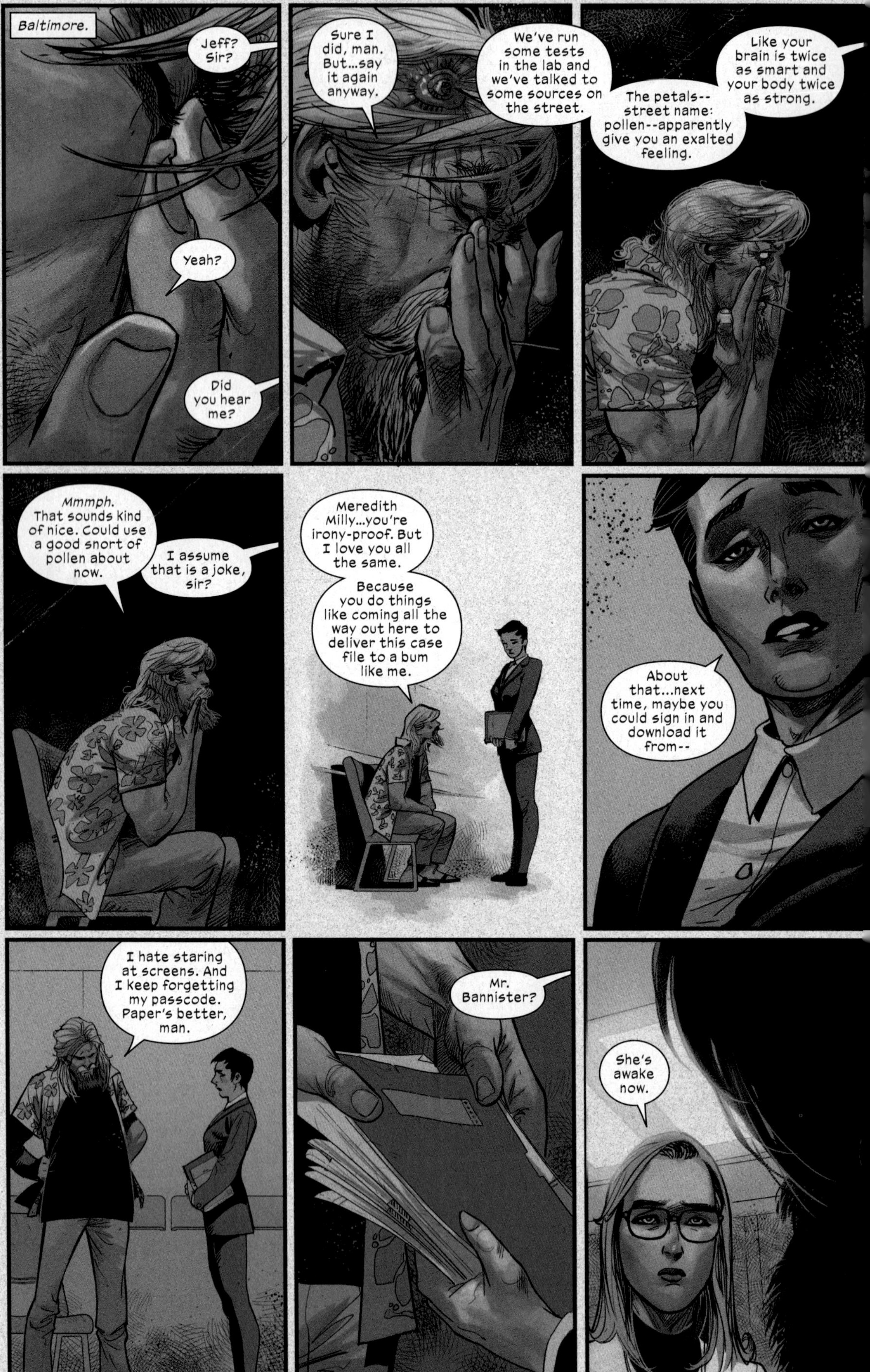
Baltimore.
Jeff? Sir?
Yeah?
Did you hear me?
Sure I did, man. But...say it again anyway.
We've run some tests in the lab and we've talked to some sources on the street.
The petals--street name: pollen--apparently give you an exalted feeling.
Like your brain is twice as smart and your body twice as strong.
Mmmph. That sounds kind of nice. Could use a good snort of pollen about now.
I assume that is a joke, sir?
Meredith Milly...you're irony-proof. But I love you all the same.
Because you do things like coming all the way out here to deliver this case file to a bum like me.
About that...next time, maybe you could sign in and download it from--
I hate staring at screens. And I keep forgetting my passcode. Paper's better, man.
Mr. Bannister?
She's awake now.

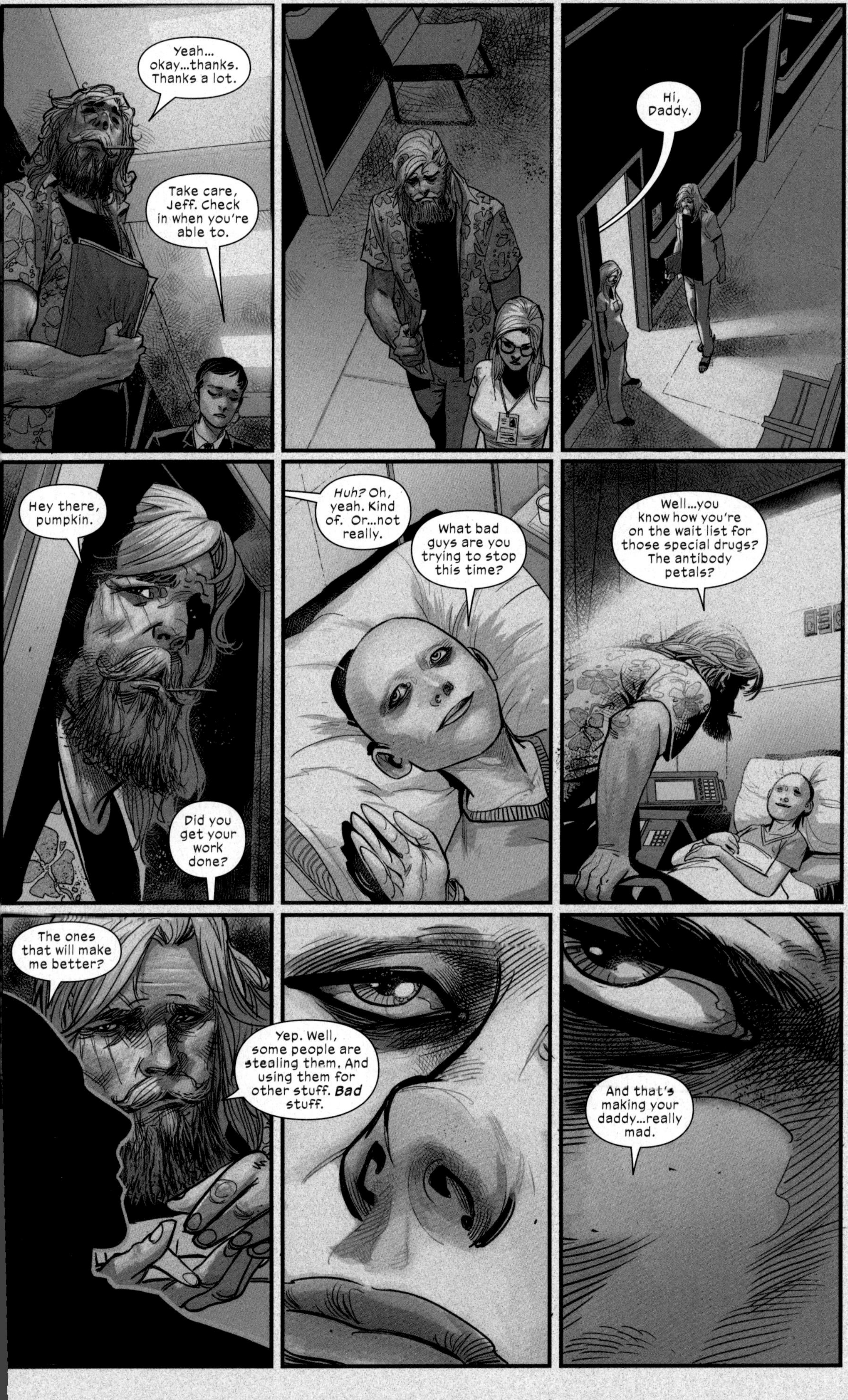
Yeah... okay...thanks. Thanks a lot.
Take care, Jeff. Check in when you're able to.
Hi, Daddy.
Hey there, pumpkin.
Did you get your work done?
Huh? Oh, yeah. Kind of. Or...not really.
What bad guys are you trying to stop this time?
Well...you know how you're on the wait list for those special drugs? The antibody petals?
The ones that will make me better?
Yep. Well, some people are stealing them. And using them for other stuff. *Bad* stuff.
And that's making your daddy...really mad.

THE ORDER OF X

There have always been those humans who recognized mutants as higher beings, touched by divinity. But since the declaration of sovereignty, their numbers have grown dramatically, as if the new dawn broke with an ethereal light.

At this time, the Order of X has no definitive leader or practice or text or belief system. No roof over its church, so to speak.

But there are commonalities evolving among the various branches and thousands of parishioners worldwide.

They regularly gather around Krakoan gates, prostrating their bodies, praying and pleading. Should a mutant appear, some parishioners will collapse in seizure and speak in tongues. Others will rush the mutant, their hands hungry for a touch, as if some essence might carry over to them.

There have been reports of men and women disrobing and offering themselves naked to the mutants. Their bodies are altars upon which they might produce the ultimate form of worship: a child that carries the X-Gene.

Some branches wear an X around their necks like a crucifix or Star of David, but scarification and branding seems to be the standard for adornment. Xs are sometimes carved over the eyes or across the chest or the face, but the mouth is the most frequent site for etching.

Though their overall theology appears to be based on devotion and humility, there are extremists who appear to believe that the sacrifice and consumption of *Homo superior* is the path to a higher plane.

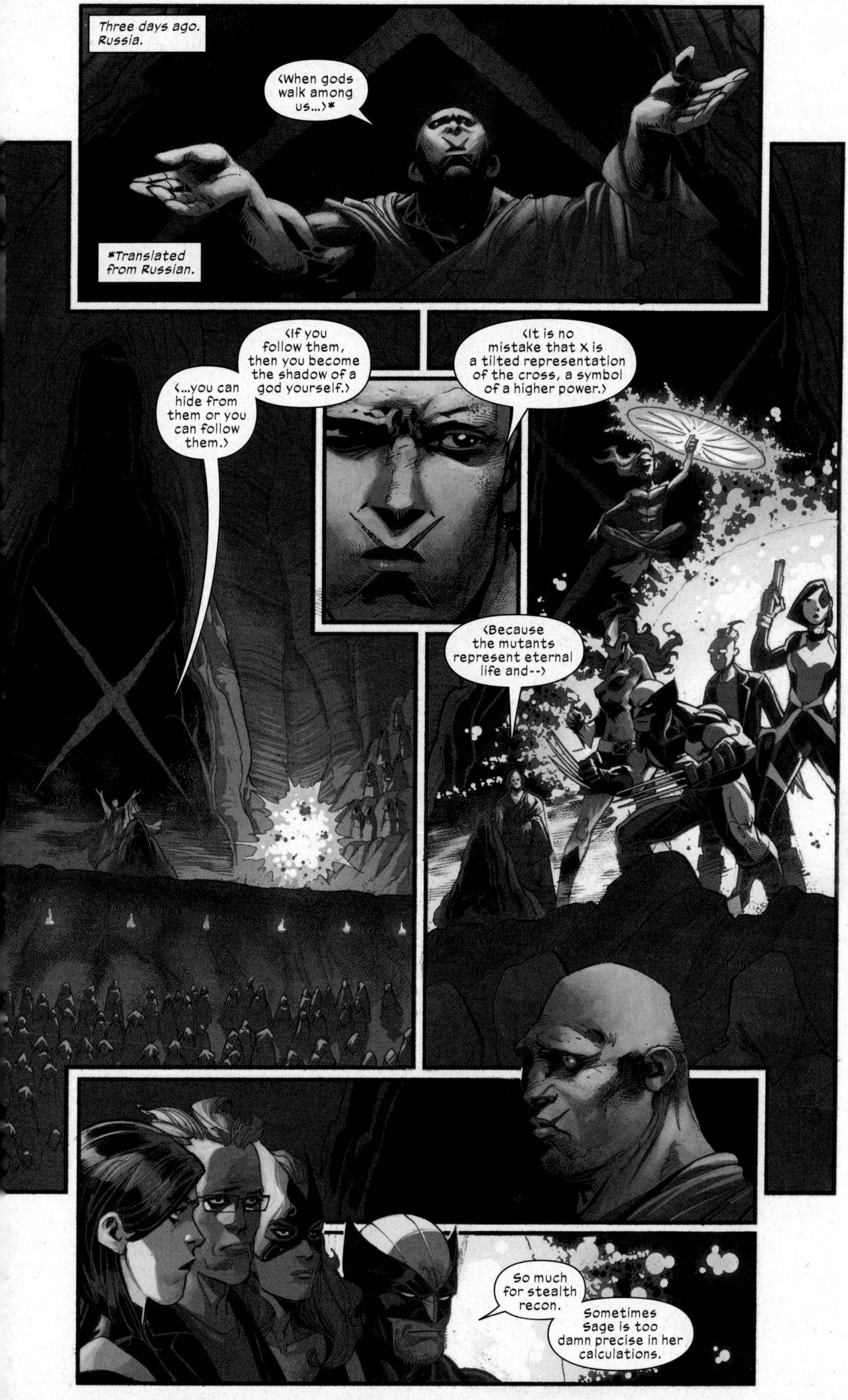
Three days ago. Russia.
<When gods walk among us...>*
*Translated from Russian.
<...you can hide from them or you can follow them.>
<If you follow them, then you become the shadow of a god yourself.>
<It is no mistake that X is a tilted representation of the cross, a symbol of a higher power.>
<Because the mutants represent eternal life and-->
So much for stealth recon.
Sometimes Sage is too damn precise in her calculations.

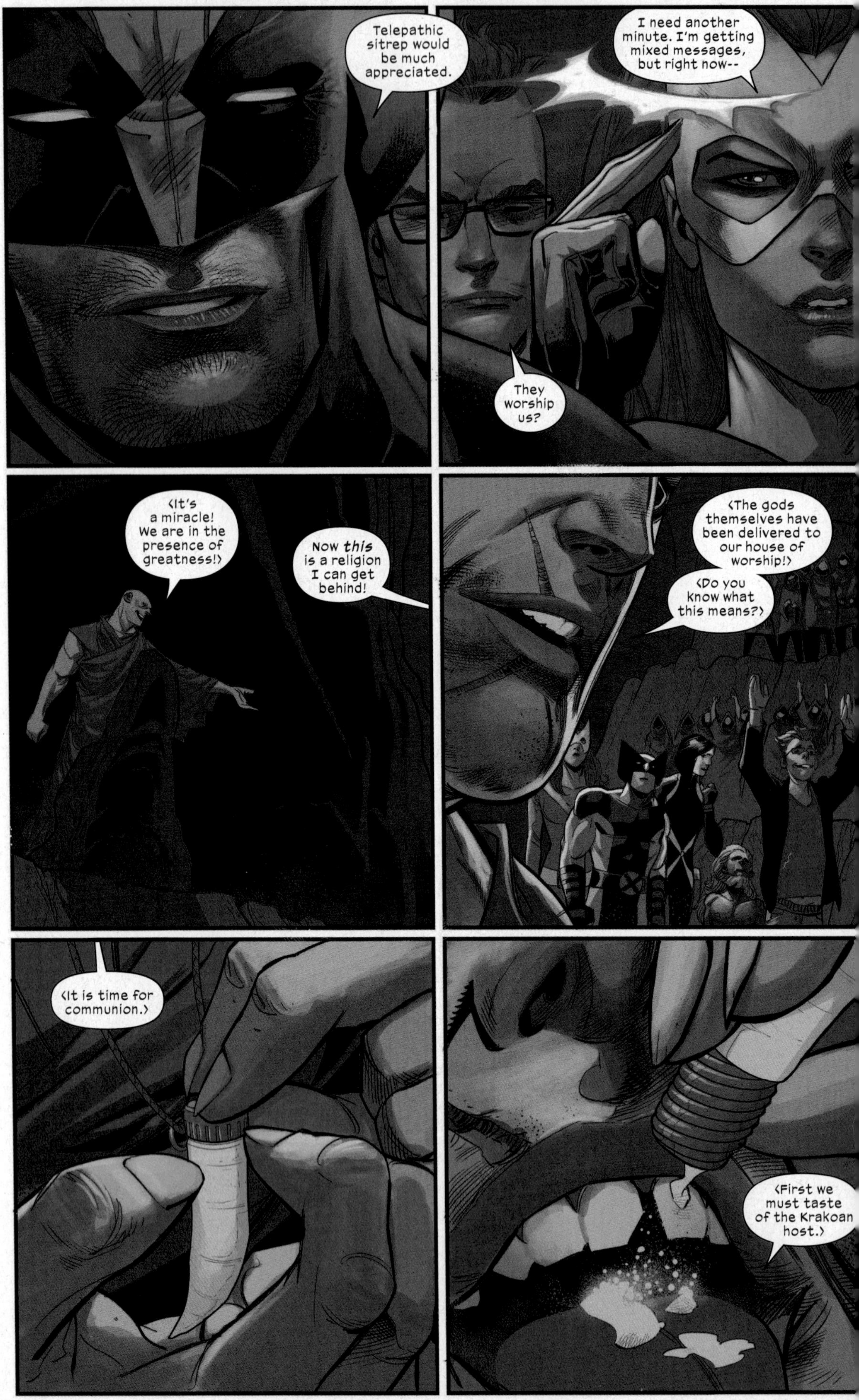
Telepathic sitrep would be much appreciated.
I need another minute. I'm getting mixed messages, but right now--
They worship us?
<It's a miracle! We are in the presence of greatness!>
Now *this* is a religion I can get behind!
<The gods themselves have been delivered to our house of worship!>
<Do you know what this means?>
<It is time for communion.>
<First we must taste of the Krakoan host.>

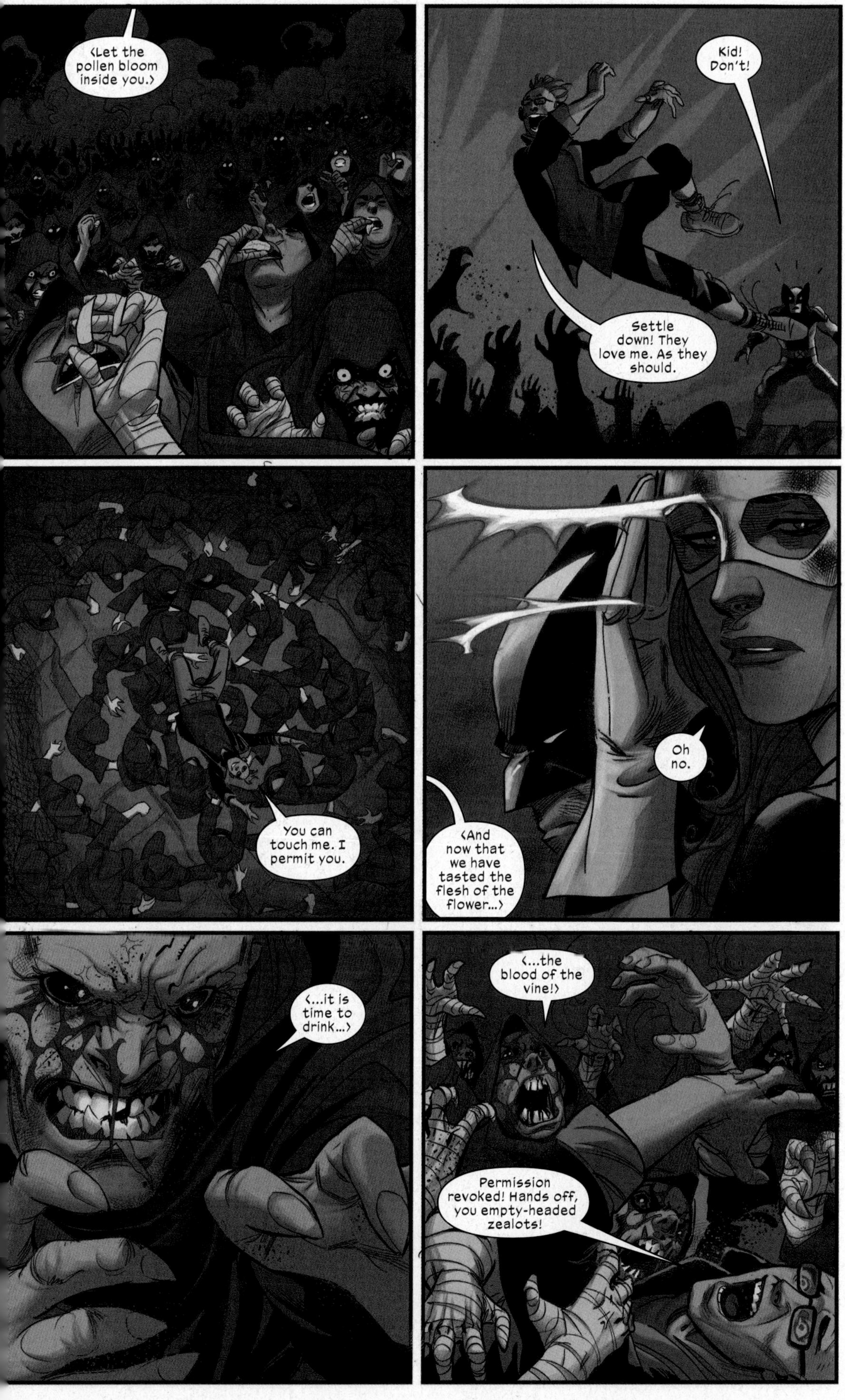
‹Let the pollen bloom inside you.›
Kid! Don't!
Settle down! They love me. As they should.
You can touch me. I permit you.
Oh no.
‹And now that we have tasted the flesh of the flower...›
‹...it is time to drink...›
‹...the blood of the vine!›
Permission revoked! Hands off, you empty-headed zealots!

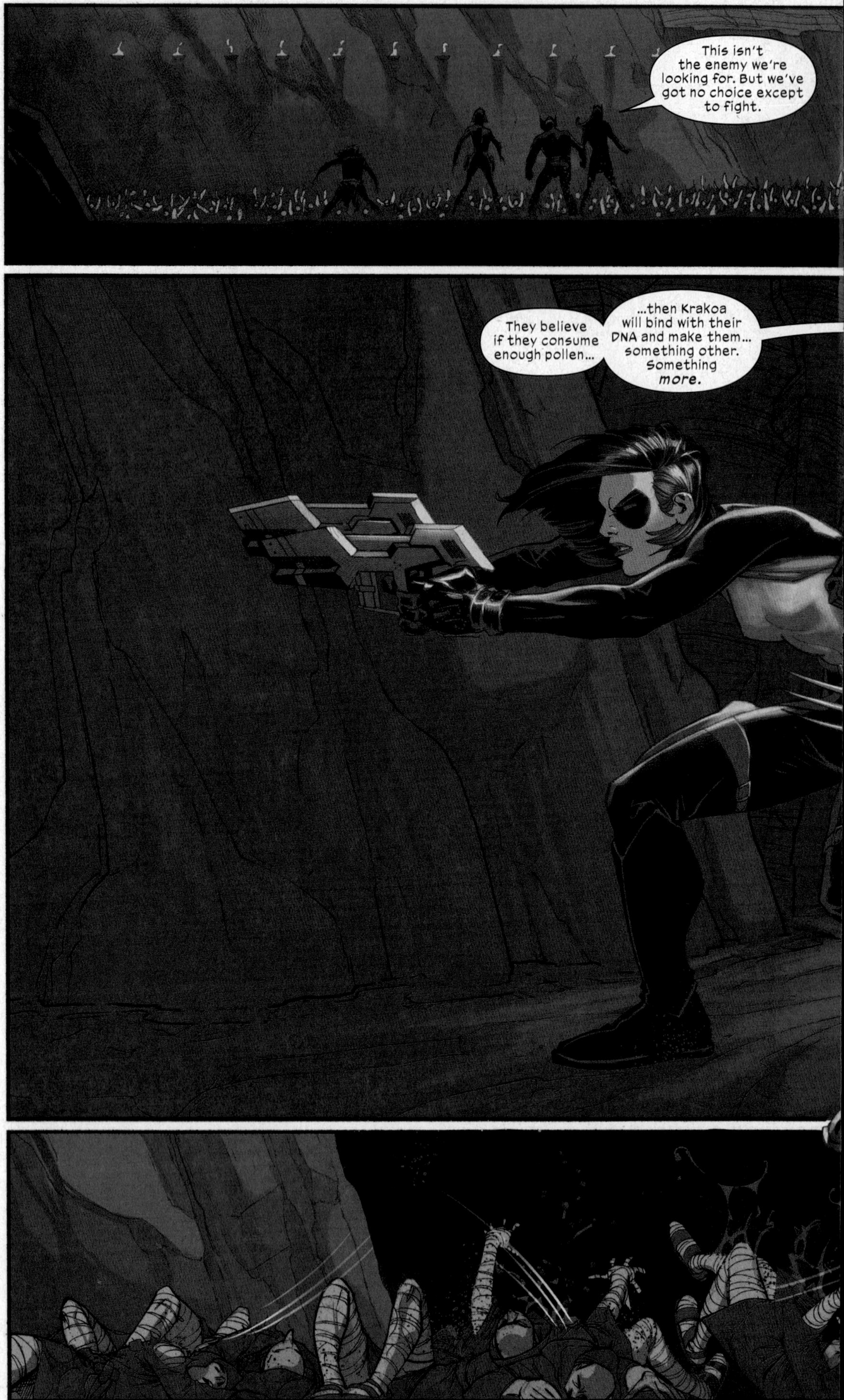
This isn't the enemy we're looking for. But we've got no choice except to fight.
They believe if they consume enough pollen...
...then Krakoa will bind with their DNA and make them... something other. Something *more.*

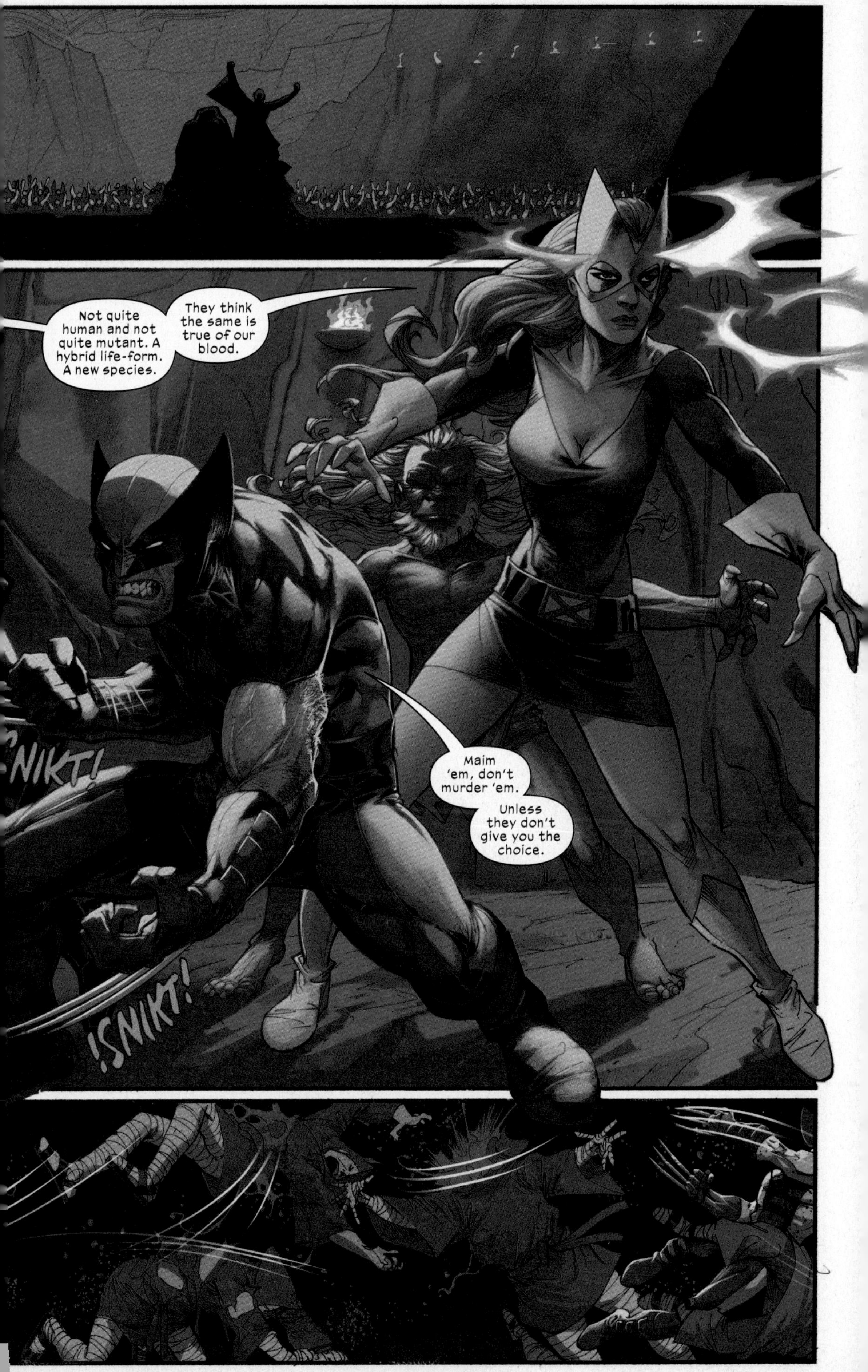
Not quite human and not quite mutant. A hybrid life-form. A new species.
They think the same is true of our blood.
SNIKT!
Maim 'em, don't murder 'em.
Unless they don't give you the choice.
SNIKT!

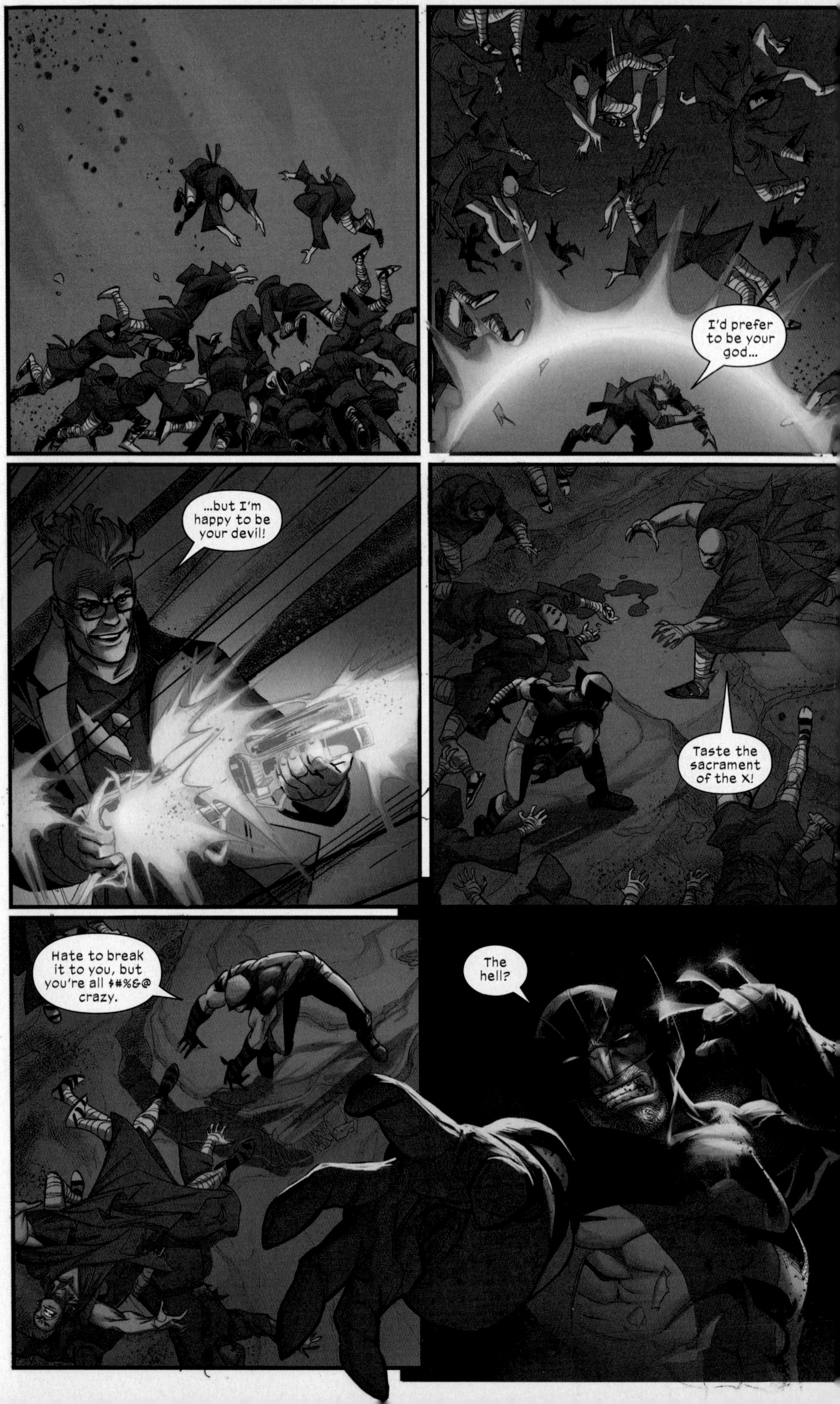
I'd prefer to be your god...
...but I'm happy to be your devil!
Taste the sacrament of the X!
Hate to break it to you, but you're all $#%&@ crazy.
The hell?

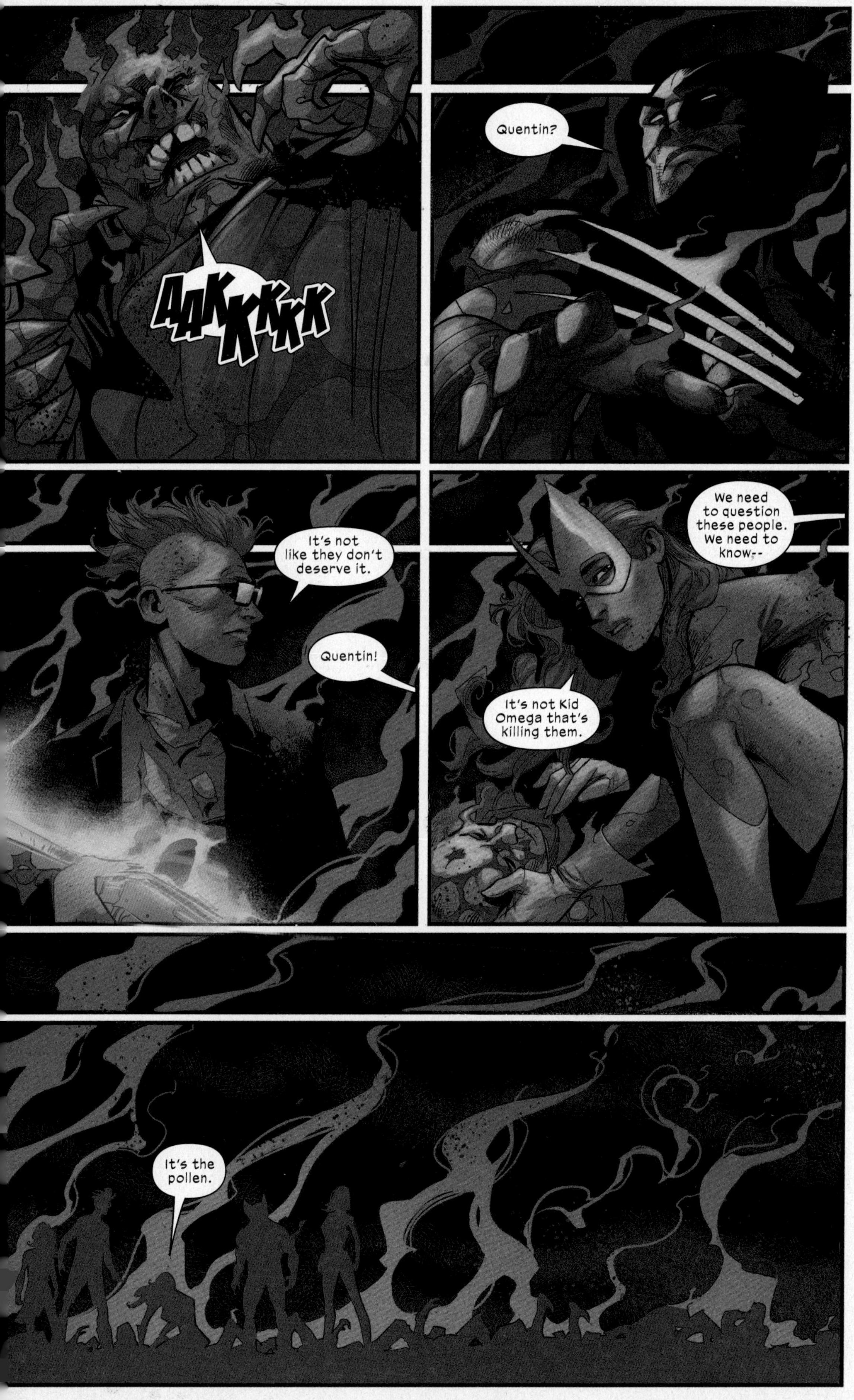
AAKKKKKK
Quentin?
It's not like they don't deserve it.
Quentin!
We need to question these people. We need to know--
It's not Kid Omega that's killing them.
It's the pollen.

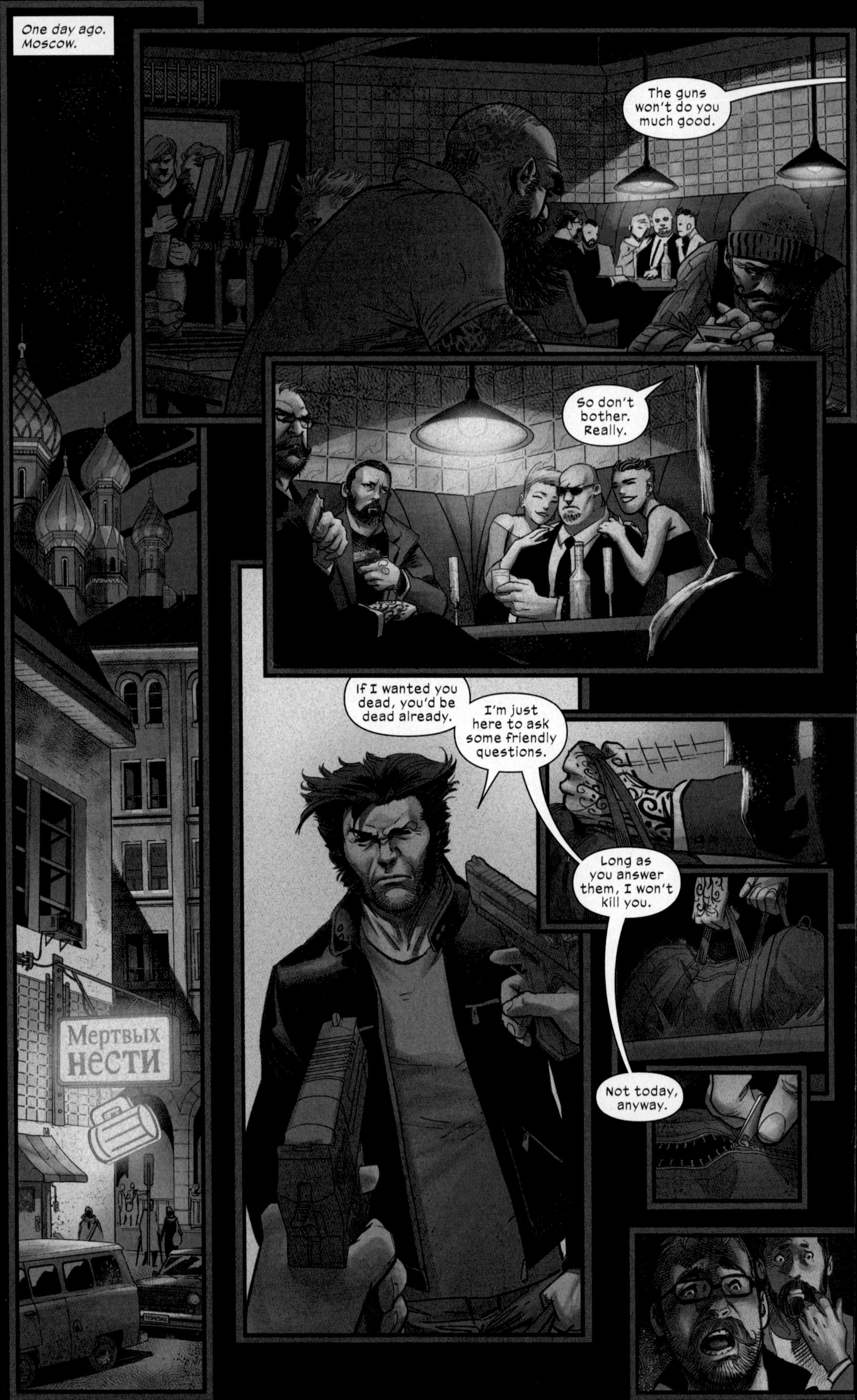

One day ago.
Moscow.
The guns won't do you much good.
So don't bother. Really.
Мертвых Нести
If I wanted you dead, you'd be dead already.
I'm just here to ask some friendly questions.
Long as you answer them, I won't kill you.
Not today, anyway.

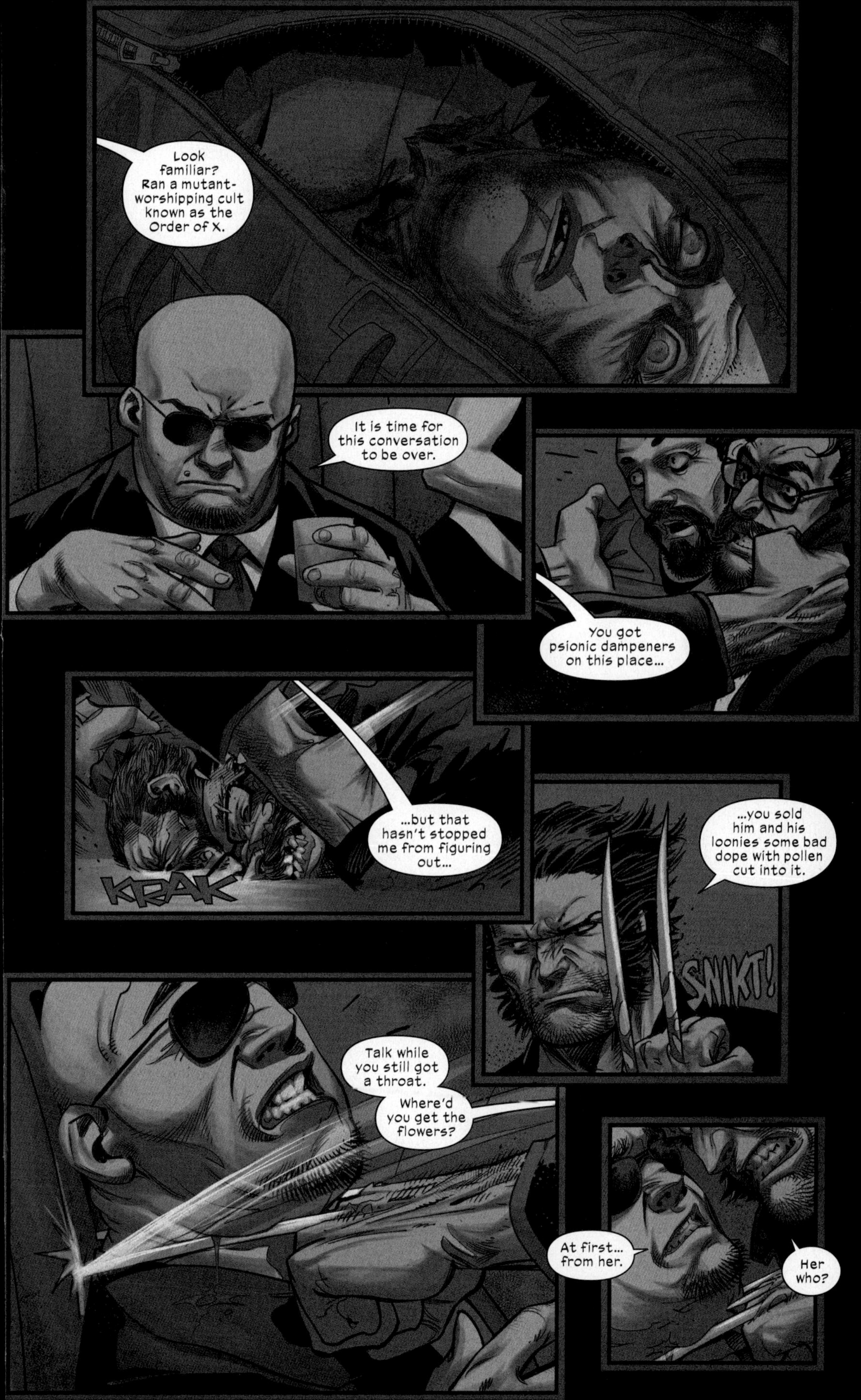
Look familiar? Ran a mutant-worshipping cult known as the Order of X.
It is time for this conversation to be over.
You got psionic dampeners on this place...
...but that hasn't stopped me from figuring out...
KRAK
...you sold him and his loonies some bad dope with pollen cut into it.
SNIKT!
Talk while you still got a throat.
Where'd you get the flowers?
At first... from her.
Her who?

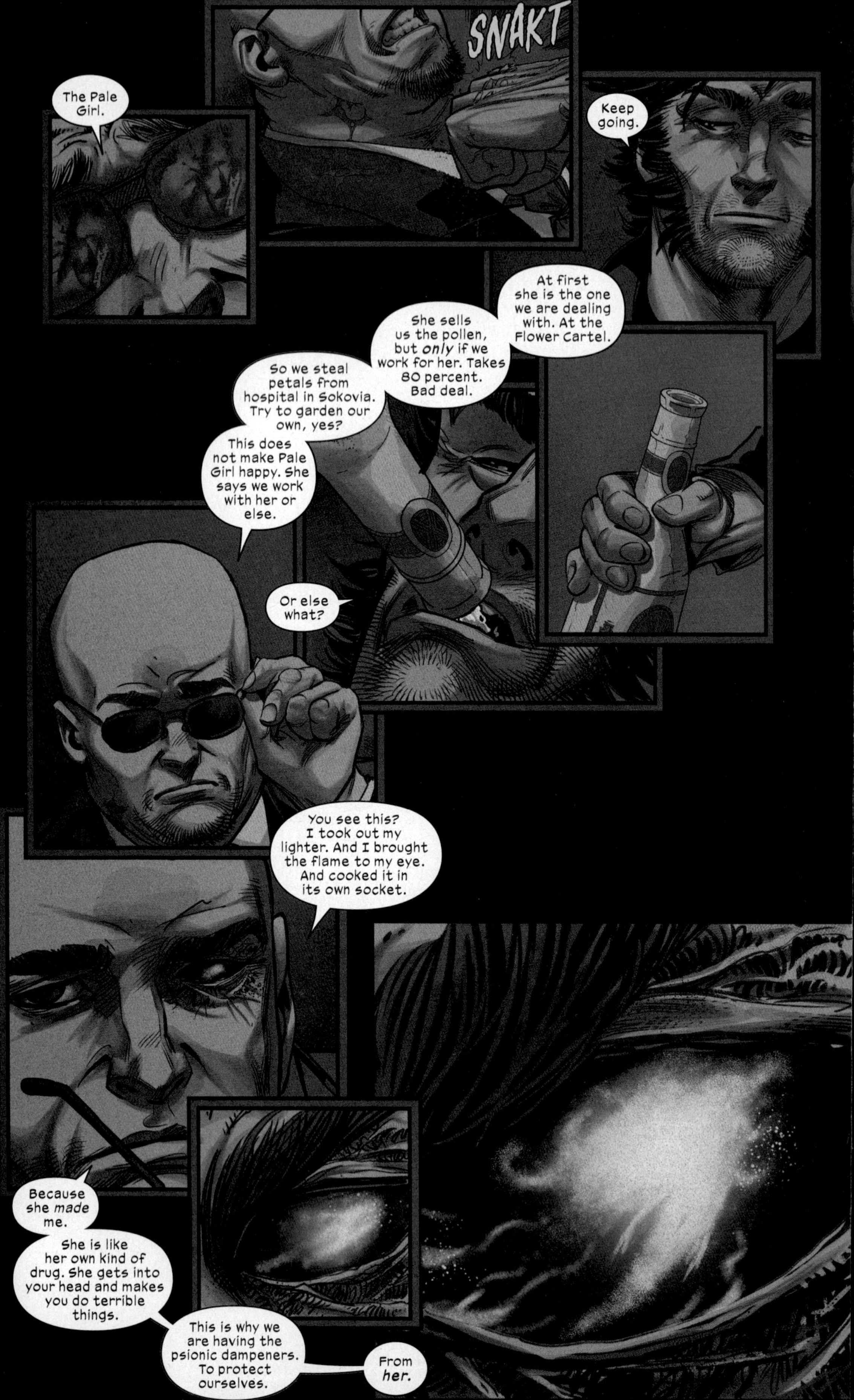
SNAKT
The Pale Girl.
Keep going.
At first she is the one we are dealing with. At the Flower Cartel.
She sells us the pollen, but *only* if we work for her. Takes 80 percent. Bad deal.
So we steal petals from hospital in Sokovia. Try to garden our own, yes?
This does not make Pale Girl happy. She says we work with her or else.
Or else what?
You see this? I took out my lighter. And I brought the flame to my eye. And cooked it in its own socket.
Because she *made* me.
She is like her own kind of drug. She gets into your head and makes you do terrible things.
This is why we are having the psionic dampeners. To protect ourselves.
From *her*.

*Earlier today.
The Pointe. Krakoa.*

Pollen isn't everywhere, but it's taken to the wind, so to speak.

*C.I.A. headquarters.
Langley, VA.*

L.A. Rio. Mumbai. Johannesburg.

We're tracking the feeds. News, police, social media, the dark web. More people are talking about it than actually using it.

But people are dying, man.

From the synthetic knockoffs, yeah. But more so from the Flower Cartel taking over or taking down any competition.

There appears to be a new drug war brewing.

And we're to blame.

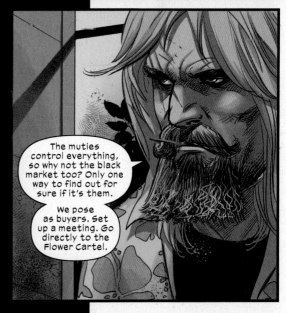

The muties control everything, so why not the black market too? Only one way to find out for sure if it's them.

We pose as buyers. Set up a meeting. Go directly to the Flower Cartel.

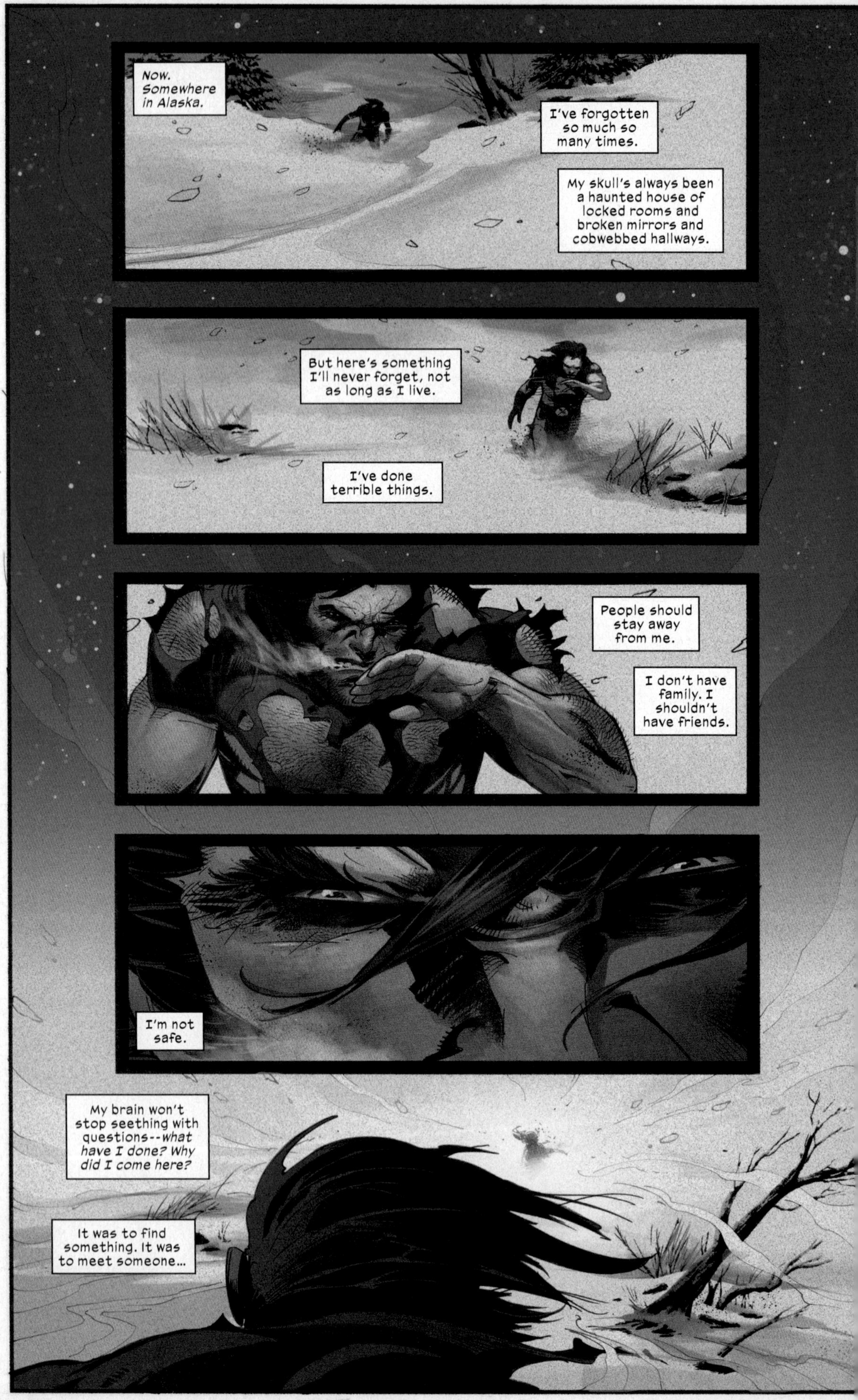
Now. Somewhere in Alaska.
I've forgotten so much so many times.
My skull's always been a haunted house of locked rooms and broken mirrors and cobwebbed hallways.
But here's something I'll never forget, not as long as I live.
I've done terrible things.
People should stay away from me.
I don't have family. I shouldn't have friends.
I'm not safe.
My brain won't stop seething with questions--*what have I done? Why did I come here?*
It was to find something. It was to meet someone...

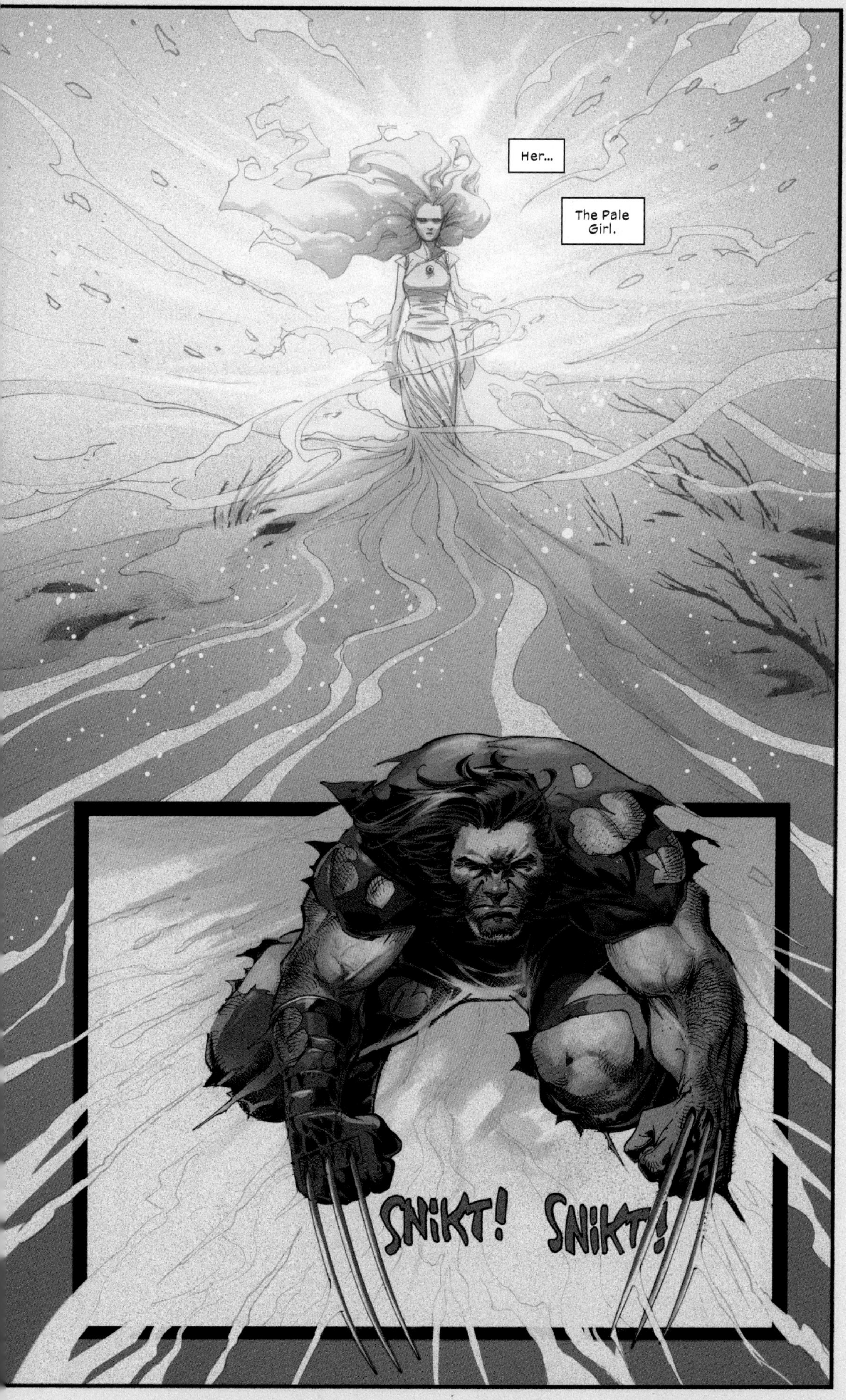
Her...
The Pale Girl.
SNIKT! SNIKT!

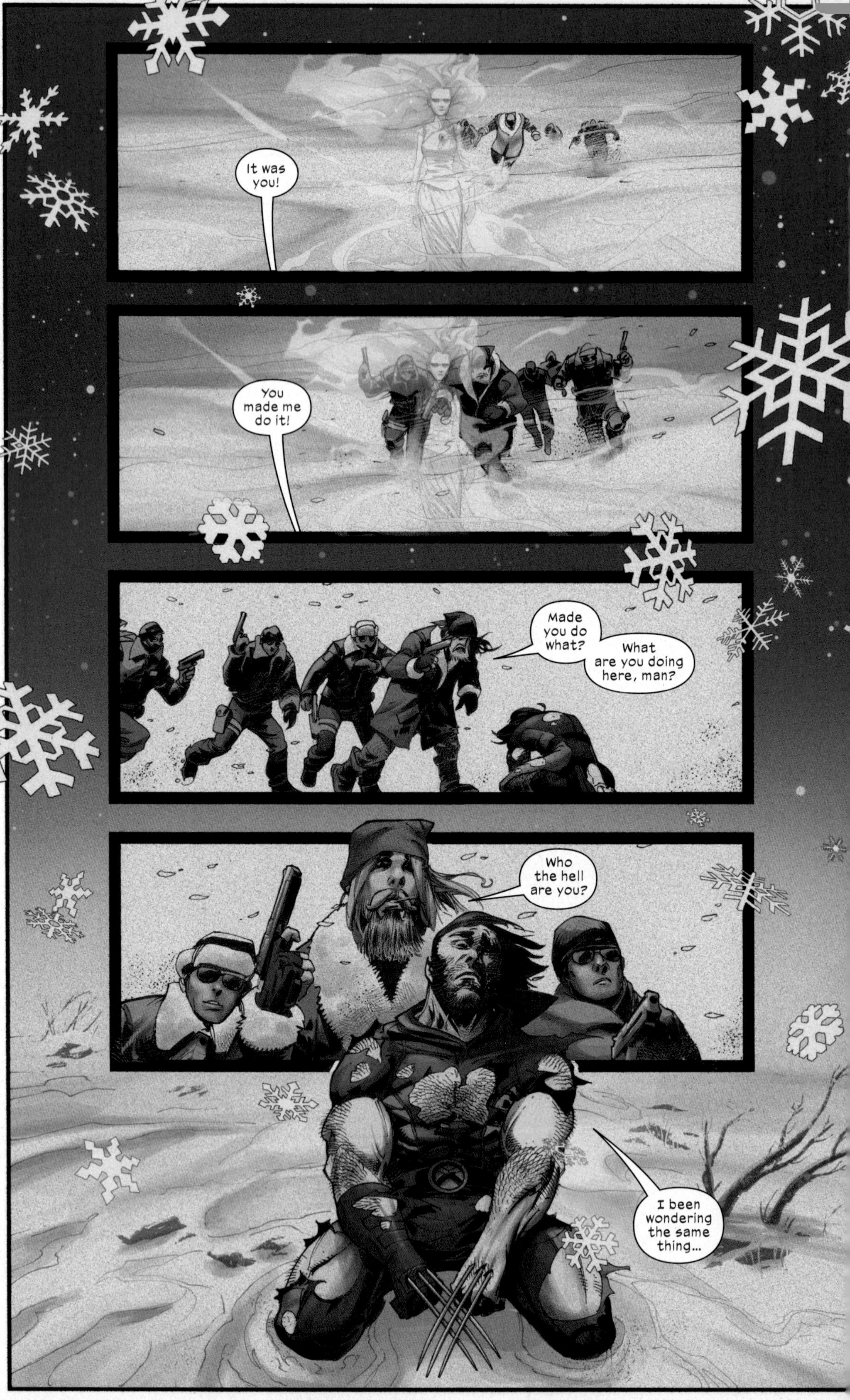
It was you!
You made me do it!
Made you do what?
What are you doing here, man?
Who the hell are you?
I been wondering the same thing...

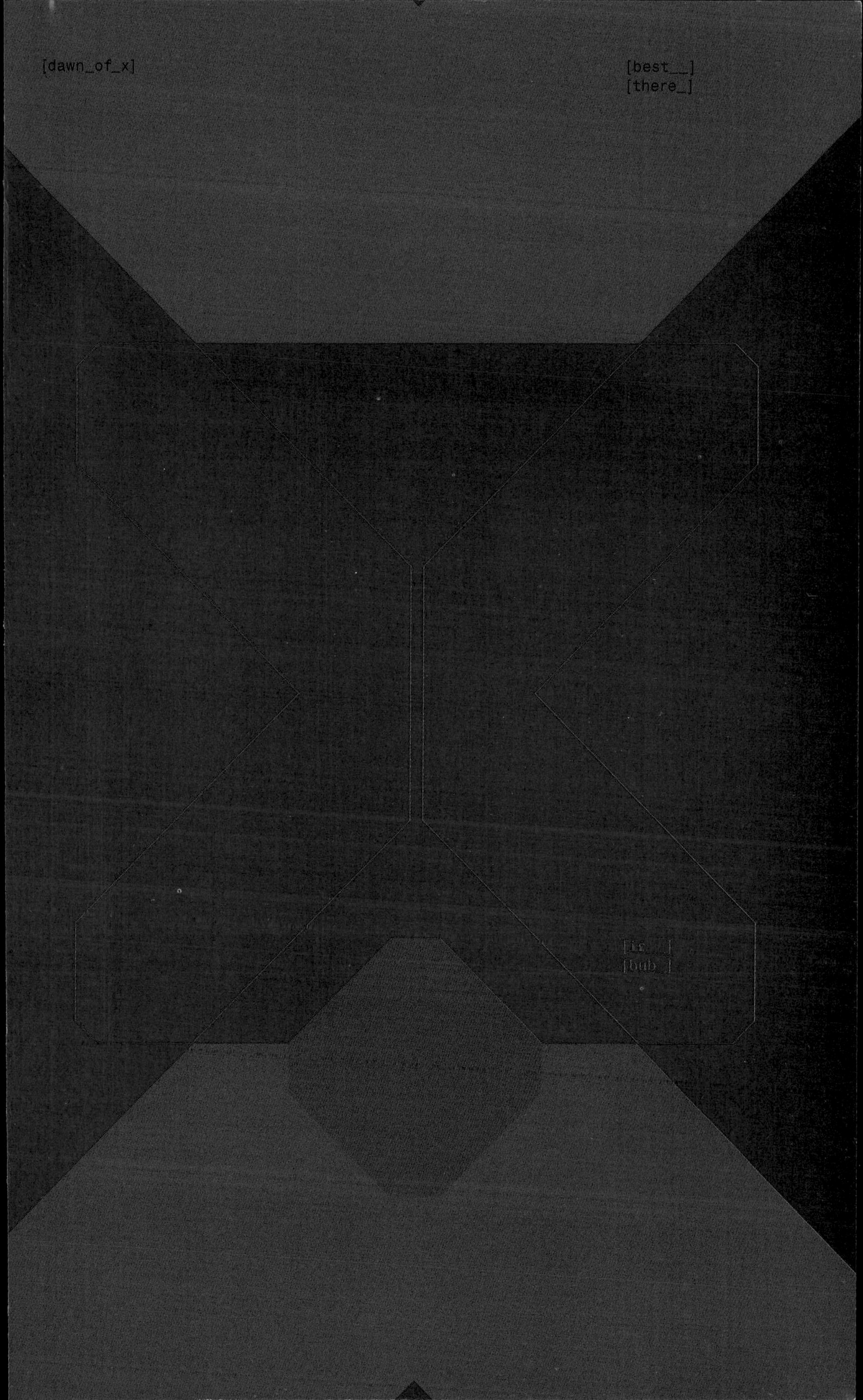
[dawn_of_x]
[best__]
[there_]
[is__]
[bub_]

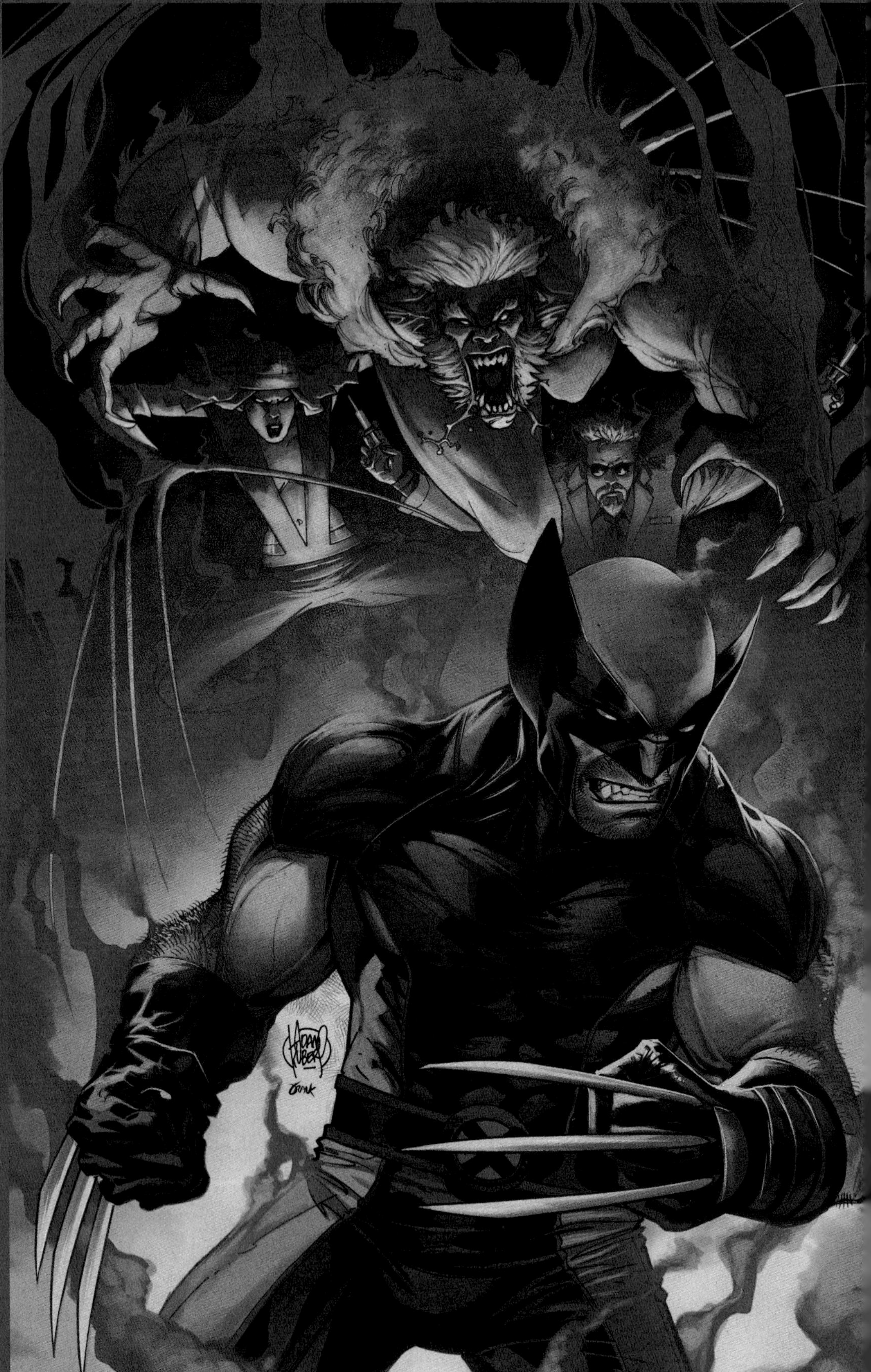

Your Own Worst Enemy

The Marauder.
Somewhere in the Pacific.
The vessel is off course.

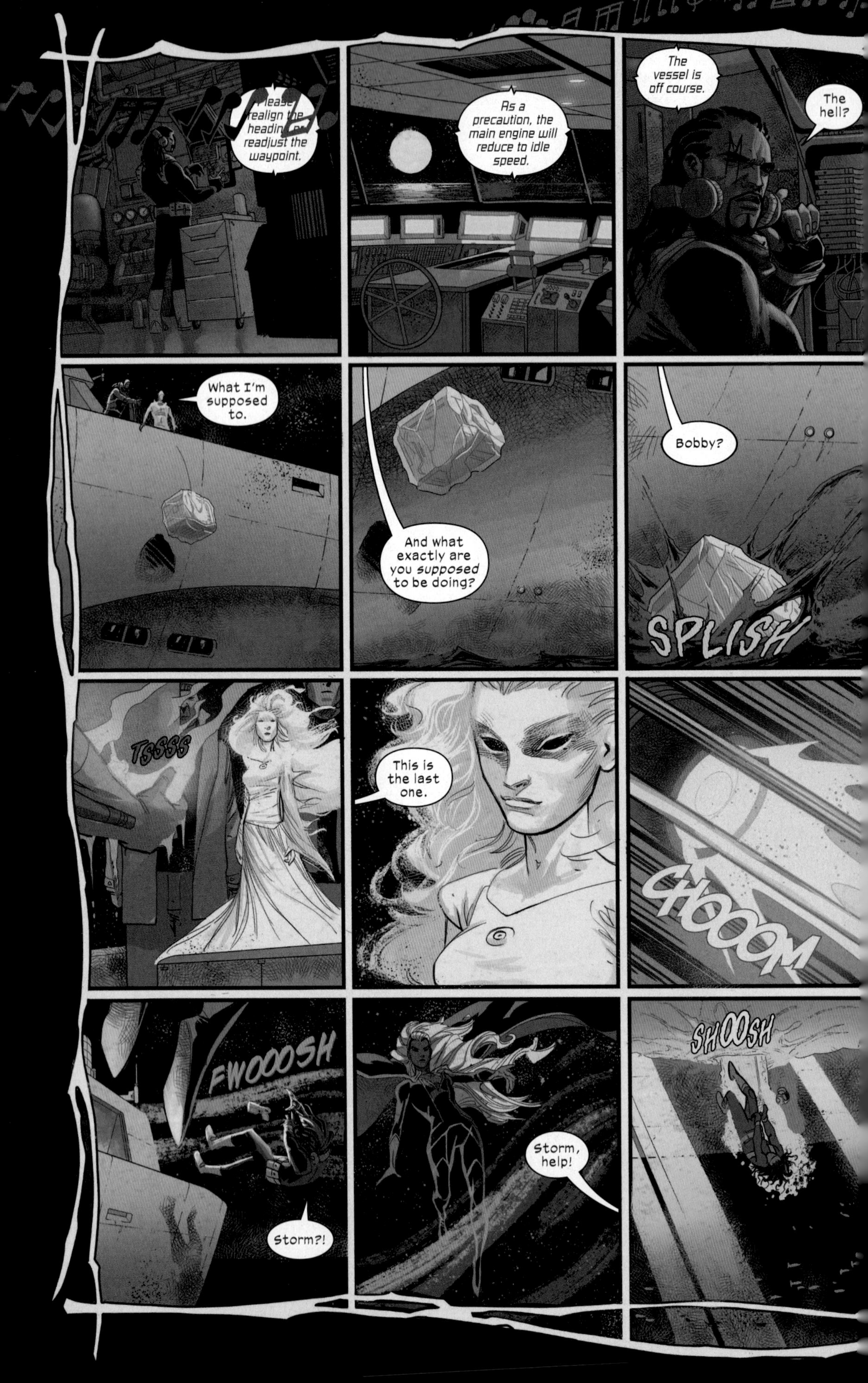
Please realign the heading or readjust the waypoint.
As a precaution, the main engine will reduce to idle speed.
The vessel is off course.
The hell?
What I'm supposed to.
And what exactly are you *supposed* to be doing?
Bobby?
SPLISH
TSSSS
This is the last one.
CHOOOM
FWOOOSH
Storm?!
Storm, help!
SHOOSH

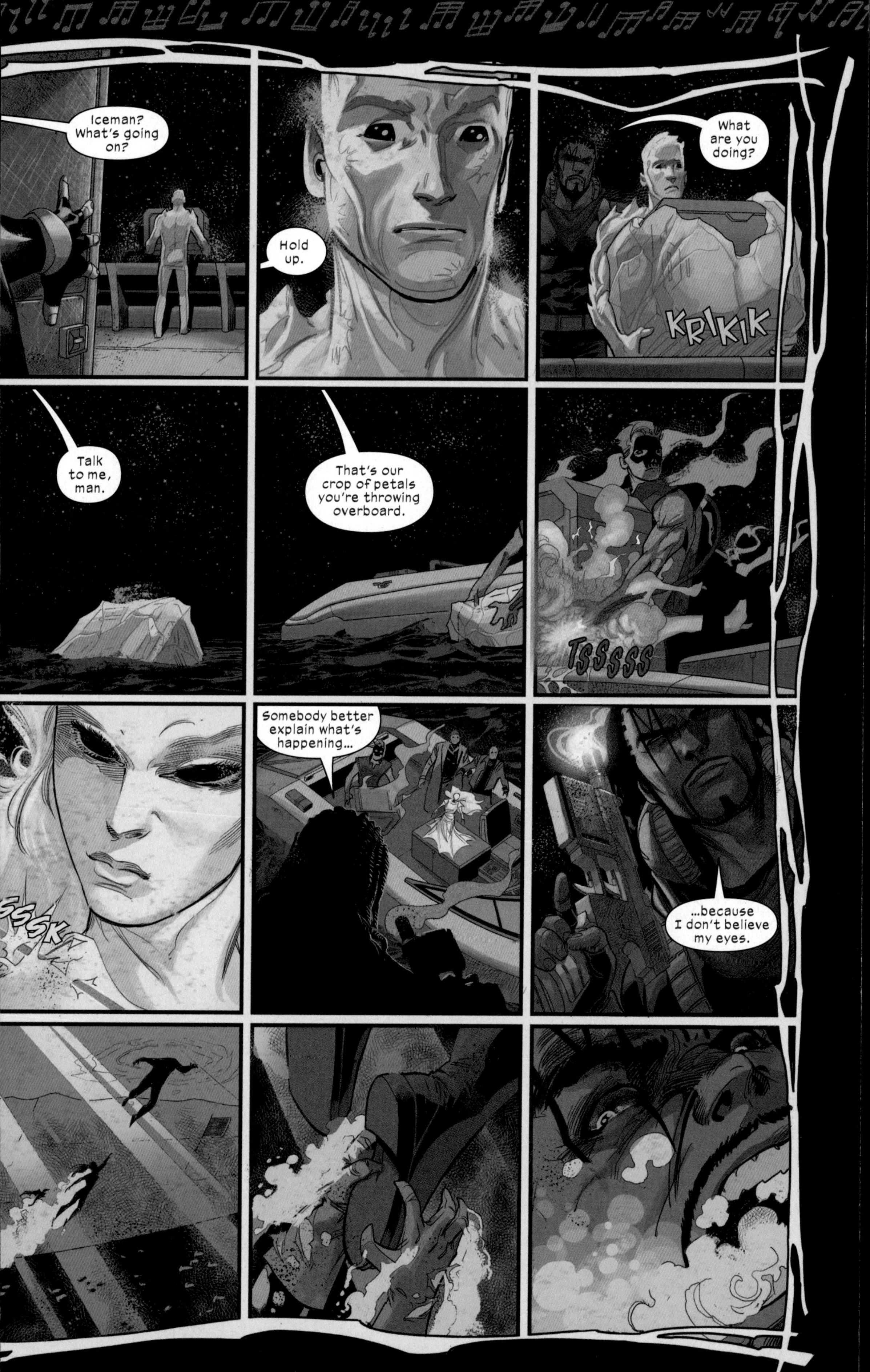
Iceman? What's going on?
Hold up.
What are you doing?
KRIKIK
Talk to me, man.
That's our crop of petals you're throwing overboard.
TSSSSS
Somebody better explain what's happening...
...because I don't believe my eyes.

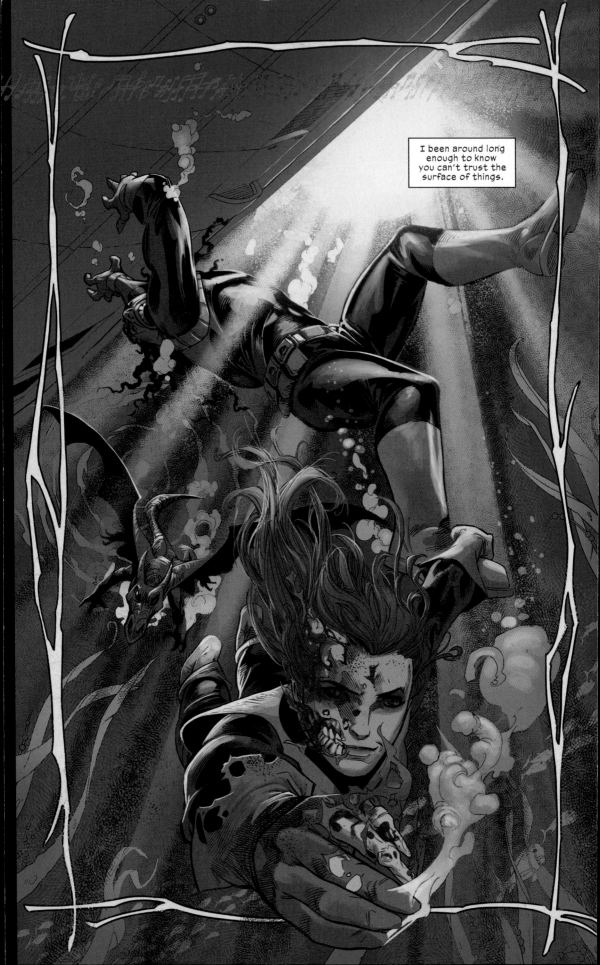

I been around long enough to know you can't trust the surface of things.

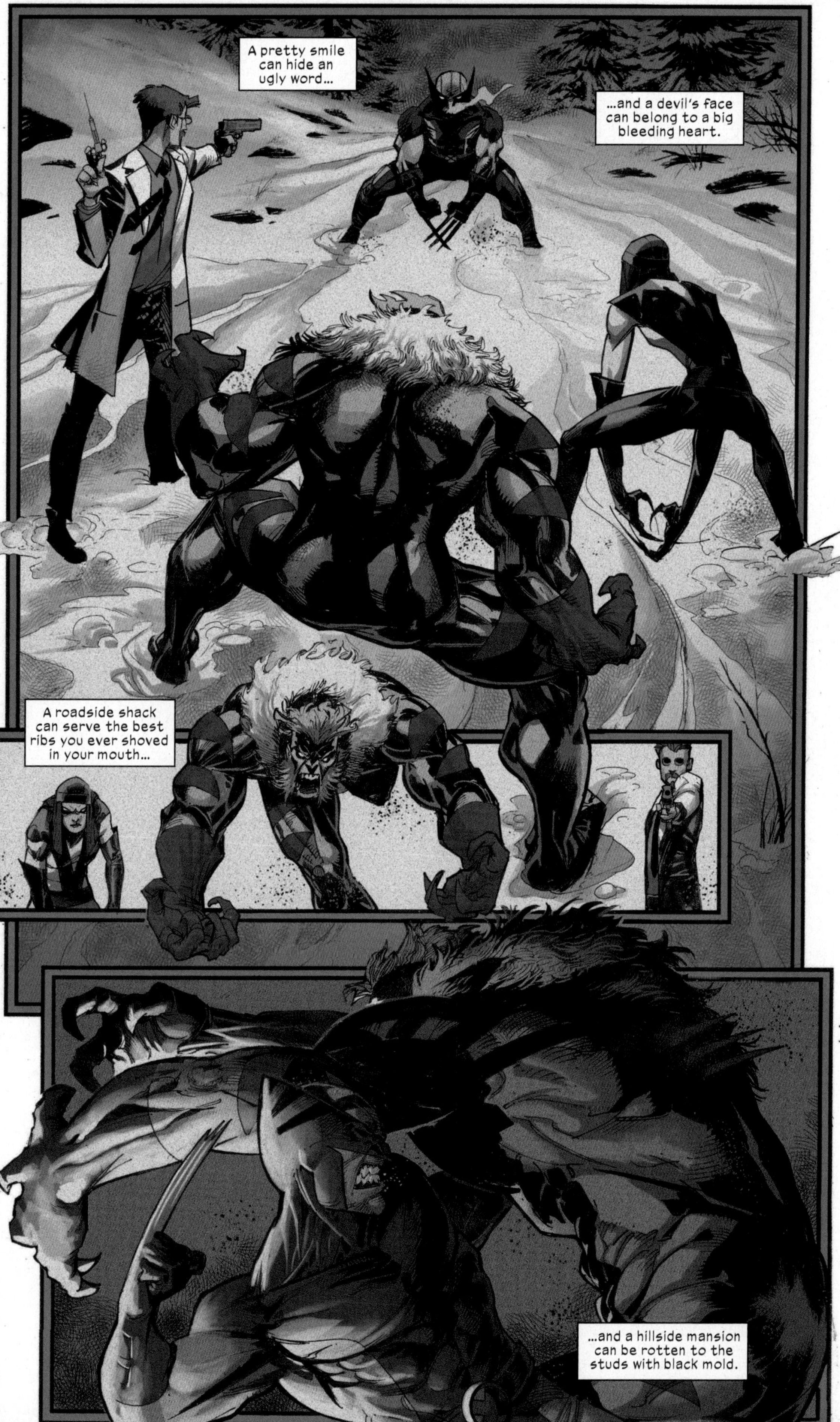
A pretty smile can hide an ugly word...
...and a devil's face can belong to a big bleeding heart.
A roadside shack can serve the best ribs you ever shoved in your mouth...
...and a hillside mansion can be rotten to the studs with black mold.

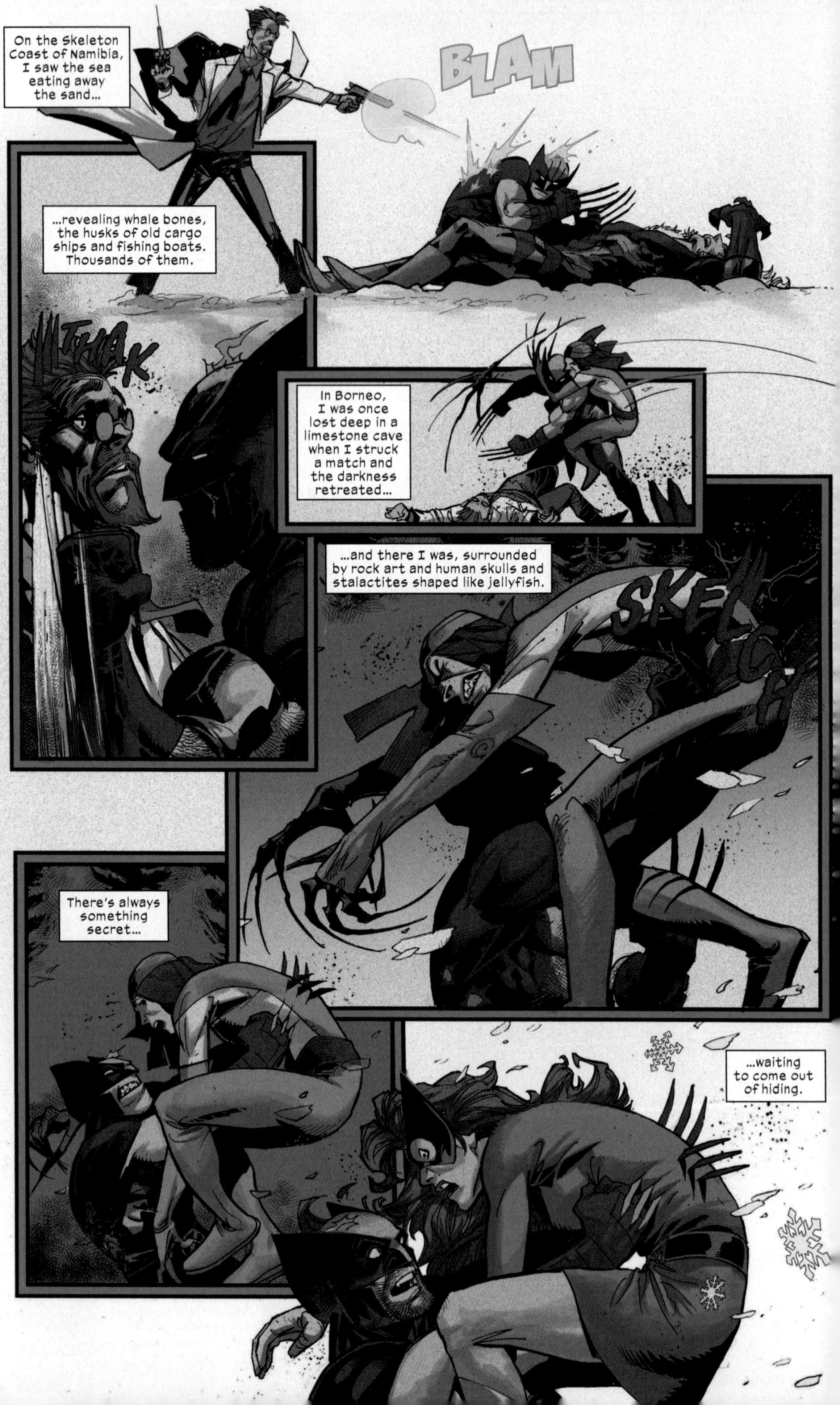
On the Skeleton Coast of Namibia, I saw the sea eating away the sand...
BLAM
...revealing whale bones, the husks of old cargo ships and fishing boats. Thousands of them.
THAK
In Borneo, I was once lost deep in a limestone cave when I struck a match and the darkness retreated...
...and there I was, surrounded by rock art and human skulls and stalactites shaped like jellyfish.
SKELCH
There's always something secret...
...waiting to come out of hiding.

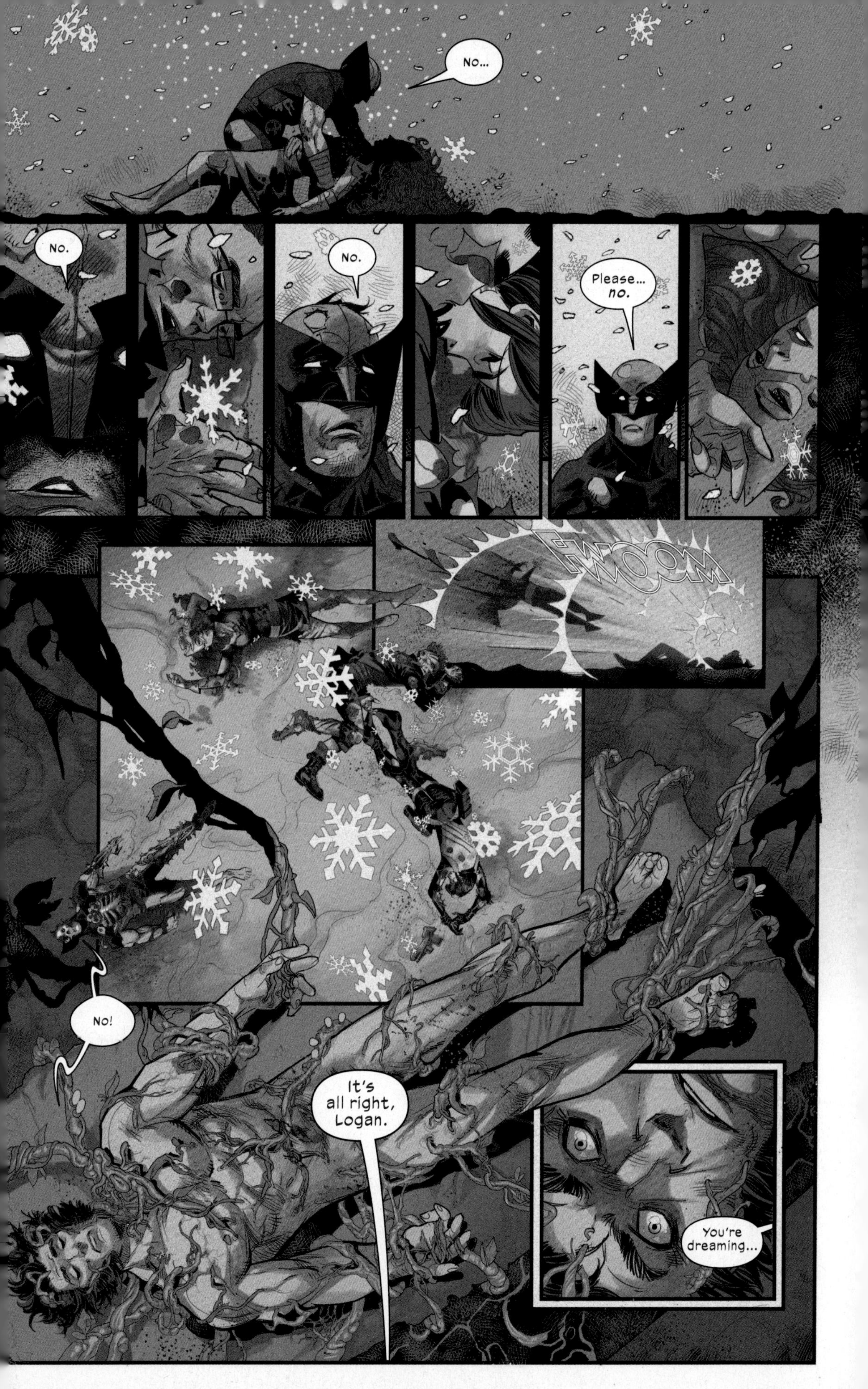
No...
No.
No.
Please... no.
FWOOM
No!
It's all right, Logan.
You're dreaming...

[best___]
[there_]

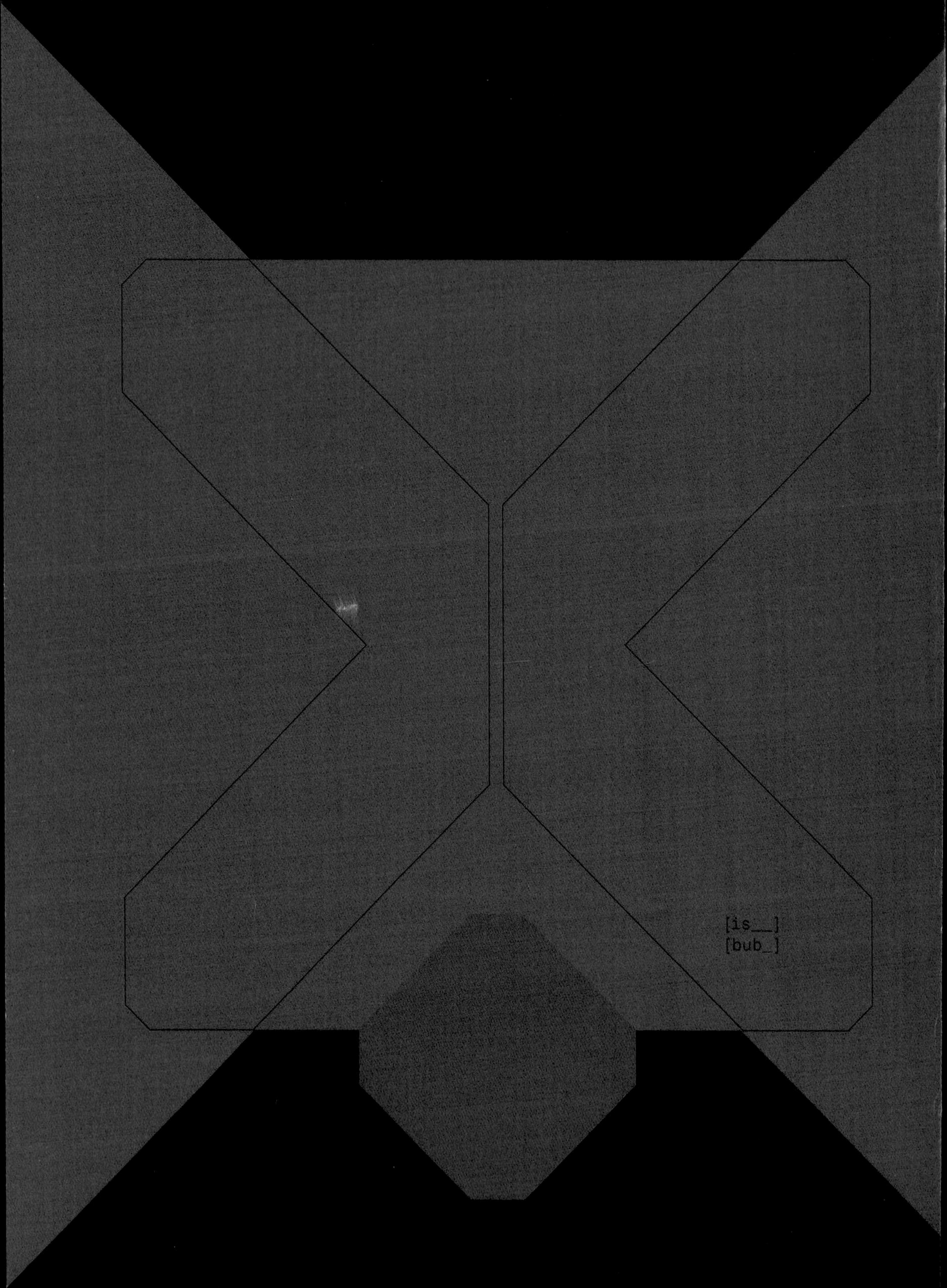
[is__]
[bub_]

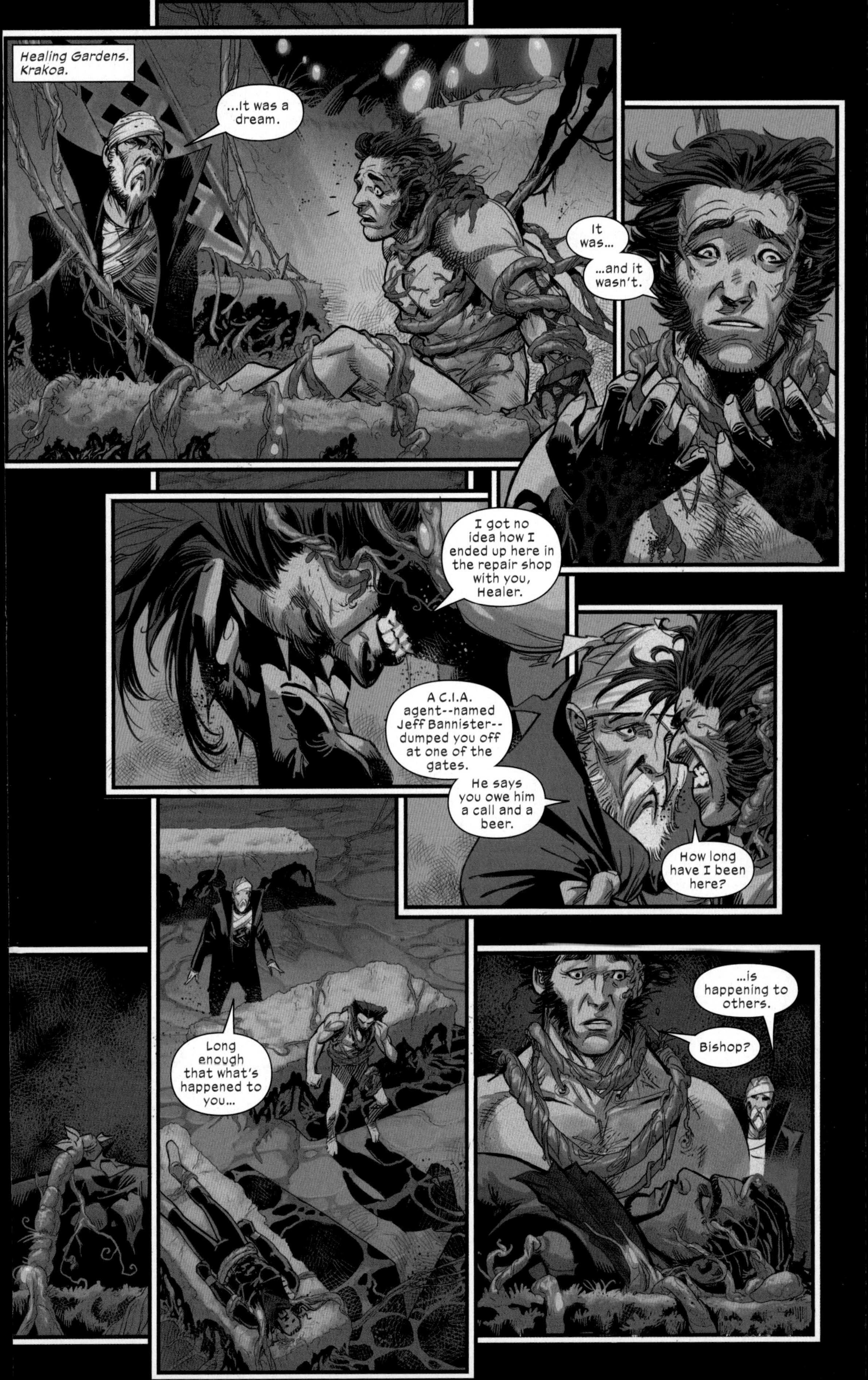
Healing Gardens. Krakoa.
...It was a dream.
It was...
...and it wasn't.
I got no idea how I ended up here in the repair shop with you, Healer.
A C.I.A. agent--named Jeff Bannister--dumped you off at one of the gates.
He says you owe him a call and a beer.
How long have I been here?
Long enough that what's happened to you...
...is happening to others.
Bishop?

PORT OF ENTRY REPORT

The ship's log discloses that for twenty minutes, the *Marauder* vessel was adrift two hundred miles off the coast of Chile.

No one on board could account for the lapse in course, but all report feeling confused, exhausted and even dizzy.

A series of radiant blasts were noticed off the stern, and further investigation revealed that Lucas Bishop had gone overboard. By the time of his recovery, nearly two miles off the wake of the vessel, he was almost drowned and hypothermic. He has no memory of the event. A full recovery is expected.

Inventory exposes the loss of a dozen crates of petals.

Brain scans of each crew member reveal neural patterns indicative of transient ischemic attacks.

A psionic threat is suspected, likely working on behalf of the Flower Cartel responsible for the current pollen epidemic.

—

—

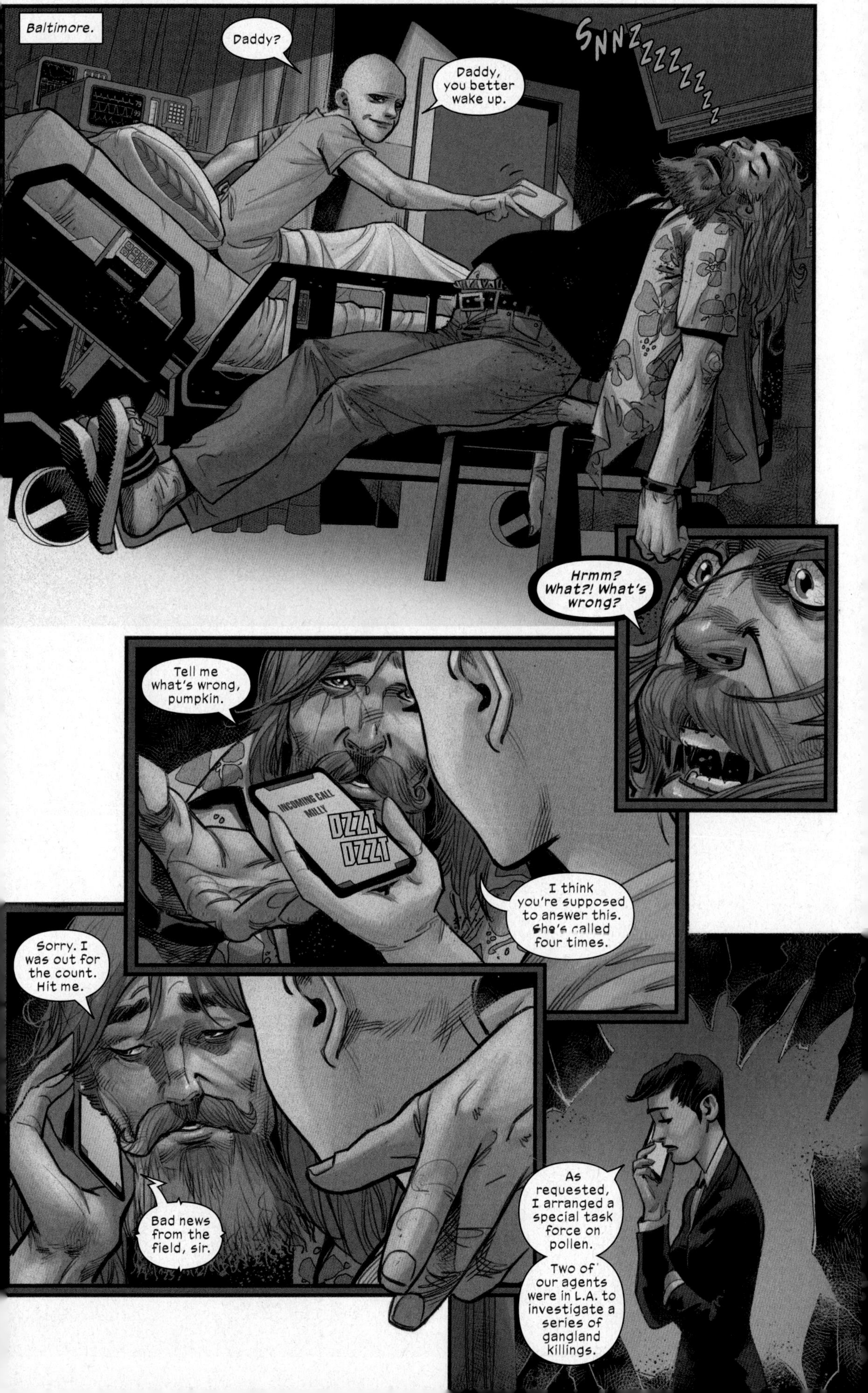
Baltimore.
Daddy?
Daddy, you better wake up.
SNNZZZZZZZZ
Hrmm? What?! What's wrong?
Tell me what's wrong, pumpkin.
INCOMING CALL MILLY
DZZT DZZT
I think you're supposed to answer this. She's called four times.
Sorry. I was out for the count. Hit me.
Bad news from the field, sir.
As requested, I arranged a special task force on pollen.
Two of our agents were in L.A. to investigate a series of gangland killings.

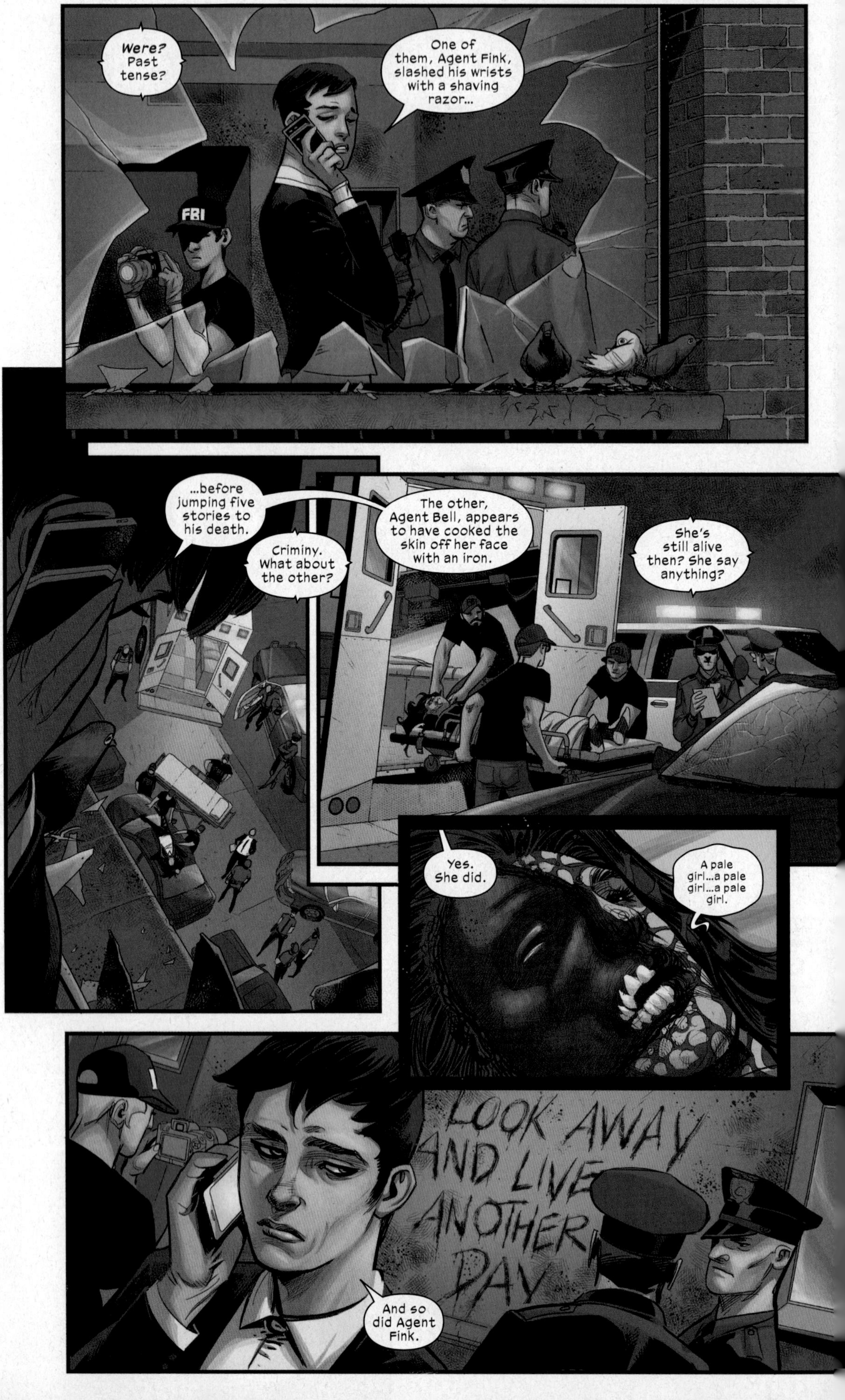
Were? Past tense?
One of them, Agent Fink, slashed his wrists with a shaving razor...
FBI
...before jumping five stories to his death.
Criminy. What about the other?
The other, Agent Bell, appears to have cooked the skin off her face with an iron.
She's still alive then? She say anything?
FBI
Yes. She did.
A pale girl...a pale girl...a pale girl.
LOOK AWAY AND LIVE ANOTHER DAY
And so did Agent Fink.

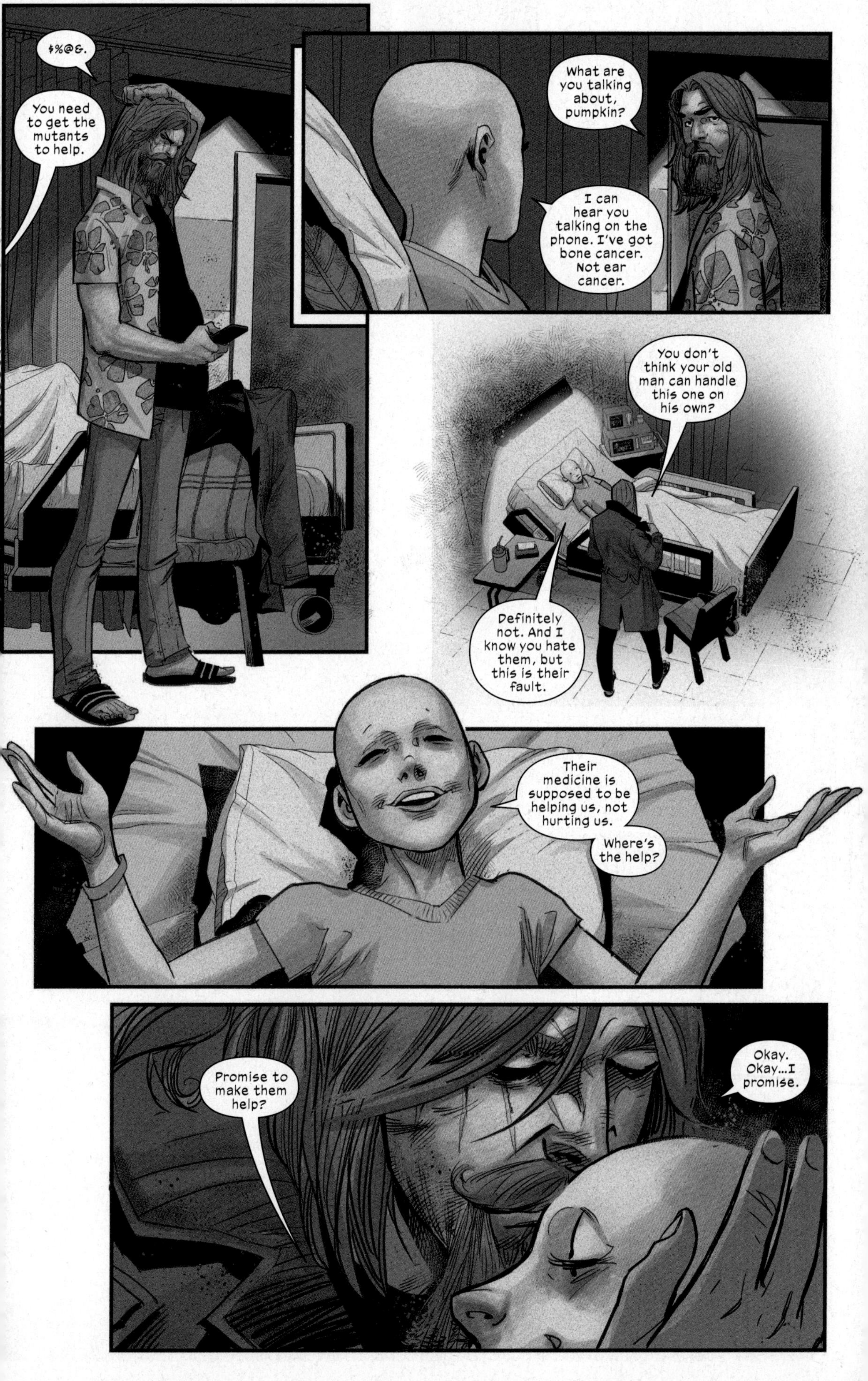
$%@&.
You need to get the mutants to help.
What are you talking about, pumpkin?
I can hear you talking on the phone. I've got bone cancer. Not ear cancer.
You don't think your old man can handle this one on his own?
Definitely not. And I know you hate them, but this is their fault.
Their medicine is supposed to be helping us, not hurting us.
Where's the help?
Promise to make them help?
Okay. Okay...I promise.

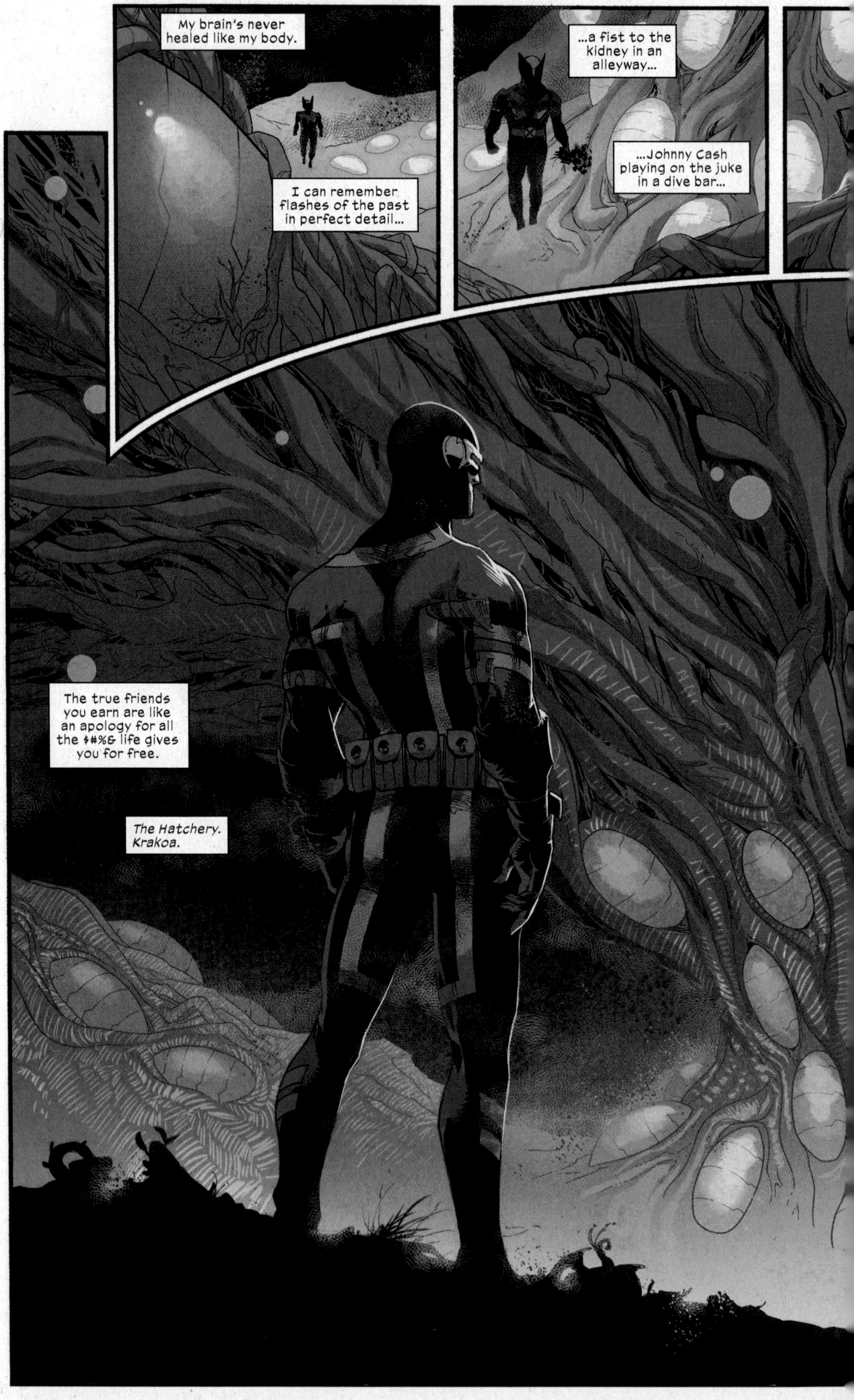

My brain's never healed like my body.
I can remember flashes of the past in perfect detail...
...a fist to the kidney in an alleyway...
...Johnny Cash playing on the juke in a dive bar...
The true friends you earn are like an apology for all the $#%& life gives you for free.
The Hatchery. Krakoa.

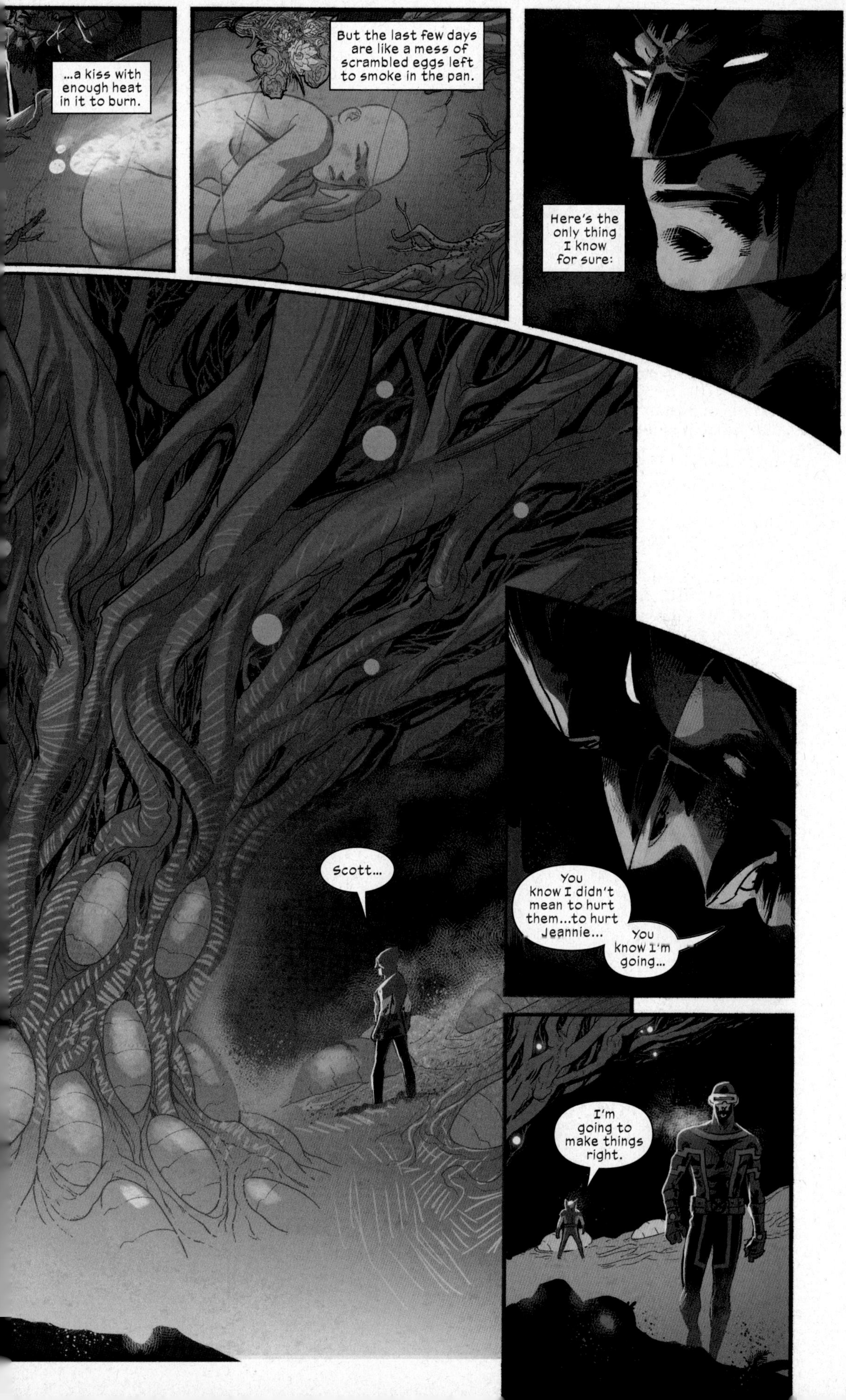
...a kiss with enough heat in it to burn.
But the last few days are like a mess of scrambled eggs left to smoke in the pan.
Here's the only thing I know for sure:
Scott...
You know I didn't mean to hurt them...to hurt Jeannie...
You know I'm going...
I'm going to make things right.

PROFIT AND LOSS ANALYSIS OF PETAL SHIPMENTS

From farm to factory to pharmacy, the Hellfire Trading Company controls the shipping of all Krakoan petals. This is necessarily inefficient. When the oversight is so complete, the losses are few.

But beyond their product, there is another kind of loss that bears accounting.

Fifty million people worldwide have dementia, with nearly ten million new diagnoses each year.

There were seventeen million new cases of cancer last year and nearly ten million deaths.

The mutants are hopeful that within the next five years, a waitlist will no longer be necessary for all their medicines. But at present, the demand for antibody petals is greater than the capacity.

—

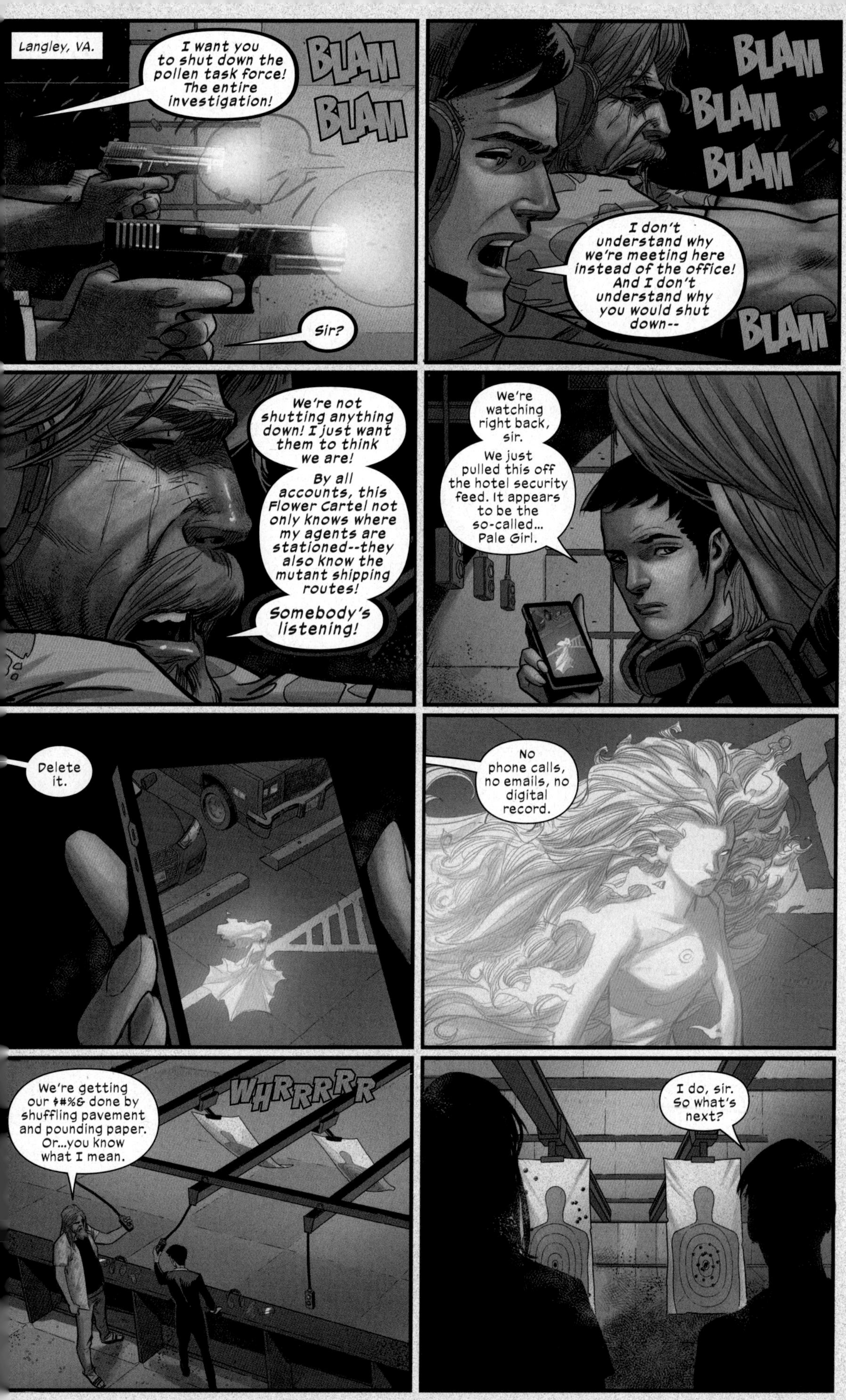

Langley, VA.
I want you to shut down the pollen task force! The entire investigation!
BLAM
BLAM
Sir?
BLAM
BLAM
BLAM
I don't understand why we're meeting here instead of the office! And I don't understand why you would shut down--
BLAM
We're not shutting anything down! I just want them to think we are!
By all accounts, this Flower Cartel not only knows where my agents are stationed--they also know the mutant shipping routes!
Somebody's listening!
We're watching right back, sir.
We just pulled this off the hotel security feed. It appears to be the so-called... Pale Girl.
Delete it.
No phone calls, no emails, no digital record.
WHRRRRRR
We're getting our $#%& done by shuffling pavement and pounding paper. Or...you know what I mean.
I do, sir. So what's next?

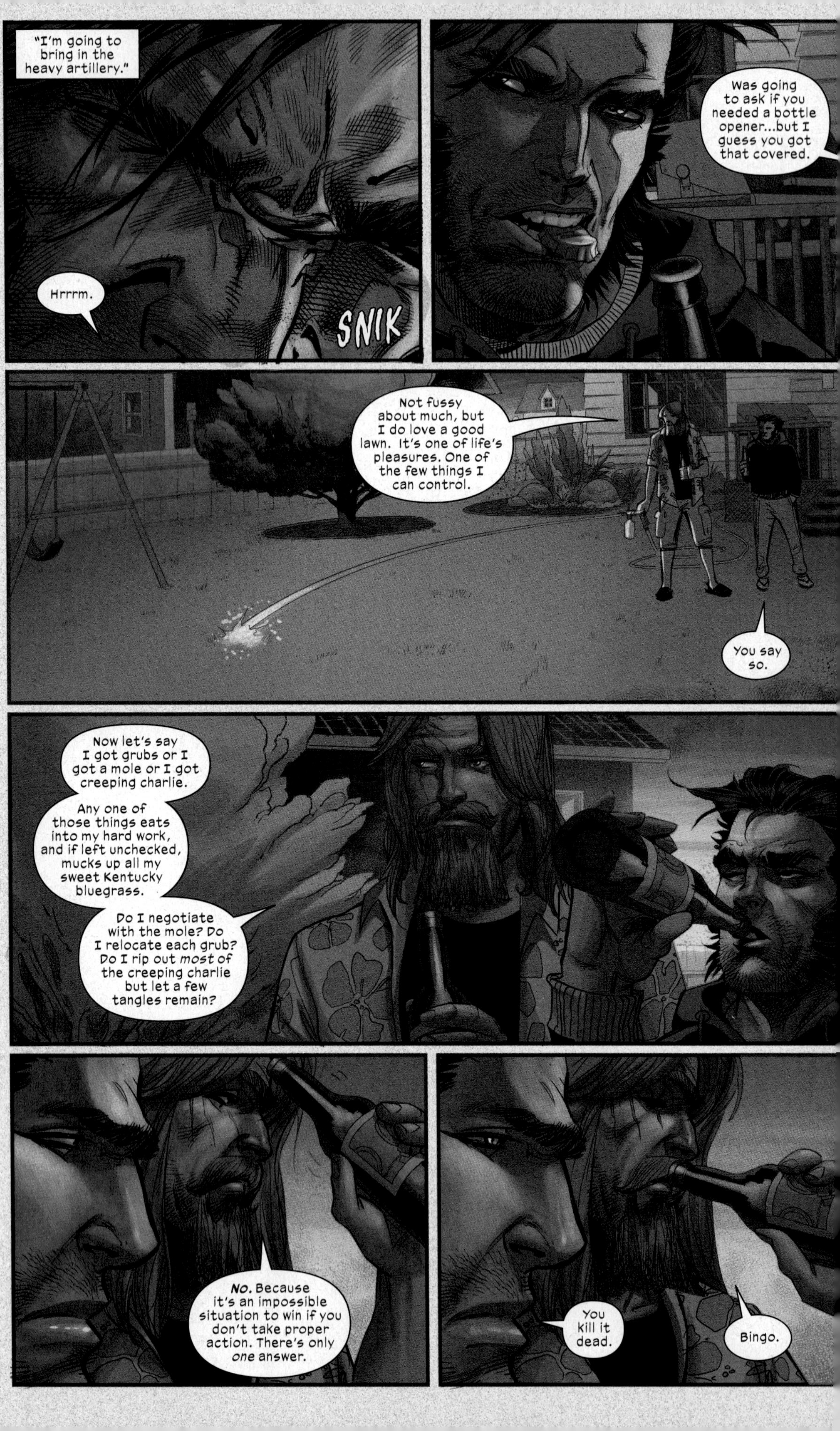
"I'm going to bring in the heavy artillery."
Hrrrm.
SNIK
Was going to ask if you needed a bottle opener...but I guess you got that covered.
Not fussy about much, but I do love a good lawn. It's one of life's pleasures. One of the few things I can control.
You say so.
Now let's say I got grubs or I got a mole or I got creeping charlie.
Any one of those things eats into my hard work, and if left unchecked, mucks up all my sweet Kentucky bluegrass.
Do I negotiate with the mole? Do I relocate each grub? Do I rip out *most* of the creeping charlie but let a few tangles remain?
No. Because it's an impossible situation to win if you don't take proper action. There's only *one* answer.
You kill it dead.
Bingo.

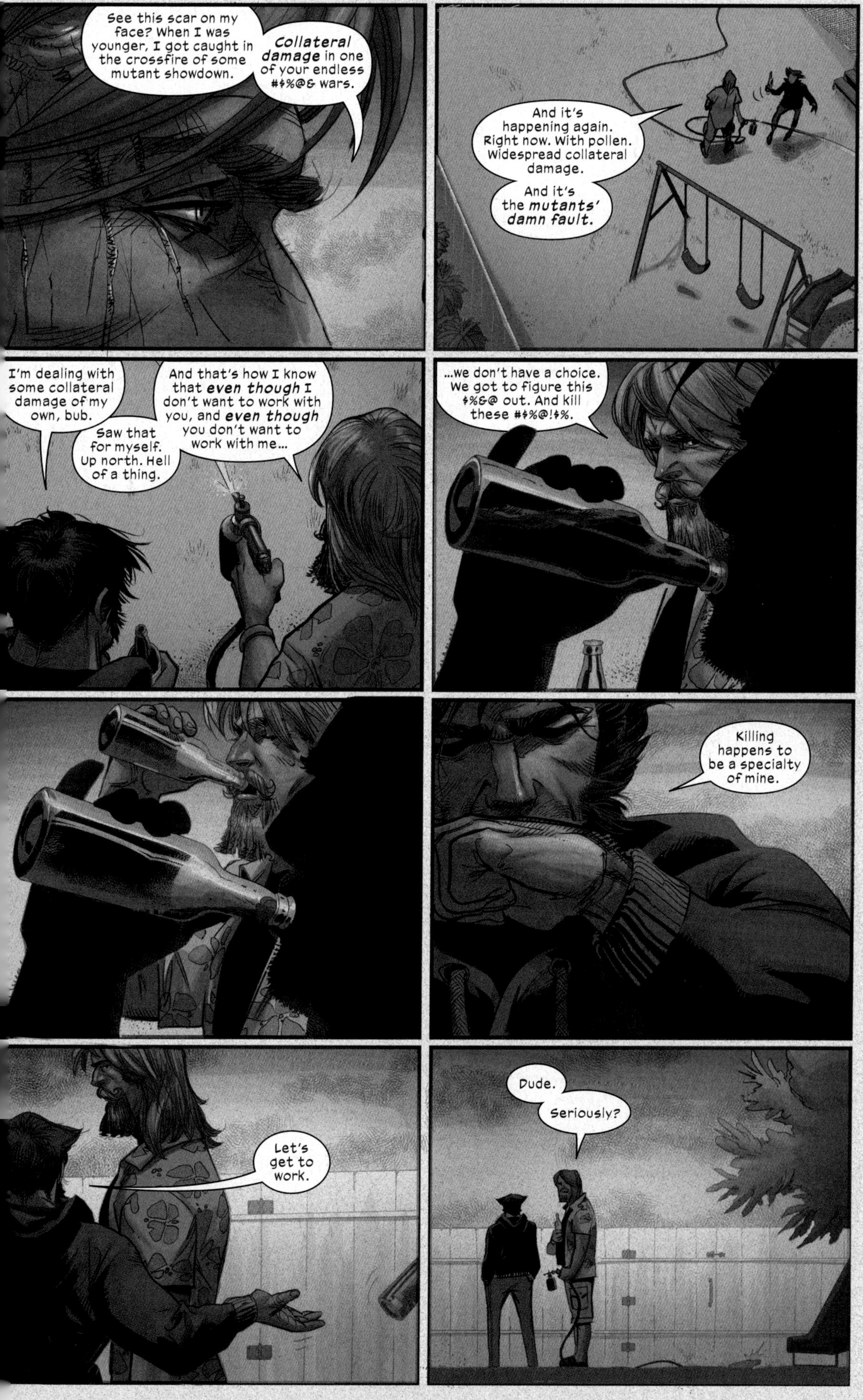
See this scar on my face? When I was younger, I got caught in the crossfire of some mutant showdown.
Collateral damage in one of your endless #$%@& wars.
And it's happening again. Right now. With pollen. Widespread collateral damage.
And it's the *mutants' damn fault.*
I'm dealing with some collateral damage of my own, bub.
Saw that for myself. Up north. Hell of a thing.
And that's how I know that *even though* I don't want to work with you, and *even though* you don't want to work with me...
...we don't have a choice. We got to figure this $%&@ out. And kill these #$%@!$%.
Killing happens to be a specialty of mine.
Let's get to work.
Dude.
Seriously?

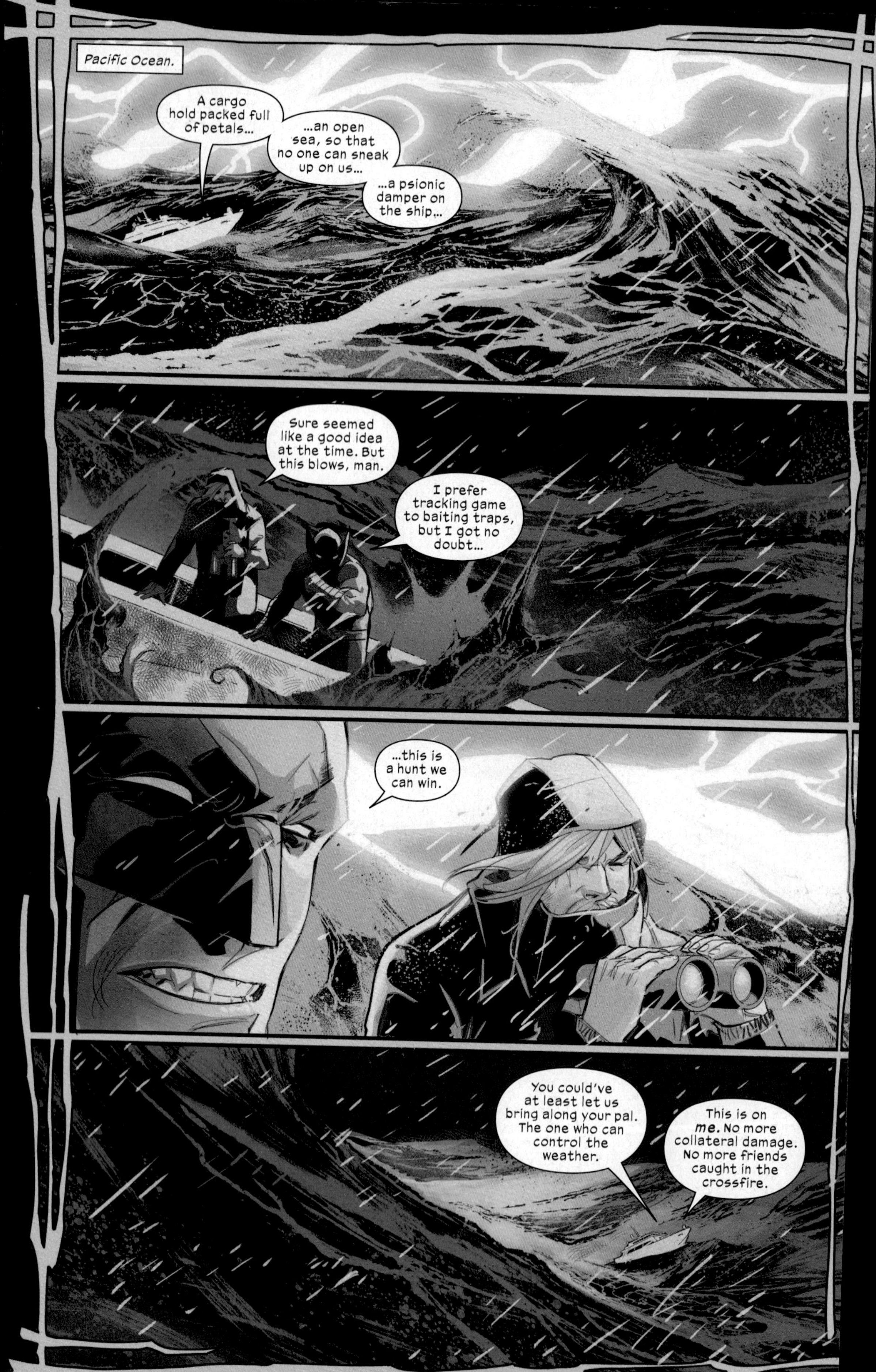

Pacific Ocean.
A cargo hold packed full of petals...
...an open sea, so that no one can sneak up on us...
...a psionic damper on the ship...
Sure seemed like a good idea at the time. But this blows, man.
I prefer tracking game to baiting traps, but I got no doubt...
...this is a hunt we can win.
You could've at least let us bring along your pal. The one who can control the weather.
This is on *me.* No more collateral damage. No more friends caught in the crossfire.

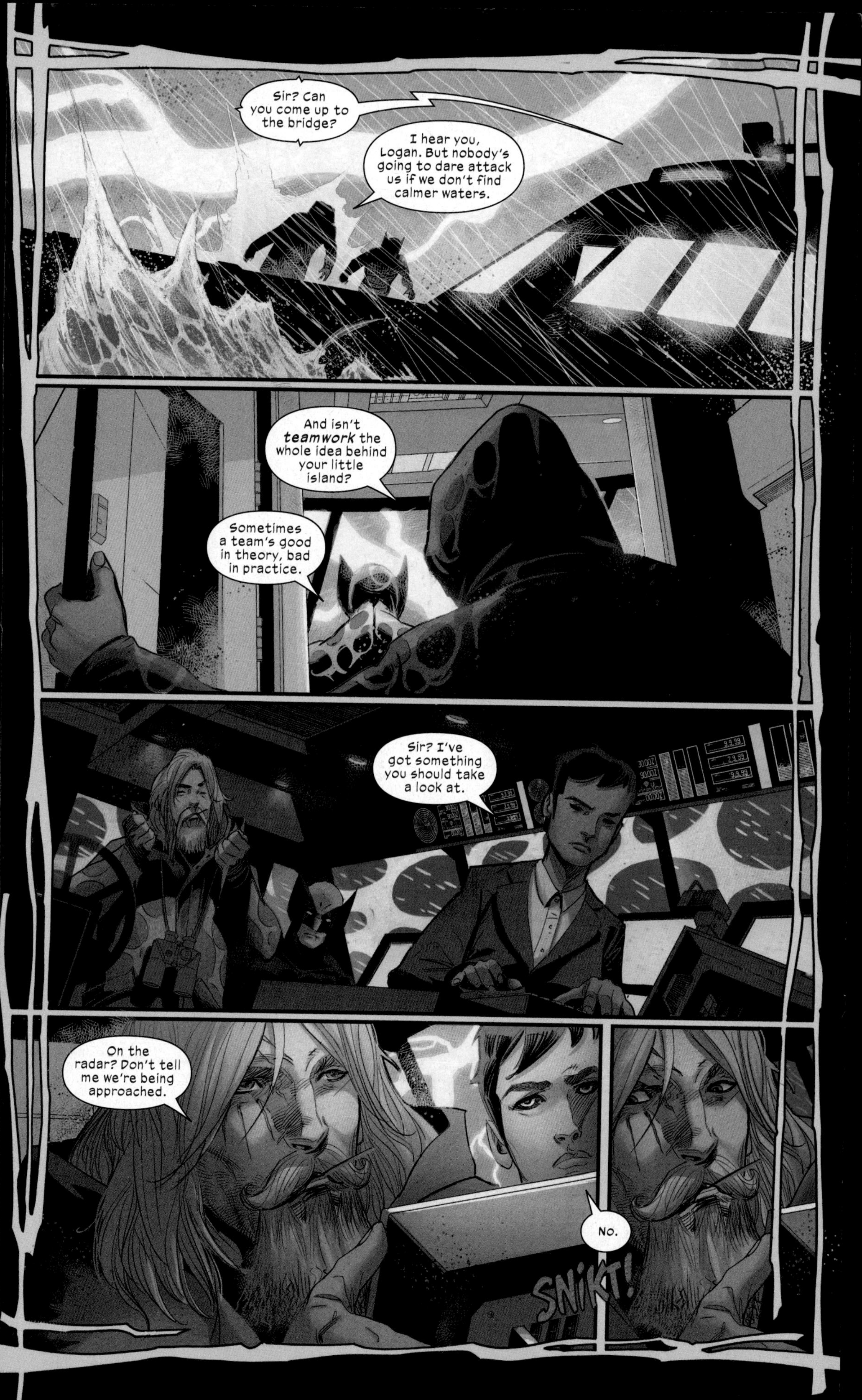
Sir? Can you come up to the bridge?
I hear you, Logan. But nobody's going to dare attack us if we don't find calmer waters.
And isn't *teamwork* the whole idea behind your little island?
Sometimes a team's good in theory, bad in practice.
Sir? I've got something you should take a look at.
On the radar? Don't tell me we're being approached.
No.
SNIKT!

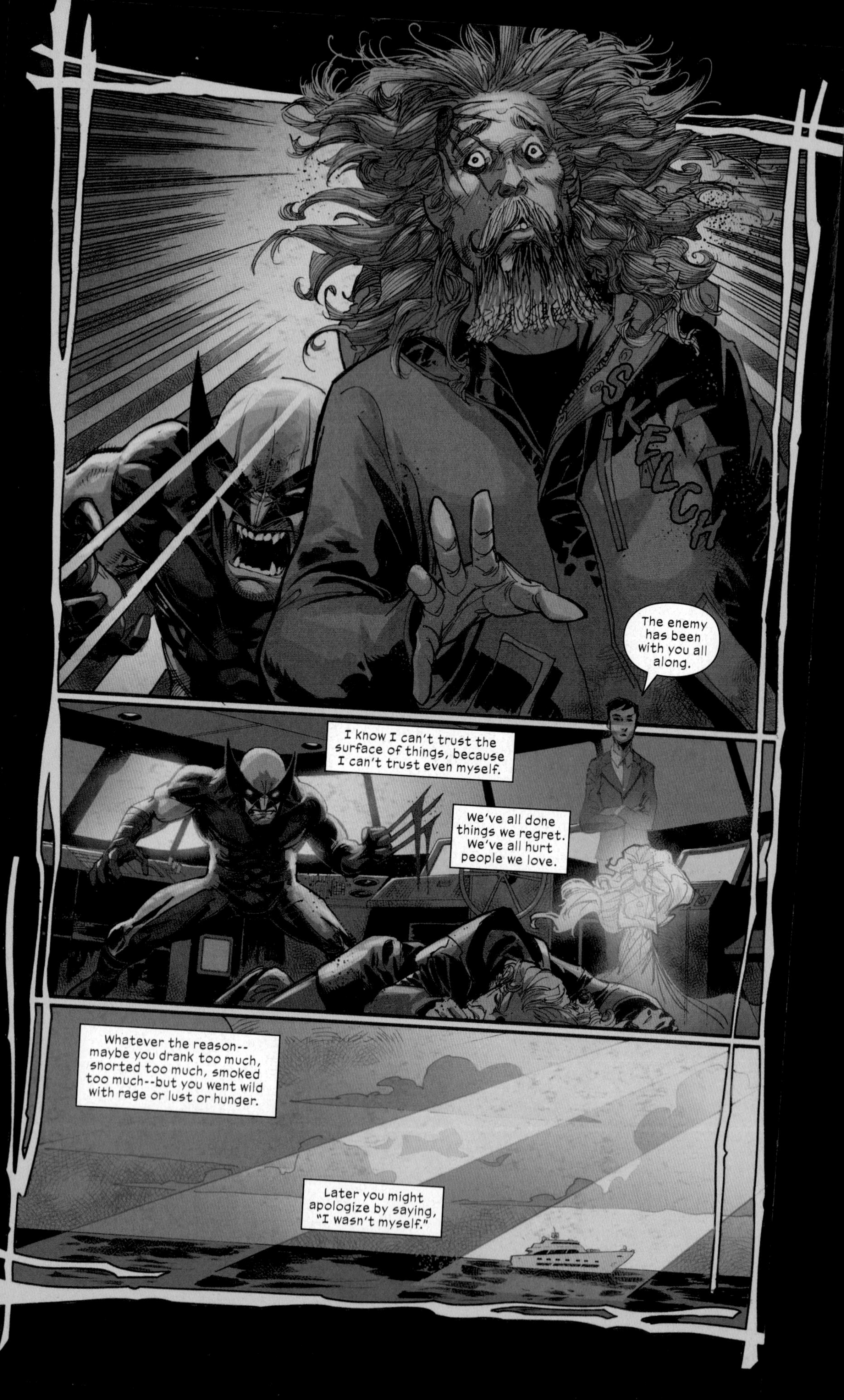
SKELCH
The enemy has been with you all along.
I know I can't trust the surface of things, because I can't trust even myself.
We've all done things we regret. We've all hurt people we love.
Whatever the reason-- maybe you drank too much, snorted too much, smoked too much--but you went wild with rage or lust or hunger.
Later you might apologize by saying, "I wasn't myself."

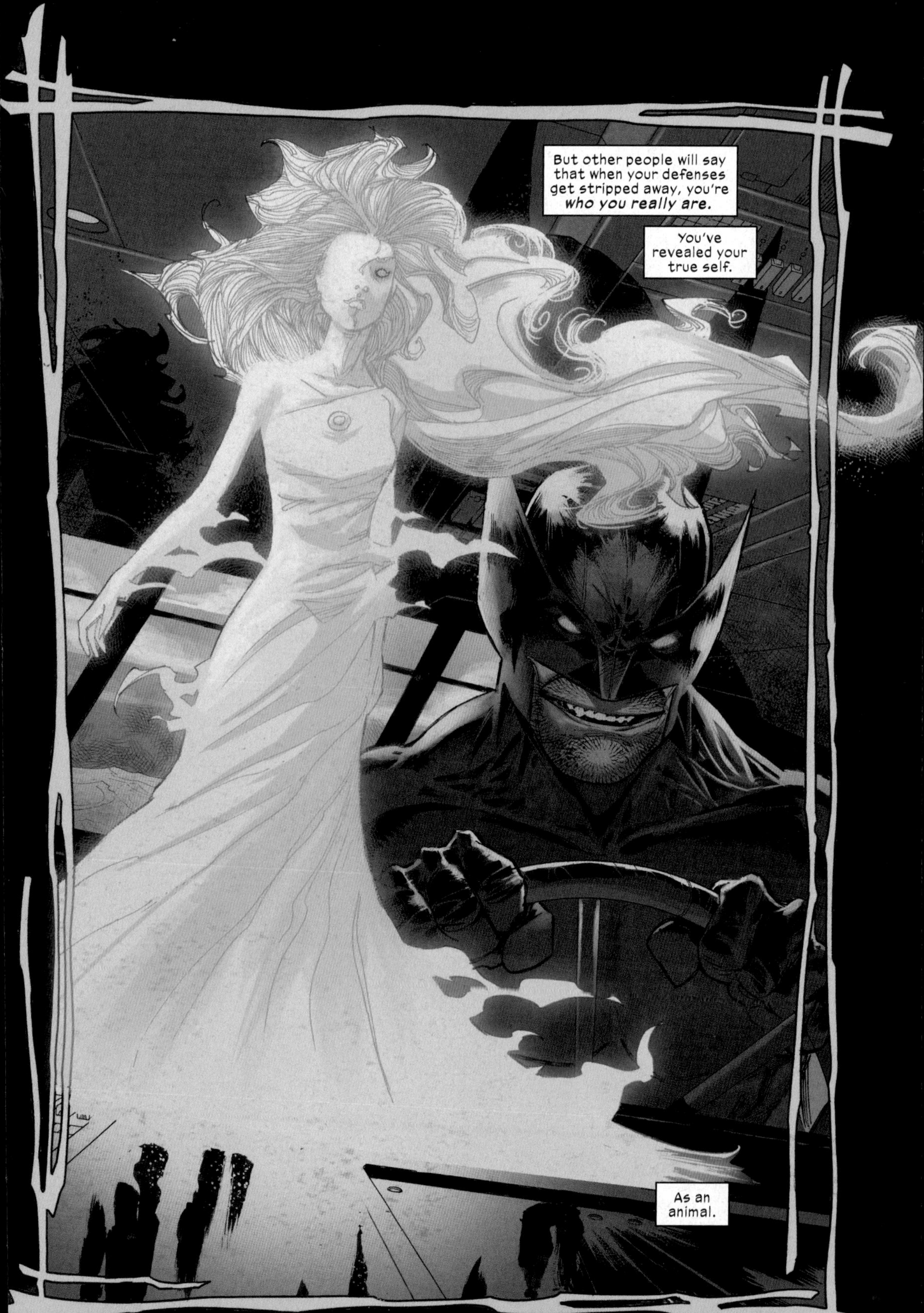
But other people will say that when your defenses get stripped away, you're *who you really are.*
You've revealed your true self.
As an animal.

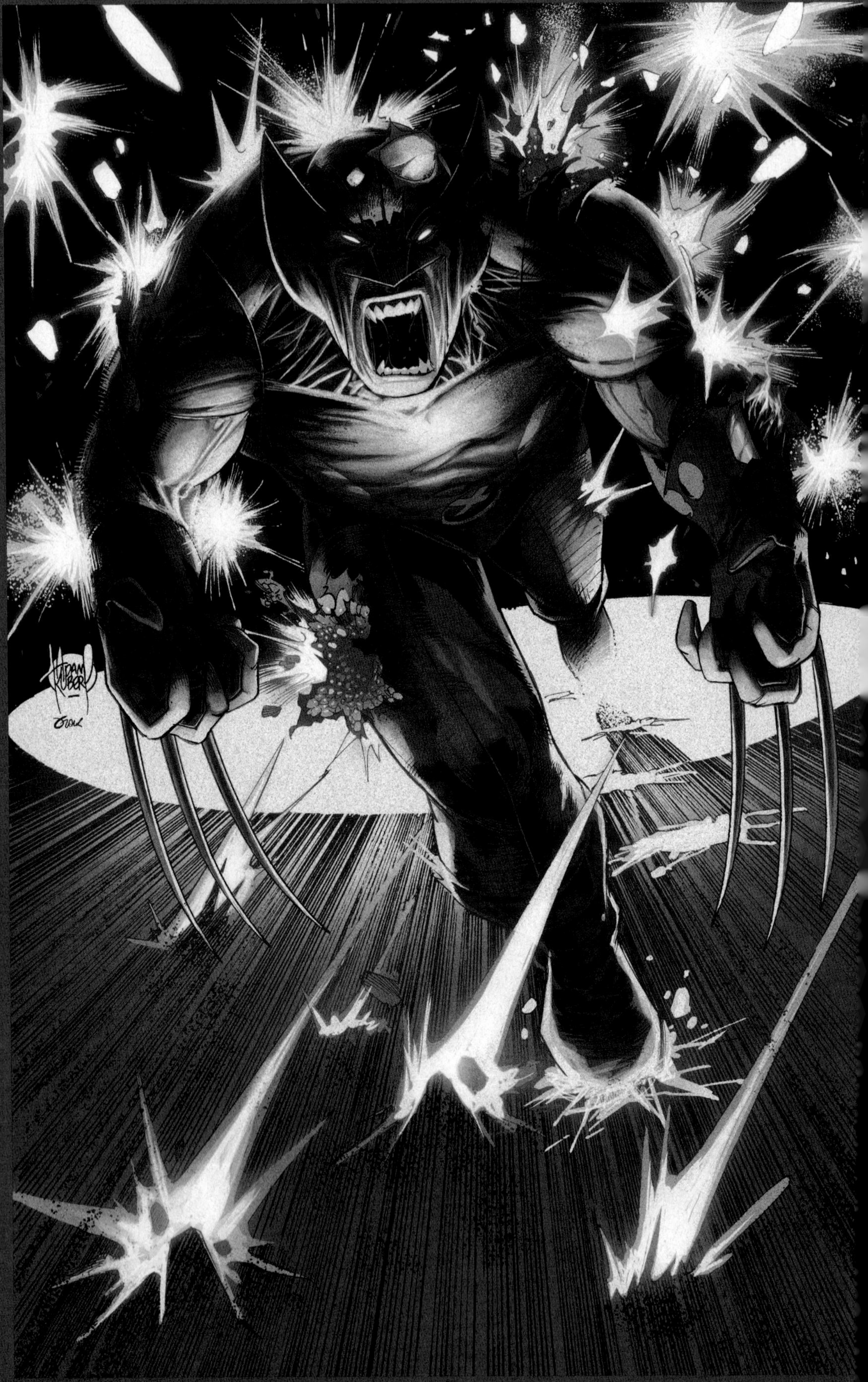

You Didn't See Nothing

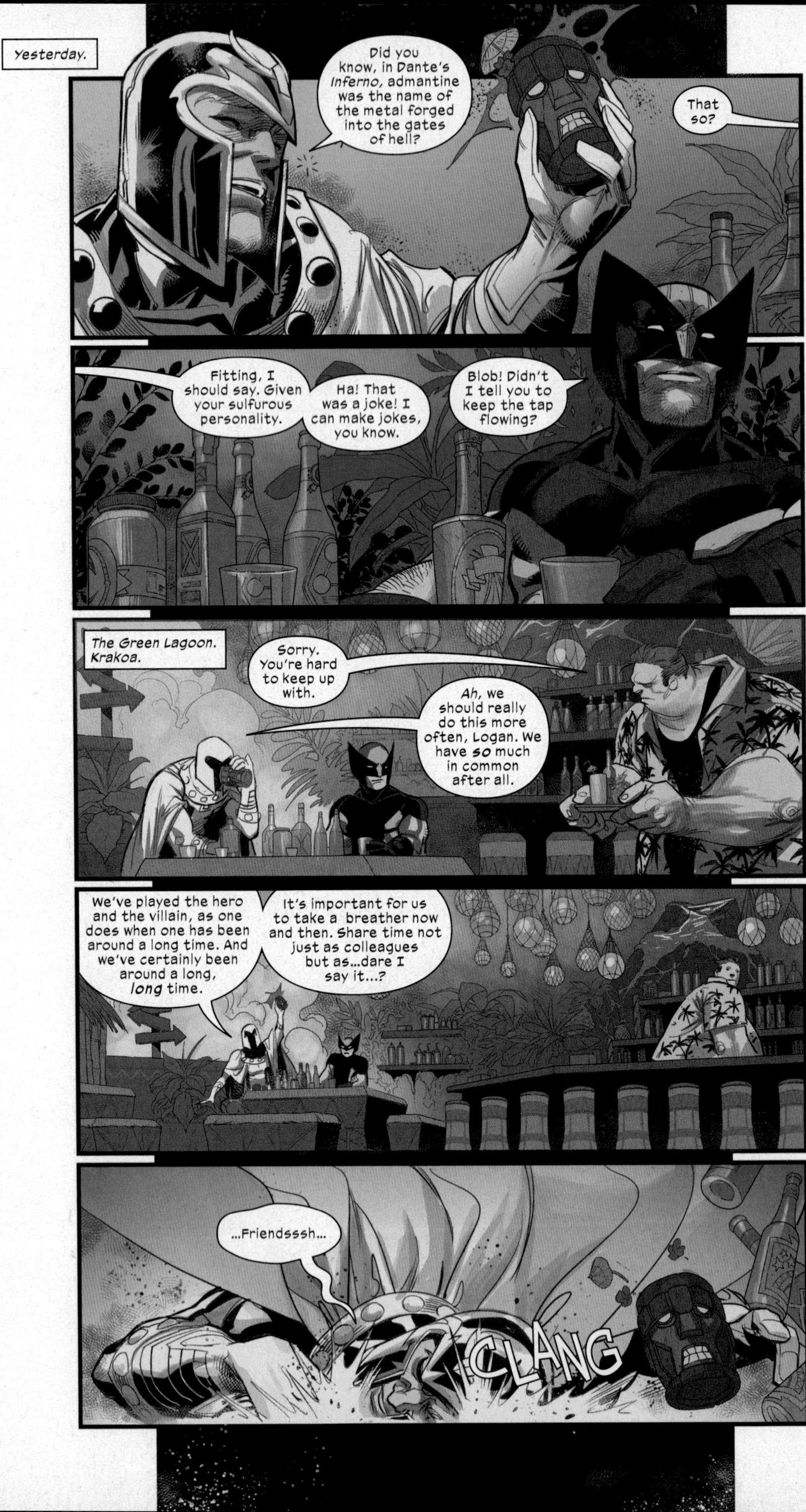

Yesterday.
Did you know, in Dante's *Inferno,* admantine was the name of the metal forged into the gates of hell?
That so?
Fitting, I should say. Given your sulfurous personality.
Ha! That was a joke! I can make jokes, you know.
Blob! Didn't I tell you to keep the tap flowing?
The Green Lagoon. Krakoa.
Sorry. You're hard to keep up with.
Ah, we should really do this more often, Logan. We have **so** much in common after all.
We've played the hero and the villain, as one does when one has been around a long time. And we've certainly been around a long, *long* time.
It's important for us to take a breather now and then. Share time not just as colleagues but as...dare I say it...?
...Friendsssh...
CLANG

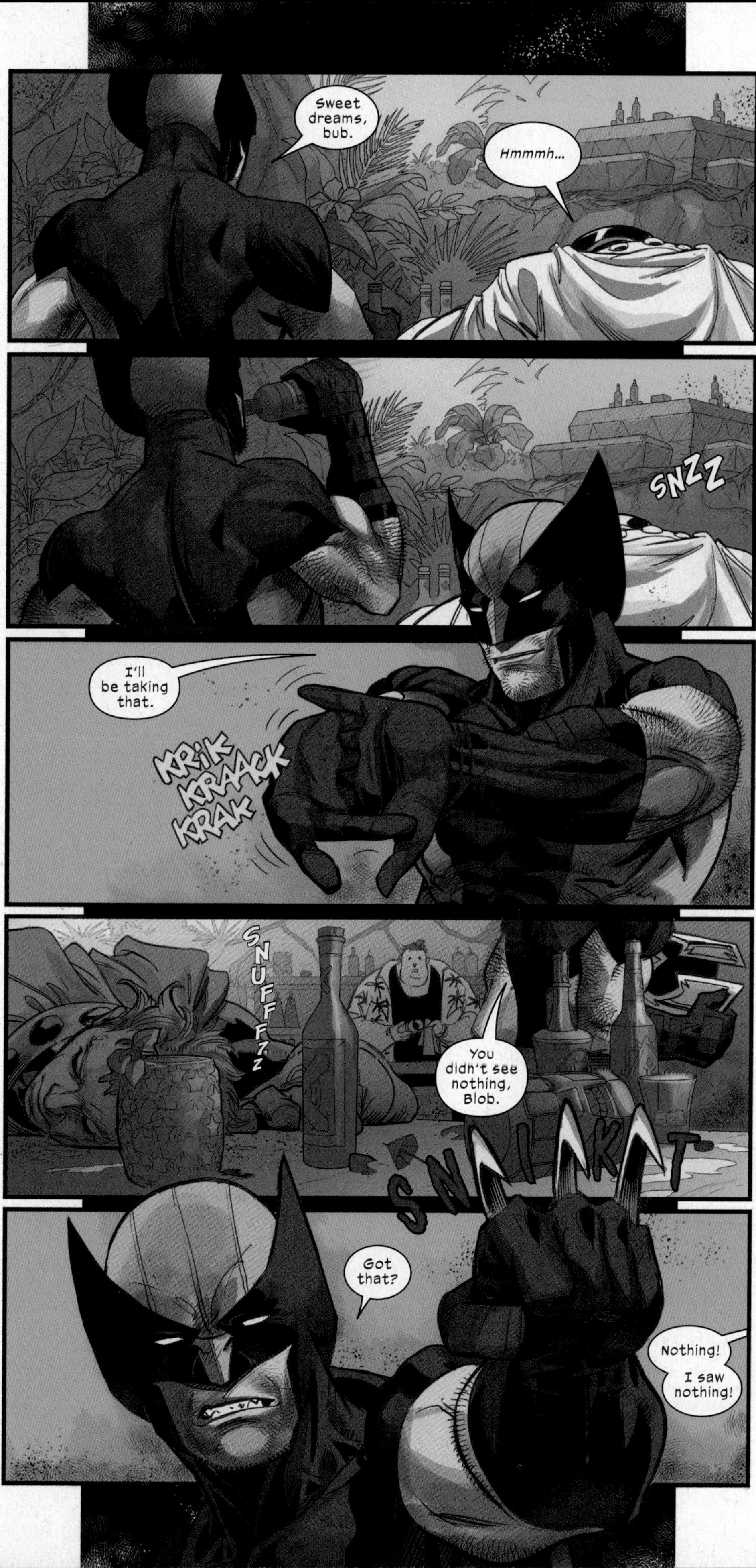
Sweet dreams, bub.
Hmmmh...
SNZZ
I'll be taking that.
KRIK KRAACK KRAK
SNUFFFZZ
You didn't see nothing, Blob.
SNIKT
Got that?
Nothing! I saw nothing!

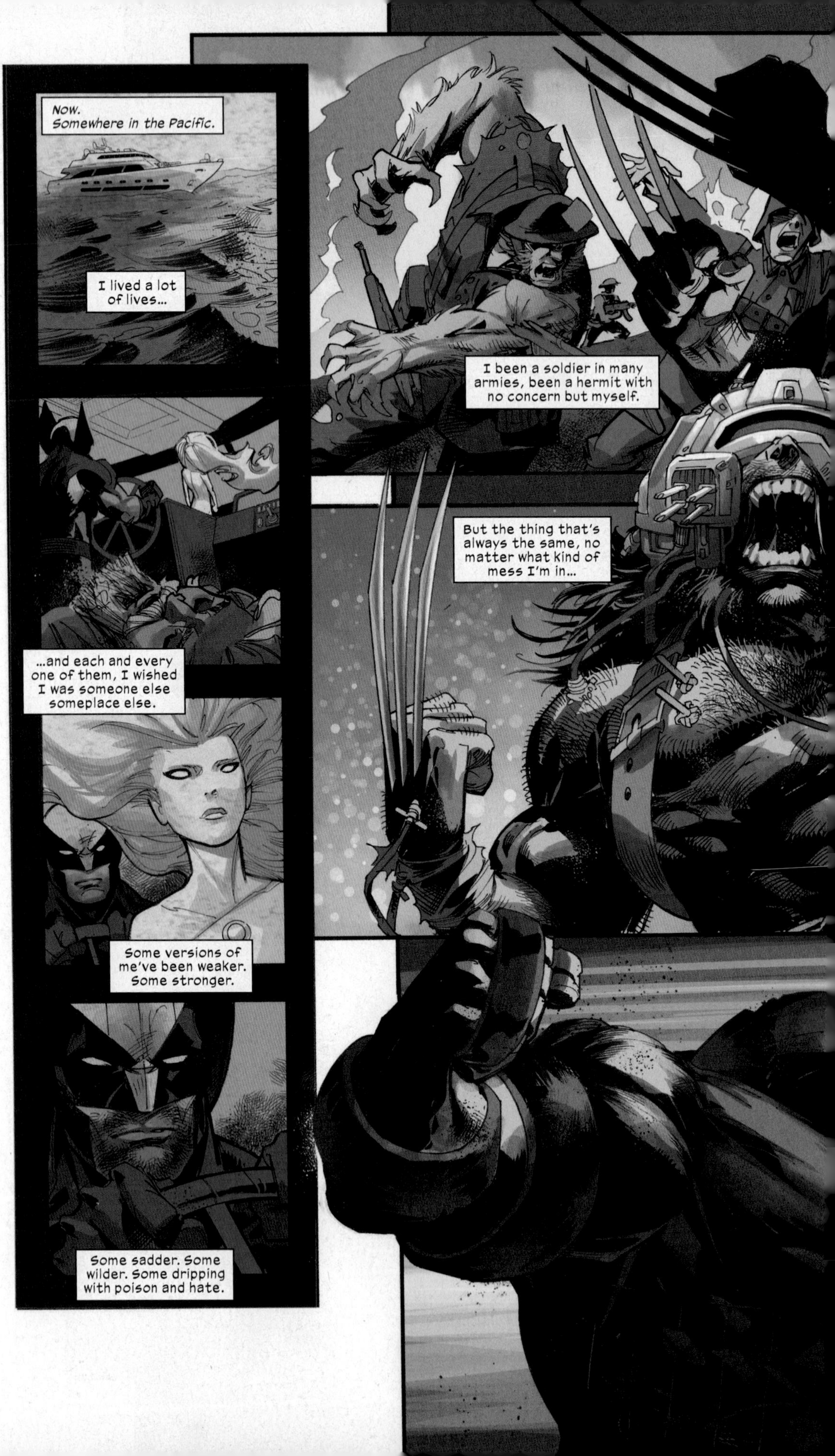
Now.
Somewhere in the Pacific.
I lived a lot of lives...
...and each and every one of them, I wished I was someone else someplace else.
Some versions of me've been weaker. Some stronger.
Some sadder. Some wilder. Some dripping with poison and hate.
I been a soldier in many armies, been a hermit with no concern but myself.
But the thing that's always the same, no matter what kind of mess I'm in...

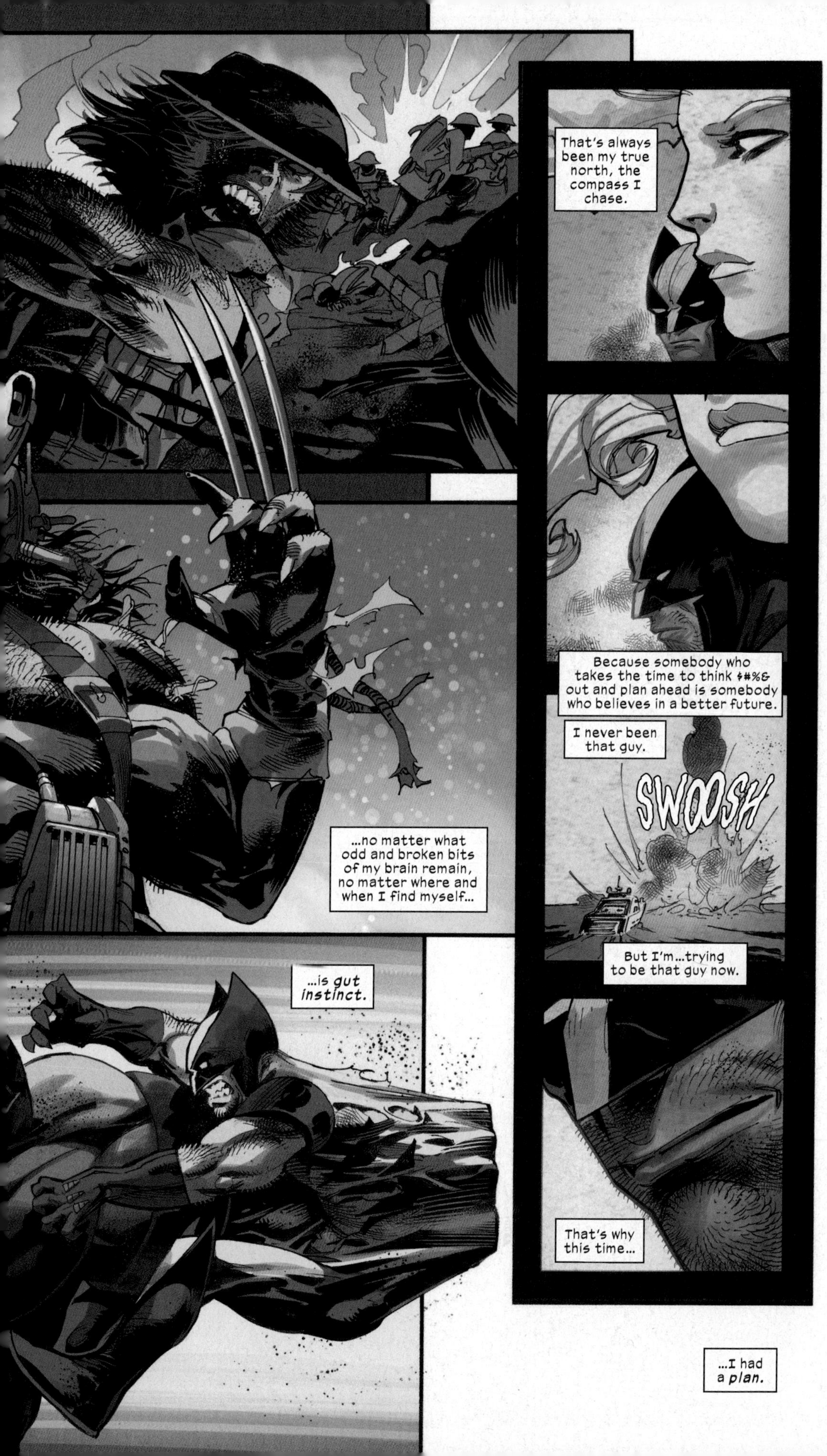
...no matter what odd and broken bits of my brain remain, no matter where and when I find myself...
...is *gut instinct.*
That's always been my true north, the compass I chase.
Because somebody who takes the time to think $#%& out and plan ahead is somebody who believes in a better future.
I never been that guy.
SWOOSH
But I'm...trying to be that guy now.
That's why this time...
...I had a *plan.*

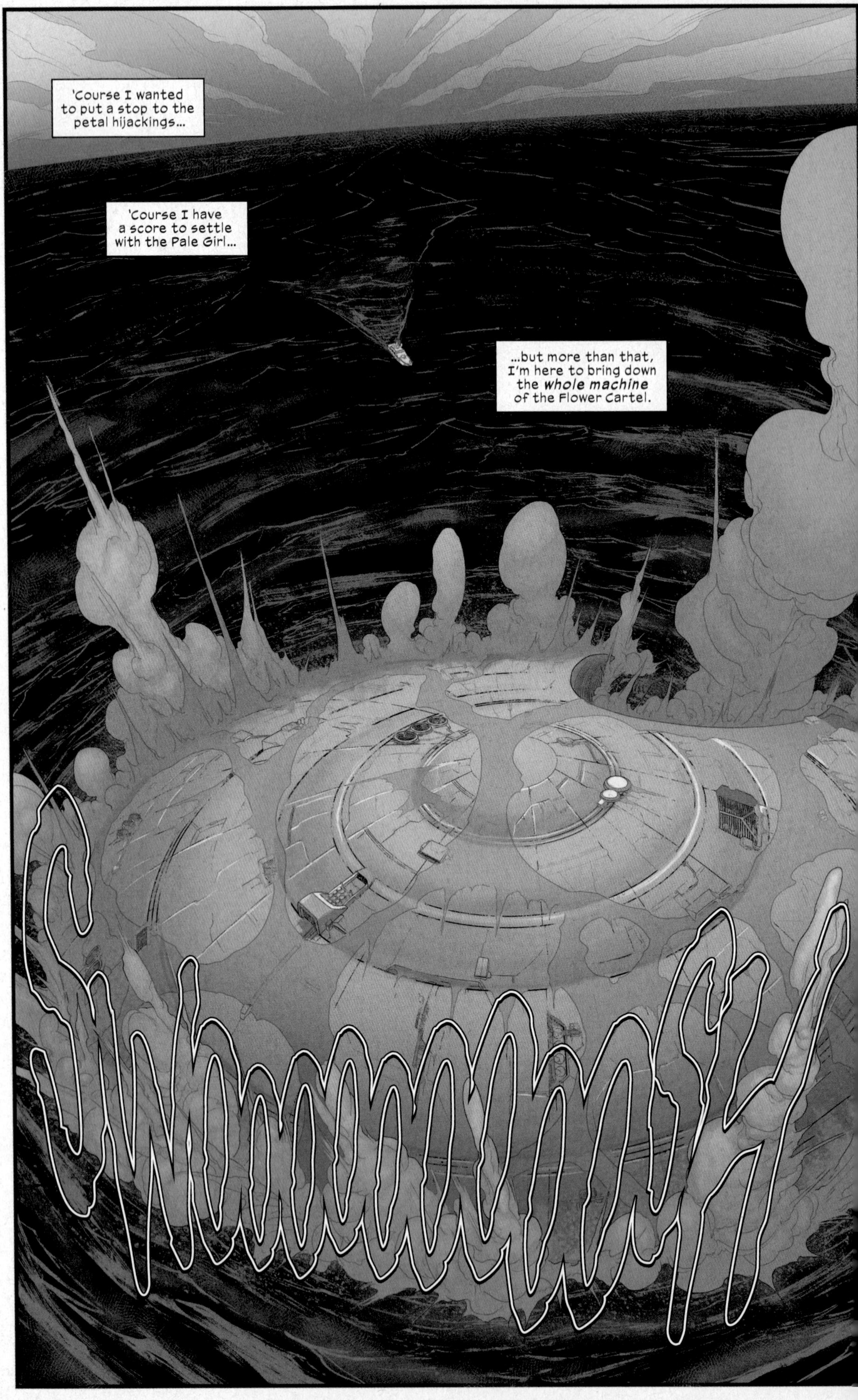
'Course I wanted to put a stop to the petal hijackings...
'Course I have a score to settle with the Pale Girl...
...but more than that, I'm here to bring down the *whole machine* of the Flower Cartel.
Shwoooooom!

Yesterday. Krakoa.

No. One hundred percent no. One **thousand** percent no!

Though I do love seeing you grovel, so feel free to continue.

Maybe try showering me with heart-shaped compliments and see if that works.

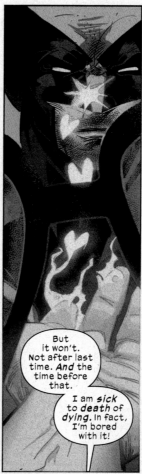

But it won't. Not after last time. **And** the time before that.

I am **sick** to **death** of **dying.** In fact, I'm bored with it!

Did you hear me? **Death** is boring.

Scared?

Scared? Scared! You and the rest of the clueless olds have no sway over me.

Don't think for a second you can manipulate...

...the master... manipulator.

Quentin...

Um. *≠koff≠* Salutations, Cuckoos!

I mean... how you doing, ladies?

We just wanted to say...

...how hot, hot, hot it is...

...that you're taking on the Pale Girl.

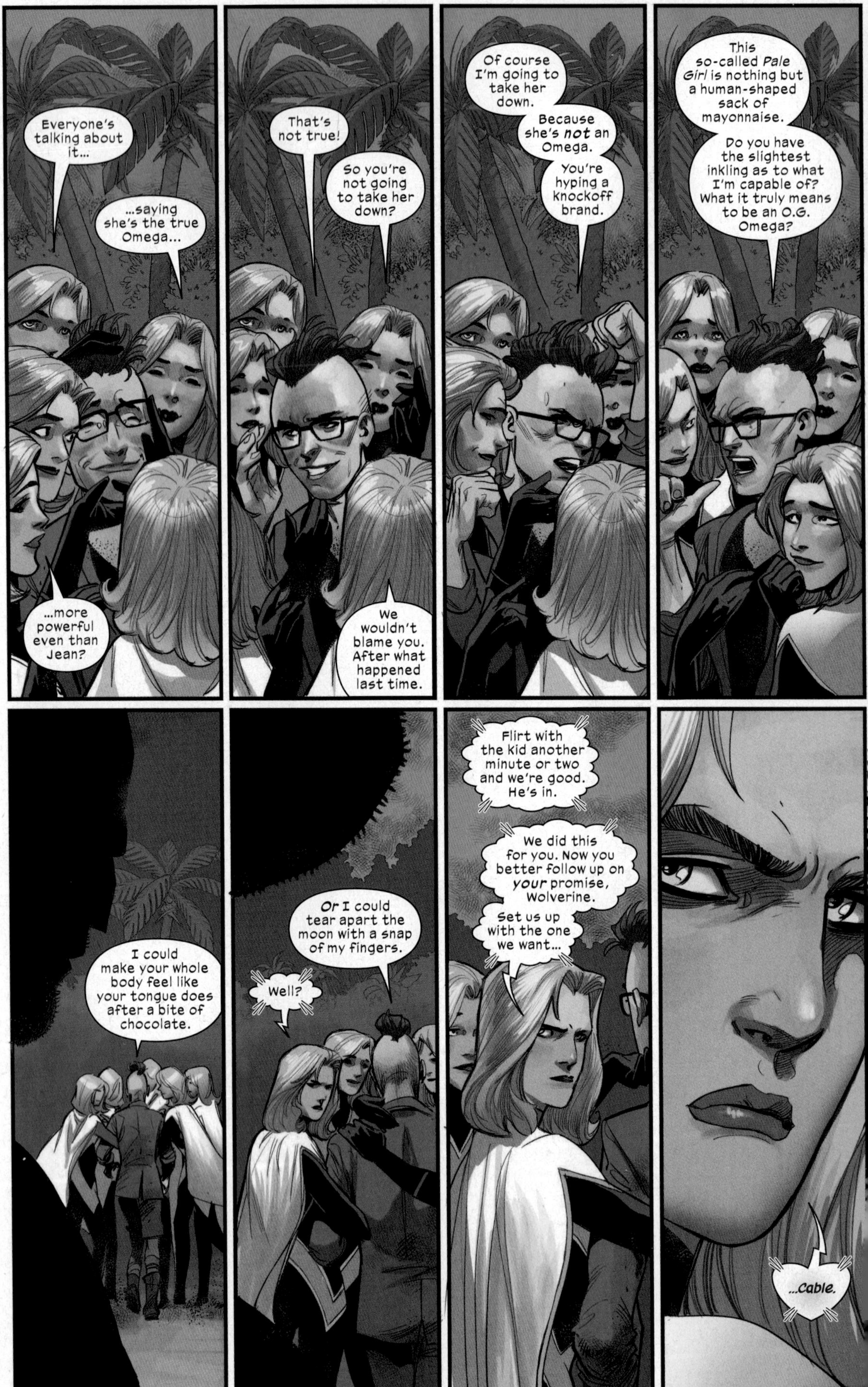

Everyone's talking about it...
...saying she's the true Omega...
...more powerful even than Jean?
That's not true!
So you're not going to take her down?
We wouldn't blame you. After what happened last time.
Of course I'm going to take her down.
Because she's *not* an Omega.
You're hyping a knockoff brand.
This so-called *Pale Girl* is nothing but a human-shaped sack of mayonnaise.
Do you have the slightest inkling as to what I'm capable of? What it truly means to be an O.G. Omega?
I could make your whole body feel like your tongue does after a bite of chocolate.
Or I could tear apart the moon with a snap of my fingers.
Well?
Flirt with the kid another minute or two and we're good. He's in.
We did this for you. Now you better follow up on *your* promise, Wolverine.
Set us up with the one we want...
...Cable.

BEAST'S LOGBOOK: INTERFERENCE

Xavier came to speak with me today about the possibility of psychic aberrations or a technical malfunction with Cerebro.

In Alaska, after the Pale Girl wrested control of Logan's mind and puppeted him into killing his teammates, the professor told me that he began a hunt of his own.

I'll admit some jealousy at the sensation he must experience each time he places Cerebro over his head. I imagine the gentle quake that must run through his body, almost seismic, as he expands, a whole world growing inside him. A mindscape he can travel to seek out each and every mutant...

But here is what matters: when he searched for the one everyone calls the Pale Girl...he couldn't find her.

She must derive her abilities from a different source, he concluded.

But I am not so certain of this. And now neither is he.

Some time later -- just this morning, in fact -- as he discussed tariffs and trade deals with the Quiet Council, he paused mid-conversation and stood from his seat and looked east.

Because there was a flicker. He described it as a static hiss in the space between radio stations. It lasted only a moment, but it was enough to come rushing to the fore of his mind.

His fellow council members asked him what was wrong, and he said maybe nothing...or maybe something. For a moment, just a moment, he felt plugged into...what wasn't there before.

"It reminded me of Jean," he told me. "Except...other."

It was then that Xavier realized something. Something that worried him deeply. Something he scolded himself for not recognizing sooner. That is why he came to me.

Russia -- as a whole -- is unavailable to him. Like a section of the sky that carries no stars.

What did this mean? Has the country killed off all of its mutants?

Or...

—

CENTRAL INTELLIGENCE AGENCY
TRANSCRIPTION OF INTEROFFICE CONVERSATION

JEFF BANNISTER: [unintelligible]

DELORES RAMIREZ: Hello?

BANNISTER: Hello?

RAMIREZ: Yes, is this Agent Jeff Bannister? In Narcotics?

BANNISTER: Wait, did I call you or did you call me?

RAMIREZ: I'm calling you. From across the campus here at Langley.

BANNISTER: Oh! Weird, man. I just picked up the phone to order some pizza and there you were.

RAMIREZ: My name is Delores Ramirez and I work at the X-Desk.

BANNISTER: The sex desk? We're investigating sex now?

RAMIREZ: The X-Desk. We're a special unit tasked with keeping an eye on the mutants.

BANNISTER: Huh. Never heard of it.

RAMIREZ: I'd say that's a good thing, except that I've left you several emails and voicemails.

BANNISTER: Huh. Yeah, man. Not going to get into the dirty details, but I'm chasing something right now, something big, and it's become clear somebody's watching. So I'm going old school. No computers. No phones.

RAMIREZ: Except to order pizza?

BANNISTER: Now you're talking!

RAMIREZ: You mentioned that you're chasing something...big. I was wondering if we -- the X-Desk -- might offer our assistance.

BANNISTER: Nope. Thanks though.

RAMIREZ: We understand that you're in touch with the mutant known as Wolverine — that you've formed a kind of partnership?

BANNISTER: [silence of fifteen seconds] Who told you that?

RAMIREZ: It's a two-way street, Jeff. You give me some information, and I'll give you some information, and we'll all be better off.

BANNISTER: Huh. Yeah. No. In fact, ▓▓▓▓ off. I'm gonna order an extra-large pie stacked with ham and pineapple.

<end of conversation>

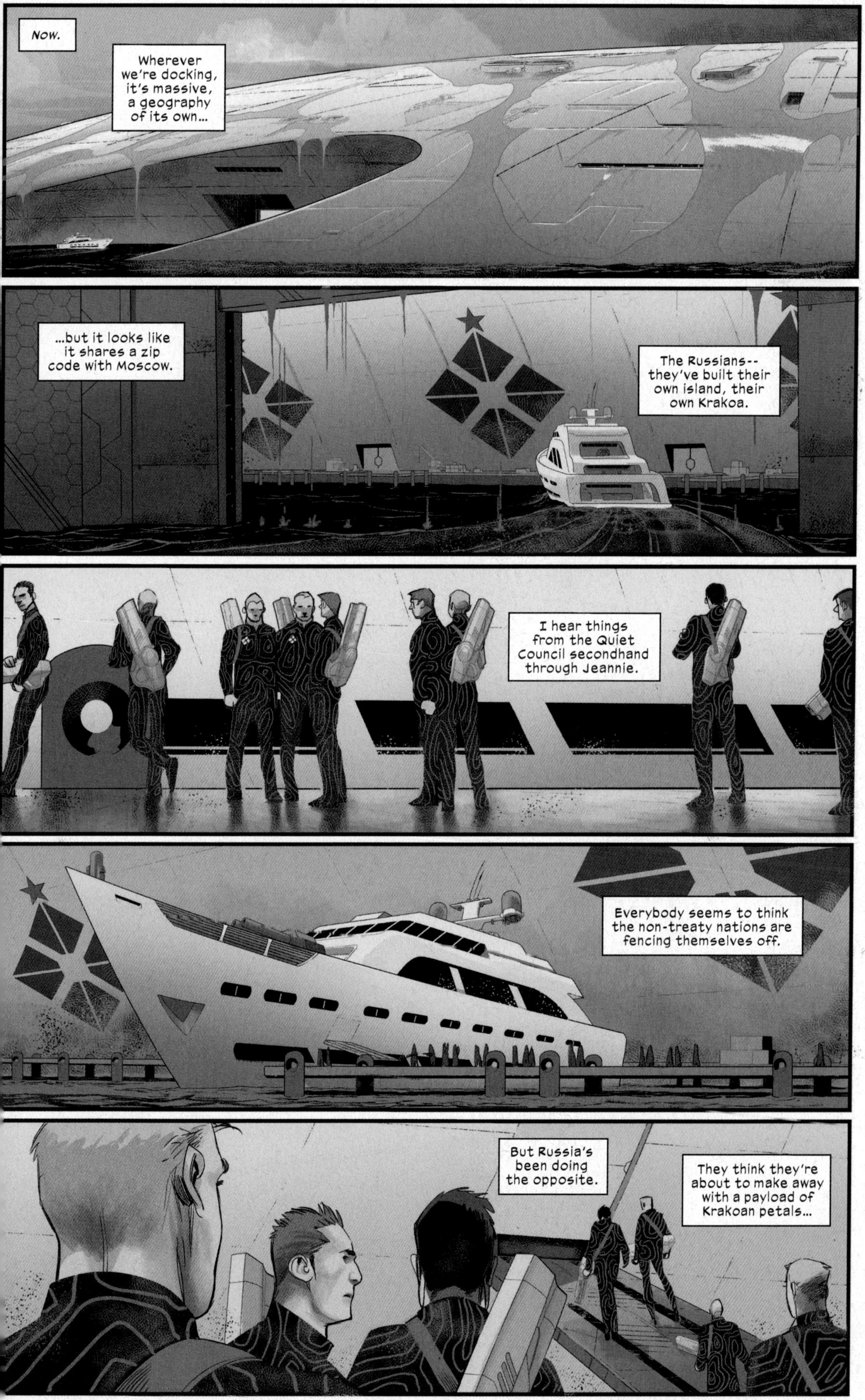
Now.
Wherever we're docking, it's massive, a geography of its own...
...but it looks like it shares a zip code with Moscow.
The Russians-- they've built their own island, their own Krakoa.
I hear things from the Quiet Council secondhand through Jeannie.
Everybody seems to think the non-treaty nations are fencing themselves off.
But Russia's been doing the opposite.
They think they're about to make away with a payload of Krakoan petals...

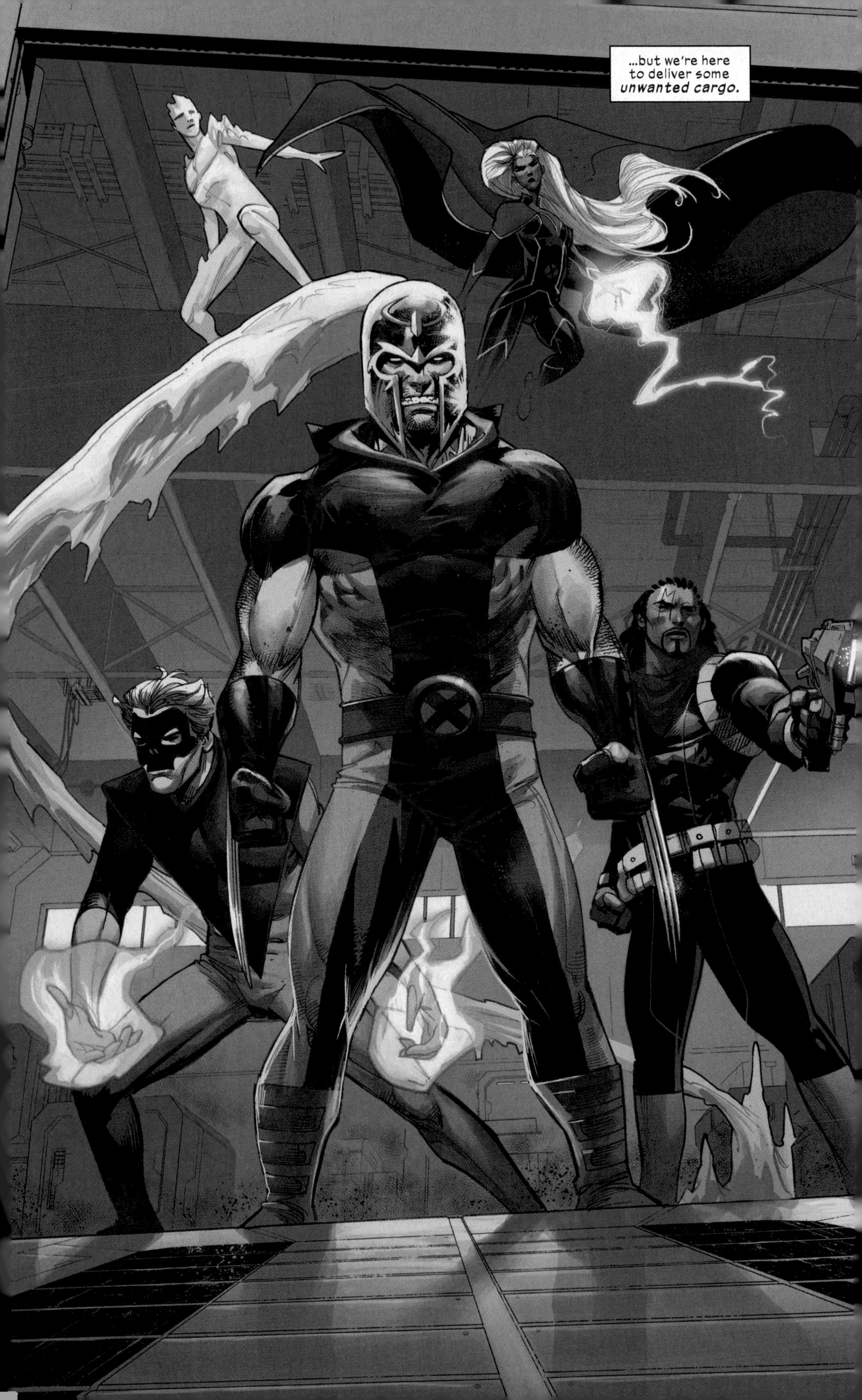
...but we're here to deliver some *unwanted cargo.*

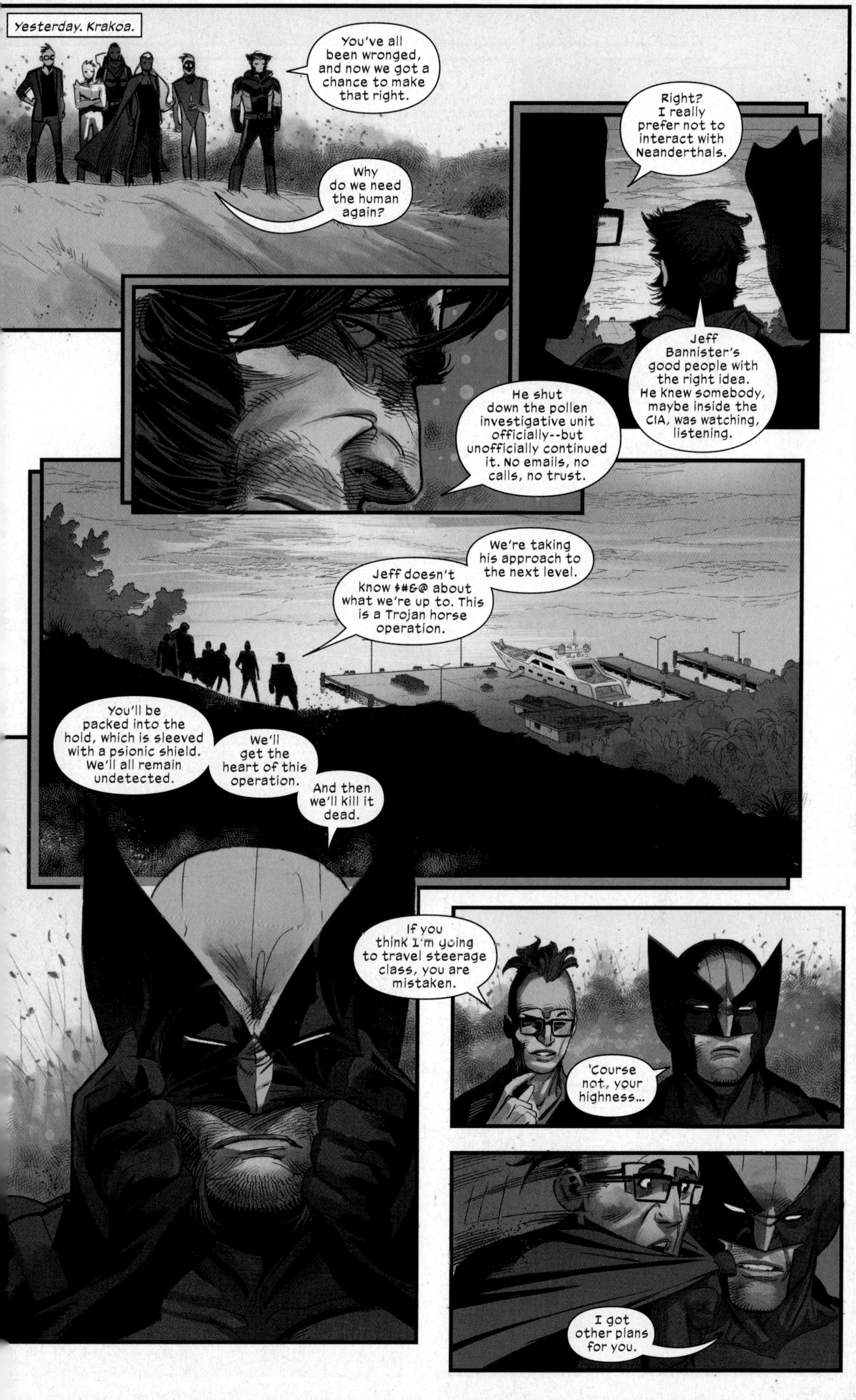
Yesterday. Krakoa.
You've all been wronged, and now we got a chance to make that right.
Why do we need the human again?
Right? I really prefer not to interact with Neanderthals.
Jeff Bannister's good people with the right idea. He knew somebody, maybe inside the CIA, was watching, listening.
He shut down the pollen investigative unit officially--but unofficially continued it. No emails, no calls, no trust.
We're taking his approach to the next level.
Jeff doesn't know $#&@ about what we're up to. This is a Trojan horse operation.
You'll be packed into the hold, which is sleeved with a psionic shield. We'll all remain undetected.
We'll get the heart of this operation.
And then we'll kill it dead.
If you think I'm going to travel steerage class, you are mistaken.
'Course not, your highness...
I got other plans for you.

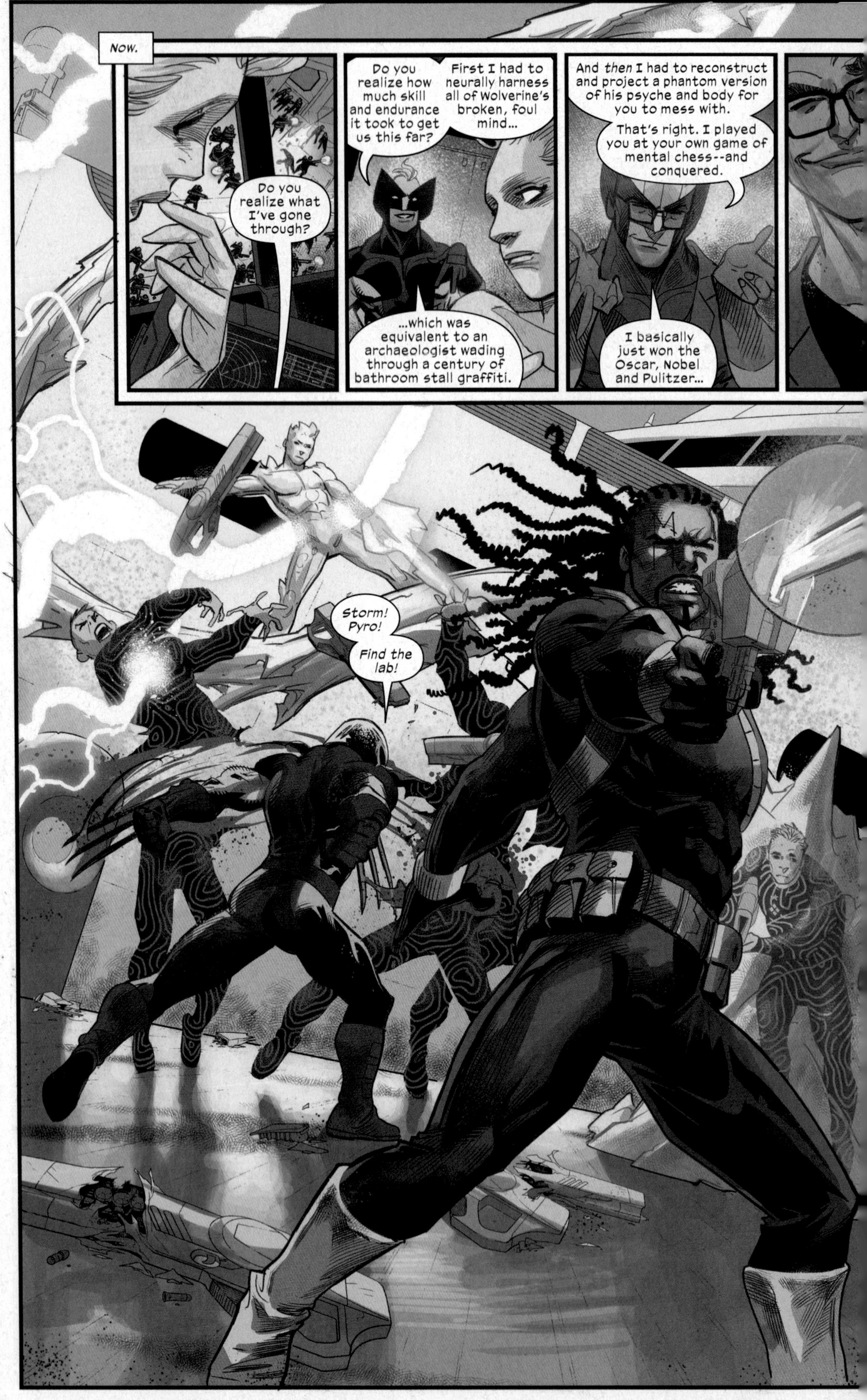
NOW.
Do you realize what I've gone through?
Do you realize how much skill and endurance it took to get us this far?
First I had to neurally harness all of Wolverine's broken, foul mind...
...which was equivalent to an archaeologist wading through a century of bathroom stall graffiti.
And then I had to reconstruct and project a phantom version of his psyche and body for you to mess with.
That's right. I played you at your own game of mental chess--and conquered.
I basically just won the Oscar, Nobel and Pulitzer...
Storm! Pyro!
Find the lab!

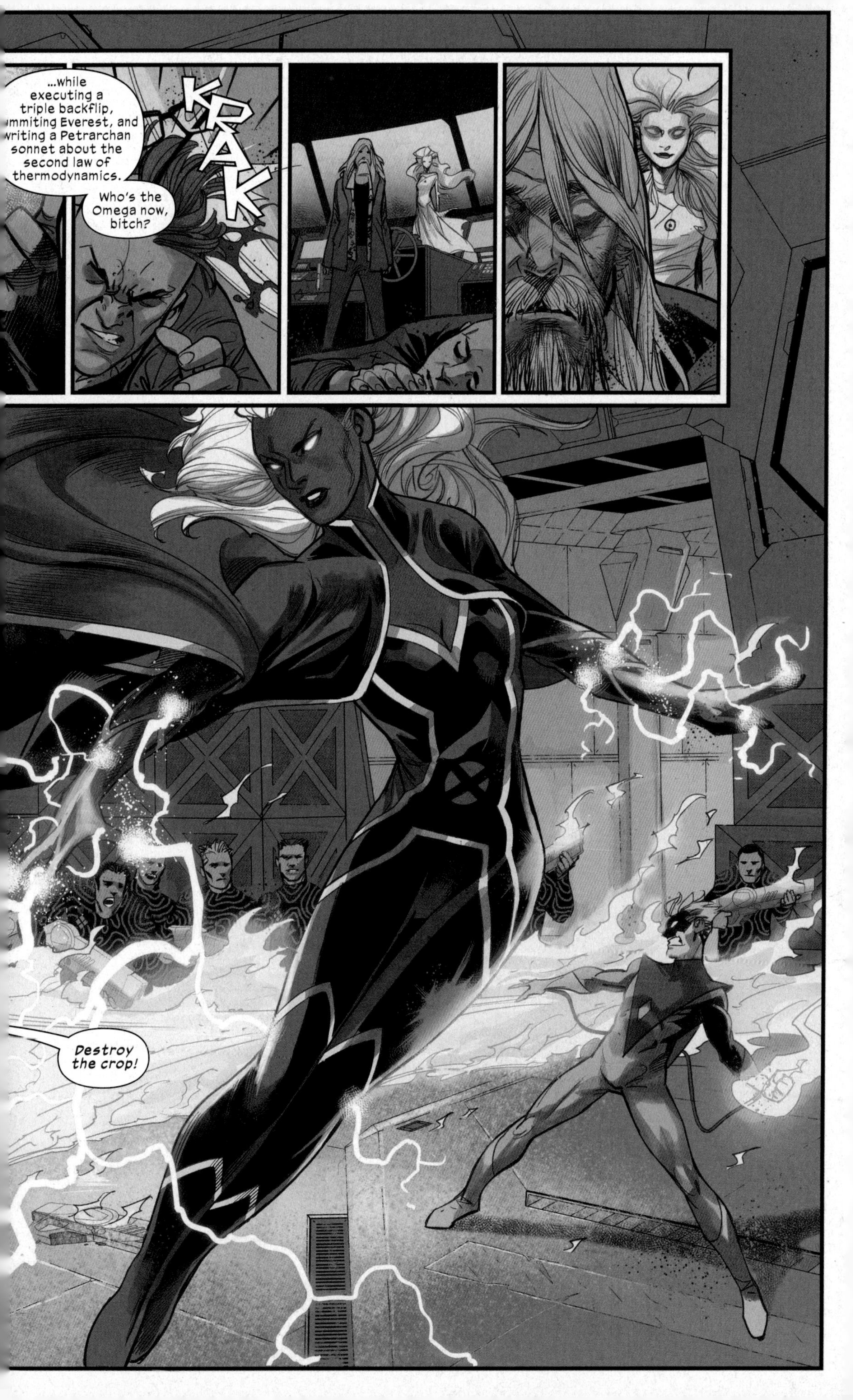

...while executing a triple backflip, ummiting Everest, and riting a Petrarchan sonnet about the second law of thermodynamics.
Who's the Omega now, bitch?
KRAK
Destroy the crop!

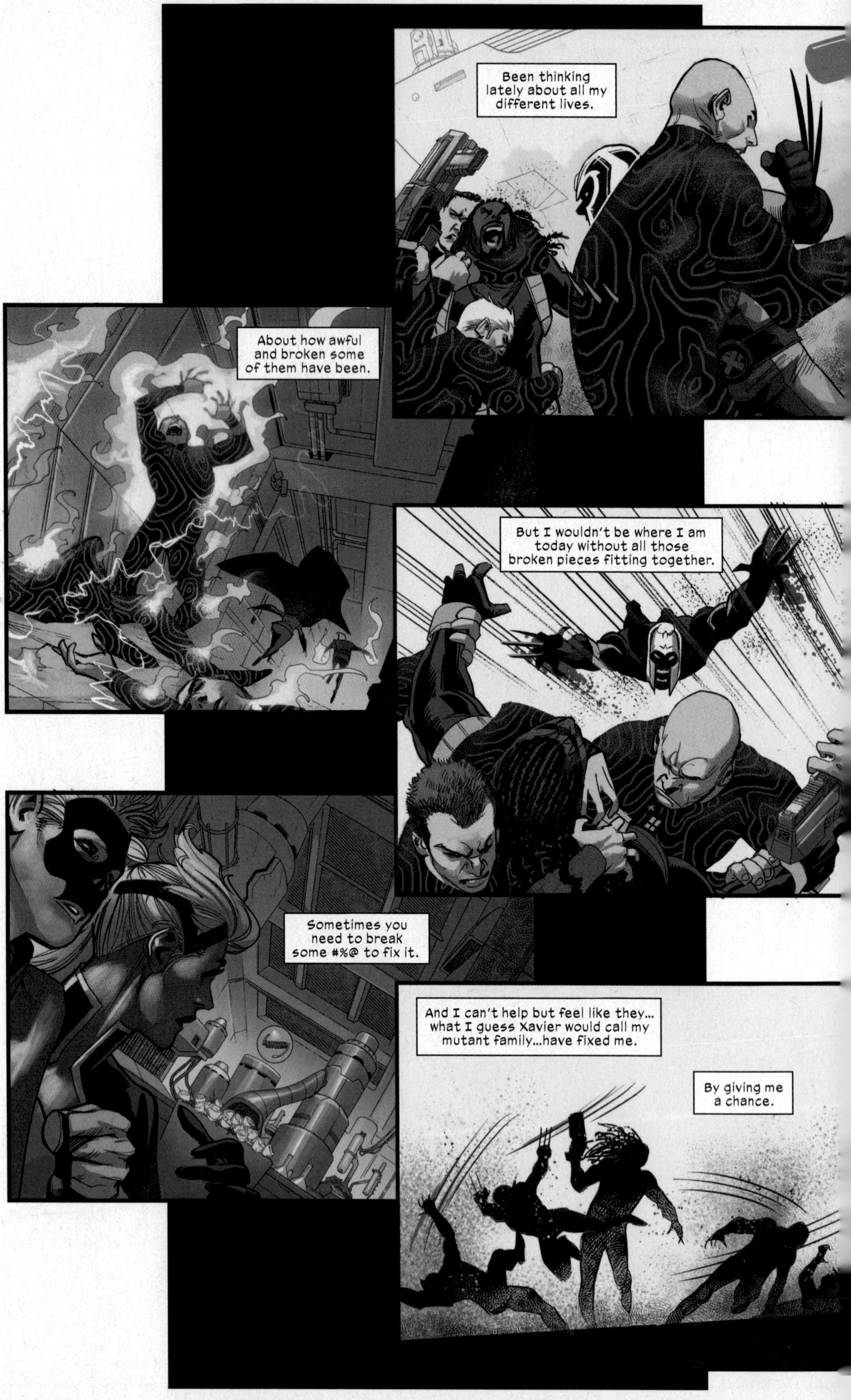
Been thinking lately about all my different lives.
About how awful and broken some of them have been.
But I wouldn't be where I am today without all those broken pieces fitting together.
Sometimes you need to break some #%@ to fix it.
And I can't help but feel like they... what I guess Xavier would call my mutant family...have fixed me.
By giving me a chance.

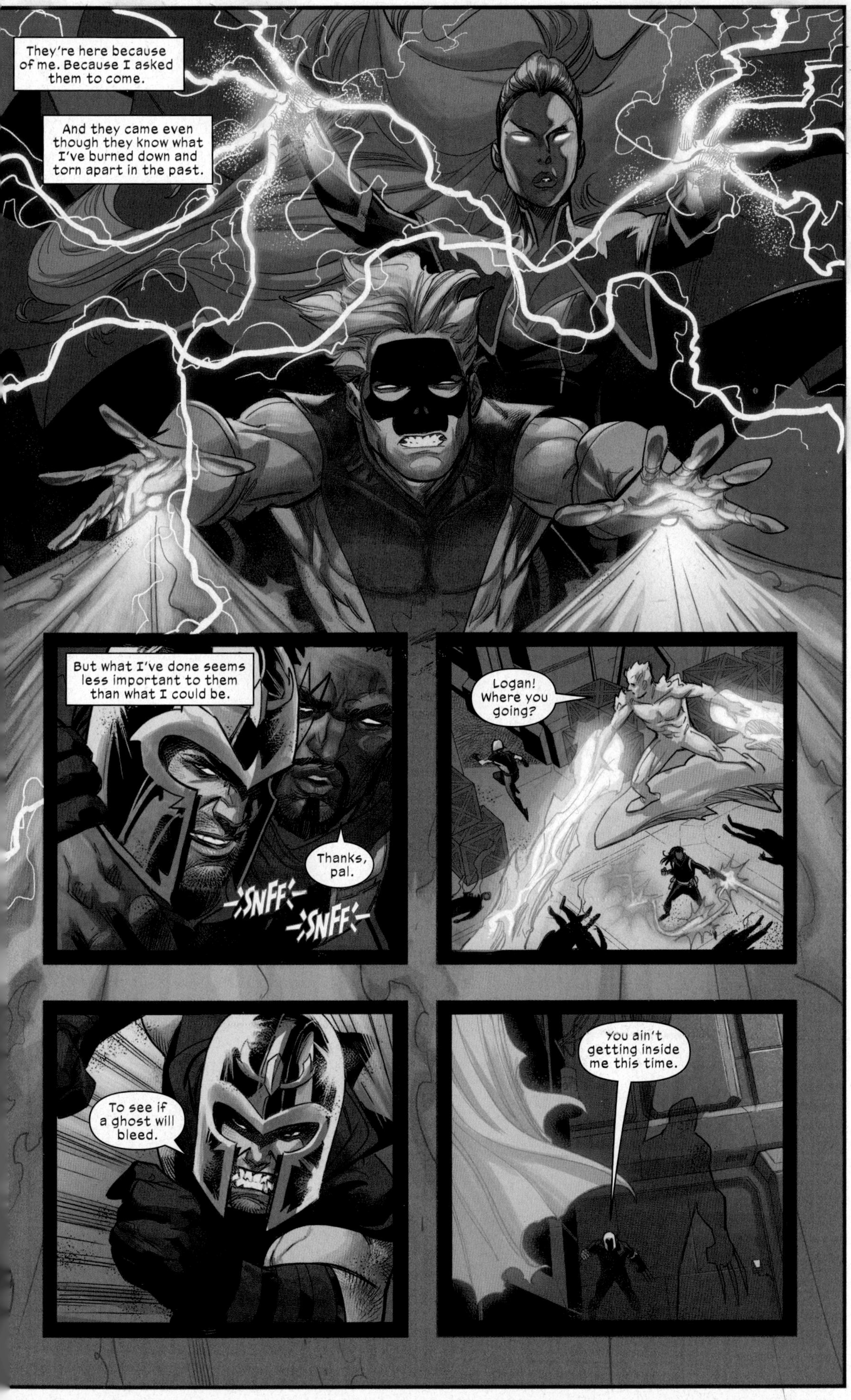
They're here because of me. Because I asked them to come.
And they came even though they know what I've burned down and torn apart in the past.
But what I've done seems less important to them than what I could be.
Thanks, pal.
SNFF
SNFF
Logan! Where you going?
To see if a ghost will bleed.
You ain't getting inside me this time.

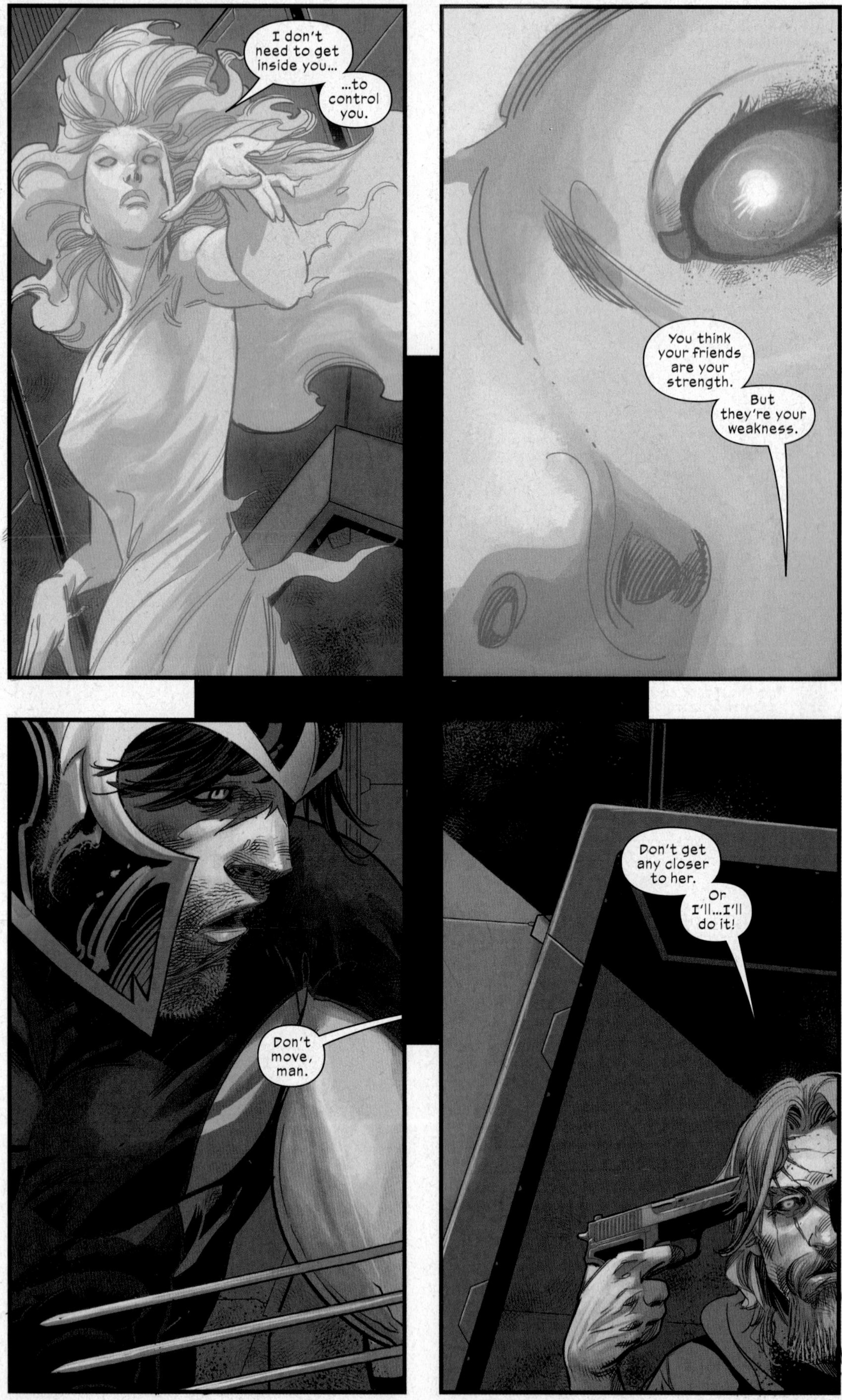

I don't need to get inside you...
...to control you.
You think your friends are your strength.
But they're your weakness.
Don't move, man.
Don't get any closer to her.
Or I'll...I'll do it!

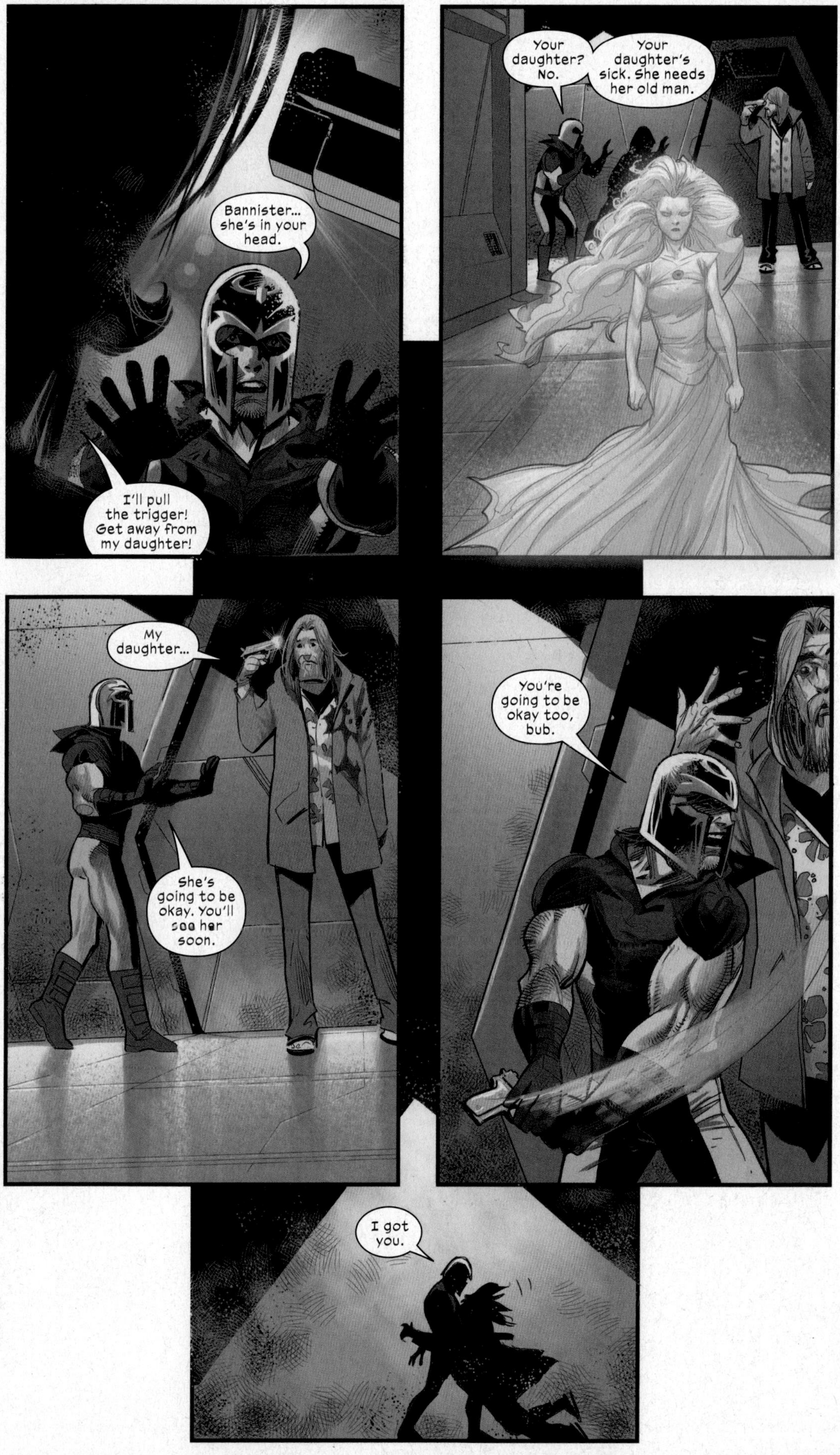
Bannister... she's in your head.
I'll pull the trigger! Get away from my daughter!
Your daughter? No.
Your daughter's sick. She needs her old man.
My daughter...
She's going to be okay. You'll see her soon.
You're going to be okay too, bub.
I got you.

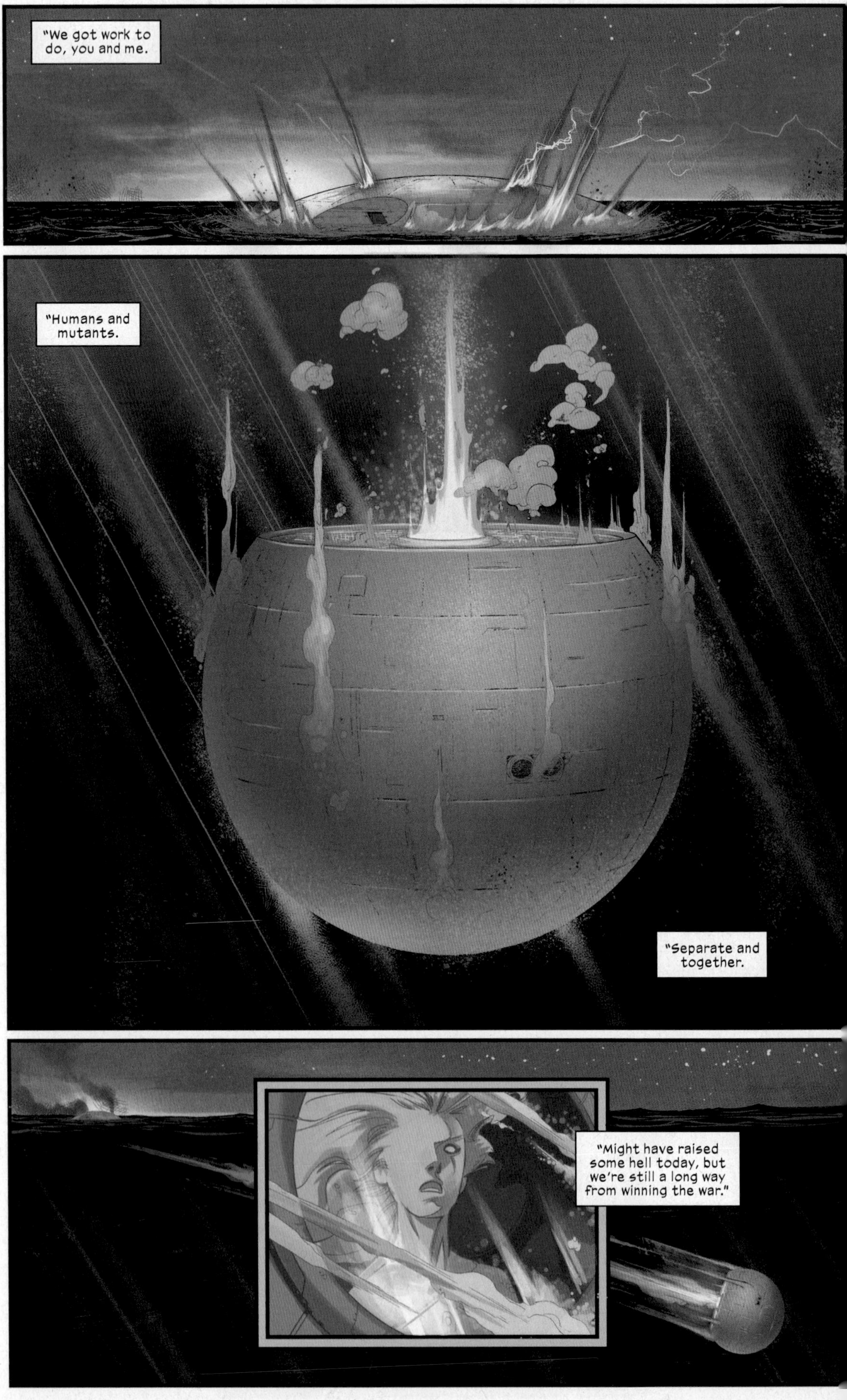
"We got work to do, you and me.
"Humans and mutants.
"Separate and together.
"Might have raised some hell today, but we're still a long way from winning the war."

BEAST'S LOGBOOK:
The Problem with Russia

From the very beginning, Xavier predicted that Russia would reject mutant sovereignty. Because of this, he asked Colossus (Piotr "Peter" Nikolayevich Rasputin) to quietly gather any mutant citizens who wished to escape and ready them for extraction.

A whisper network revealed their plan -- and military forces set upon them. Those who escaped barely survived.

Since then, little is known about Russia. As a non-treaty nation, it is in a state of exile.

But instead of turning inward, it appears to have been quietly expanding its influence -- economically, politically, militarily.

There is something particularly disconcerting about 1) the standardized uniform of the troops on board this vessel, and 2) the Soviet emblem -- with its traditional sickle and hammer now offset by an X instead of a star.

Though this is conjecture...it may imply a rival mutant society.

The Flower Cartel, it is now clear, is not simply a criminal organization, but a government-sponsored organization that has been interrupting mutant trade routes and processing the petals into pollen for global distribution.

This is not only an economic boon; it is an effort at destabilization. They are undermining the new geopolitical reality by turning the mutant's olive branch -- petals -- into a diseased crop.

Their goal appears to be to profiteering addiction, but within Russia's borders, pollen is being used as propaganda. Recently a branch of the Order of X -- a mutant-worshipping cult -- died as a result of a bad batch of pollen, and it is now widely believed this was intentionally meant to inspire fearfulness and distrust of the Krakoan source material.

At this juncture, I have requested a sit-down with Colossus and Omega Red for both a debriefing on everything they know about their mother country and the possibility of joining a special task force.

—

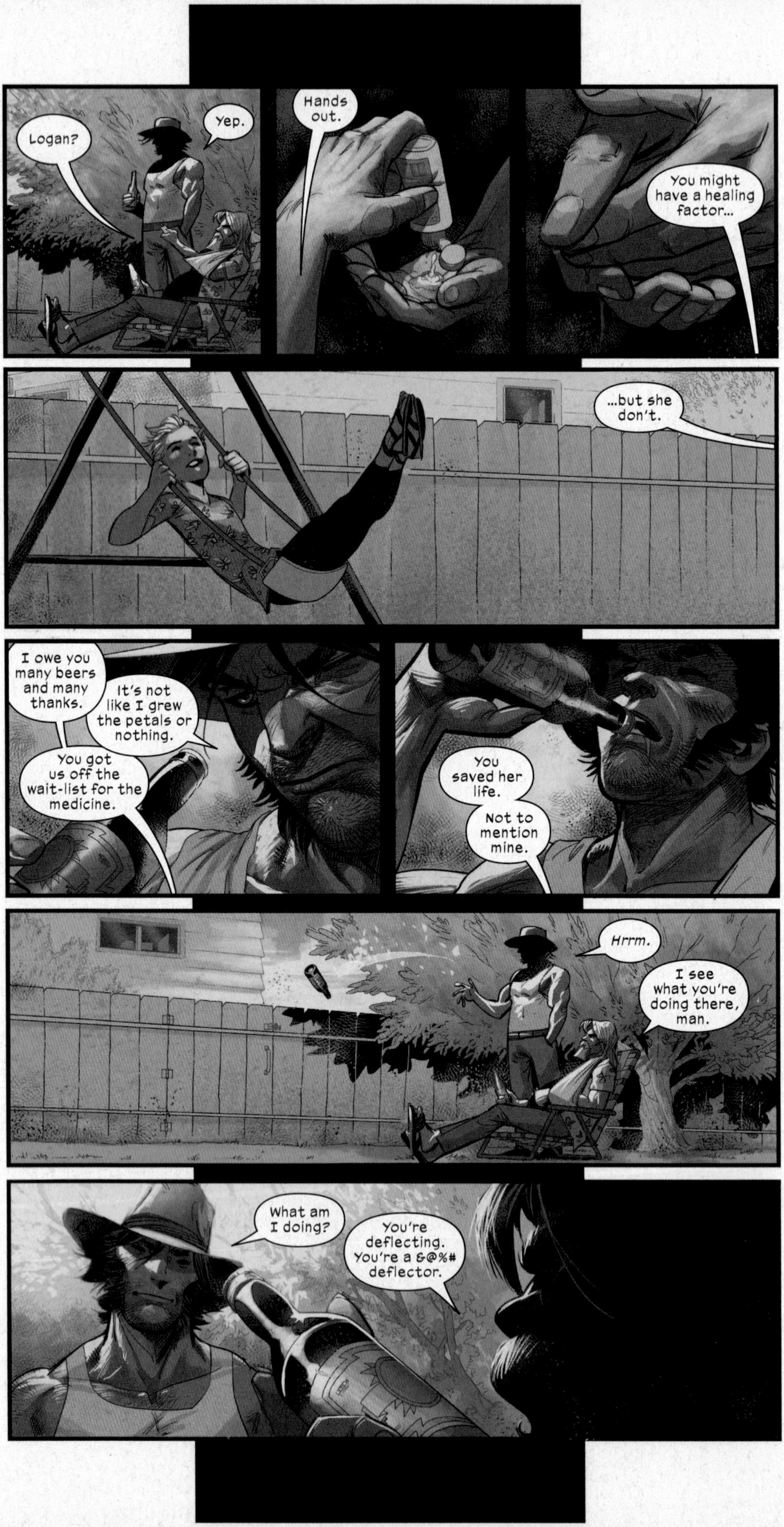
Logan?
Yep.
Hands out.
You might have a healing factor...
...but she don't.
I owe you many beers and many thanks.
It's not like I grew the petals or nothing.
You got us off the wait-list for the medicine.
You saved her life.
Not to mention mine.
Hrrm.
I see what you're doing there, man.
What am I doing?
You're deflecting. You're a &@%# deflector.

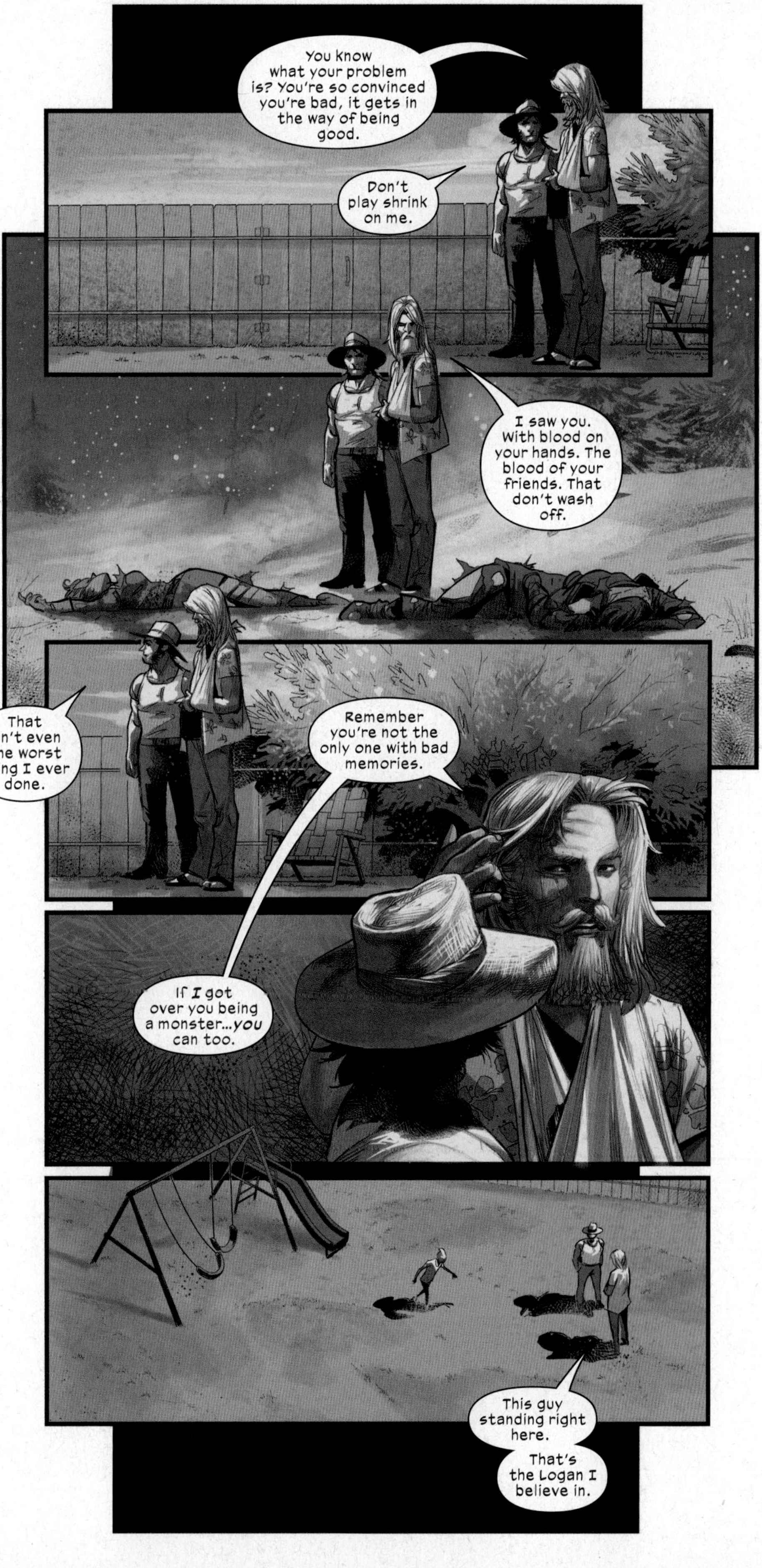
You know what your problem is? You're so convinced you're bad, it gets in the way of being good.
Don't play shrink on me.
I saw you. With blood on your hands. The blood of your friends. That don't wash off.
That ain't even the worst thing I ever done.
Remember you're not the only one with bad memories.
If *I* got over you being a monster...*you* can too.
This guy standing right here.
That's the Logan I believe in.

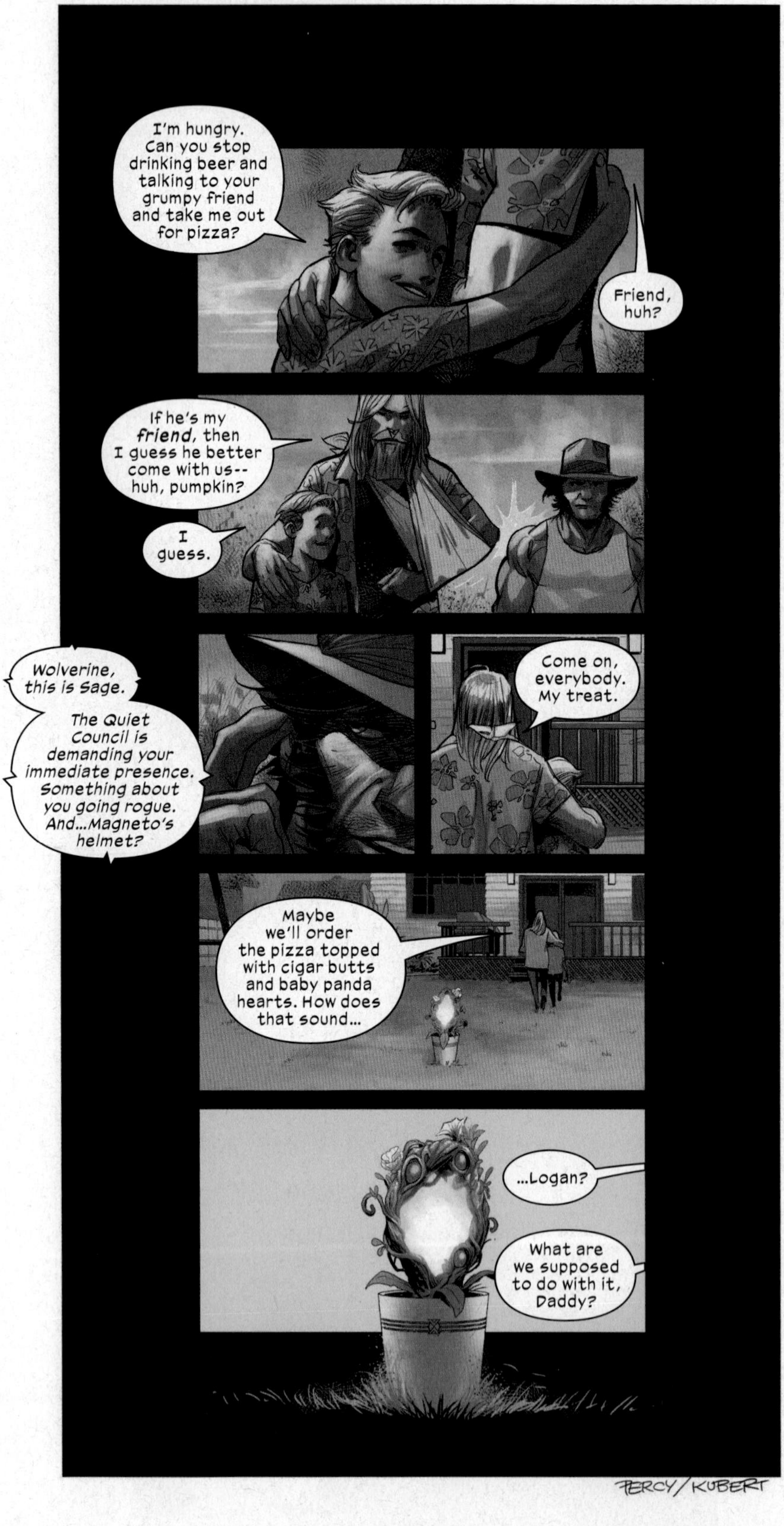
I'm hungry. Can you stop drinking beer and talking to your grumpy friend and take me out for pizza?
Friend, huh?
If he's my *friend*, then I guess he better come with us-- huh, pumpkin?
I guess.
Wolverine, this is Sage.
The Quiet Council is demanding your immediate presence. Something about you going rogue. And...Magneto's helmet?
Come on, everybody. My treat.
Maybe we'll order the pizza topped with cigar butts and baby panda hearts. How does that sound...
...Logan?
What are we supposed to do with it, Daddy?
PERCY/KUBERT

[dawn_of_x]

[best__]
[there_]

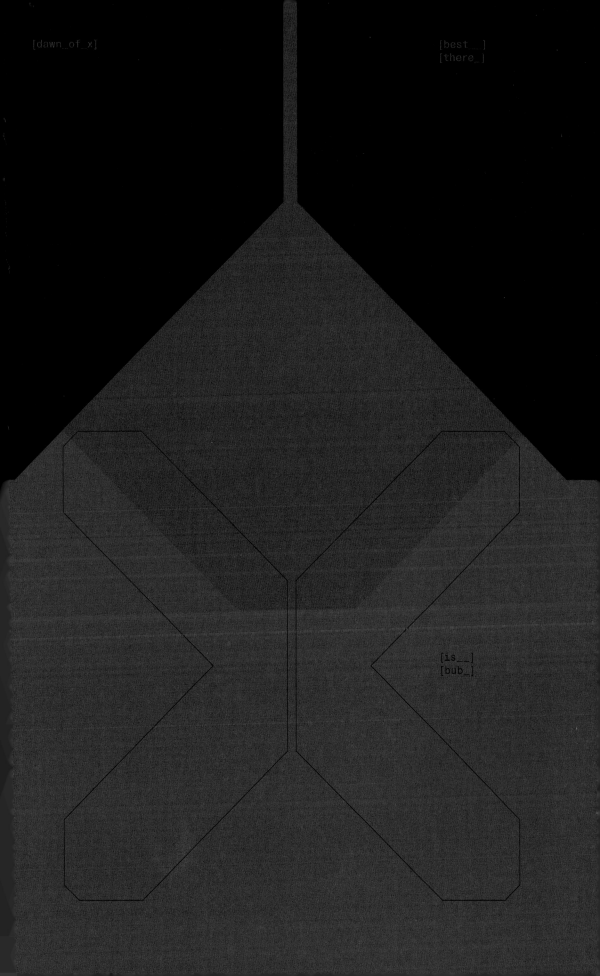

[is__]
[bub_]

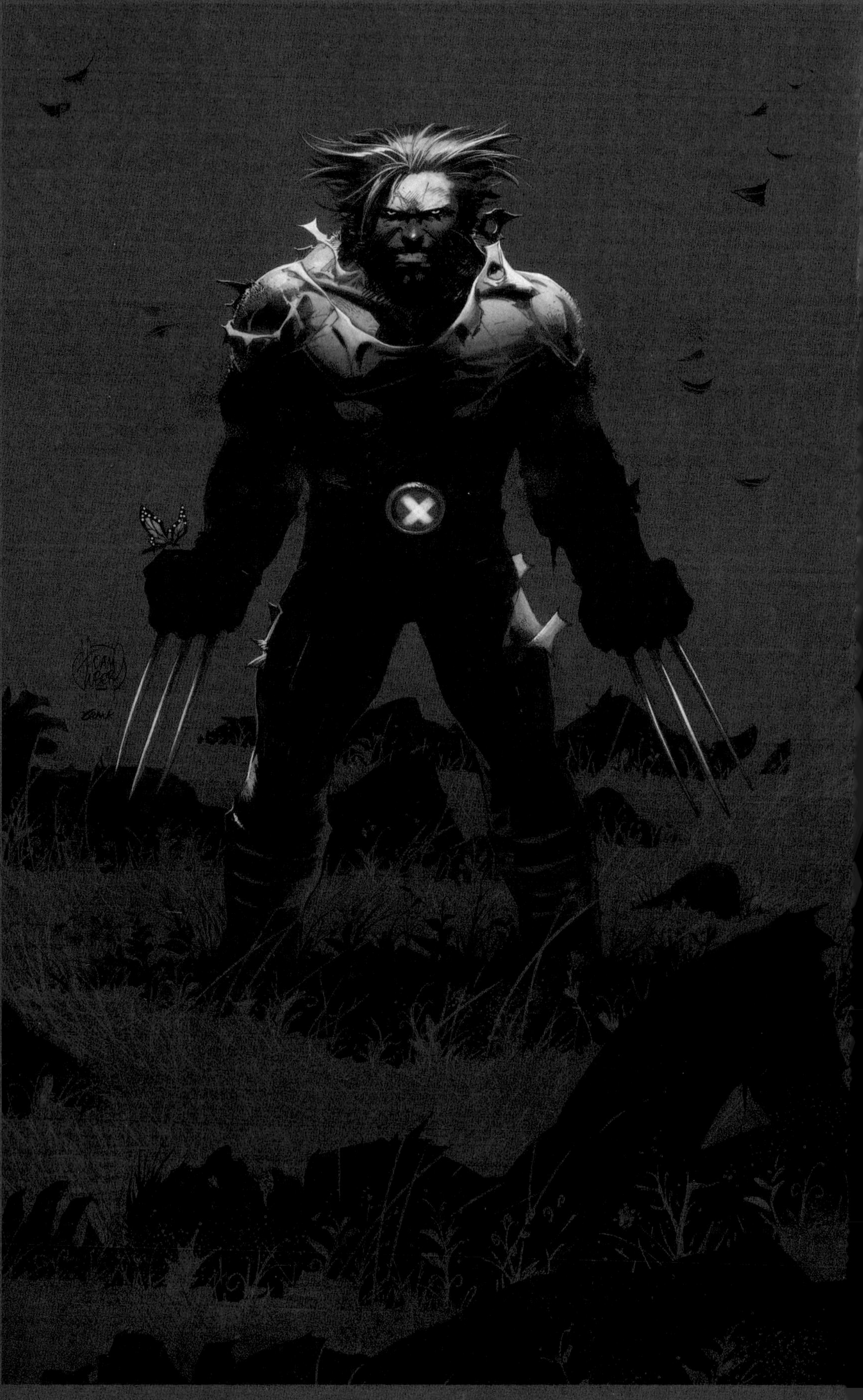

Catacombs

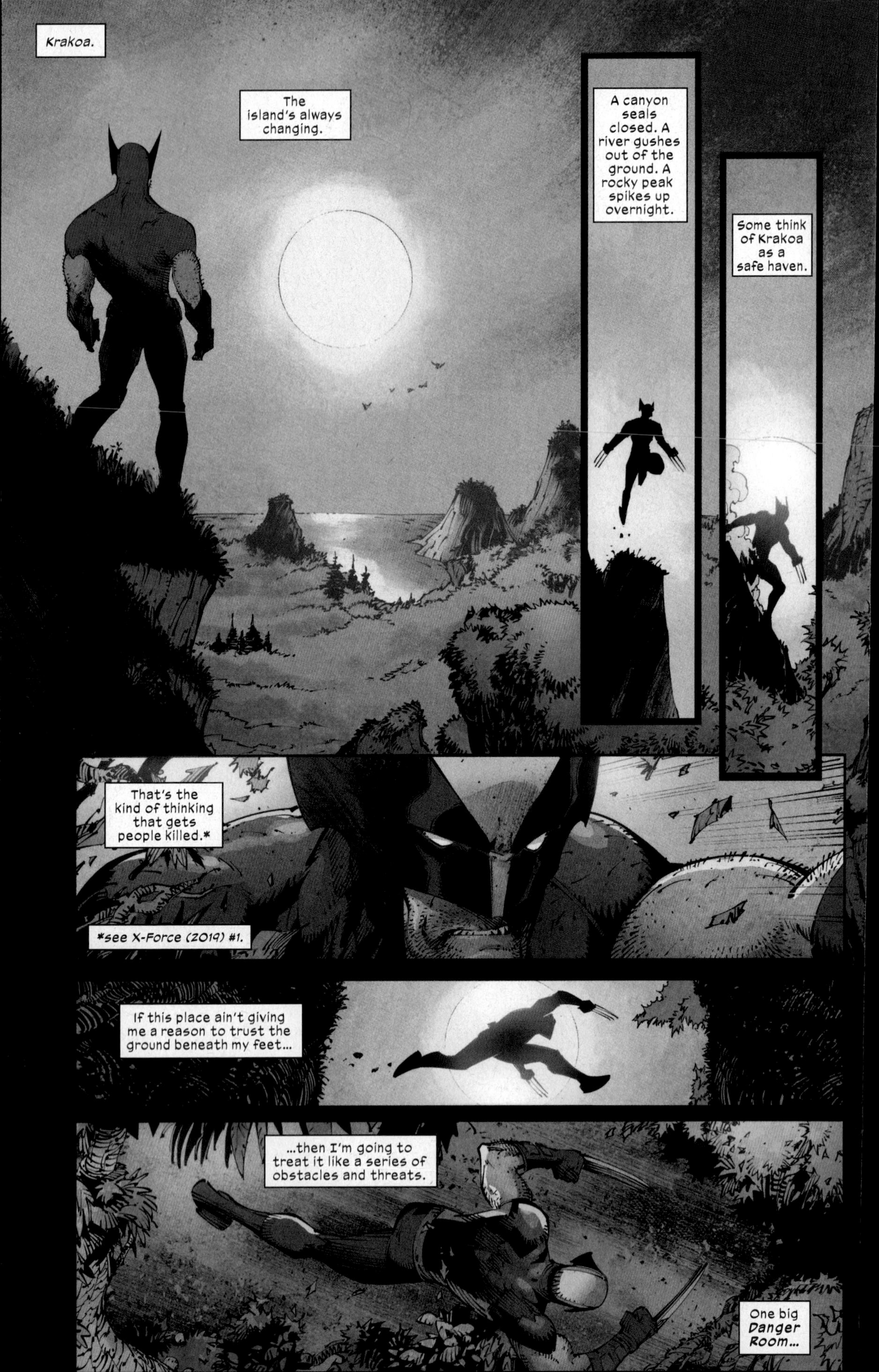
Krakoa.
The island's always changing.
A canyon seals closed. A river gushes out of the ground. A rocky peak spikes up overnight.
Some think of Krakoa as a safe haven.
That's the kind of thinking that gets people killed.*
*see X-Force (2019) #1.
If this place ain't giving me a reason to trust the ground beneath my feet...
...then I'm going to treat it like a series of obstacles and threats.
One big Danger Room...

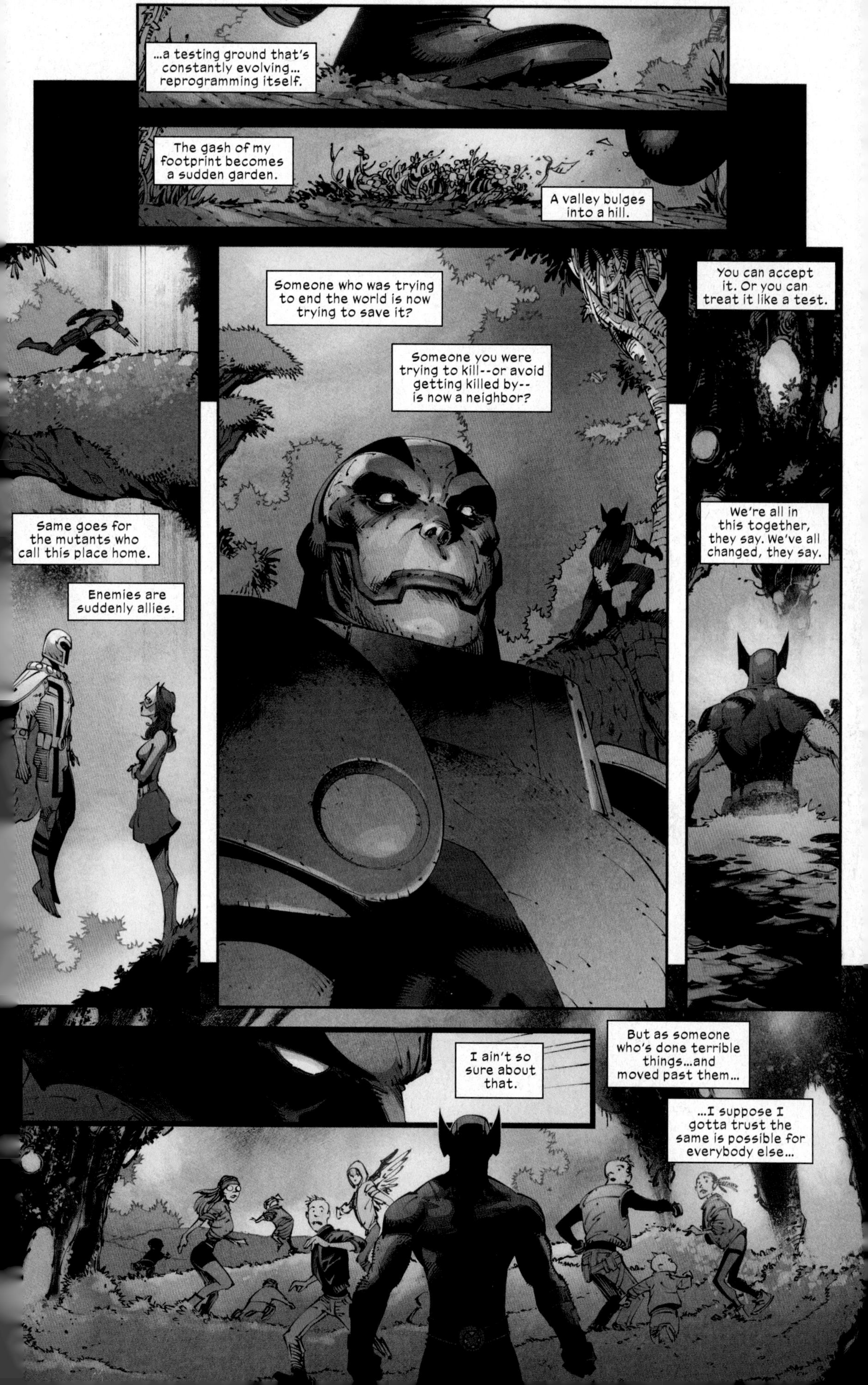

...a testing ground that's constantly evolving... reprogramming itself.
The gash of my footprint becomes a sudden garden.
A valley bulges into a hill.
Same goes for the mutants who call this place home.
Enemies are suddenly allies.
Someone who was trying to end the world is now trying to save it?
Someone you were trying to kill--or avoid getting killed by--is now a neighbor?
You can accept it. Or you can treat it like a test.
We're all in this together, they say. We've all changed, they say.
I ain't so sure about that.
But as someone who's done terrible things...and moved past them...
...I suppose I gotta trust the same is possible for everybody else...

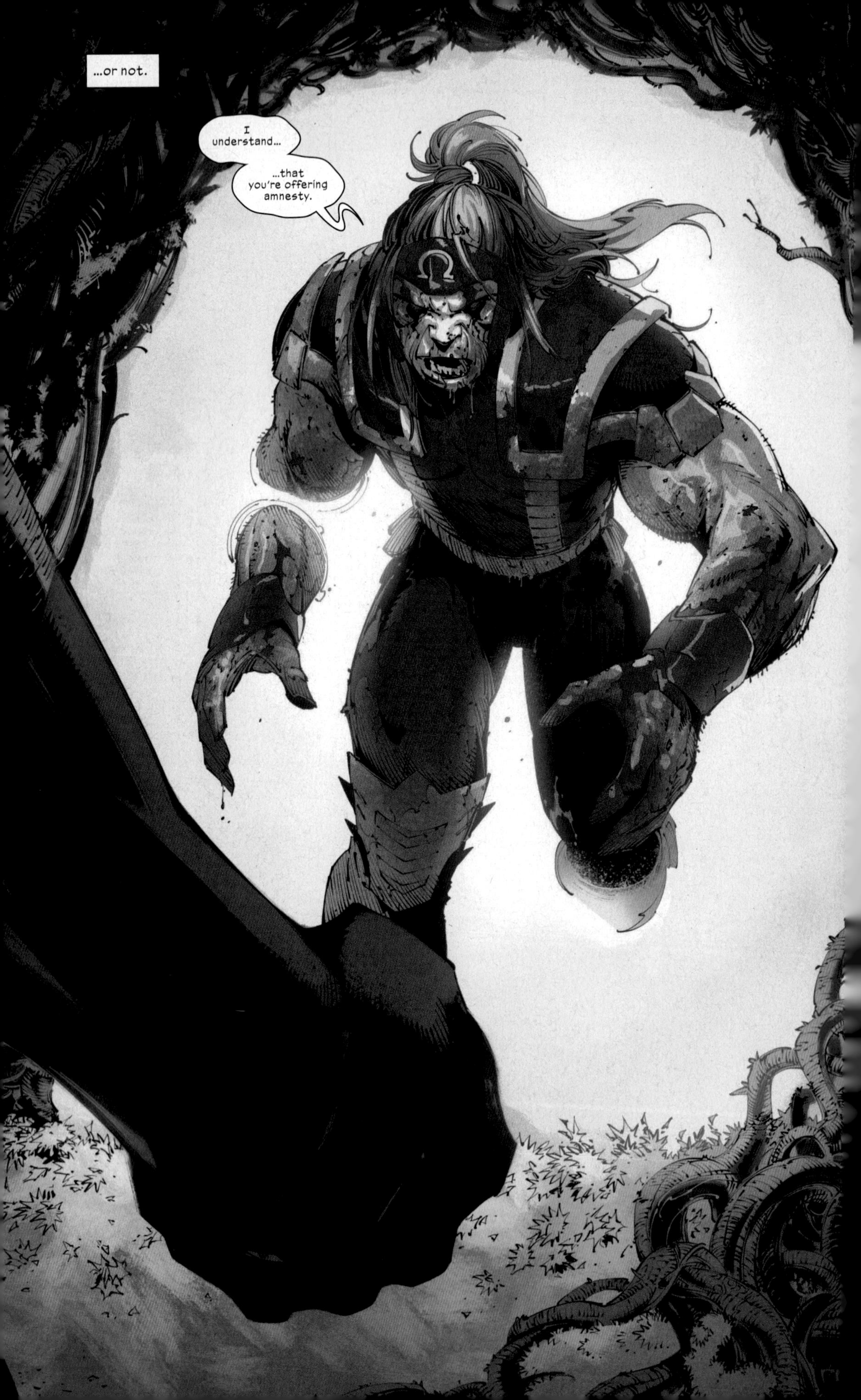
...or not.
I understand...
...that you're offering amnesty.

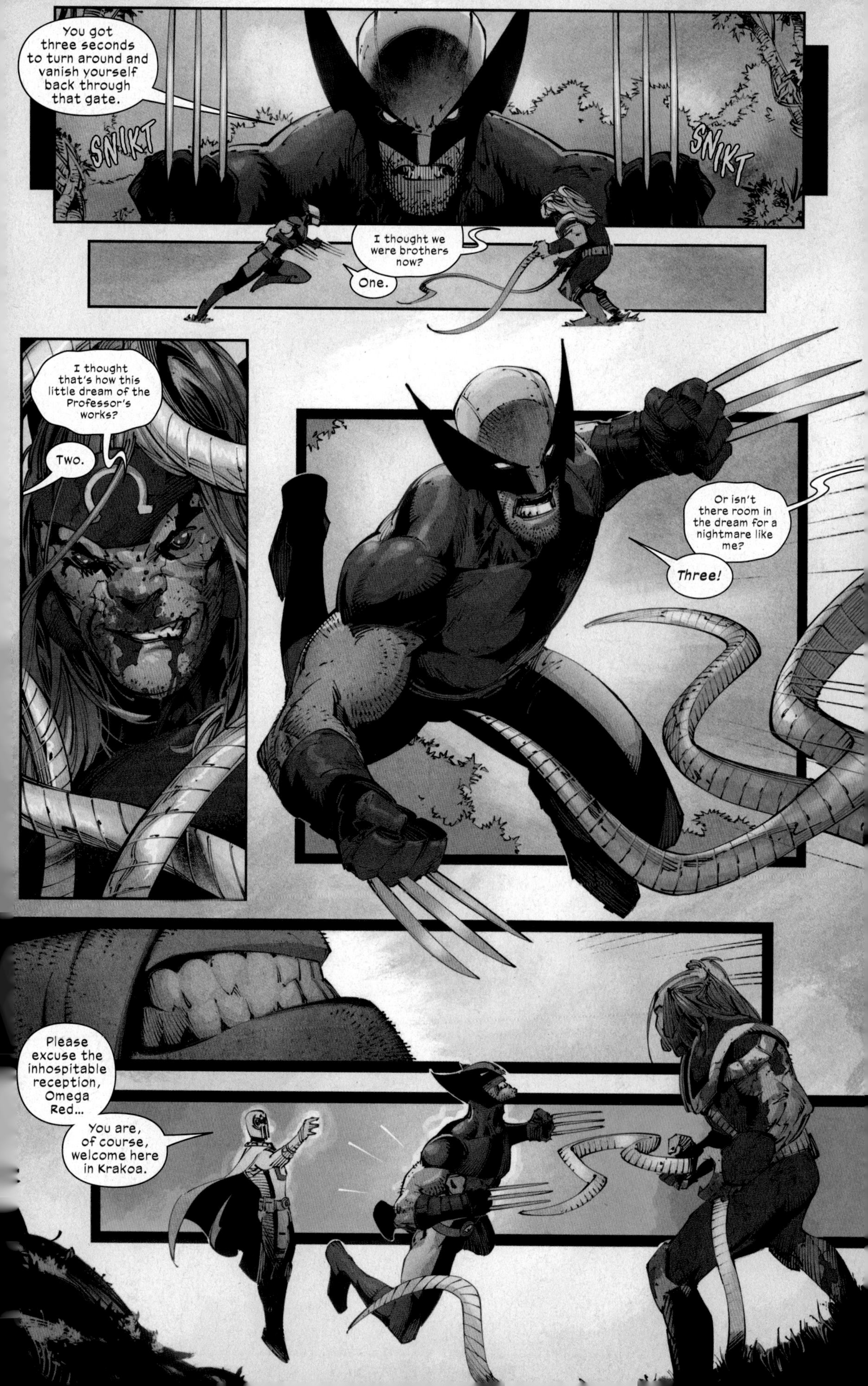

You got three seconds to turn around and vanish yourself back through that gate.
SNIKT
SNIKT
I thought we were brothers now?
One.
I thought that's how this little dream of the Professor's works?
Two.
Or isn't there room in the dream for a nightmare like me?
Three!
Please excuse the inhospitable reception, Omega Red...
You are, of course, welcome here in Krakoa.

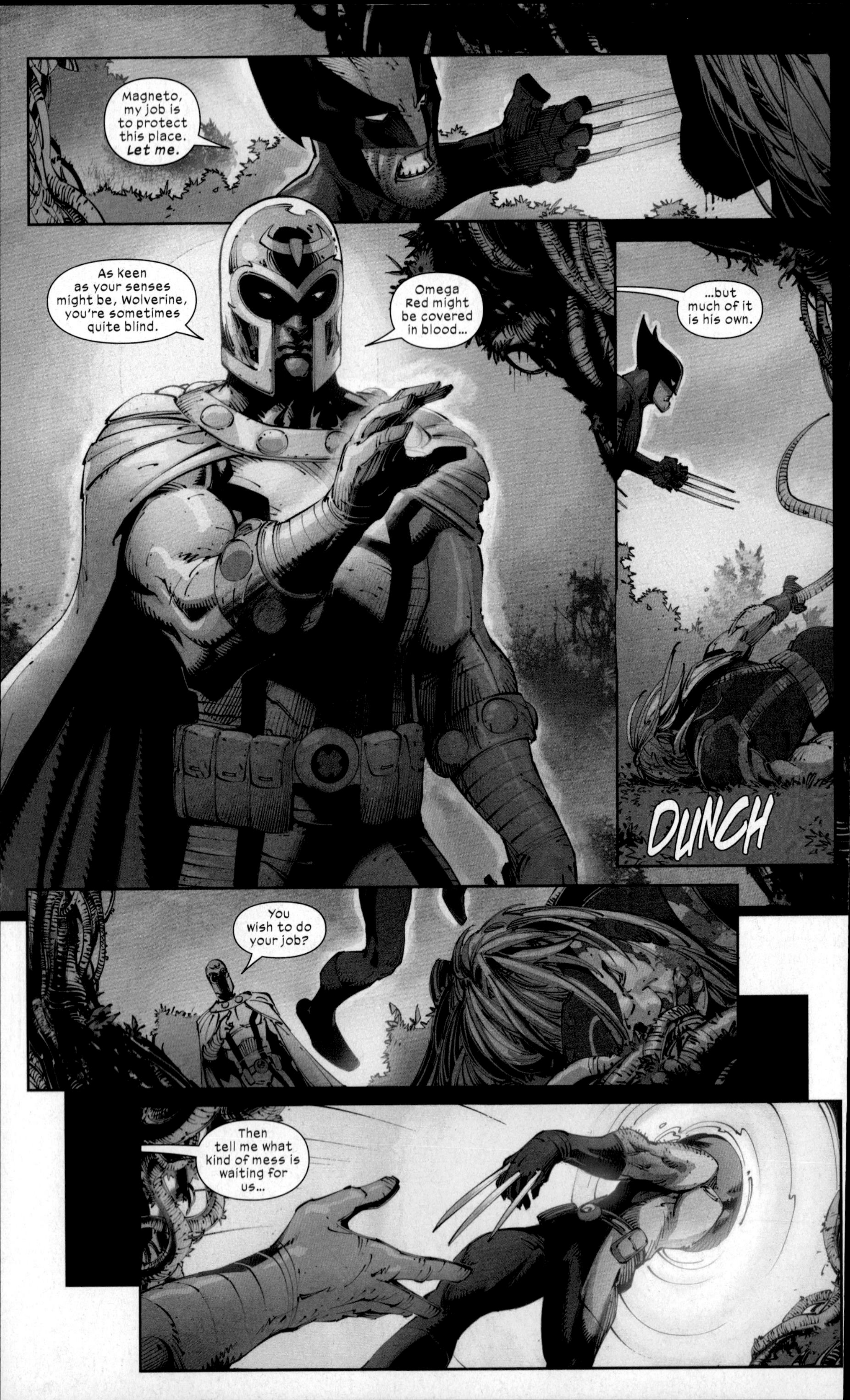
Magneto, my job is to protect this place. *Let me.*
As keen as your senses might be, Wolverine, you're sometimes quite blind.
Omega Red might be covered in blood...
...but much of it is his own.
DUNCH
You wish to do your job?
Then tell me what kind of mess is waiting for us...

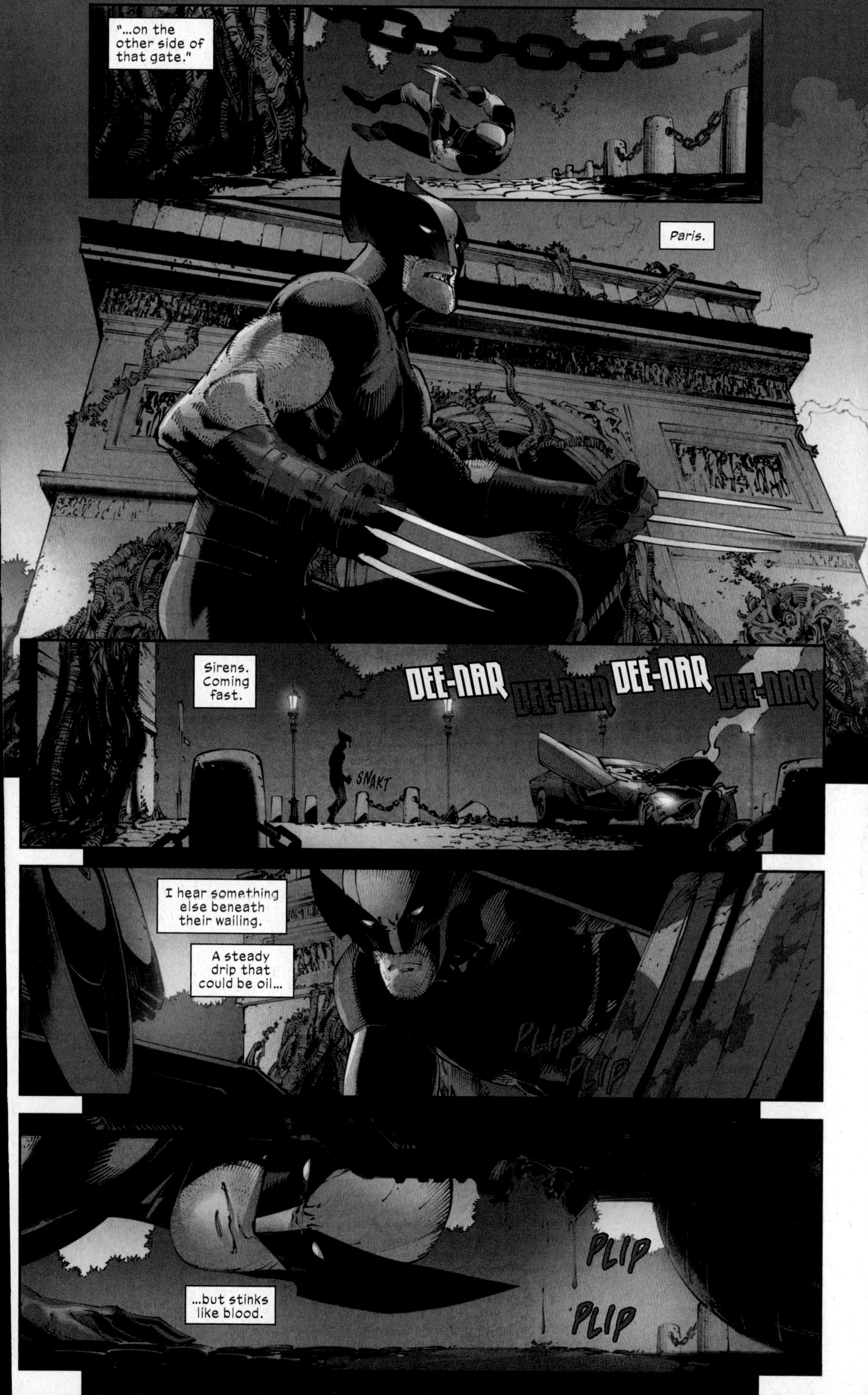
"...on the other side of that gate."
Paris.
Sirens. Coming fast.
DEE-NAR
DEE-NAR
DEE-NAR
DEE-NAR
SNAKT
I hear something else beneath their wailing.
A steady drip that could be oil...
PLIP
PLIP
...but stinks like blood.
PLIP
PLIP

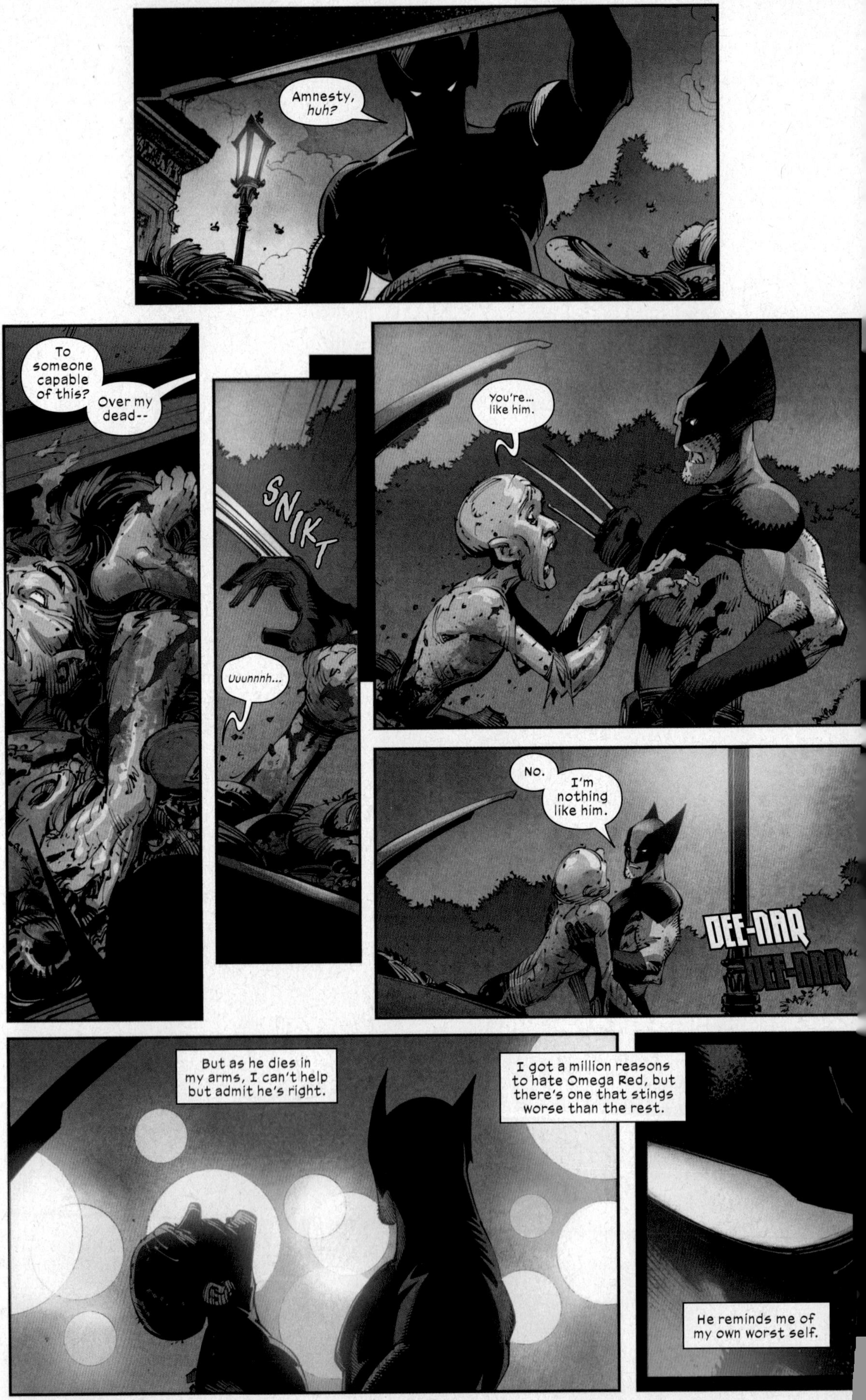
Amnesty, huh?
To someone capable of this?
Over my dead--
SNIKT
Uuunnnh...
You're... like him.
No. I'm nothing like him.
DEE-NAR
DEE-NAR
But as he dies in my arms, I can't help but admit he's right.
I got a million reasons to hate Omega Red, but there's one that stings worse than the rest.
He reminds me of my own worst self.

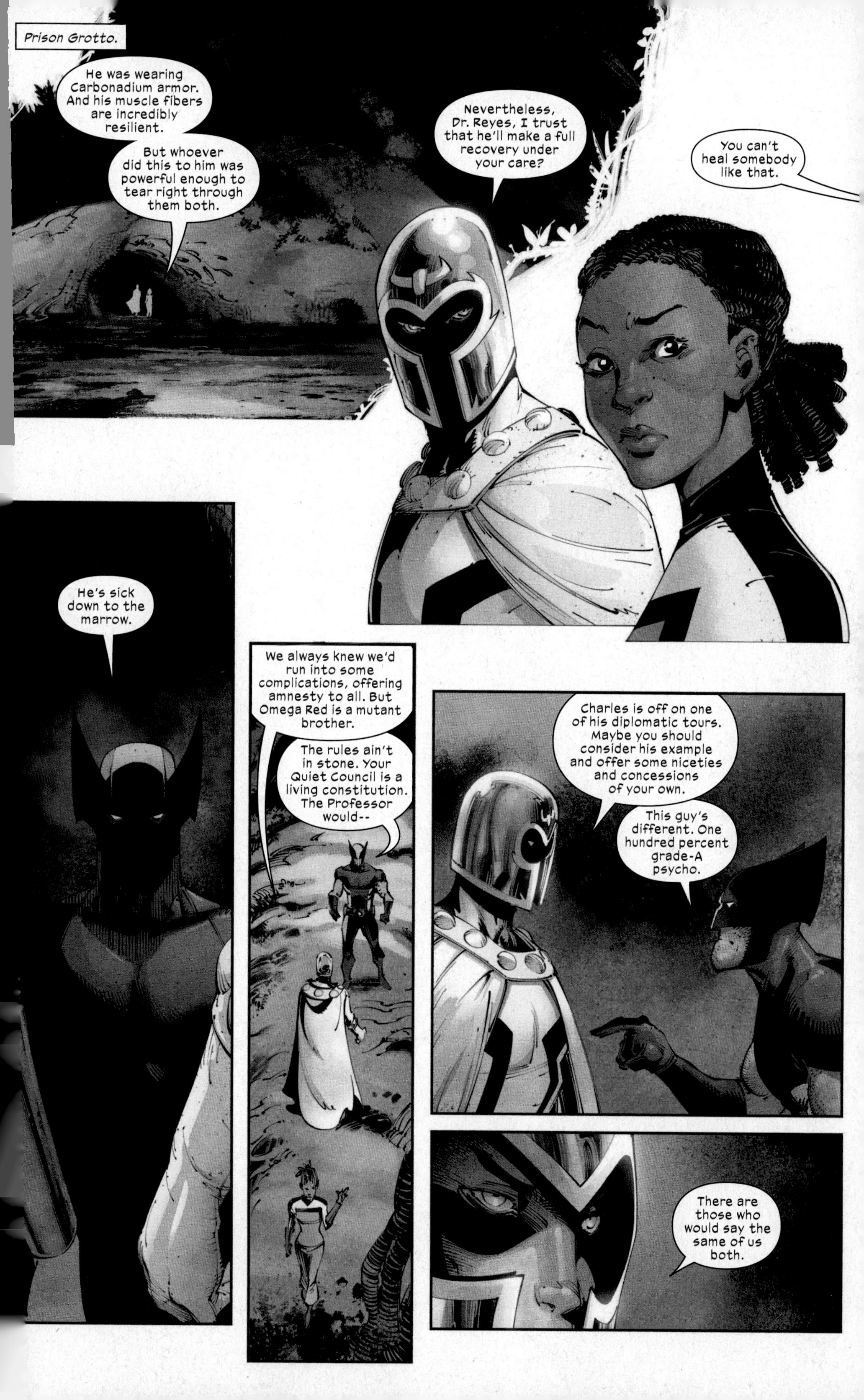
Prison Grotto.
He was wearing Carbonadium armor. And his muscle fibers are incredibly resilient.
But whoever did this to him was powerful enough to tear right through them both.
Nevertheless, Dr. Reyes, I trust that he'll make a full recovery under your care?
You can't heal somebody like that.
He's sick down to the marrow.
We always knew we'd run into some complications, offering amnesty to all. But Omega Red is a mutant brother.
The rules ain't in stone. Your Quiet Council is a living constitution. The Professor would--
Charles is off on one of his diplomatic tours. Maybe you should consider his example and offer some niceties and concessions of your own.
This guy's different. One hundred percent grade-A psycho.
There are those who would say the same of us both.

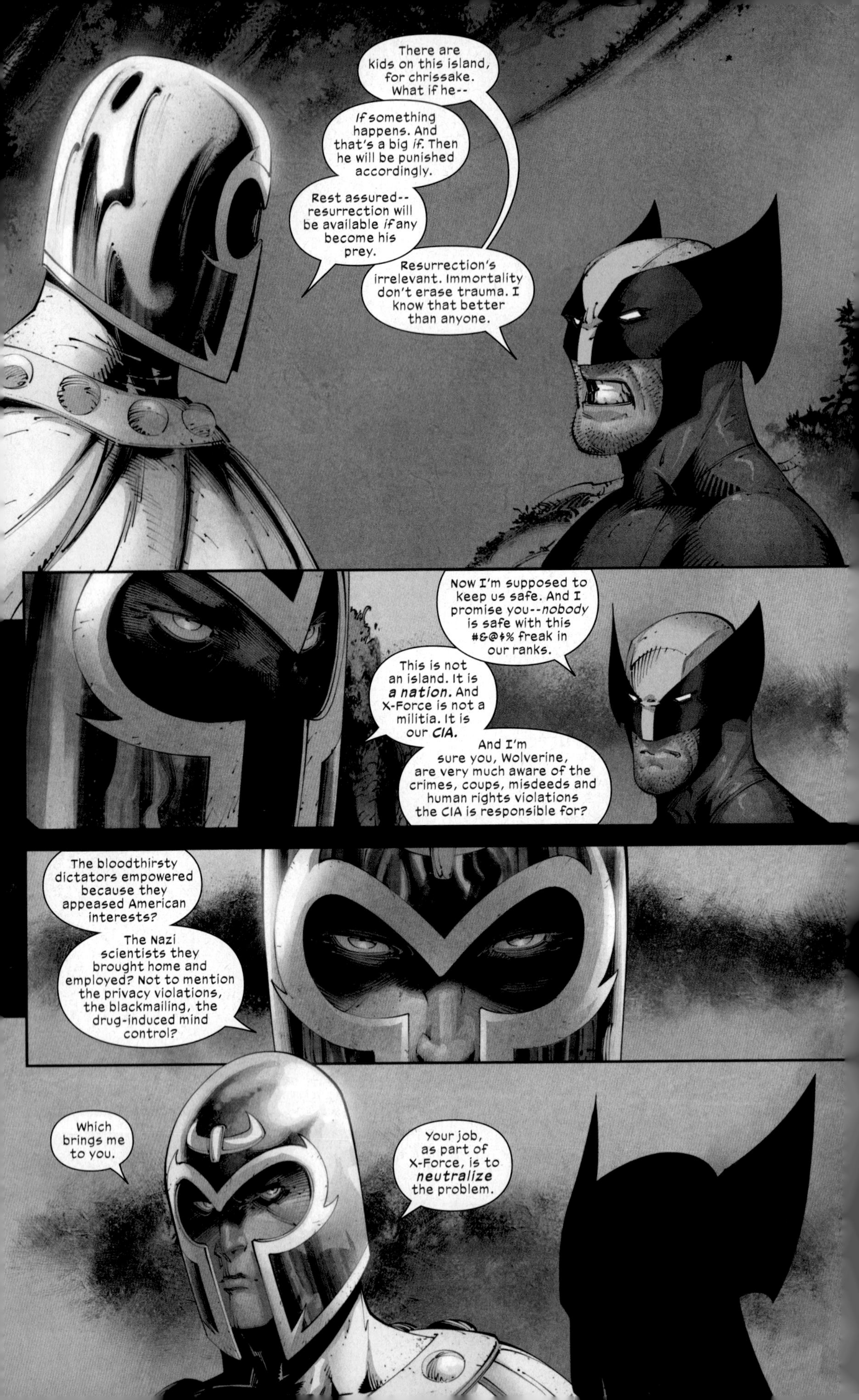
There are kids on this island, for chrissake. What if he--
If something happens. And that's a big *if*. Then he will be punished accordingly.
Rest assured--resurrection will be available *if* any become his prey.
Resurrection's irrelevant. Immortality don't erase trauma. I know that better than anyone.
Now I'm supposed to keep us safe. And I promise you--*nobody* is safe with this #&@$% freak in our ranks.
This is not an island. It is ***a nation.*** And X-Force is not a militia. It is our ***CIA.***
And I'm sure you, Wolverine, are very much aware of the crimes, coups, misdeeds and human rights violations the CIA is responsible for?
The bloodthirsty dictators empowered because they appeased American interests?
The Nazi scientists they brought home and employed? Not to mention the privacy violations, the blackmailing, the drug-induced mind control?
Which brings me to you.
Your job, as part of X-Force, is to ***neutralize*** the problem.

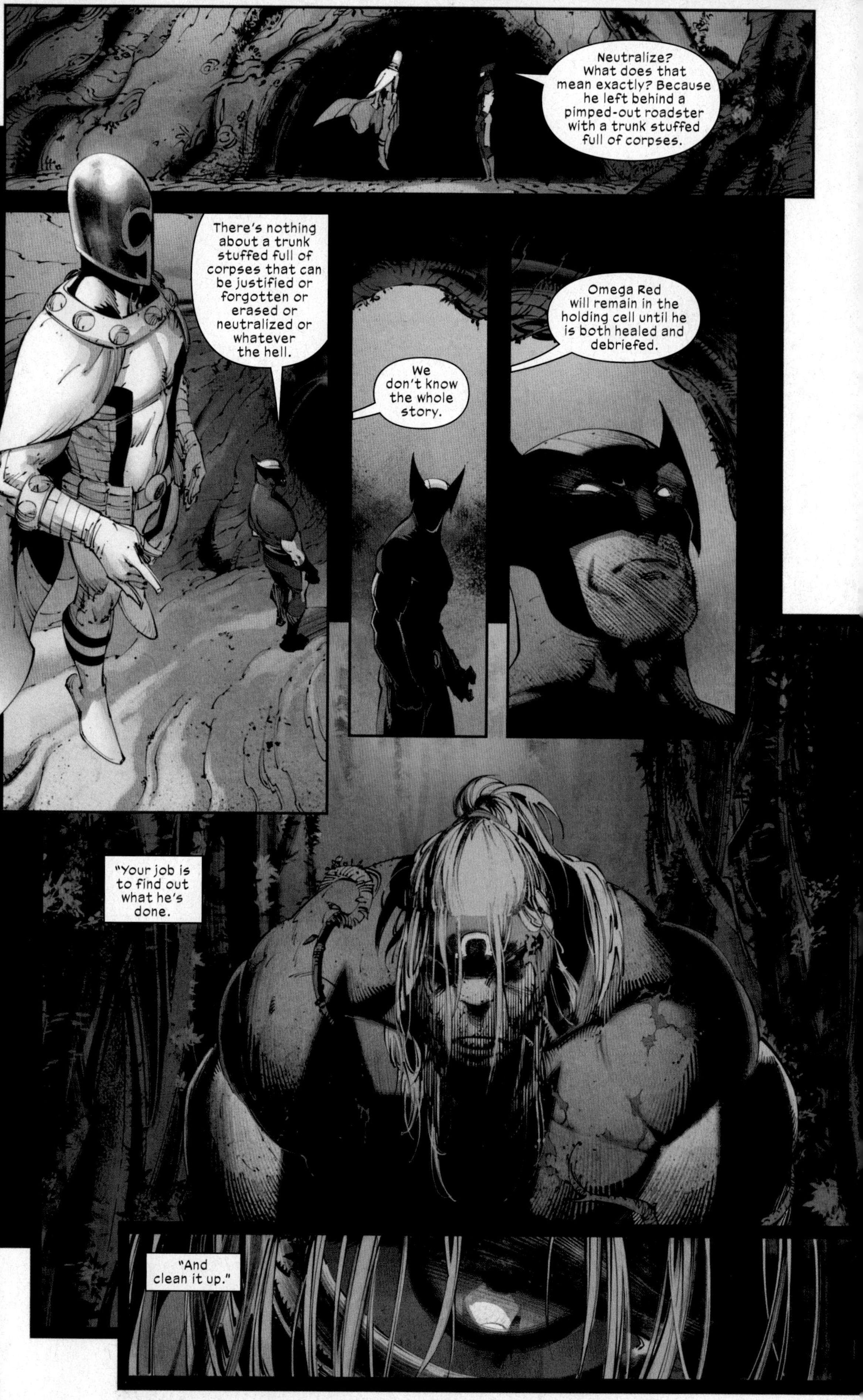
Neutralize? What does that mean exactly? Because he left behind a pimped-out roadster with a trunk stuffed full of corpses.
There's nothing about a trunk stuffed full of corpses that can be justified or forgotten or erased or neutralized or whatever the hell.
We don't know the whole story.
Omega Red will remain in the holding cell until he is both healed and debriefed.
"Your job is to find out what he's done.
"And clean it up."

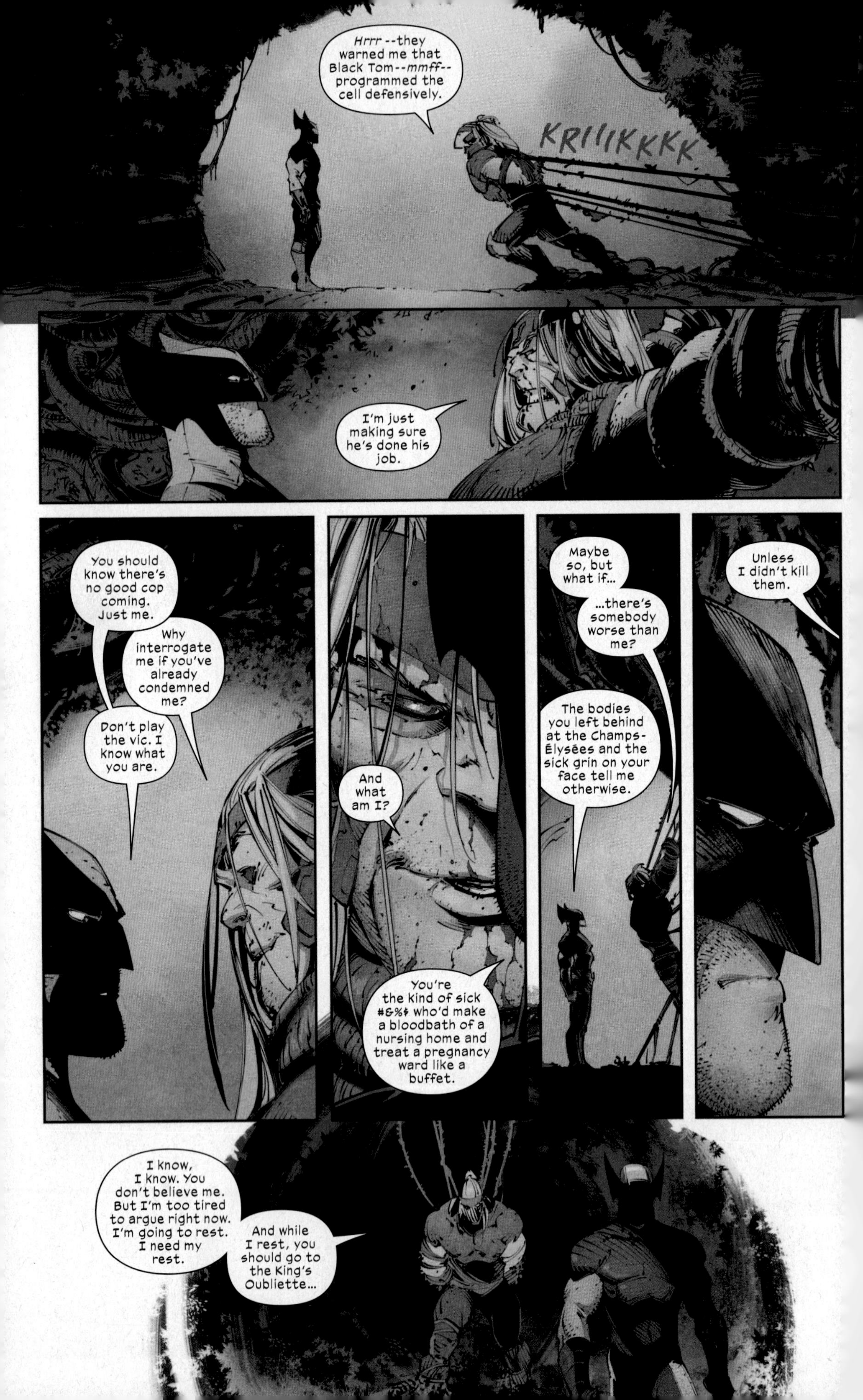

Hrrr --they warned me that Black Tom--*mmff*--programmed the cell defensively.
KRIIIKKKK
I'm just making sure he's done his job.
You should know there's no good cop coming. Just me.
Why interrogate me if you've already condemned me?
Don't play the vic. I know what you are.
And what am I?
You're the kind of sick #&%$ who'd make a bloodbath of a nursing home and treat a pregnancy ward like a buffet.
Maybe so, but what if...
...there's somebody worse than me?
The bodies you left behind at the Champs-Élysées and the sick grin on your face tell me otherwise.
Unless I didn't kill them.
I know, I know. You don't believe me. But I'm too tired to argue right now. I'm going to rest. I need my rest.
And while I rest, you should go to the King's Oubliette...

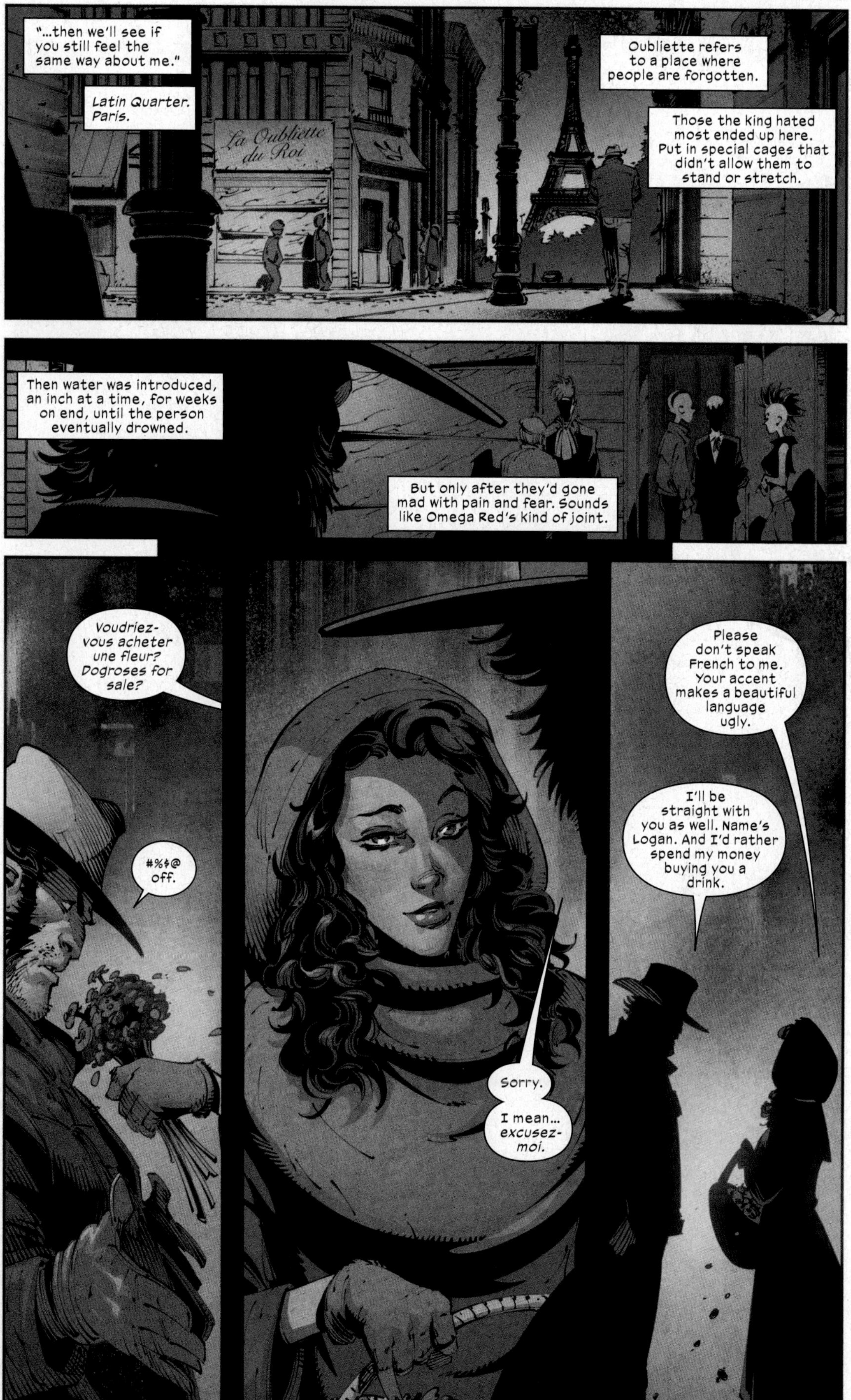
"...then we'll see if you still feel the same way about me."
Latin Quarter. Paris.
La Oubliette du Roi
Oubliette refers to a place where people are forgotten.
Those the king hated most ended up here. Put in special cages that didn't allow them to stand or stretch.
Then water was introduced, an inch at a time, for weeks on end, until the person eventually drowned.
But only after they'd gone mad with pain and fear. Sounds like Omega Red's kind of joint.
Voudriez-vous acheter une fleur? Dogroses for sale?
#%$@ off.
Sorry.
I mean... excusez-moi.
Please don't speak French to me. Your accent makes a beautiful language ugly.
I'll be straight with you as well. Name's Logan. And I'd rather spend my money buying you a drink.

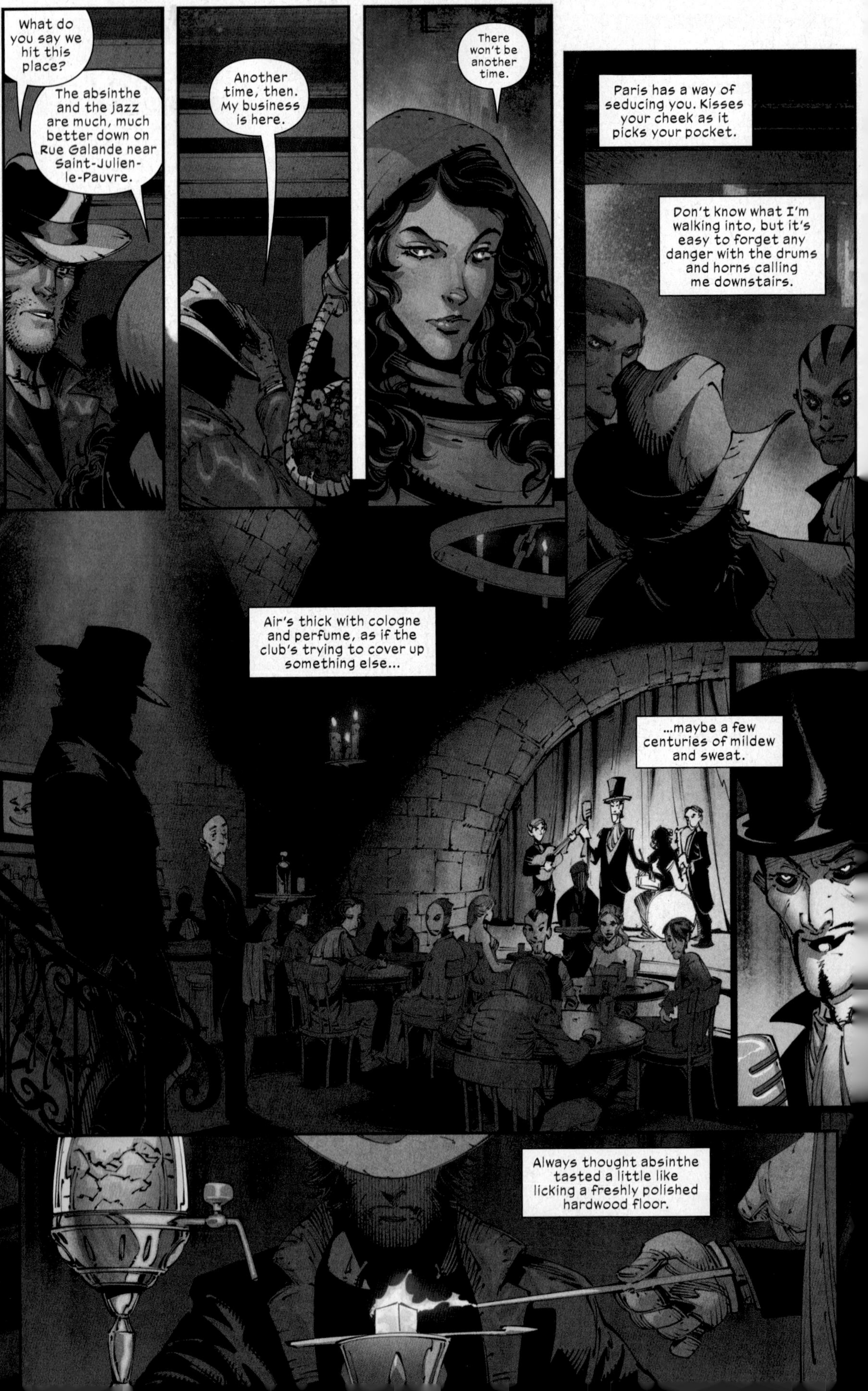
What do you say we hit this place?
The absinthe and the jazz are much, much better down on Rue Galande near Saint-Julien-le-Pauvre.
Another time, then. My business is here.
There won't be another time.
Paris has a way of seducing you. Kisses your cheek as it picks your pocket.
Don't know what I'm walking into, but it's easy to forget any danger with the drums and horns calling me downstairs.
Air's thick with cologne and perfume, as if the club's trying to cover up something else...
...maybe a few centuries of mildew and sweat.
Always thought absinthe tasted a little like licking a freshly polished hardwood floor.

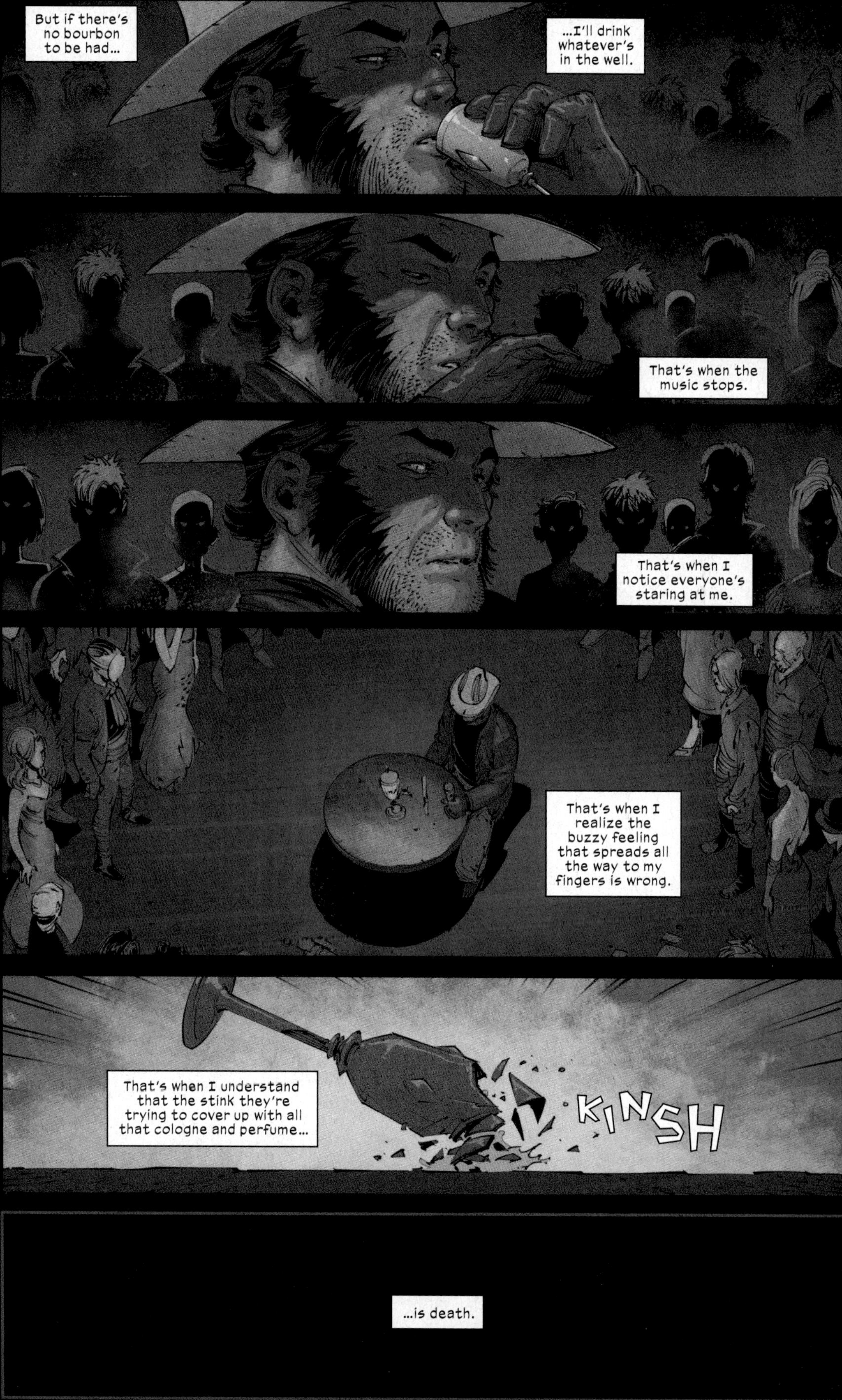

But if there's no bourbon to be had...
...I'll drink whatever's in the well.
That's when the music stops.
That's when I notice everyone's staring at me.
That's when I realize the buzzy feeling that spreads all the way to my fingers is wrong.
That's when I understand that the stink they're trying to cover up with all that cologne and perfume...
KINSH
...is death.

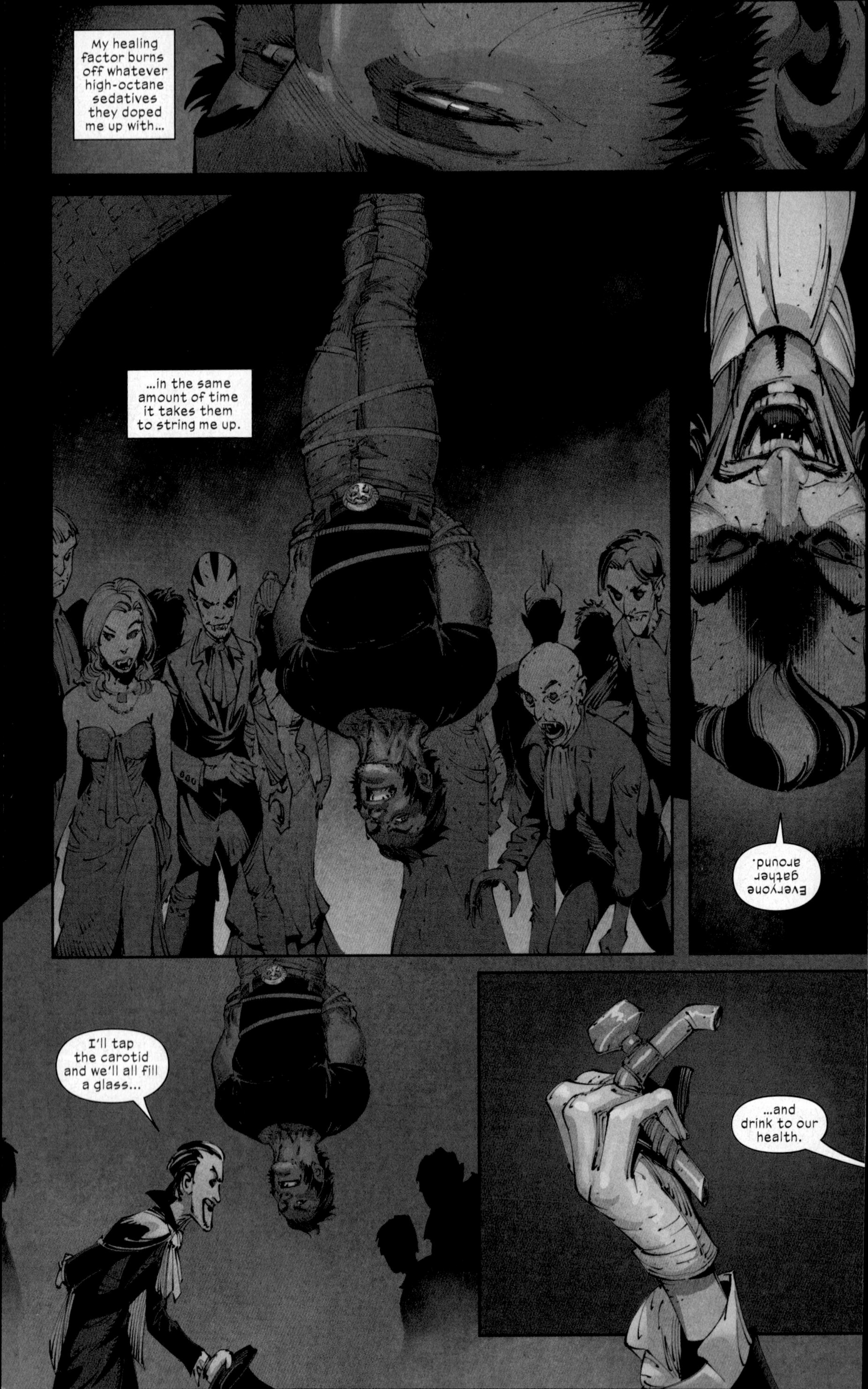
My healing factor burns off whatever high-octane sedatives they doped me up with...
...in the same amount of time it takes them to string me up.
Everyone gather around.
I'll tap the carotid and we'll all fill a glass...
...and drink to our health.

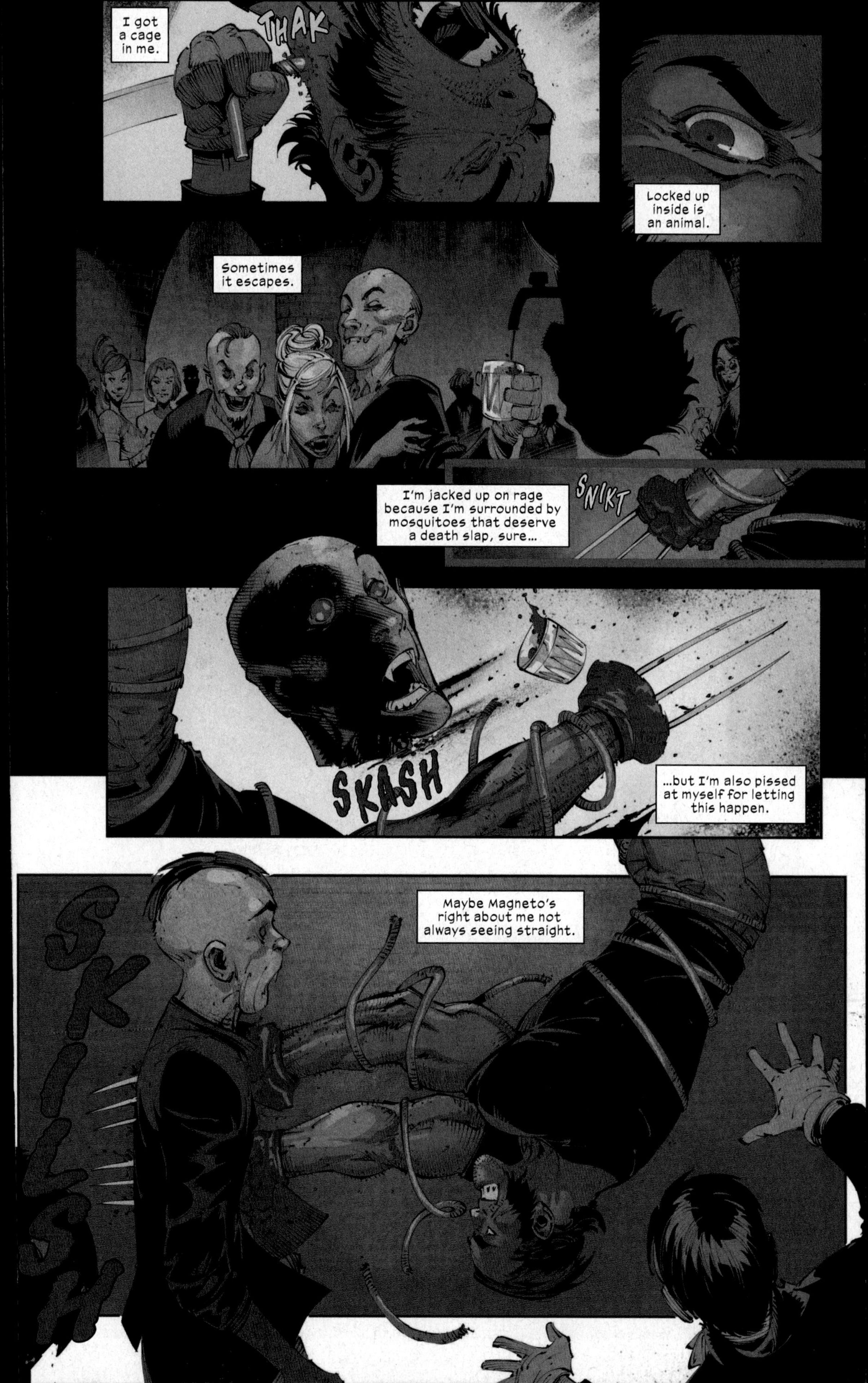
I got a cage in me.
THAK
Locked up inside is an animal.
Sometimes it escapes.
I'm jacked up on rage because I'm surrounded by mosquitoes that deserve a death slap, sure...
SNIKT
SKASH
...but I'm also pissed at myself for letting this happen.
Maybe Magneto's right about me not always seeing straight.
SKLSH

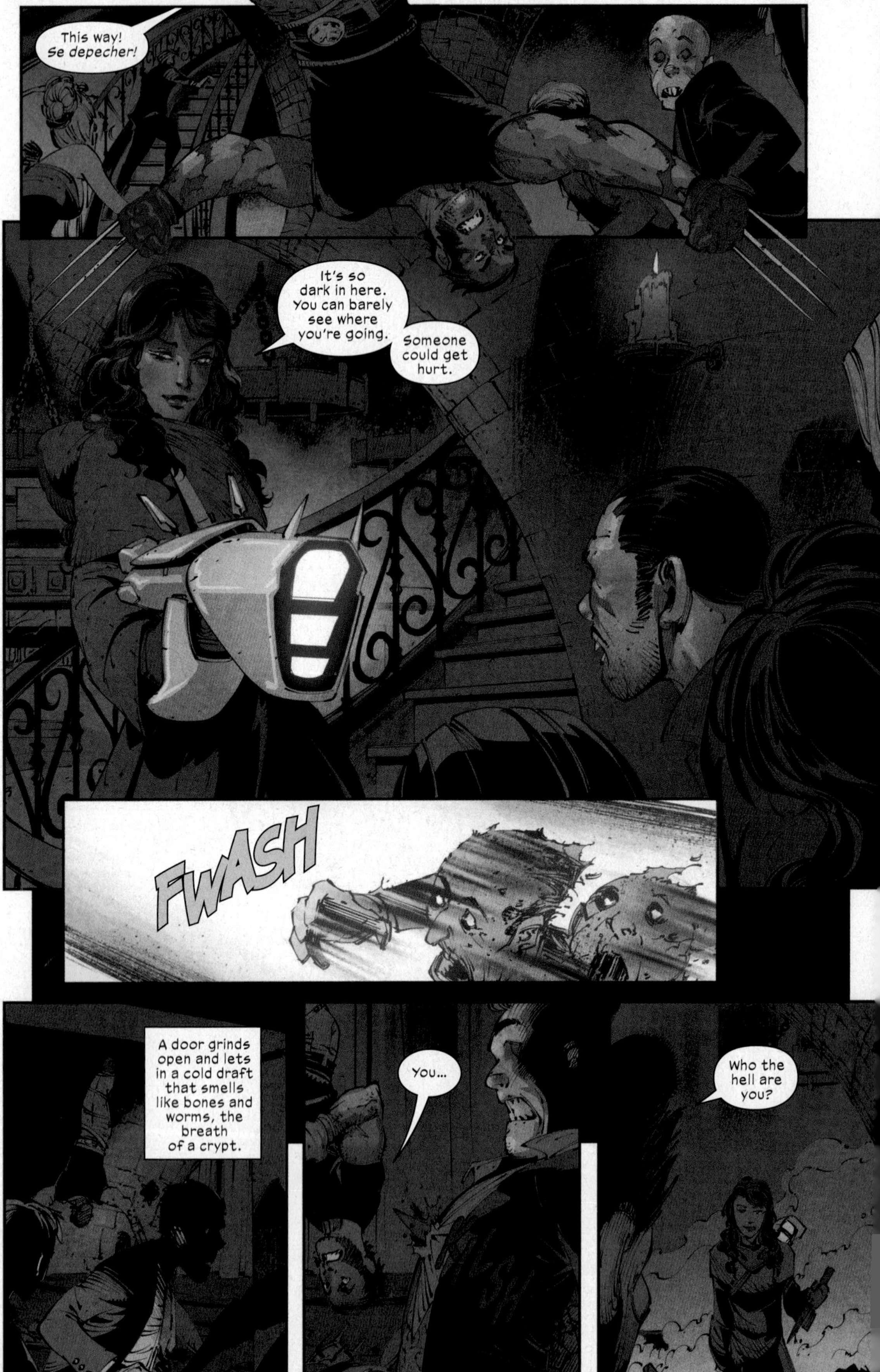
This way! Se depecher!
It's so dark in here. You can barely see where you're going.
Someone could get hurt.
FWASH
A door grinds open and lets in a cold draft that smells like bones and worms, the breath of a crypt.
You...
Who the hell are you?

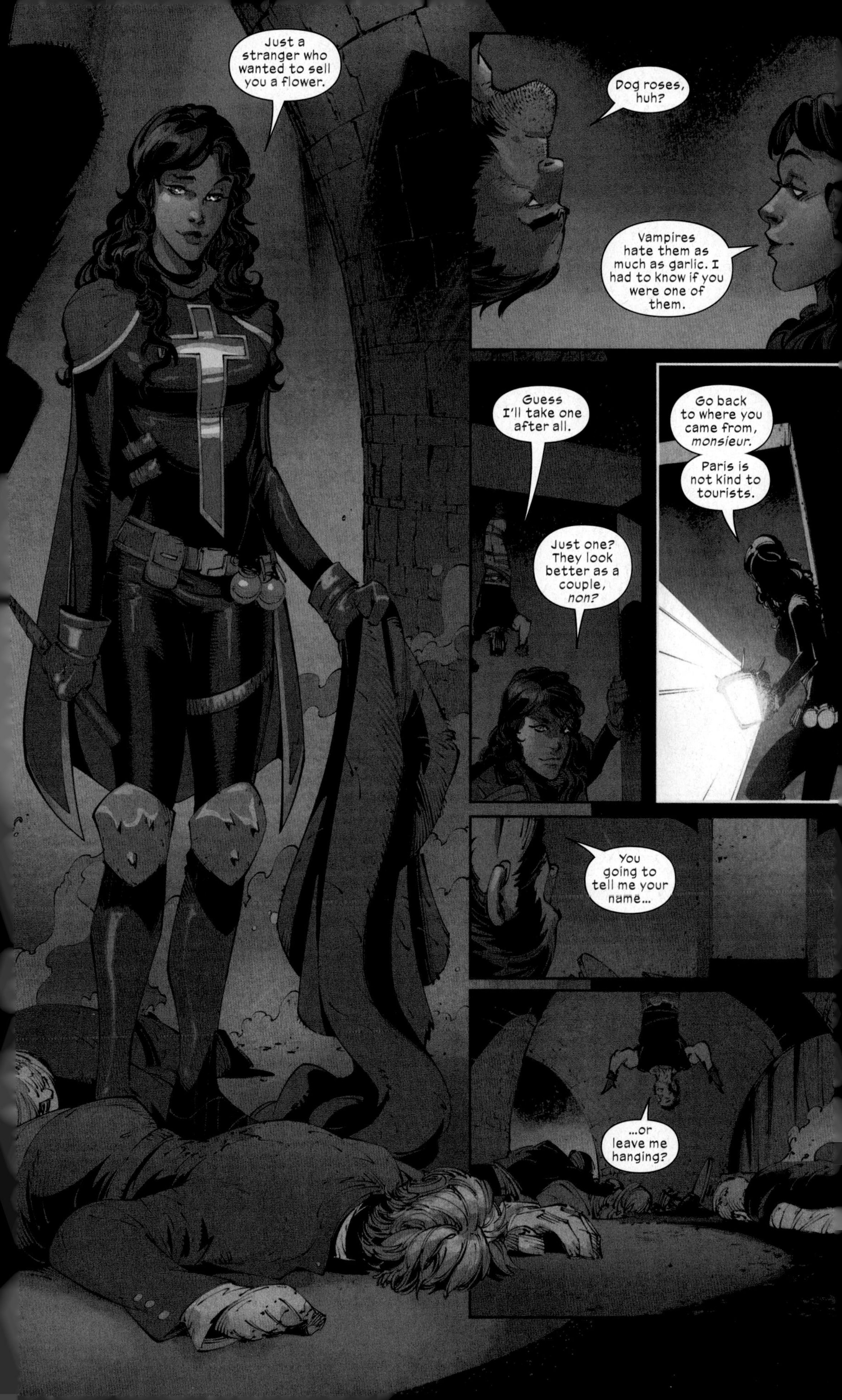

Just a stranger who wanted to sell you a flower.
Dog roses, huh?
Vampires hate them as much as garlic. I had to know if you were one of them.
Guess I'll take one after all.
Just one? They look better as a couple, *non?*
Go back to where you came from, *monsieur.*
Paris is not kind to tourists.
You going to tell me your name...
...or leave me hanging?

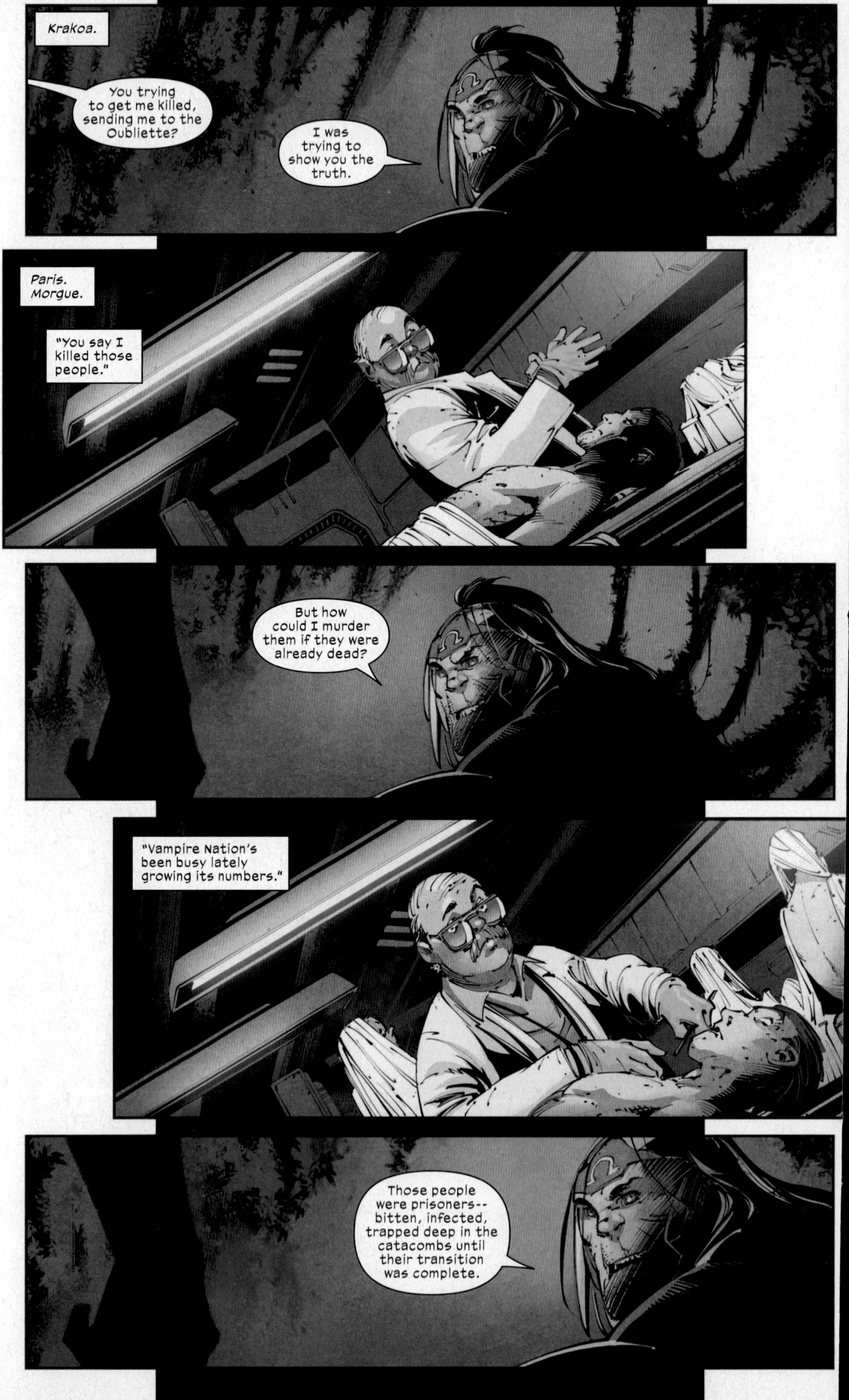
Krakoa.
You trying to get me killed, sending me to the Oubliette?
I was trying to show you the truth.
Paris. Morgue.
"You say I killed those people."
But how could I murder them if they were already dead?
"Vampire Nation's been busy lately growing its numbers."
Those people were prisoners-- bitten, infected, trapped deep in the catacombs until their transition was complete.

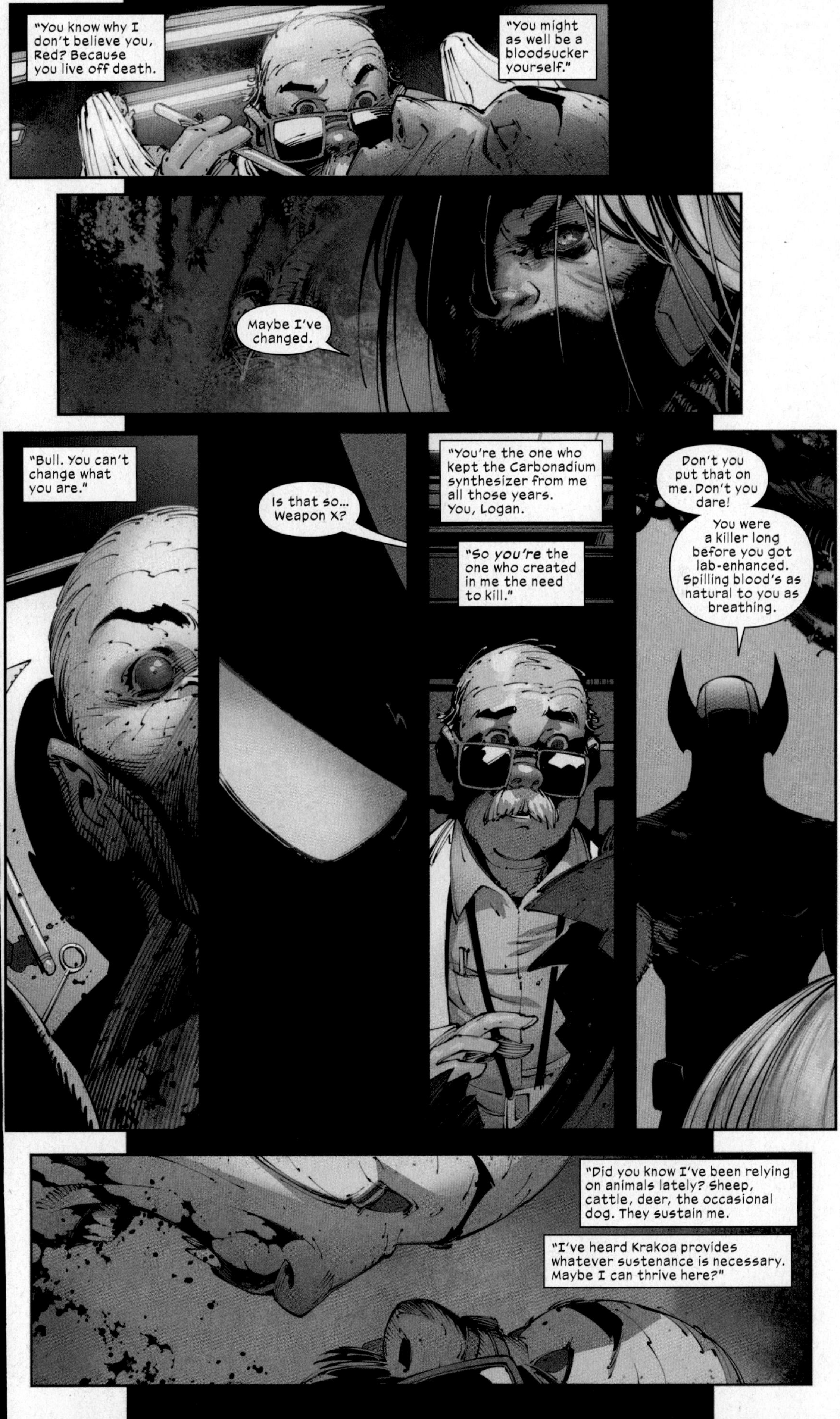
"You know why I don't believe you, Red? Because you live off death.
"You might as well be a bloodsucker yourself."
Maybe I've changed.
"Bull. You can't change what you are."
Is that so... Weapon X?
"You're the one who kept the Carbonadium synthesizer from me all those years. You, Logan.
"So *you're* the one who created in me the need to kill."
Don't you put that on me. Don't you dare!
You were a killer long before you got lab-enhanced. Spilling blood's as natural to you as breathing.
"Did you know I've been relying on animals lately? Sheep, cattle, deer, the occasional dog. They sustain me.
"I've heard Krakoa provides whatever sustenance is necessary. Maybe I can thrive here?"

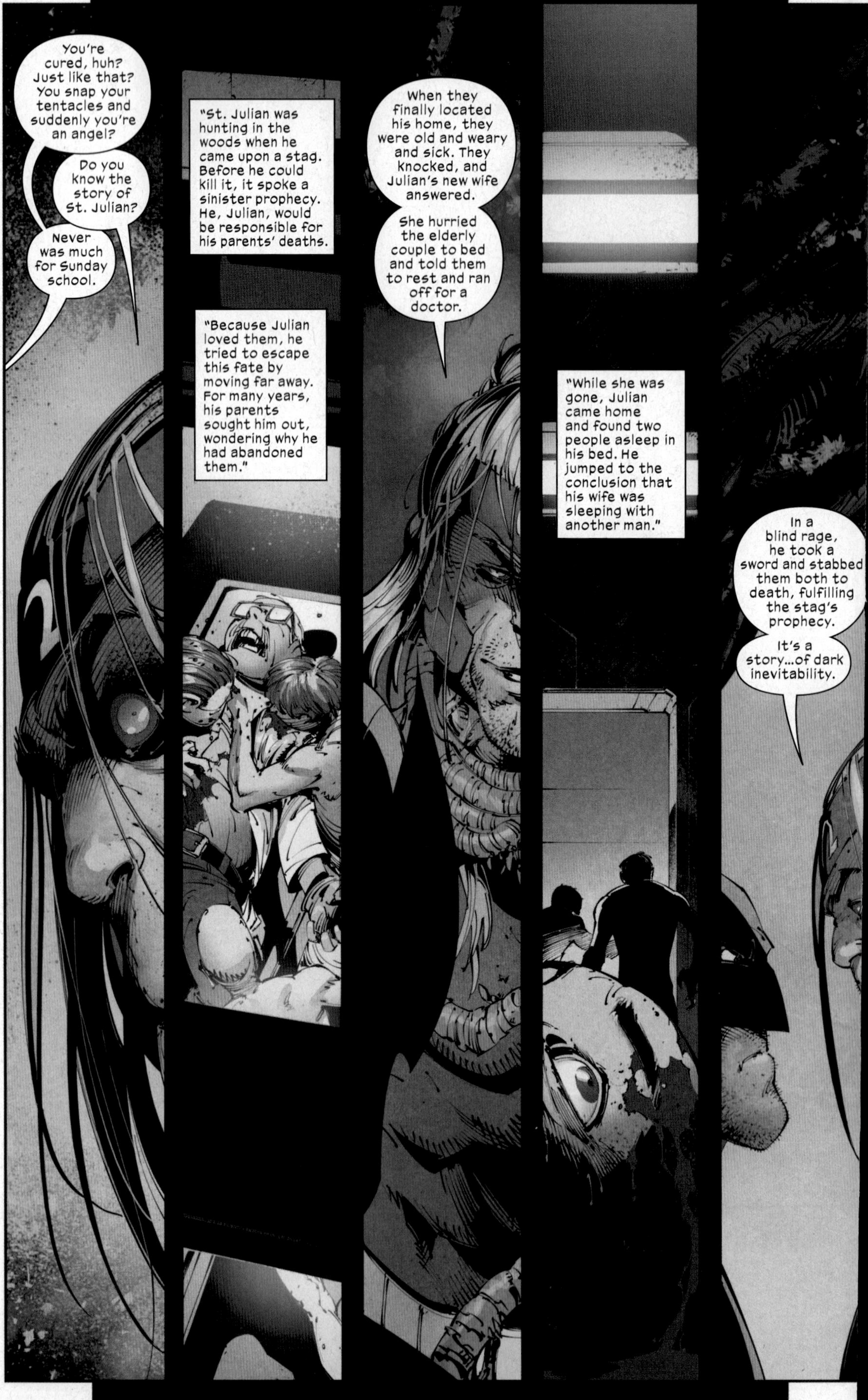
You're cured, huh? Just like that? You snap your tentacles and suddenly you're an angel?
Do you know the story of St. Julian?
Never was much for Sunday school.
"St. Julian was hunting in the woods when he came upon a stag. Before he could kill it, it spoke a sinister prophecy. He, Julian, would be responsible for his parents' deaths.
"Because Julian loved them, he tried to escape this fate by moving far away. For many years, his parents sought him out, wondering why he had abandoned them."
When they finally located his home, they were old and weary and sick. They knocked, and Julian's new wife answered.
She hurried the elderly couple to bed and told them to rest and ran off for a doctor.
"While she was gone, Julian came home and found two people asleep in his bed. He jumped to the conclusion that his wife was sleeping with another man."
In a blind rage, he took a sword and stabbed them both to death, fulfilling the stag's prophecy.
It's a story...of dark inevitability.

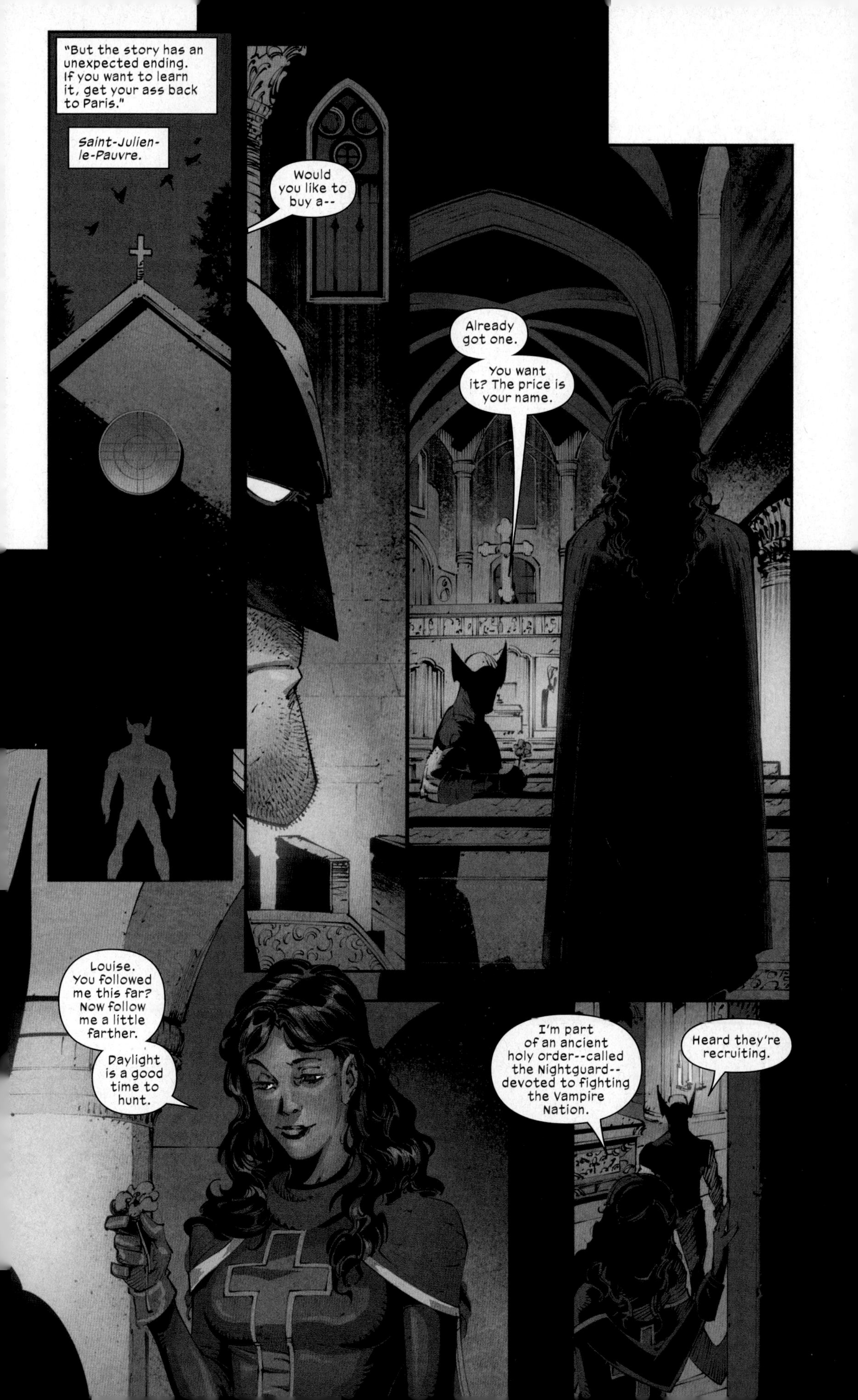
"But the story has an unexpected ending. If you want to learn it, get your ass back to Paris."
Saint-Julien-le-Pauvre.
Would you like to buy a--
Already got one.
You want it? The price is your name.
Louise. You followed me this far? Now follow me a little farther.
Daylight is a good time to hunt.
I'm part of an ancient holy order--called the Nightguard--devoted to fighting the Vampire Nation.
Heard they're recruiting.

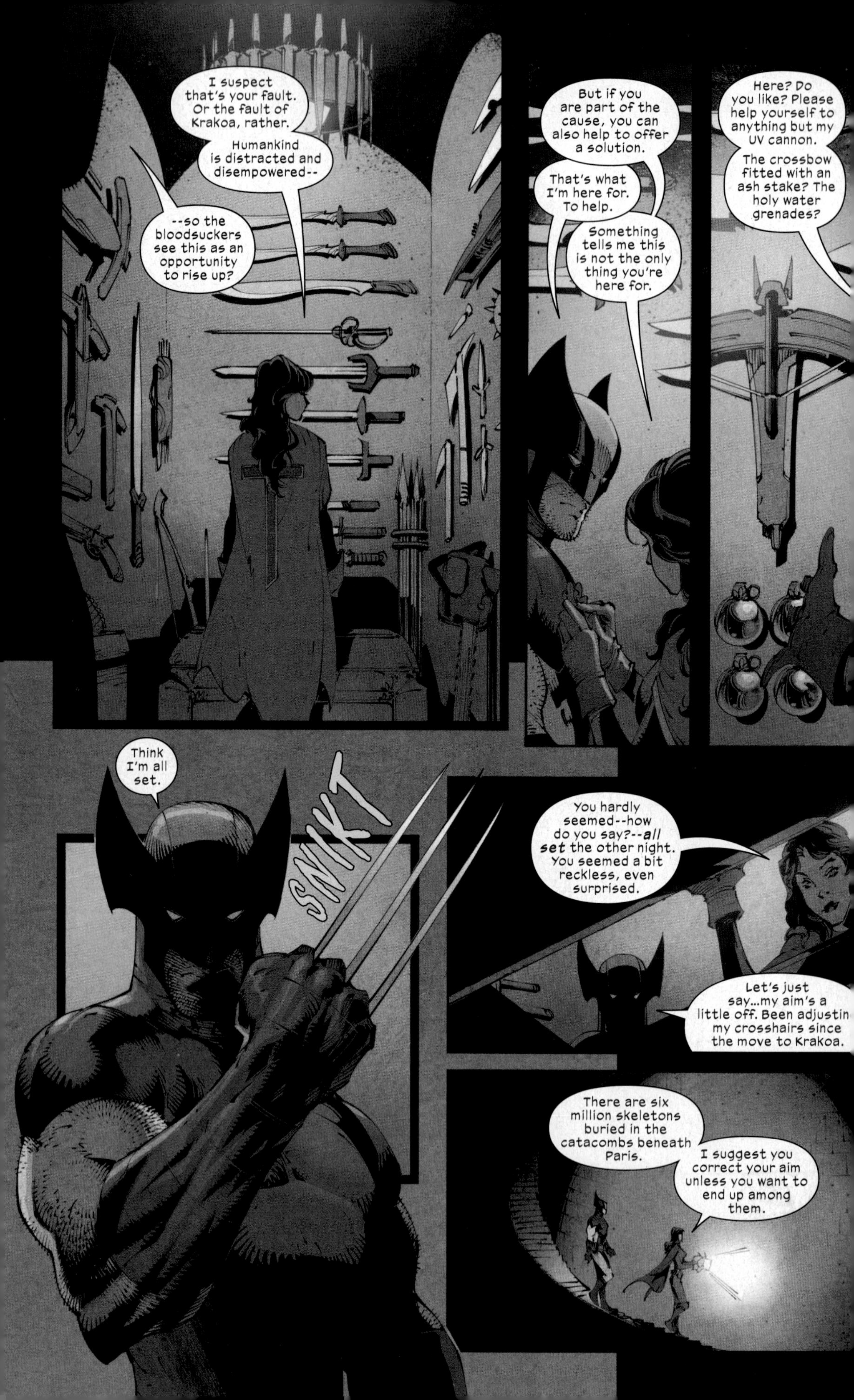
I suspect that's your fault. Or the fault of Krakoa, rather.
Humankind is distracted and disempowered--
--so the bloodsuckers see this as an opportunity to rise up?
But if you are part of the cause, you can also help to offer a solution.
That's what I'm here for. To help.
Something tells me this is not the only thing you're here for.
Here? Do you like? Please help yourself to anything but my UV cannon.
The crossbow fitted with an ash stake? The holy water grenades?
Think I'm all set.
SNIKT
You hardly seemed--how do you say?--*all set* the other night. You seemed a bit reckless, even surprised.
Let's just say...my aim's a little off. Been adjustin my crosshairs since the move to Krakoa.
There are six million skeletons buried in the catacombs beneath Paris.
I suggest you correct your aim unless you want to end up among them.

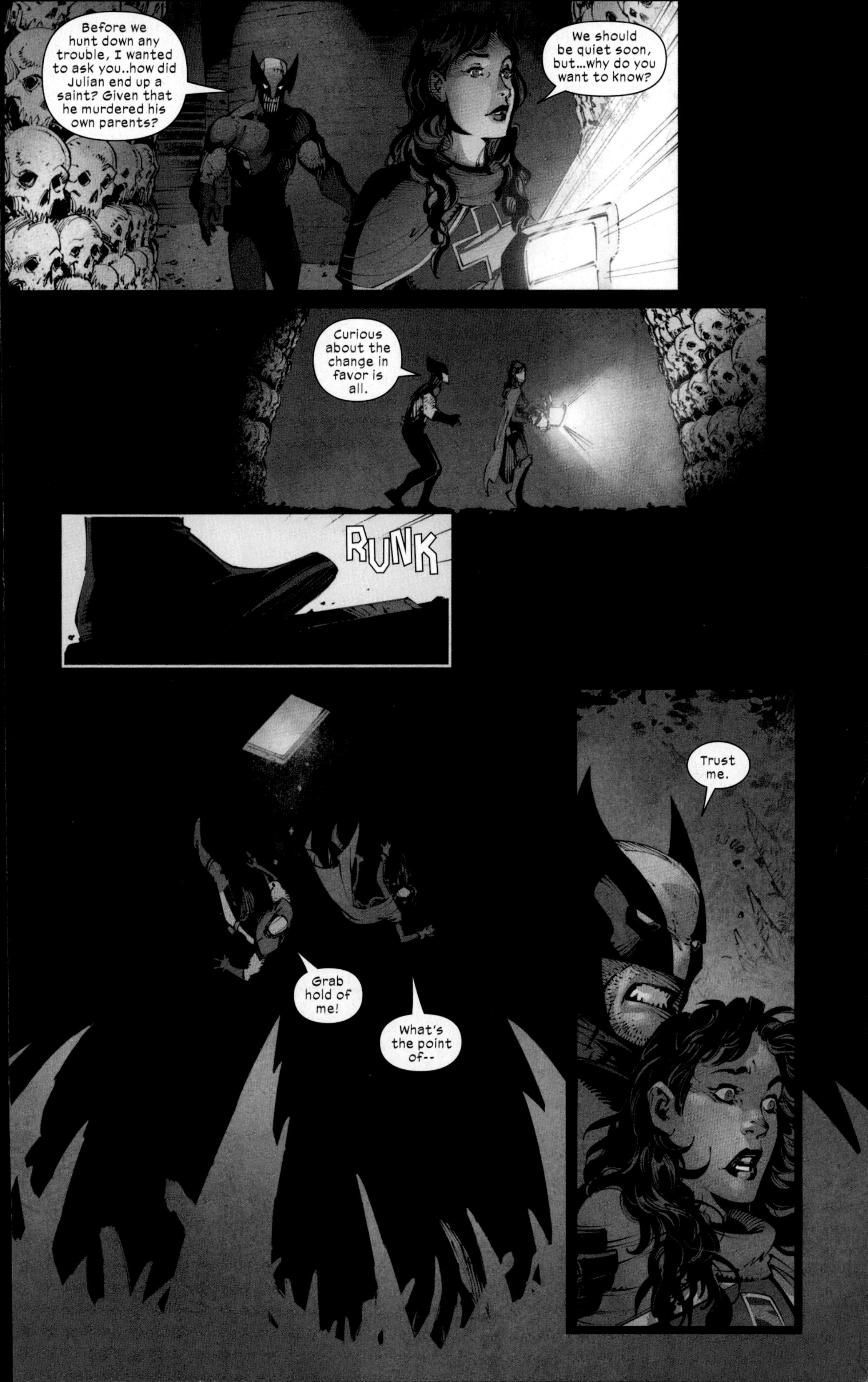
Before we hunt down any trouble, I wanted to ask you..how did Julian end up a saint? Given that he murdered his own parents?
We should be quiet soon, but...why do you want to know?
Curious about the change in favor is all.
RUNK
Grab hold of me!
What's the point of--
Trust me.

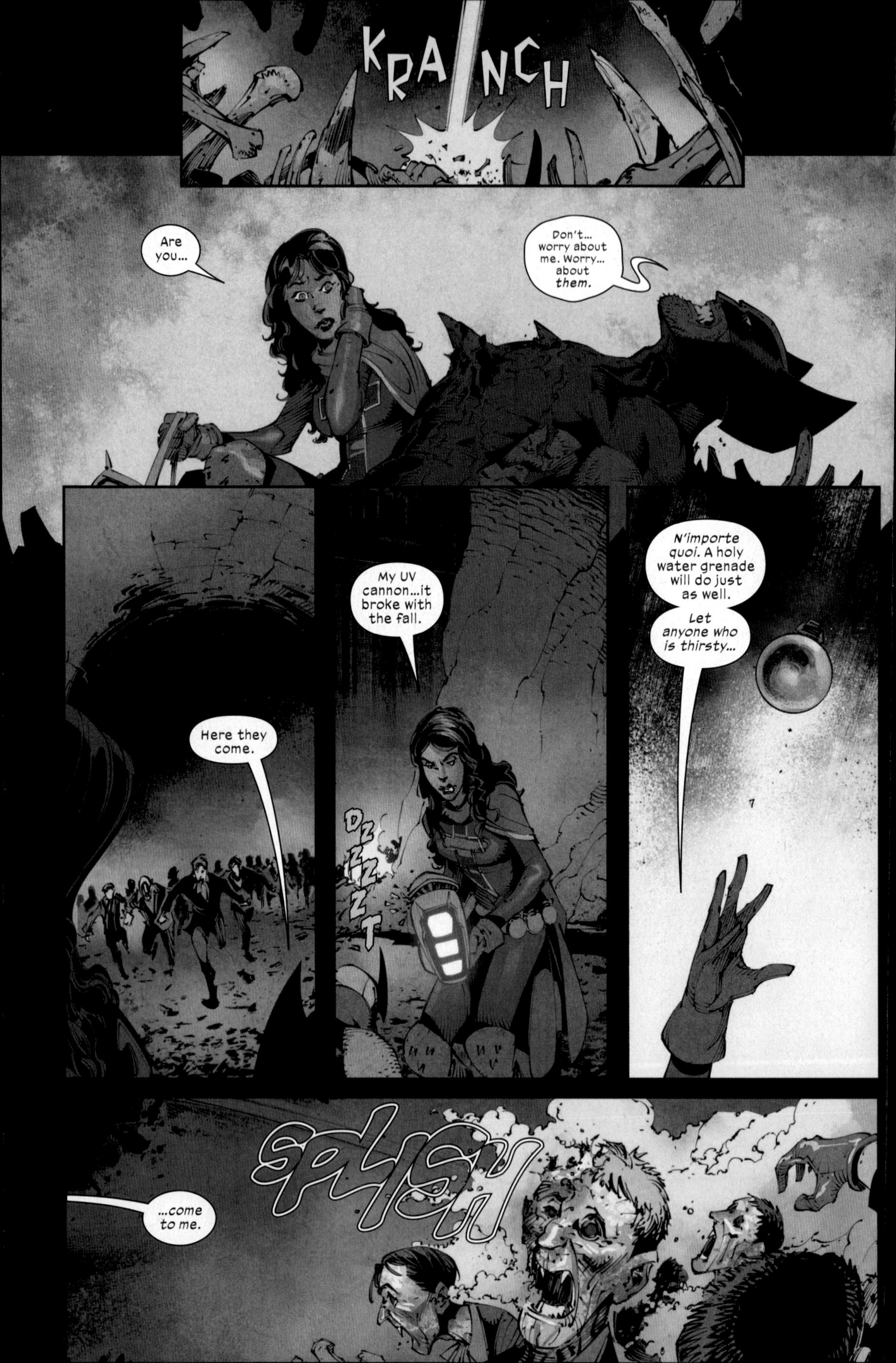
KRANCH
Are you...
Don't... worry about me. Worry... about *them.*
Here they come.
My UV cannon...it broke with the fall.
DZZZZT
N'importe quoi. A holy water grenade will do just as well.
Let anyone who is thirsty...
SPLISH
...come to me.

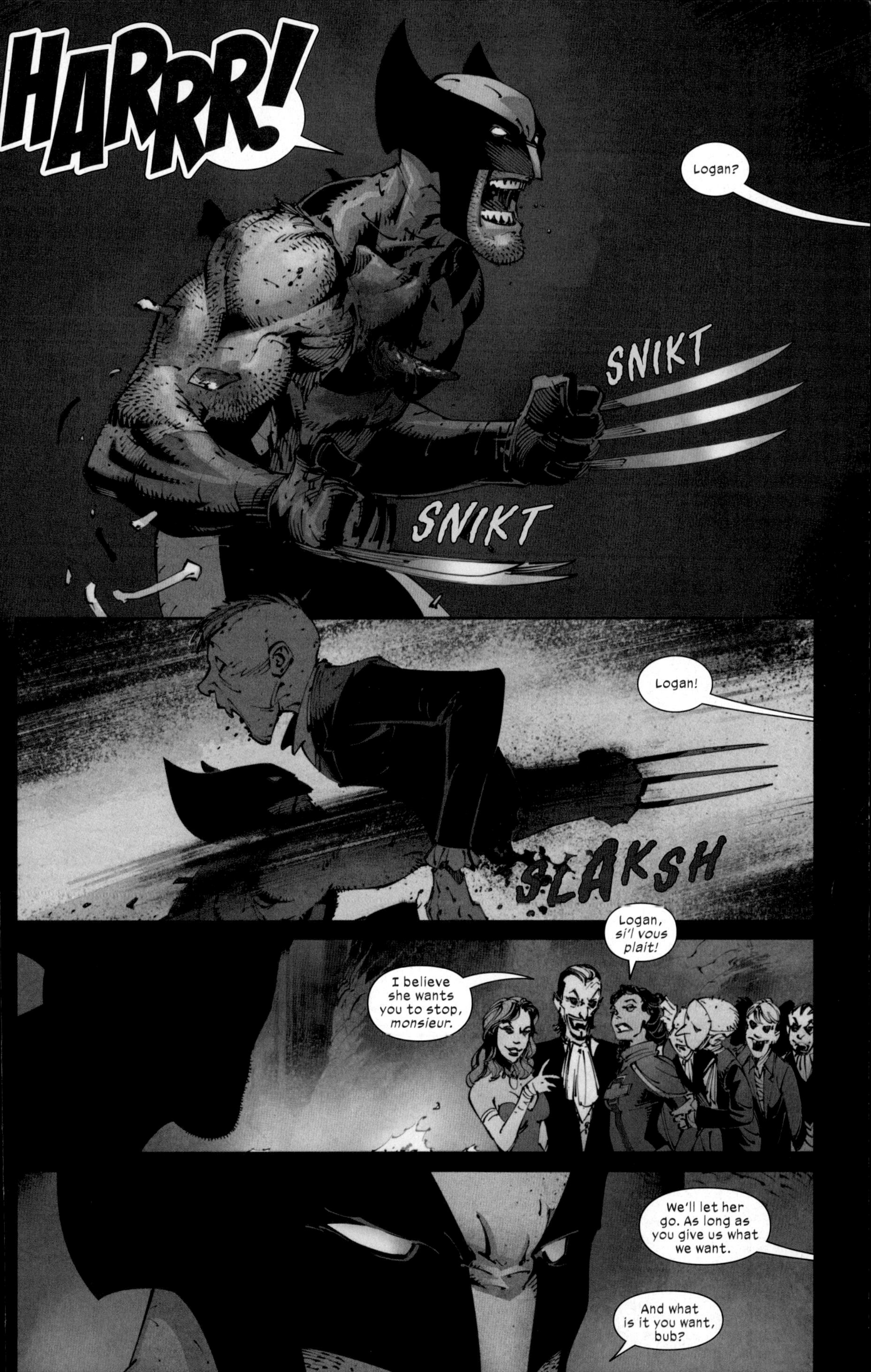
HARRR!
Logan?
SNIKT
SNIKT
Logan!
SLAKSH
Logan, si'l vous plait!
I believe she wants you to stop, monsieur.
We'll let her go. As long as you give us what we want.
And what is it you want, bub?

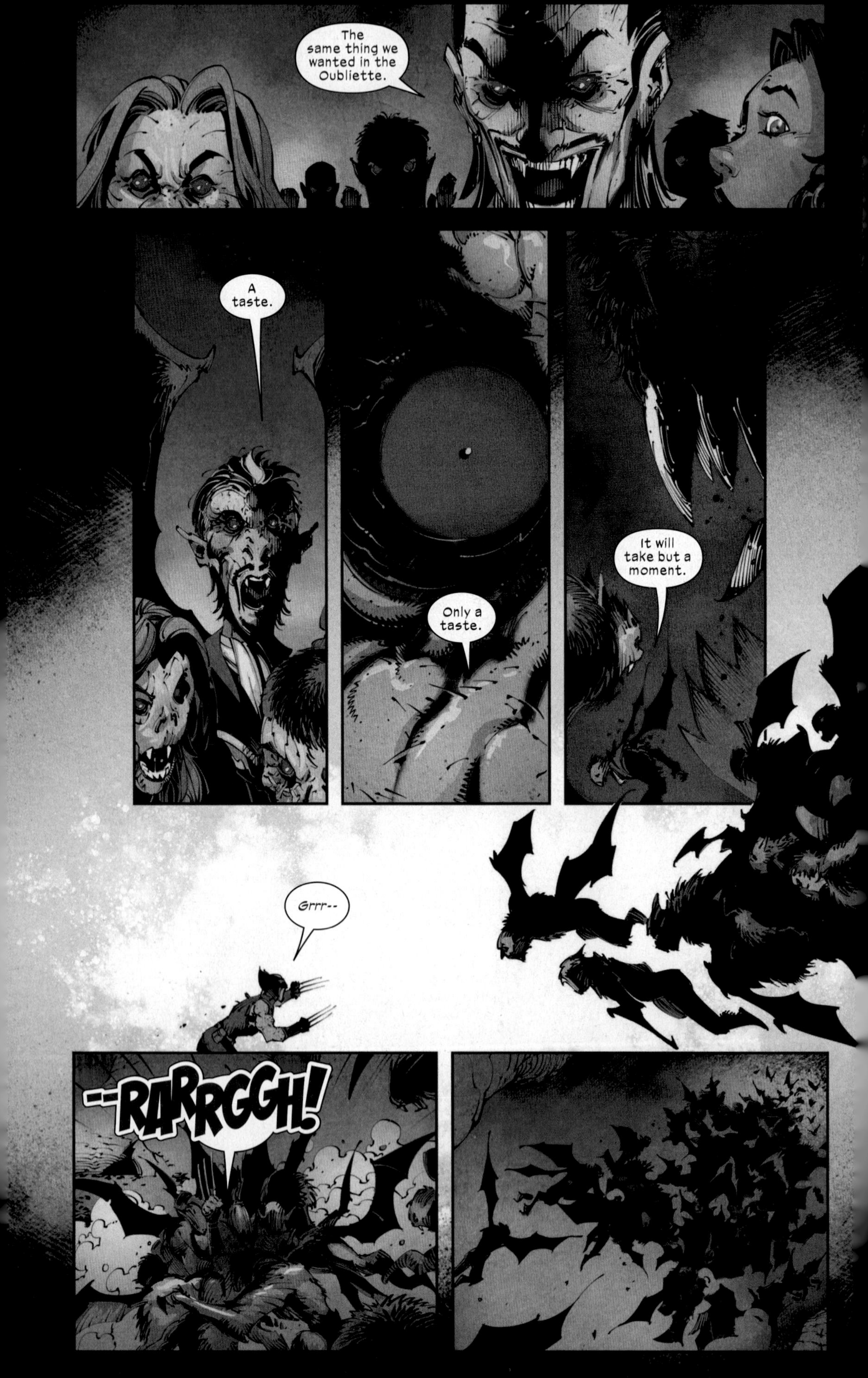
The same thing we wanted in the Oubliette.
A taste.
Only a taste.
It will take but a moment.
Grrr--
--RARRGGH!

You said not to worry about you, but...

That's because you don't need to worry about me.

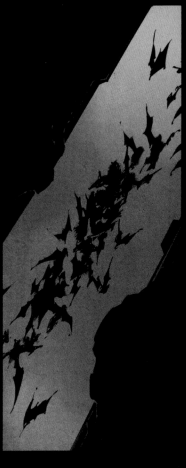

I won't turn, if that's what they were hoping for.

"My healing factor kills off the enzyme."

Anyway... one down.

And thousands to go.

"Logan...they shouldn't have left us like that..."

"Sure, they should've. I killed their leader. The rest ran off. That's good news."

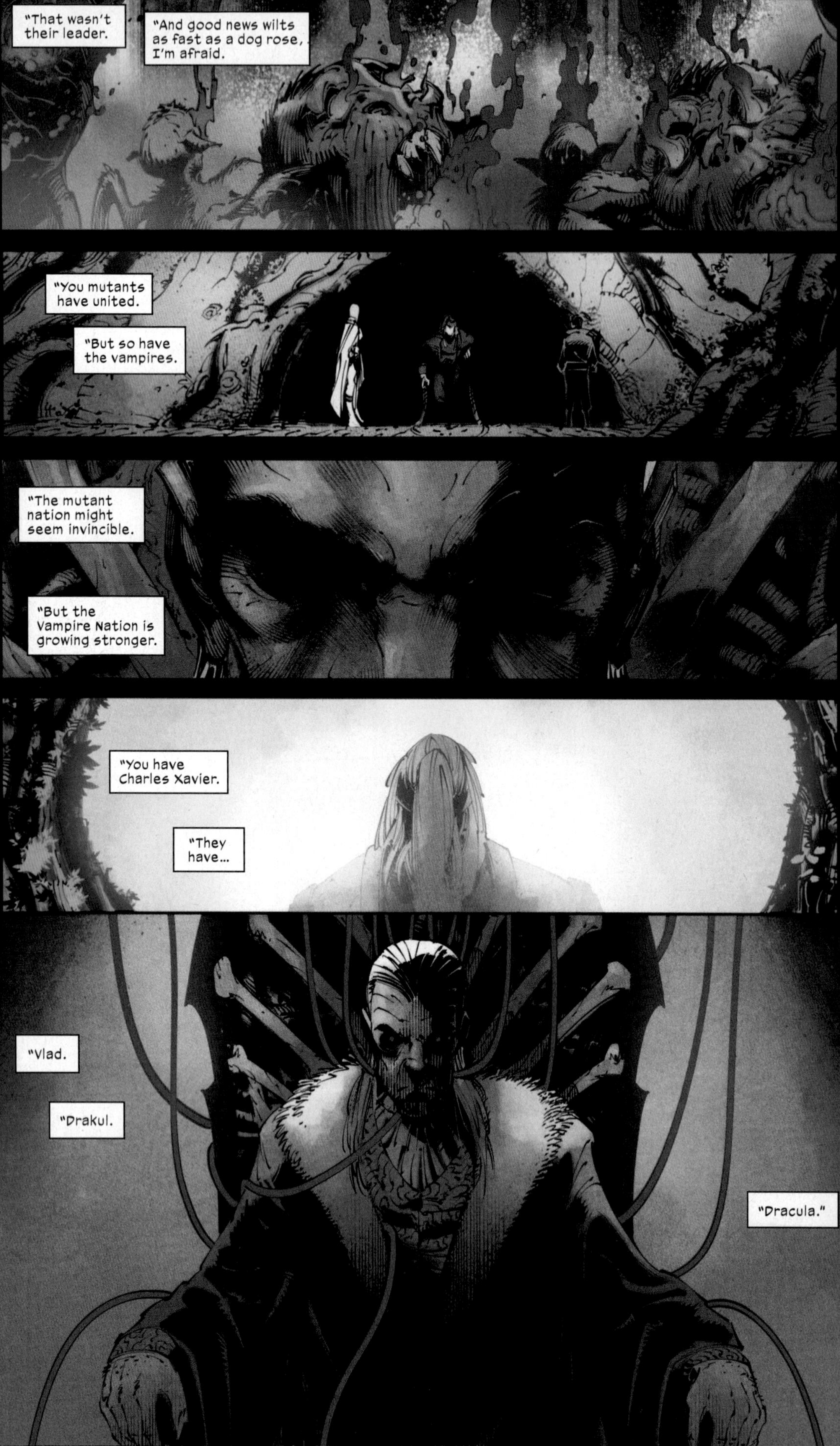
"That wasn't their leader.
"And good news wilts as fast as a dog rose, I'm afraid.
"You mutants have united.
"But so have the vampires.
"The mutant nation might seem invincible.
"But the Vampire Nation is growing stronger.
"You have Charles Xavier.
"They have...
"Vlad.
"Drakul.
"Dracula."

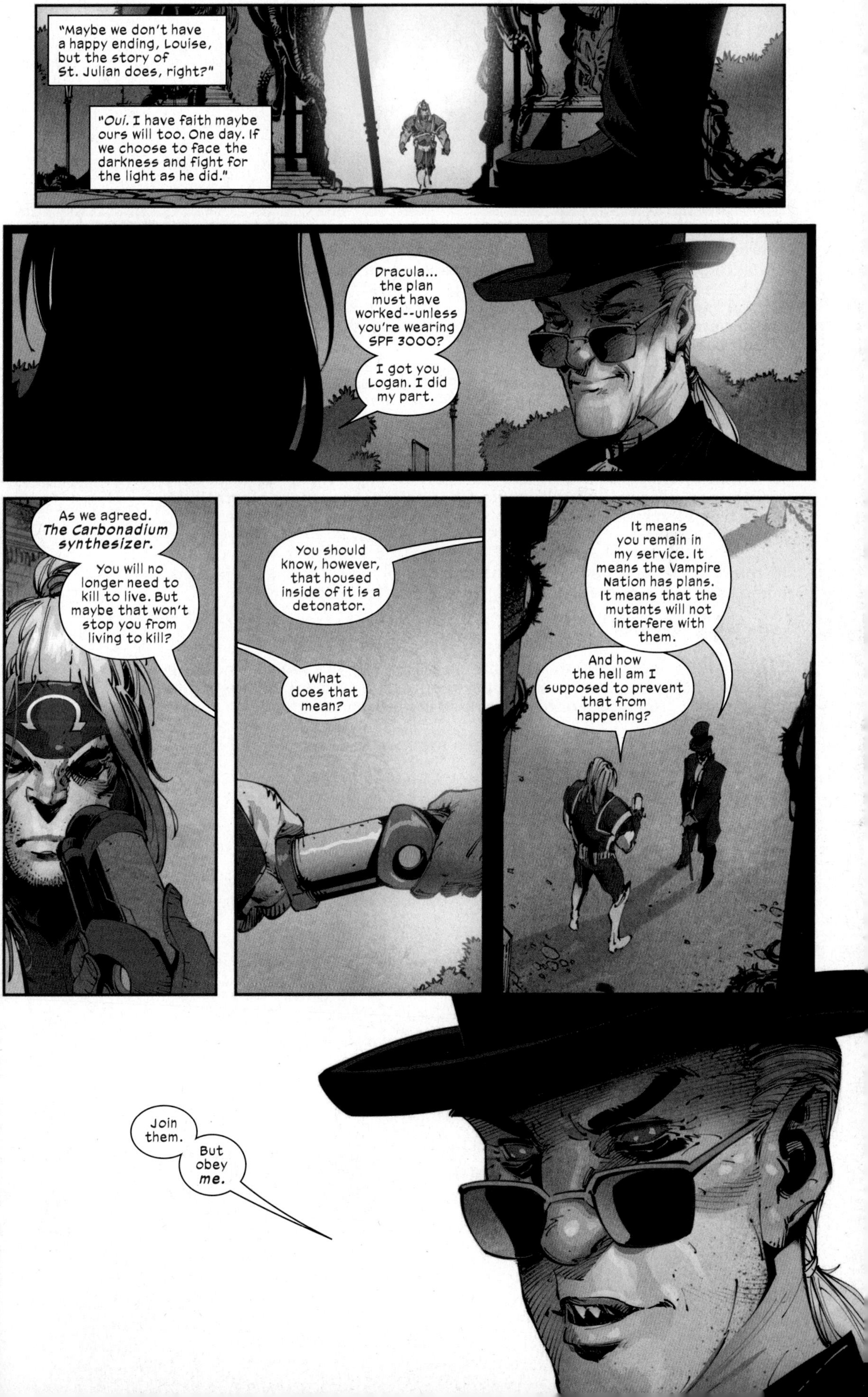
"Maybe we don't have a happy ending, Louise, but the story of St. Julian does, right?"
"*Oui.* I have faith maybe ours will too. One day. If we choose to face the darkness and fight for the light as he did."
Dracula... the plan must have worked--unless you're wearing SPF 3000?
I got you Logan. I did my part.
As we agreed. *The Carbonadium synthesizer.*
You will no longer need to kill to live. But maybe that won't stop you from living to kill?
You should know, however, that housed inside of it is a detonator.
What does that mean?
It means you remain in my service. It means the Vampire Nation has plans. It means that the mutants will not interfere with them.
And how the hell am I supposed to prevent that from happening?
Join them.
But obey *me.*

BLOODWORK

There are four groups of blood (A, B, AB, O) and each of these can be either RhD positive or RhD negative, making for a total of eight types.

But further classification is based on antibodies and antigens (such as carbohydrates and proteins), making for a known total of 36 systems and 346 antigens.

And then the math is further complicated by Wolverine.

Not all blood is alike, but that is especially true of what runs beneath his skin.

It is not merely resistant, but altogether impervious to infection, malignancy, autoimmune disorders. It is infinitely compatible with all other blood families and has been shown to have a brief, curative effect when transfused.

In this way, it bears some resemblance to blood infected (or cursed, some say) by the bite of a vampire. This is his closest cousin.

With few exceptions.

1) His body is not just the factory for his blood, it is the vault -- and once it leaves him, its powers are soon suppressed and its compatibility deteriorates. Whereas a vampire's blood is malignant, virulent.

2) His blood does not deteriorate when exposed to ultraviolet light.

You could say their blood belongs to the same group, but a different type. One positive, the other negative.

Instead of A or B or AB or O, one might call it E -- the endless.

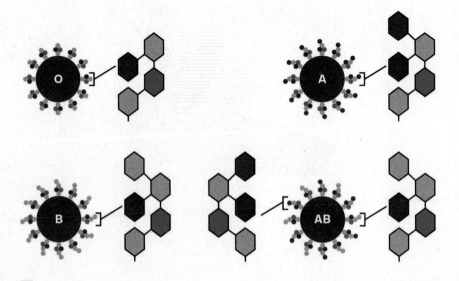

Red Blood Cell

Fucose

Galactose

N acetyl-galactosamine

N acetyl-glucosamine

[dawn_of_x]

[best__]
[there_]

[is__]
[bub_]

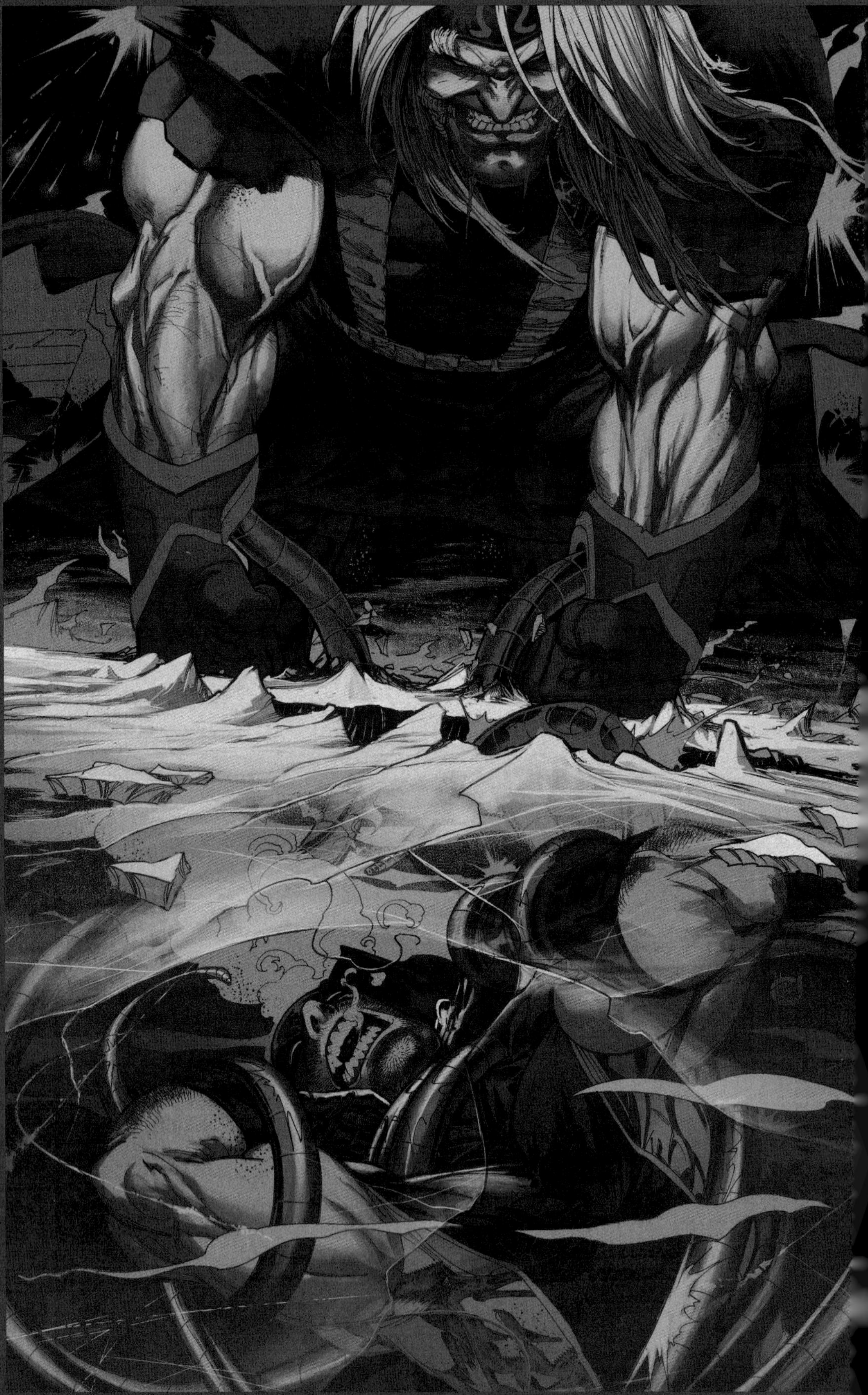

The Red Tavern

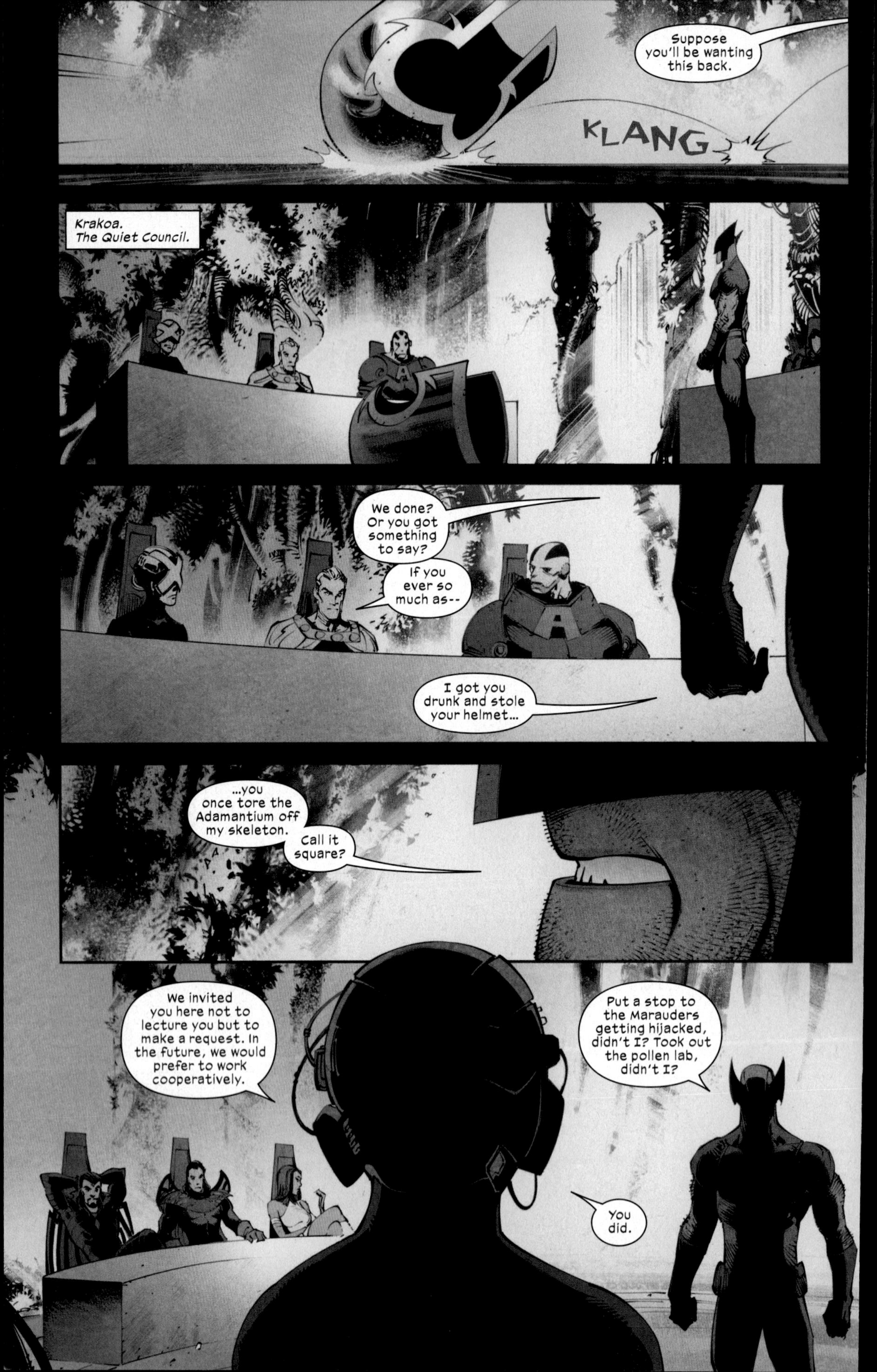

Suppose you'll be wanting this back.
KLANG
Krakoa. The Quiet Council.
We done? Or you got something to say?
If you ever so much as--
I got you drunk and stole your helmet...
...you once tore the Adamantium off my skeleton.
Call it square?
We invited you here not to lecture you but to make a request. In the future, we would prefer to work cooperatively.
Put a stop to the Marauders getting hijacked, didn't I? Took out the pollen lab, didn't I?
You did.

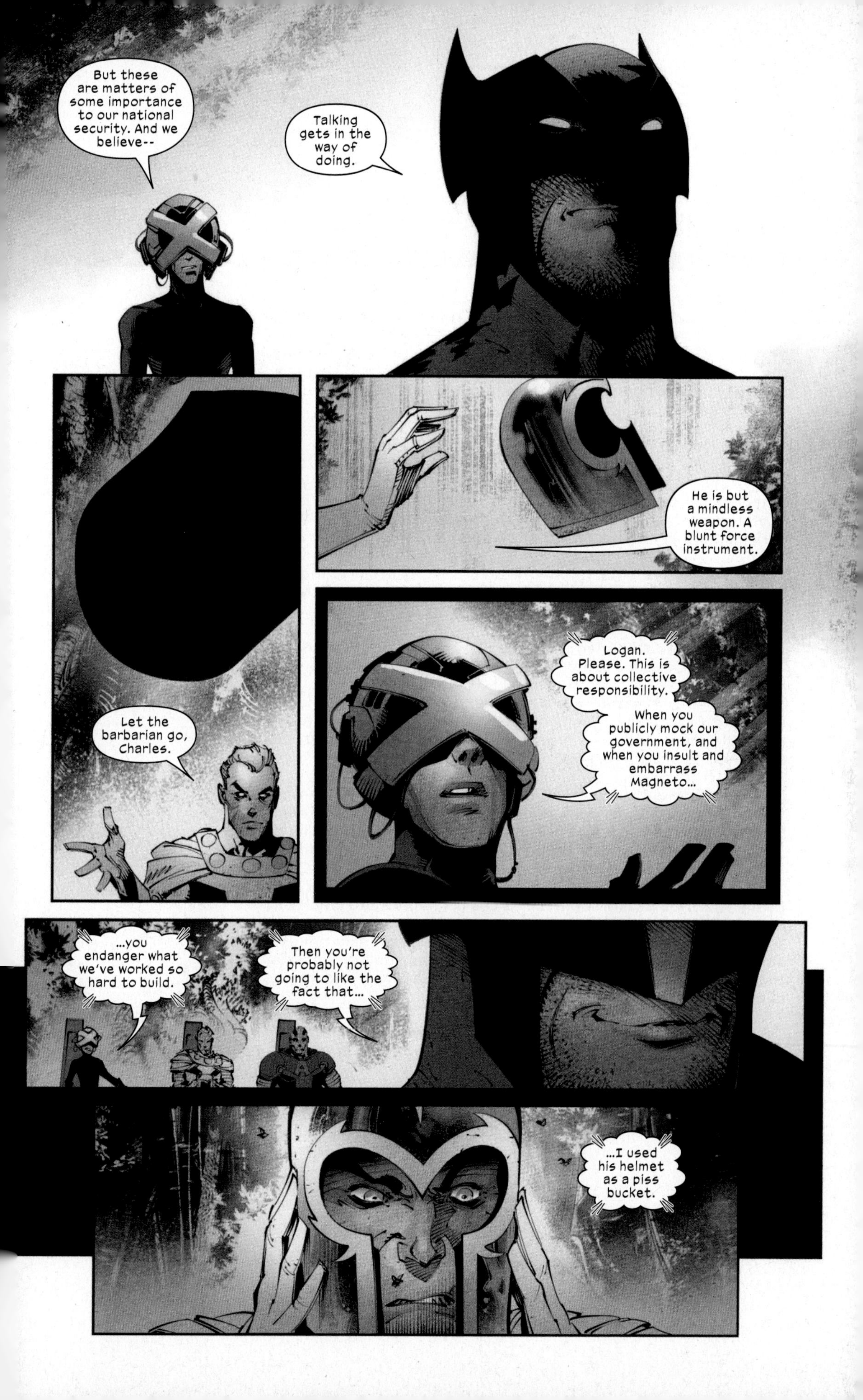

But these are matters of some importance to our national security. And we believe--
Talking gets in the way of doing.
He is but a mindless weapon. A blunt force instrument.
Let the barbarian go, Charles.
Logan. Please. This is about collective responsibility.
When you publicly mock our government, and when you insult and embarrass Magneto...
...you endanger what we've worked so hard to build.
Then you're probably not going to like the fact that...
...I used his helmet as a piss bucket.

THE HIDDEN GATE

He doesn't believe in Krakoa. He wants to, but he can't. Not yet.

Because when he takes in a big drink of this place, when he hears the children laughing and sees the flower-filled meadows and smells the salty breeze pouring off the ocean, he can't help but fall back on what he knows.

And this is what he knows...

Every time he's fallen in love, it's ended in grief or betrayal. Every time he's believed in a new beginning, it's come to an end. He's done as much wrong as right. There is a balance to life. But there's no balance here in Krakoa. Not that he sees anyway.

Even Paris, the most disgustingly beautiful city in the world, has got six million skeletons stacked in its catacombs. Six million corpses he can believe in. Shadows he can believe in.

That's where he's headed now. The shadow country. Where the sun rarely shines, and he can be alone in the company of others.

Because here, no matter where he goes, someone is always watching. Listening. Supervising. The Summerses. Xavier. Sage. Even the island itself. He feels their eyes crawling all over him like spiders. So now and then, he has to escape.

He hikes through the woods, leaving behind the perfume-bombed meadows and happy, hand-holding mutants. Sunlight filters green light through the canopy as he heads toward the center of the island, the ground angling upward gradually and then sharply into cliffs. Here he begins to climb.

As the winds knock him about, he forces his fingers into cracks, hoists himself onto rocky outcroppings and startles birds squawking from their nests. At last he reaches the ridge he seeks. He pauses here and looks about as if to take in the view -- the sunlight sparkling off the ocean, the clouds blimping through the sky -- but really he is checking to see if anyone followed him.

Then he steps into the shadows of a stony alcove. Here he has secretly planted a gate. He looks over his shoulder one last time before stepping through the shimmer of it...

летописец

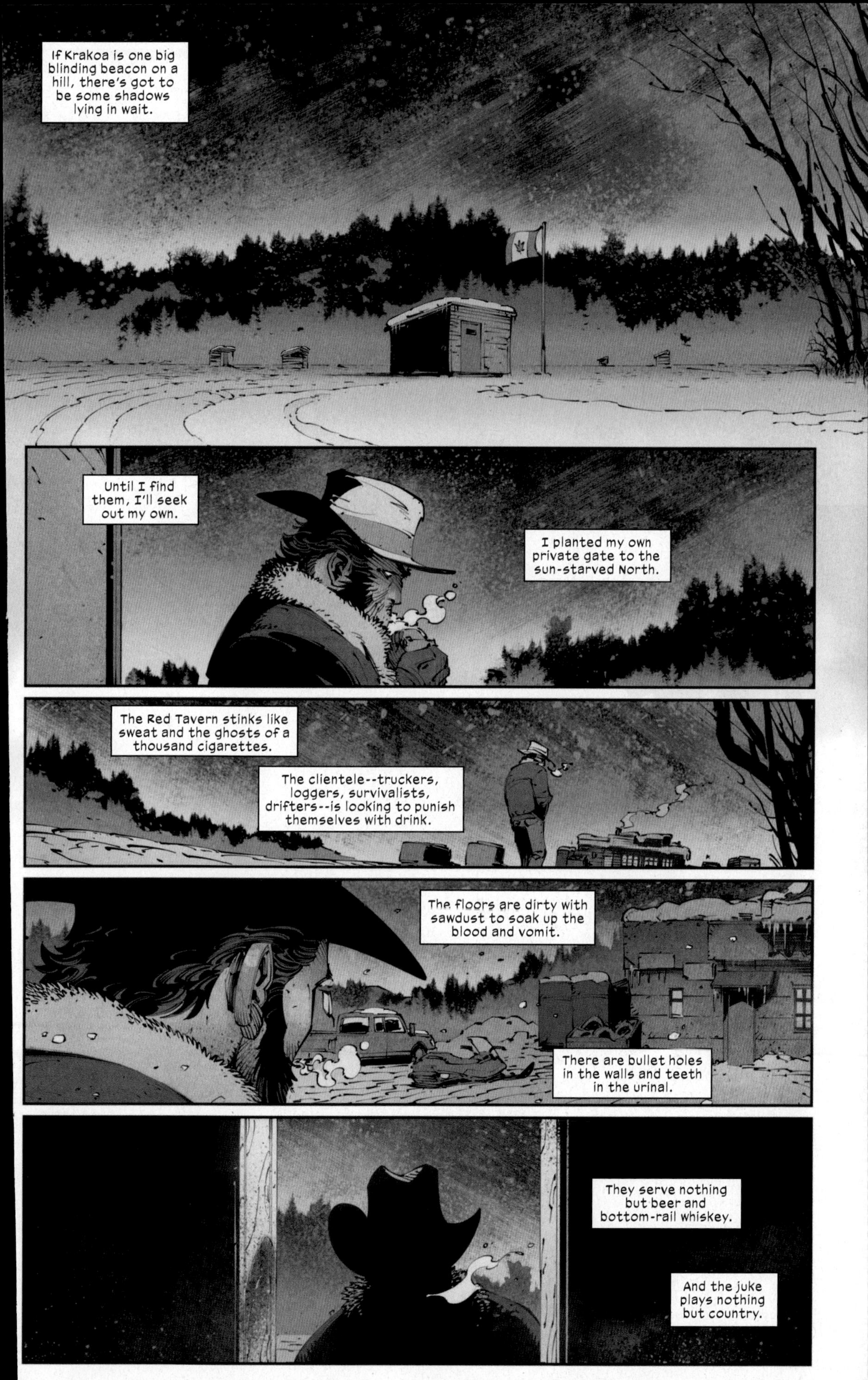
If Krakoa is one big blinding beacon on a hill, there's got to be some shadows lying in wait.
Until I find them, I'll seek out my own.
I planted my own private gate to the sun-starved North.
The Red Tavern stinks like sweat and the ghosts of a thousand cigarettes.
The clientele--truckers, loggers, survivalists, drifters--is looking to punish themselves with drink.
The floors are dirty with sawdust to soak up the blood and vomit.
There are bullet holes in the walls and teeth in the urinal.
They serve nothing but beer and bottom-rail whiskey.
And the juke plays nothing but country.

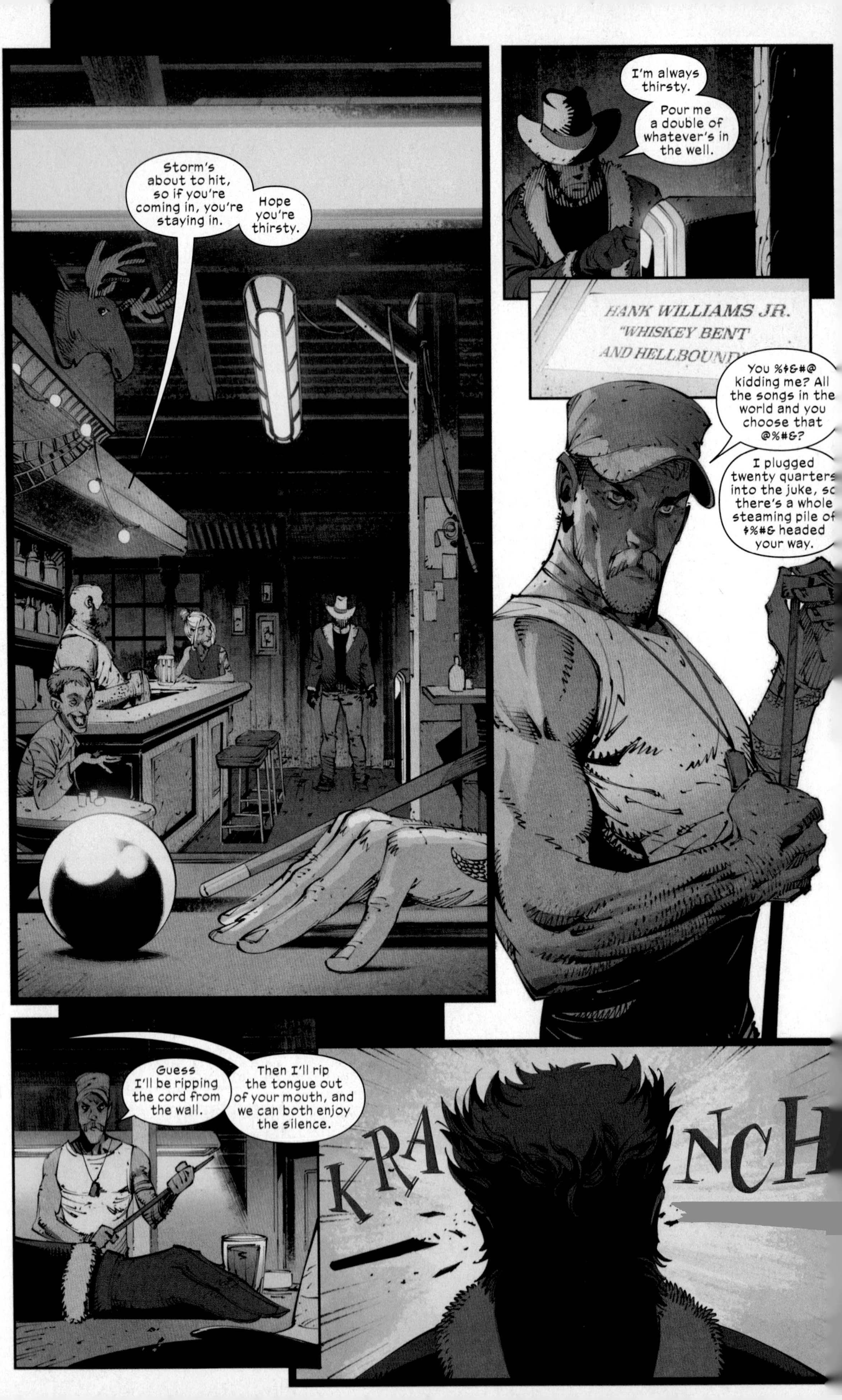

Storm's about to hit, so if you're coming in, you're staying in.
Hope you're thirsty.
I'm always thirsty.
Pour me a double of whatever's in the well.
HANK WILLIAMS JR. "WHISKEY BENT AND HELLBOUND"
You %$&#@ kidding me? All the songs in the world and you choose that @%#&?
I plugged twenty quarters into the juke, so there's a whole steaming pile of $%#& headed your way.
Guess I'll be ripping the cord from the wall.
Then I'll rip the tongue out of your mouth, and we can both enjoy the silence.
KRANCH

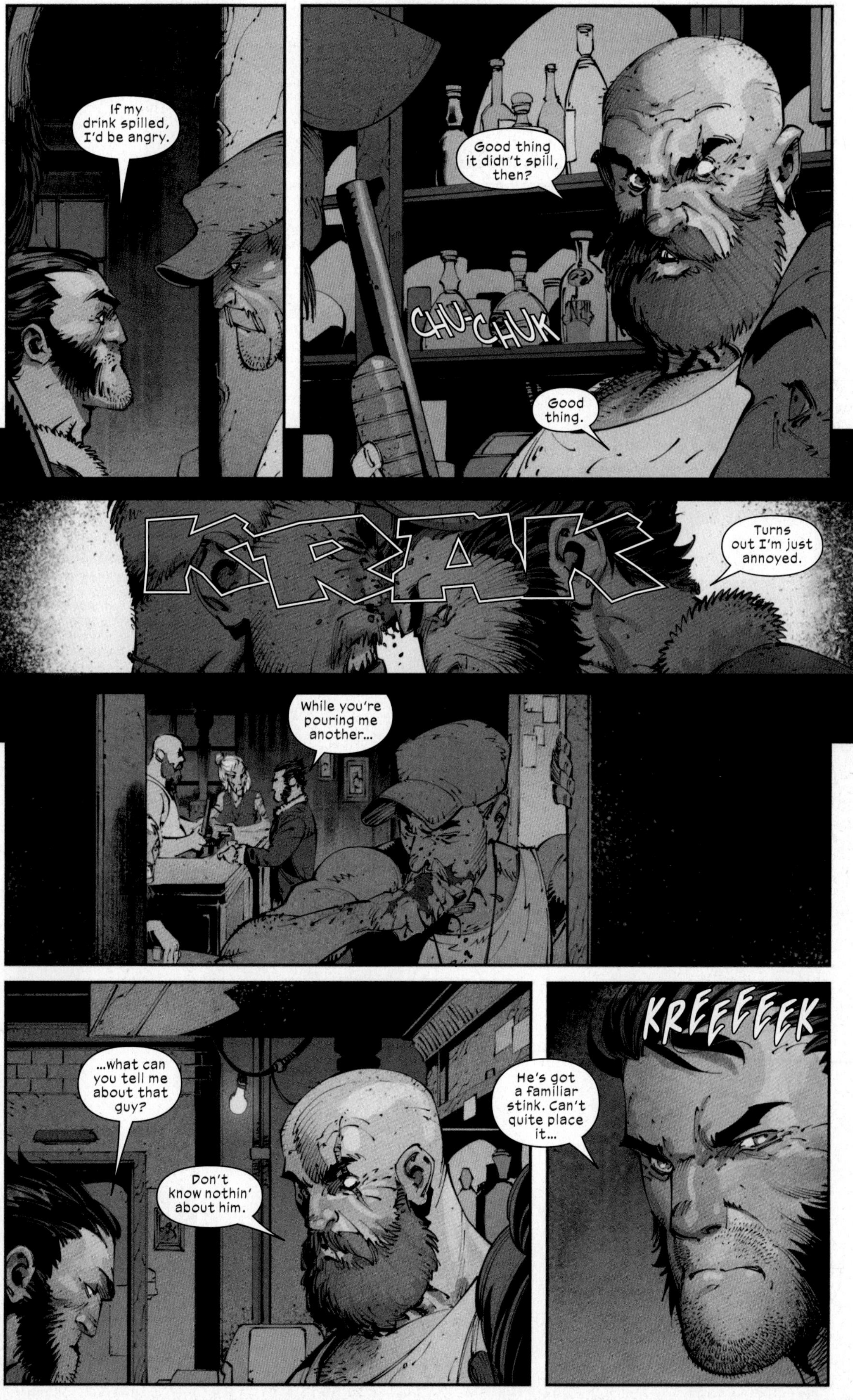
If my drink spilled, I'd be angry.
Good thing it didn't spill, then?
CHU-CHUK
Good thing.
KRAK
Turns out I'm just annoyed.
While you're pouring me another...
...what can you tell me about that guy?
Don't know nothin' about him.
He's got a familiar stink. Can't quite place it...
KREEEEEK

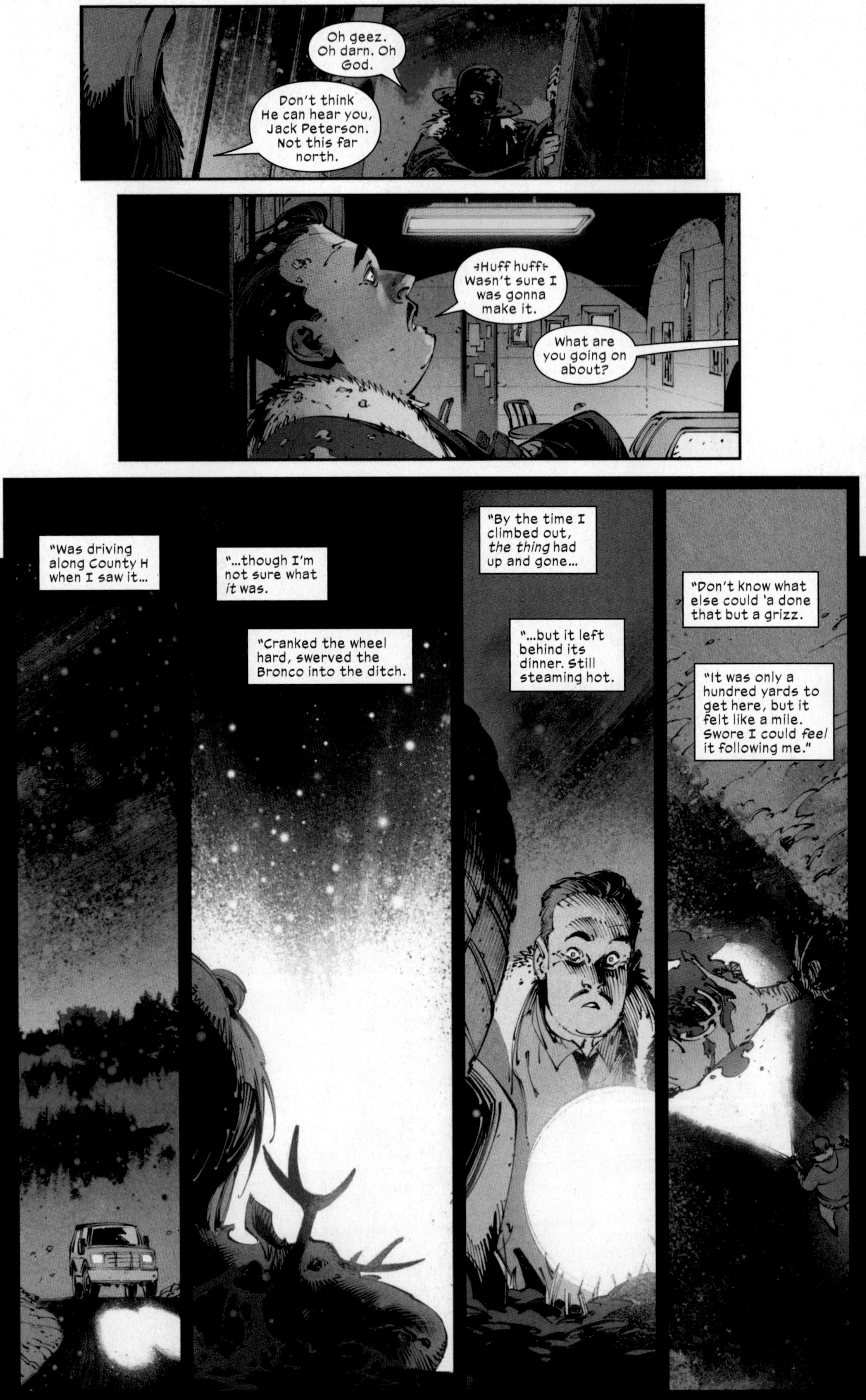

Oh geez. Oh darn. Oh God.
Don't think He can hear you, Jack Peterson. Not this far north.
-Huff huff- Wasn't sure I was gonna make it.
What are you going on about?
"Was driving along County H when I saw it...
"...though I'm not sure what *it* was.
"Cranked the wheel hard, swerved the Bronco into the ditch.
"By the time I climbed out, *the thing* had up and gone...
"...but it left behind its dinner. Still steaming hot.
"Don't know what else could 'a done that but a grizz.
"It was only a hundred yards to get here, but it felt like a mile. Swore I could *feel* it following me."

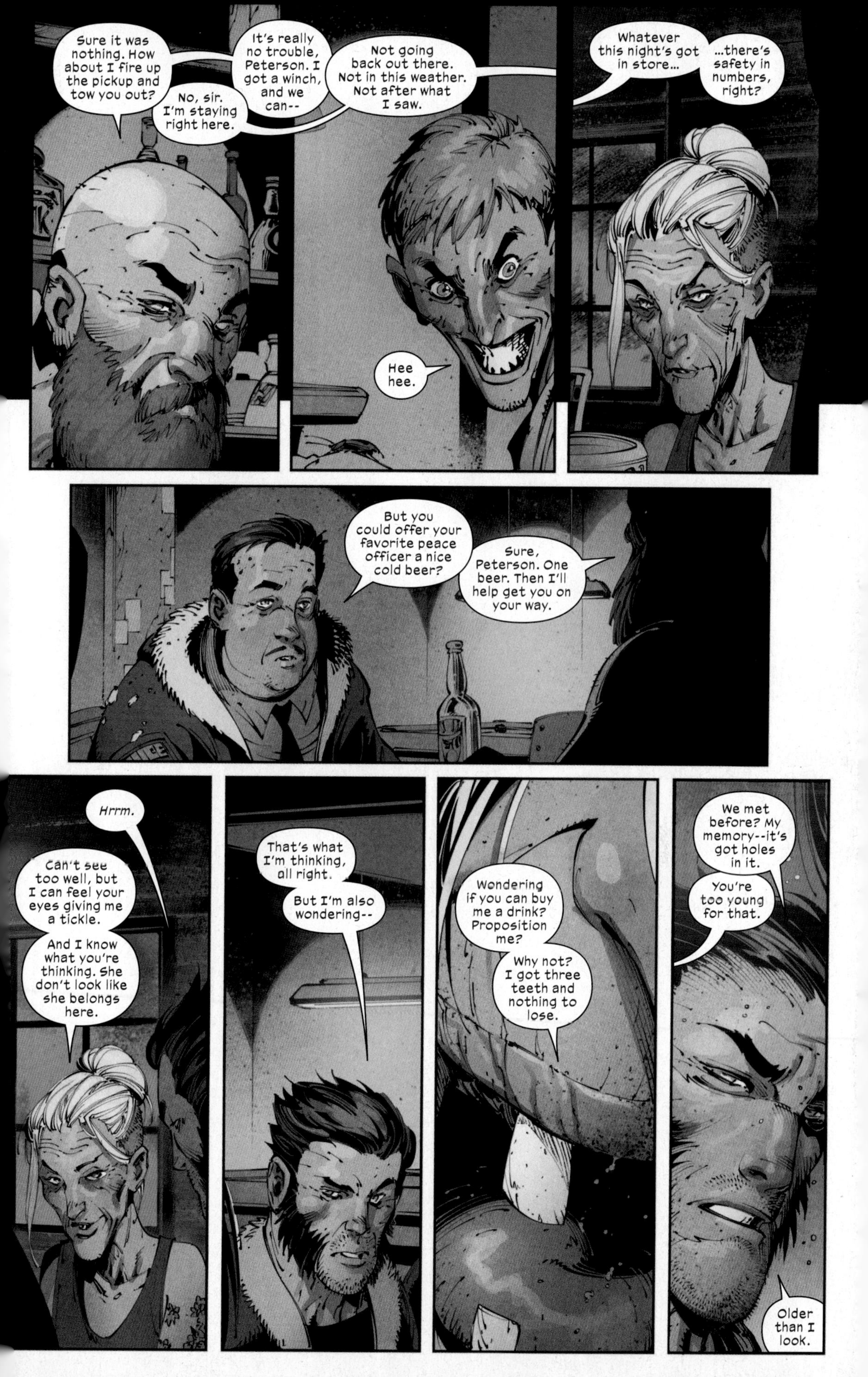
Sure it was nothing. How about I fire up the pickup and tow you out?
It's really no trouble, Peterson. I got a winch, and we can--
No, sir. I'm staying right here.
Not going back out there. Not in this weather. Not after what I saw.
Whatever this night's got in store...
...there's safety in numbers, right?
Hee hee.
But you could offer your favorite peace officer a nice cold beer?
Sure, Peterson. One beer. Then I'll help get you on your way.
Hrrm.
Can't see too well, but I can feel your eyes giving me a tickle.
And I know what you're thinking. She don't look like she belongs here.
That's what I'm thinking, all right.
But I'm also wondering--
Wondering if you can buy me a drink? Proposition me?
Why not? I got three teeth and nothing to lose.
We met before? My memory--it's got holes in it.
You're too young for that.
Older than I look.

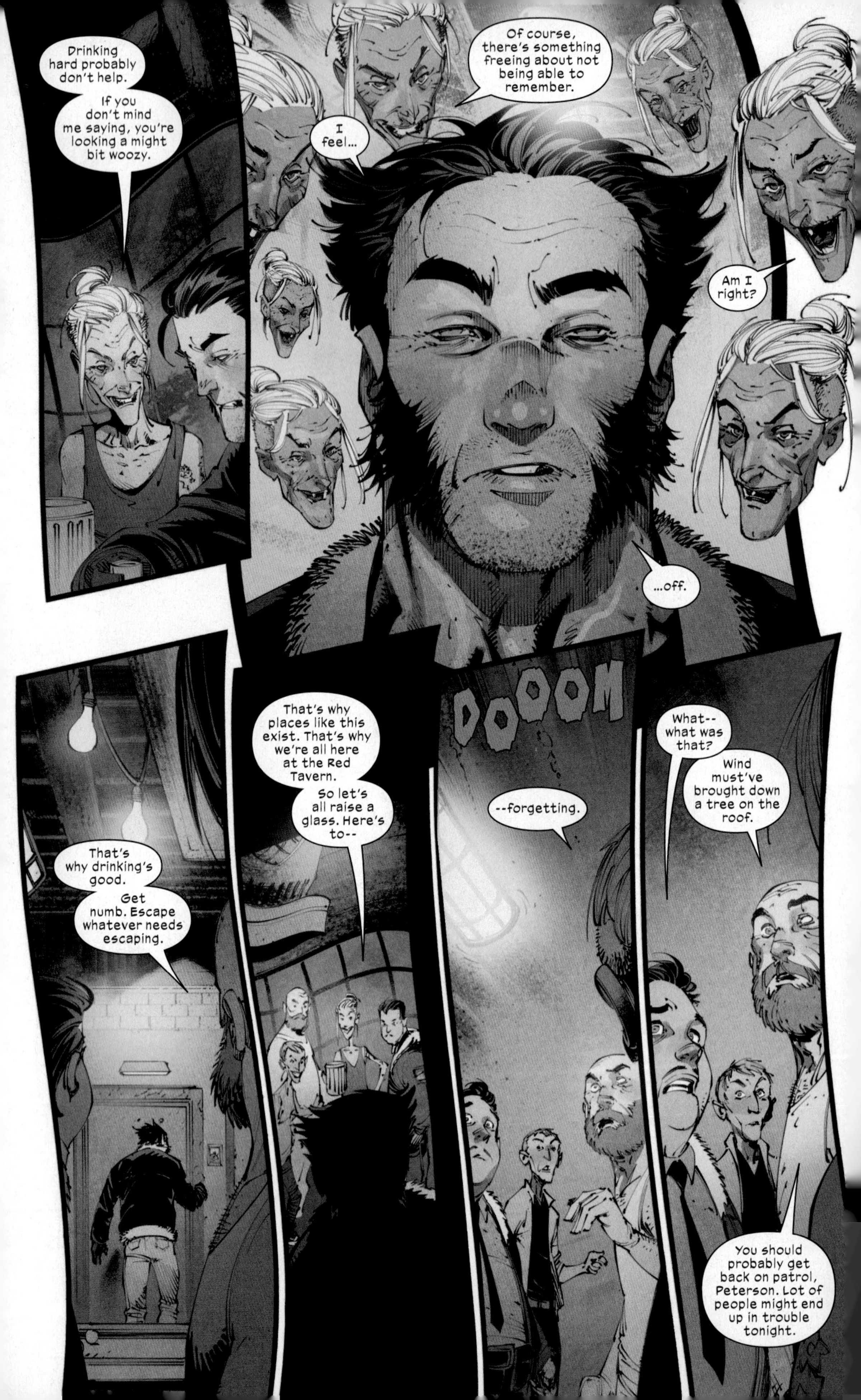
Drinking hard probably don't help.
If you don't mind me saying, you're looking a might bit woozy.
I feel...
Of course, there's something freeing about not being able to remember.
Am I right?
...off.
That's why drinking's good.
Get numb. Escape whatever needs escaping.
That's why places like this exist. That's why we're all here at the Red Tavern.
So let's all raise a glass. Here's to--
DOOOM
--forgetting.
What--what was that?
Wind must've brought down a tree on the roof.
You should probably get back on patrol, Peterson. Lot of people might end up in trouble tonight.

Welcome to the
MUTANT TRAUMA SUPPORT GROUP!

YOU ARE SAFE, VALUED AND IMPORTANT HERE!

This is an adults-only group that was founded to help all those who have suffered mental and physical damage from mutants. You are welcome to share your personal experience in this SAFE, warm, comforting place, where you will learn YOU ARE NOT ALONE.

We are not professionals, but we do offer LOVE and COMPASSION to ALL who join.

Visibility: Invitation only.

Membership: Private. Must be approved by host.

—

Rule 1: No hate speech or degrading comments EXCEPT TOWARD MUTANTS. Since they all deserve to rot in hell, LOL!

Rule 2: Respect everyone's privacy. We deserve our mutual trust. But we can ABSOLUTELY dox mutants. In fact, it is encouraged!

Rule 3: No promotions or spam, but fundraiser posts are permitted so long as they pertain to medical funds for mutant-related pain or travel/equipment funds for exacting some sweet, sweet revenge!

Rule 4: When talking about the names of mutants, use our special alpha code (in the pinned post) to camouflage who you're talking about, so that their evil web trawlers don't find us! Yikes!

Rule 5: You might be hurting today, but we can hurt them tomorrow! Again, we are NOT doctors, but vengeance is the best medicine!

—

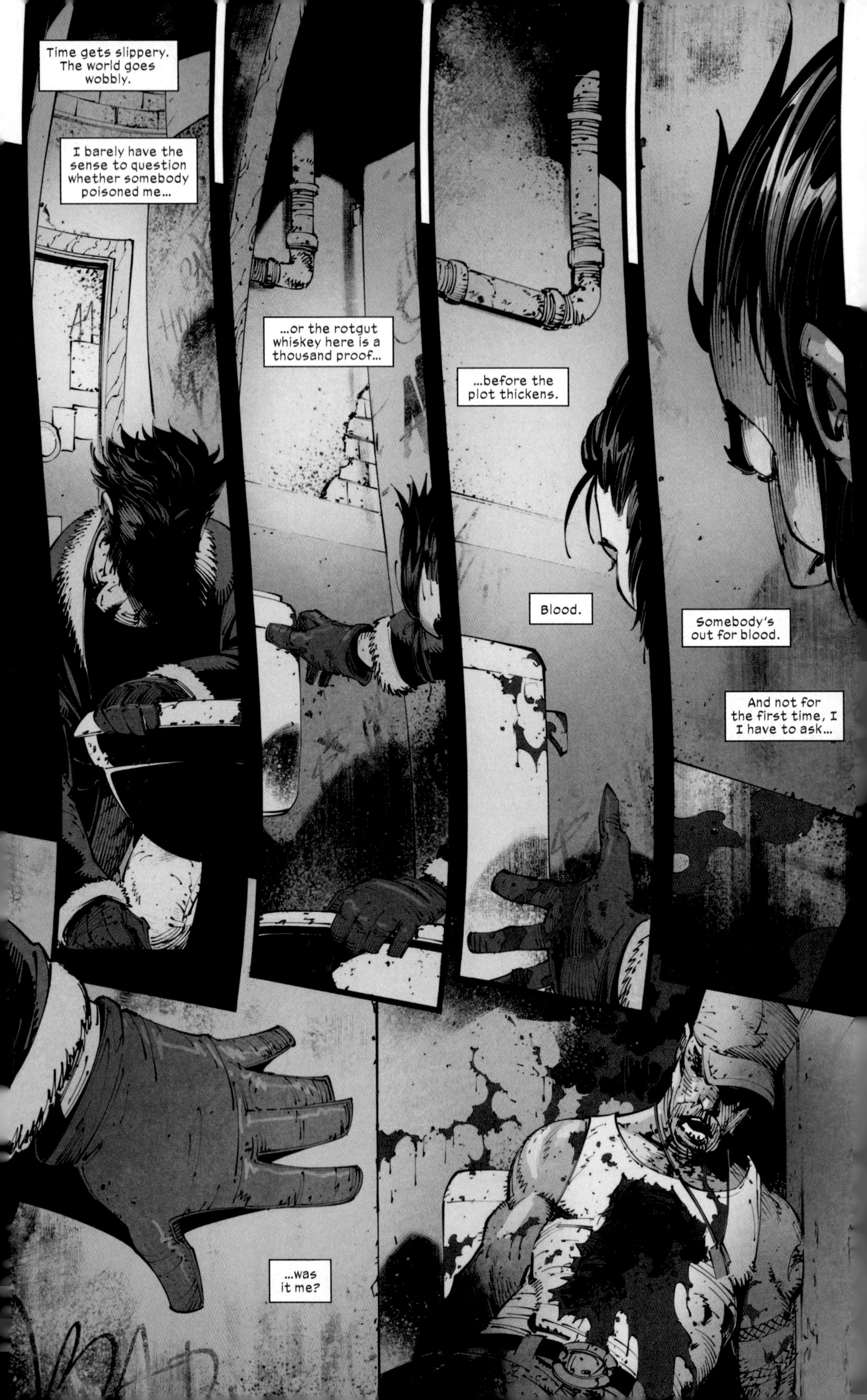
Time gets slippery. The world goes wobbly.
I barely have the sense to question whether somebody poisoned me...
...or the rotgut whiskey here is a thousand proof...
...before the plot thickens.
Blood.
Somebody's out for blood.
And not for the first time, I I have to ask...
...was it me?

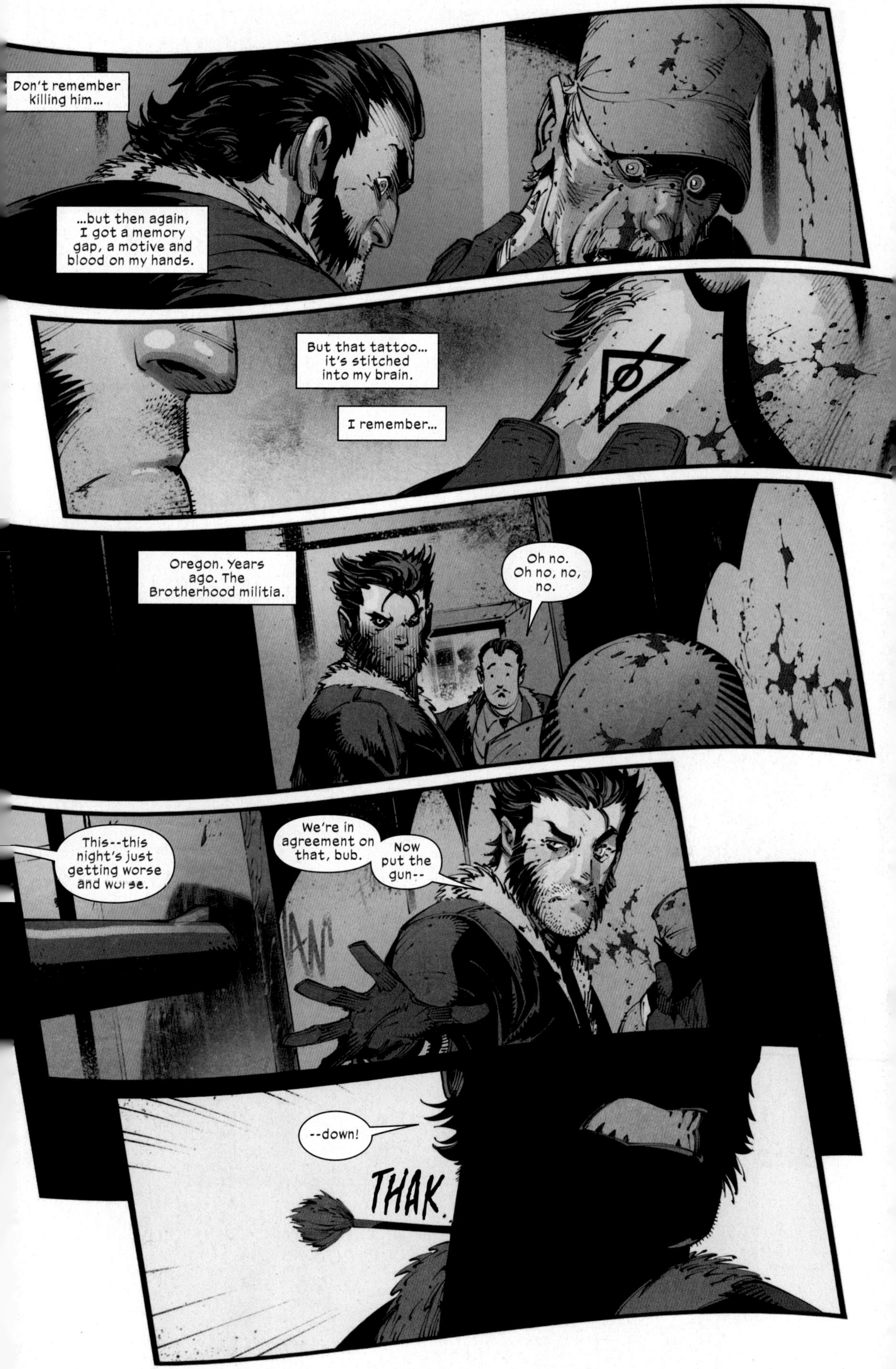
Don't remember killing him...
...but then again, I got a memory gap, a motive and blood on my hands.
But that tattoo... it's stitched into my brain.
I remember...
Oregon. Years ago. The Brotherhood militia.
Oh no. Oh no, no, no.
This--this night's just getting worse and worse.
We're in agreement on that, bub.
Now put the gun--
--down!
THAK

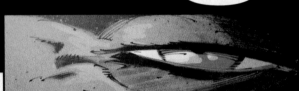

DZZZZZz

After what I seen on the road...

...I loaded my rifle with a .50 caliber ballistic syringe.

Came in handy after all.

Sure did, Peterson. You done good.

TAK

Whatever you think I did--

We all know you're guilty as hell.

Don't you go claiming amnesty.

Hee hee.

You're not going anywhere, mutie.

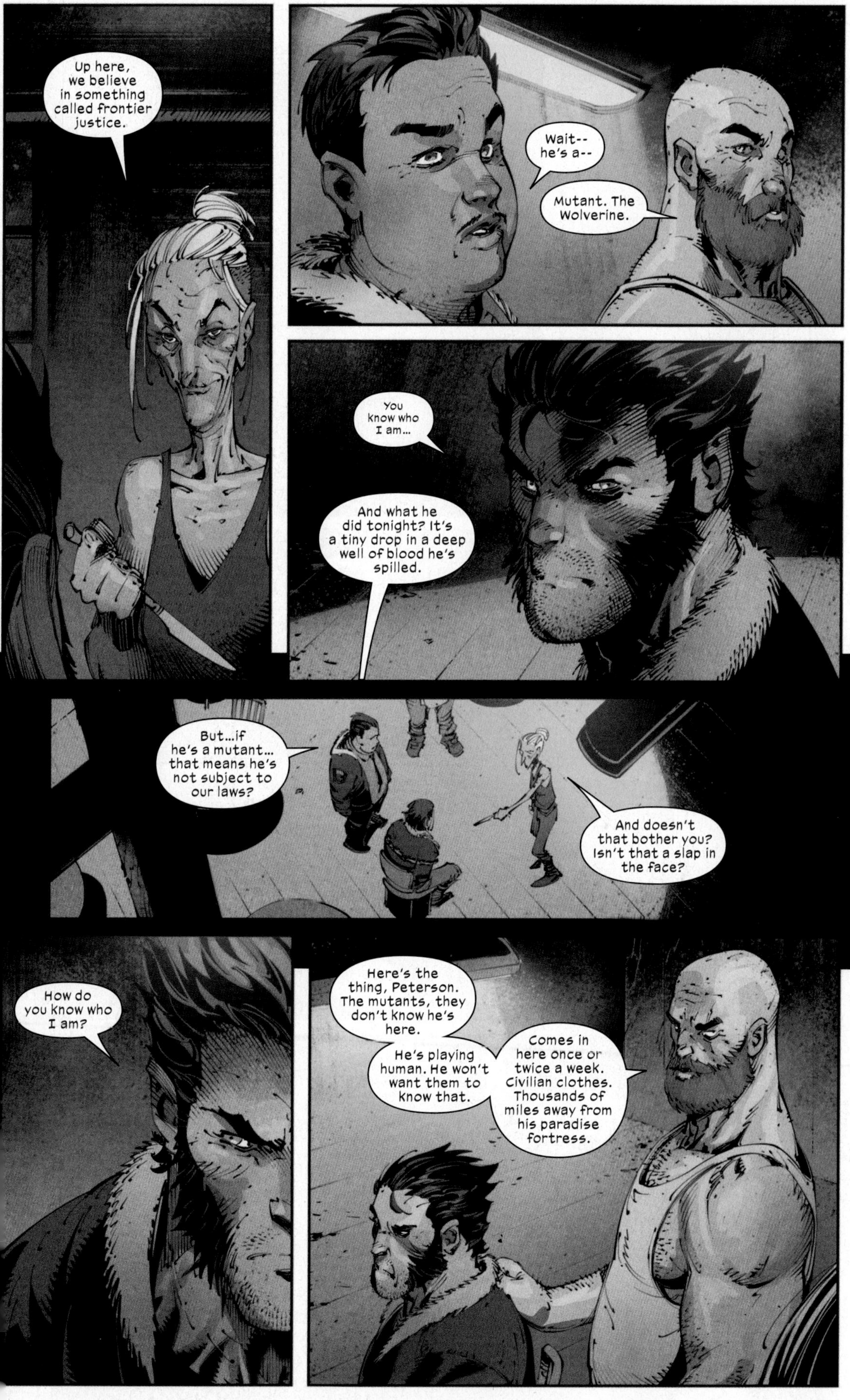
Up here, we believe in something called frontier justice.
Wait-- he's a--
Mutant. The Wolverine.
You know who I am...
And what he did tonight? It's a tiny drop in a deep well of blood he's spilled.
But...if he's a mutant... that means he's not subject to our laws?
And doesn't that bother you? Isn't that a slap in the face?
How do you know who I am?
Here's the thing, Peterson. The mutants, they don't know he's here.
He's playing human. He won't want them to know that.
Comes in here once or twice a week. Civilian clothes. Thousands of miles away from his paradise fortress.

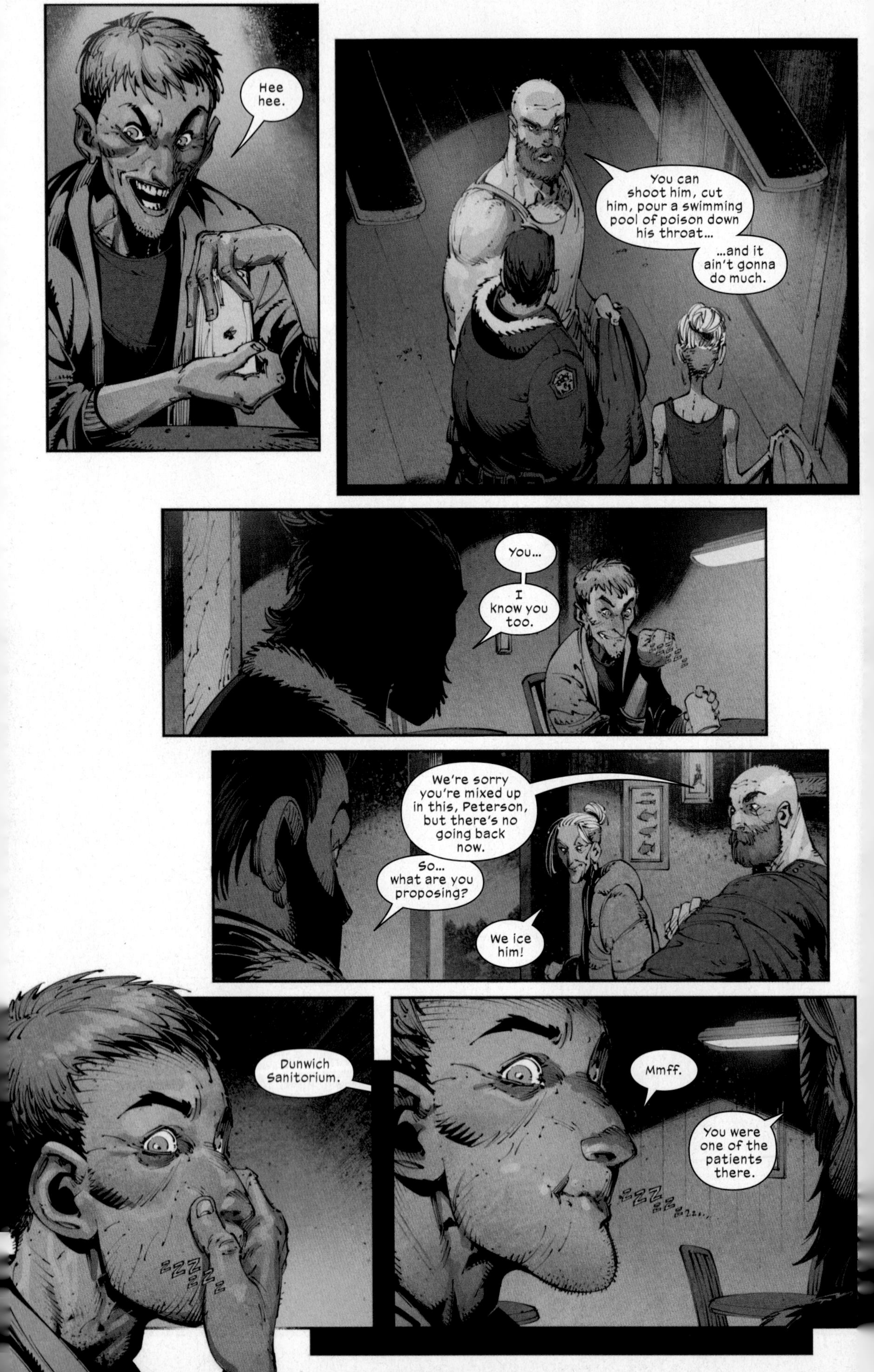
Hee hee.
You can shoot him, cut him, pour a swimming pool of poison down his throat...
...and it ain't gonna do much.
You...
I know you too.
We're sorry you're mixed up in this, Peterson, but there's no going back now.
So... what are you proposing?
We ice him!
Dunwich Sanitorium.
Mmff.
You were one of the patients there.

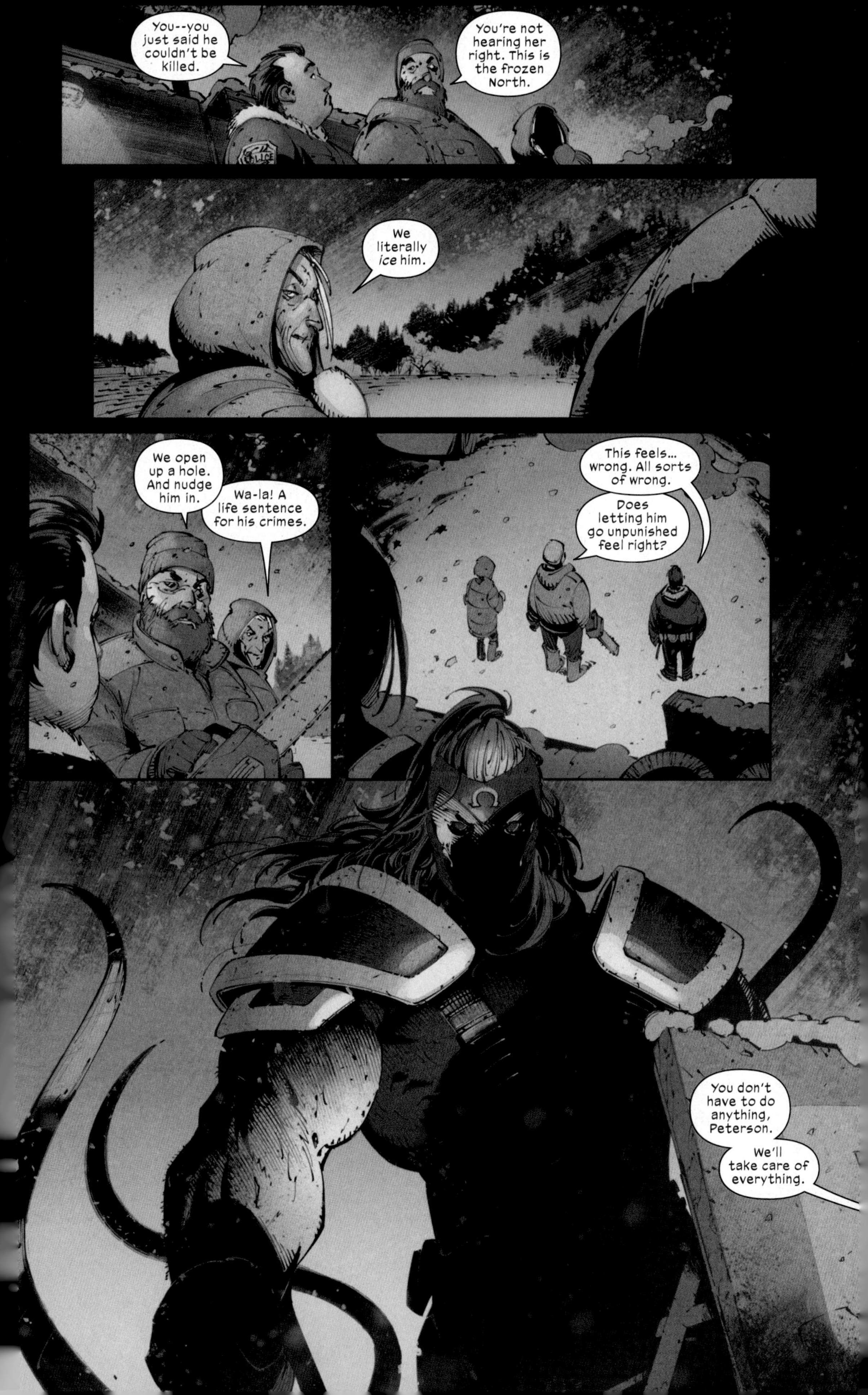
You--you just said he couldn't be killed.
You're not hearing her right. This is the frozen North.
We literally *ice* him.
We open up a hole. And nudge him in.
Wa-la! A life sentence for his crimes.
This feels... wrong. All sorts of wrong.
Does letting him go unpunished feel right?
You don't have to do anything, Peterson.
We'll take care of everything.

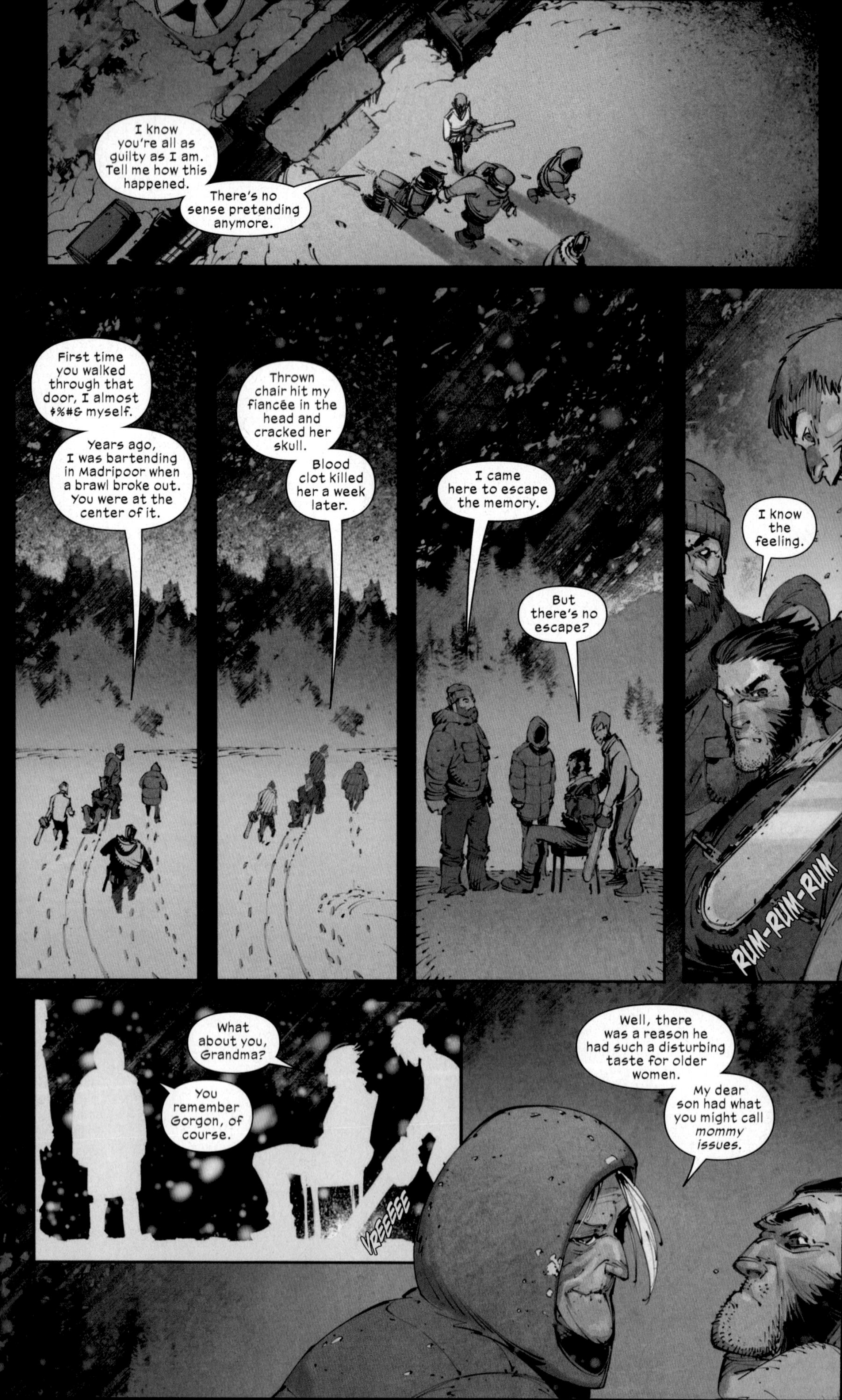

I know you're all as guilty as I am. Tell me how this happened.
There's no sense pretending anymore.
First time you walked through that door, I almost $%#& myself.
Years ago, I was bartending in Madripoor when a brawl broke out. You were at the center of it.
Thrown chair hit my fiancée in the head and cracked her skull.
Blood clot killed her a week later.
I came here to escape the memory.
But there's no escape?
I know the feeling.
RUM-RUM-RUM
What about you, Grandma?
You remember Gorgon, of course.
VREEEEE
Well, there was a reason he had such a disturbing taste for older women.
My dear son had what you might call *mommy* issues.

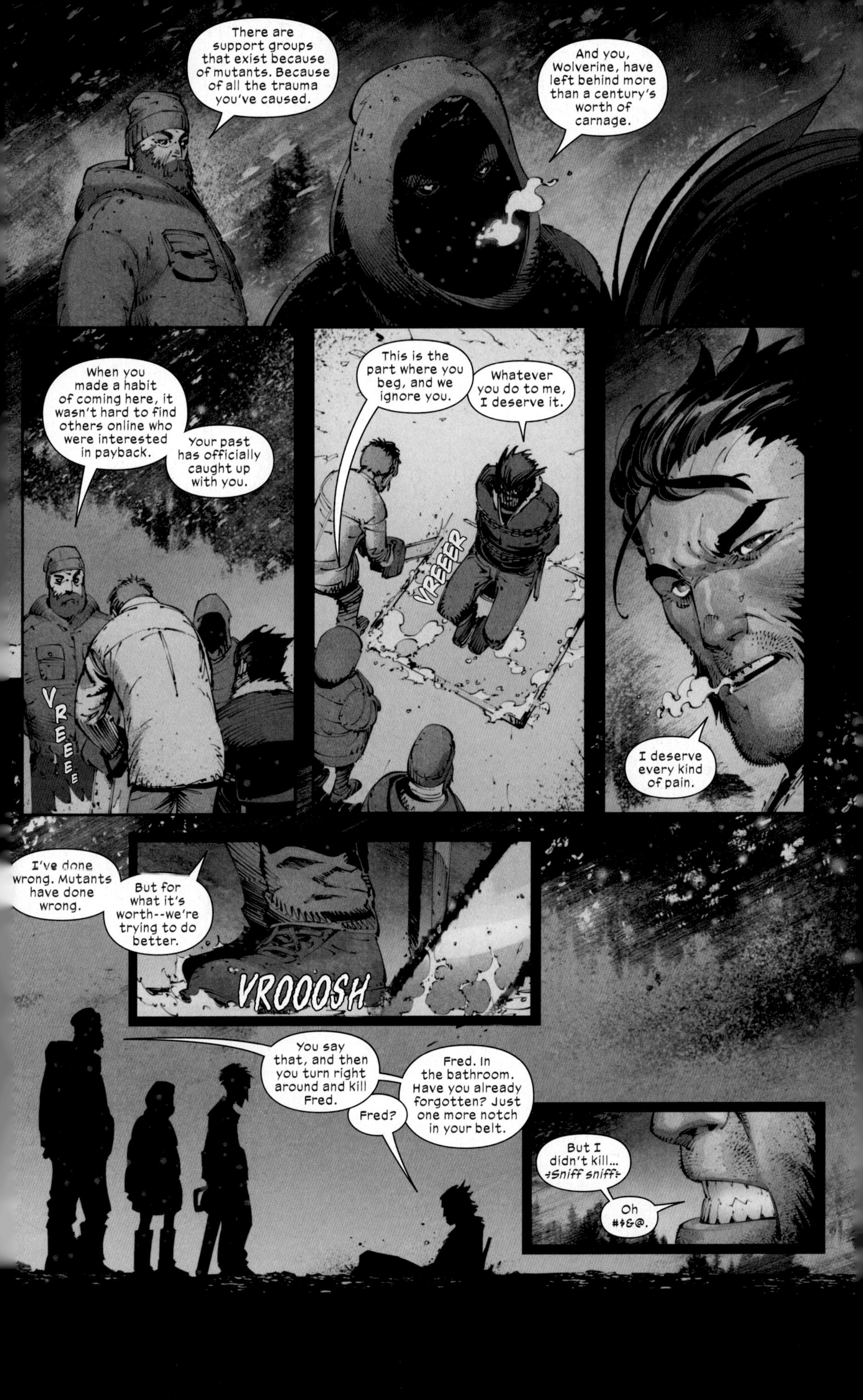
There are support groups that exist because of mutants. Because of all the trauma you've caused.
And you, Wolverine, have left behind more than a century's worth of carnage.
When you made a habit of coming here, it wasn't hard to find others online who were interested in payback.
Your past has officially caught up with you.
VREEEE
This is the part where you beg, and we ignore you.
Whatever you do to me, I deserve it.
VREEER
I deserve every kind of pain.
I've done wrong. Mutants have done wrong.
But for what it's worth--we're trying to do better.
VROOOSH
You say that, and then you turn right around and kill Fred.
Fred?
Fred. In the bathroom. Have you already forgotten? Just one more notch in your belt.
But I didn't kill... *Sniff sniff*
Oh #$&@.

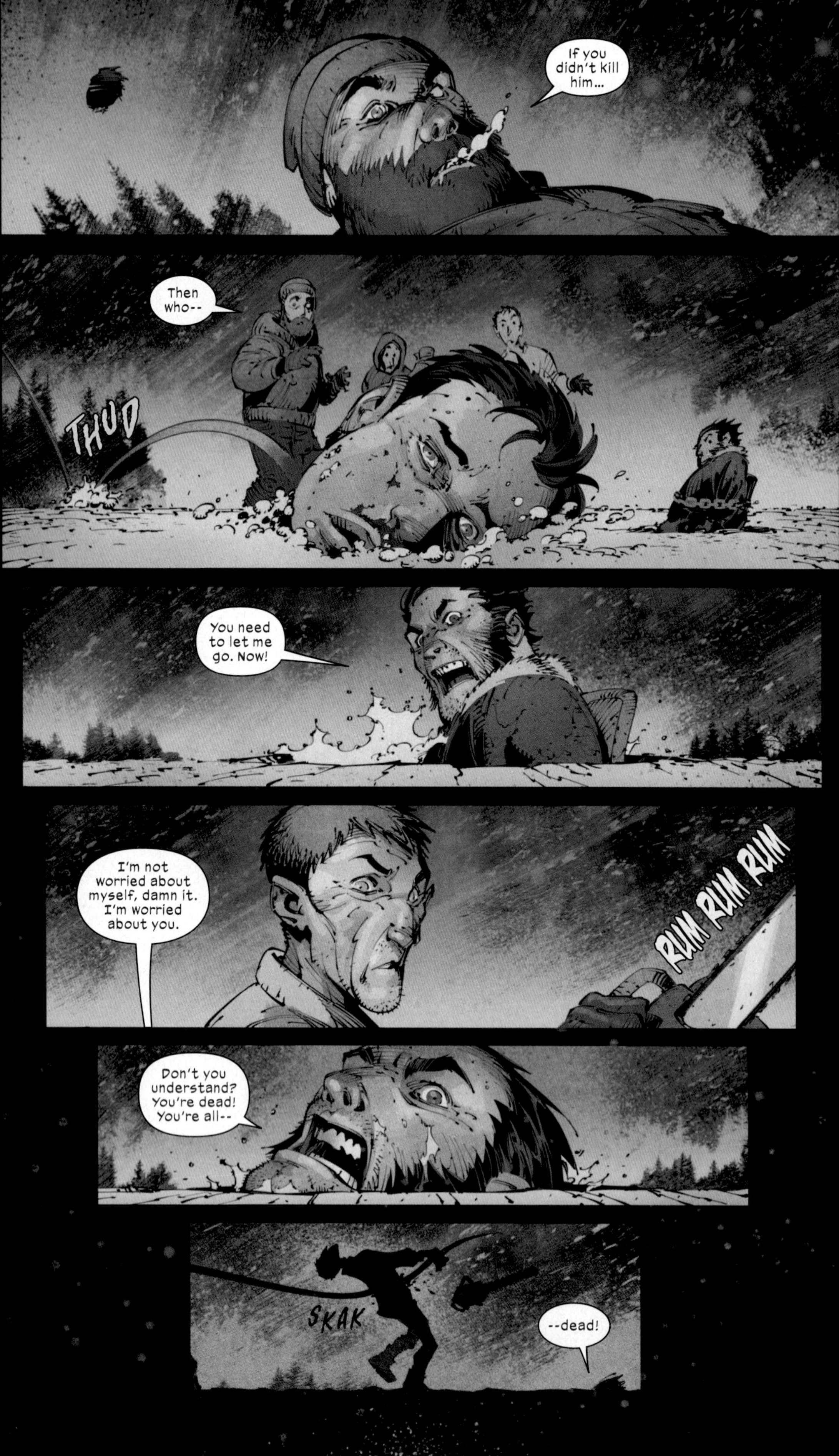
If you didn't kill him...
Then who--
THUD
You need to let me go. Now!
I'm not worried about myself, damn it. I'm worried about you.
RUM RUM RUM
Don't you understand? You're dead! You're all--
SKAK
--dead!

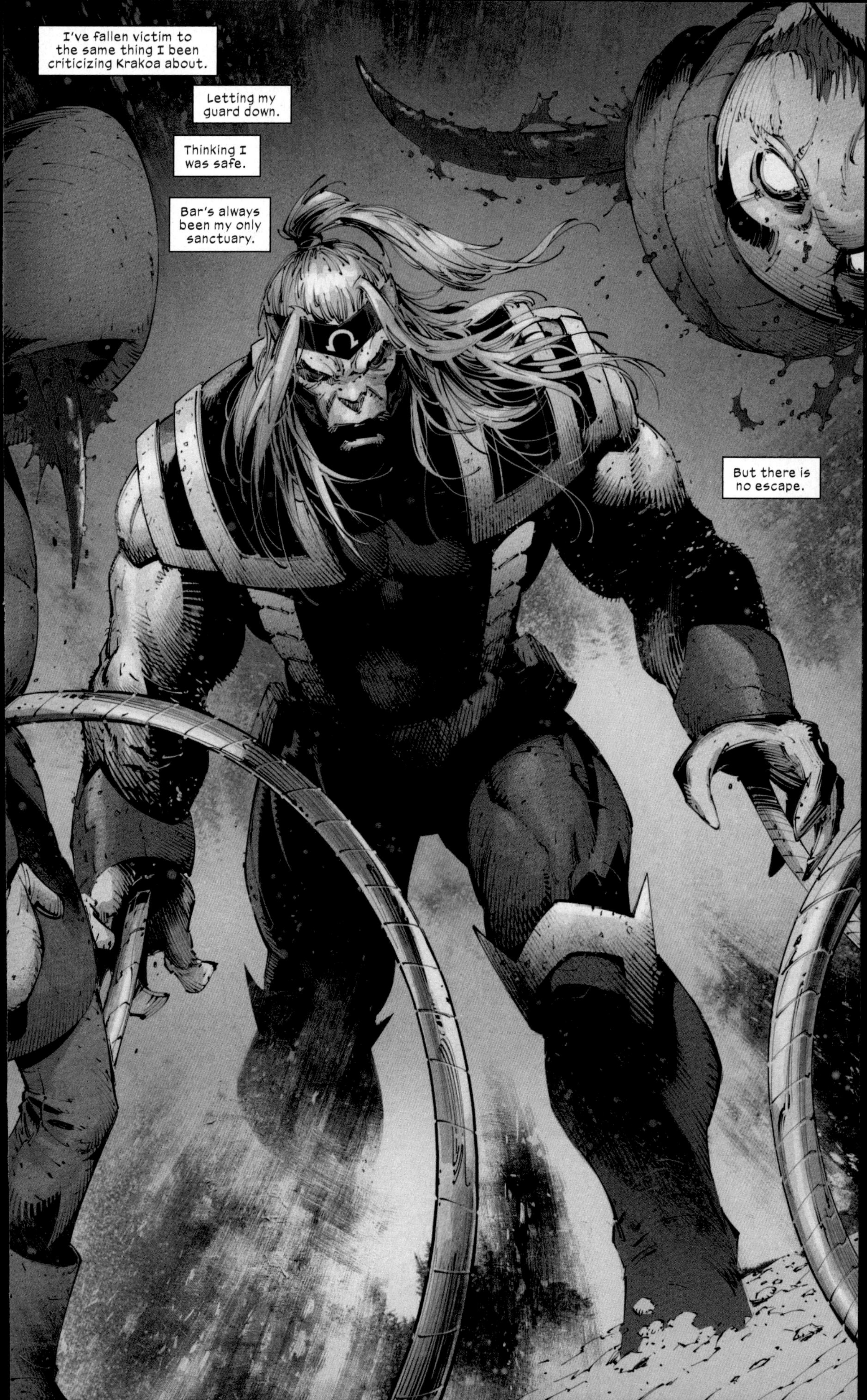
I've fallen victim to the same thing I been criticizing Krakoa about.
Letting my guard down.
Thinking I was safe.
Bar's always been my only sanctuary.
But there is no escape.

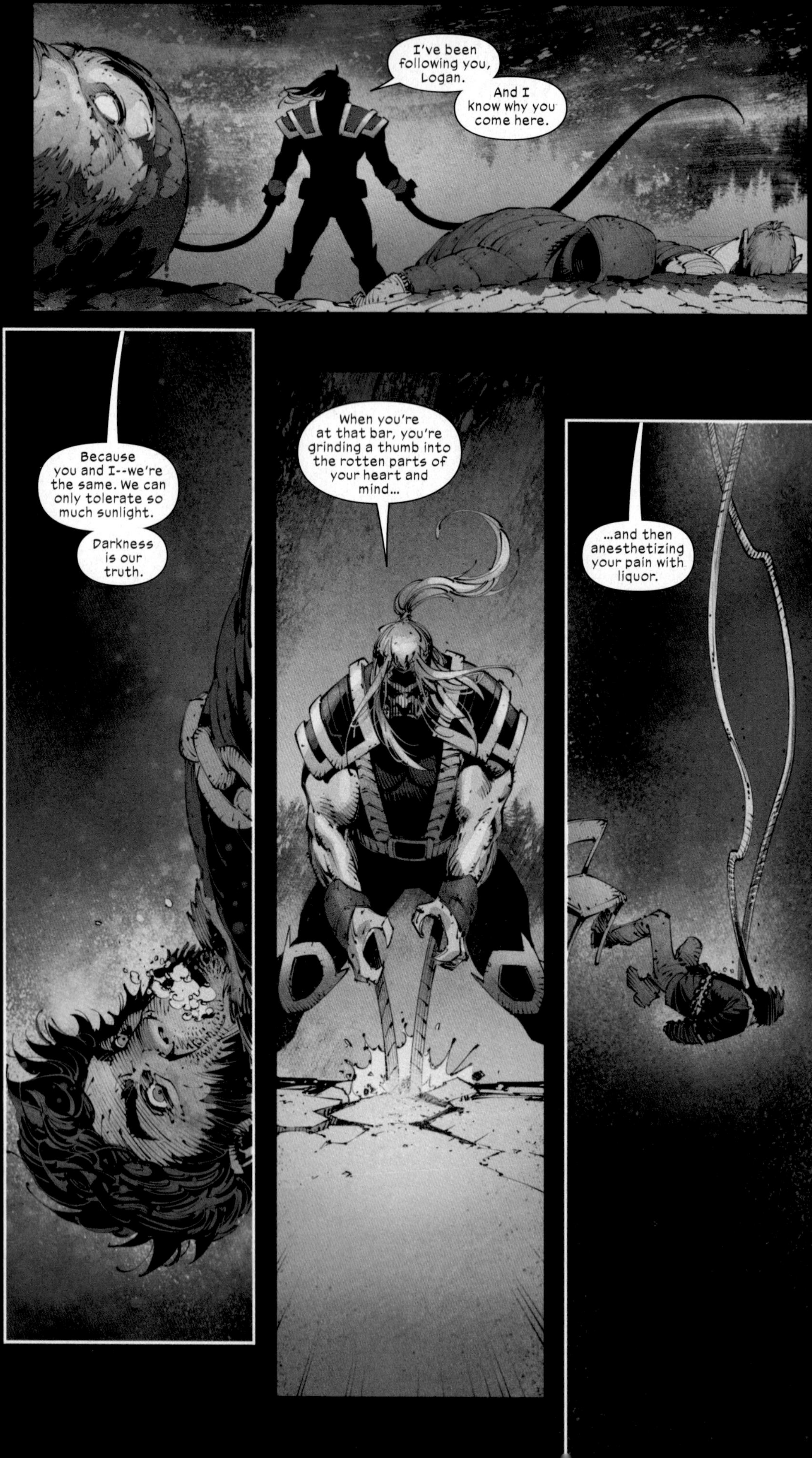
I've been following you, Logan.
And I know why you come here.
Because you and I--we're the same. We can only tolerate so much sunlight.
Darkness is our truth.
When you're at that bar, you're grinding a thumb into the rotten parts of your heart and mind...
...and then anesthetizing your pain with liquor.

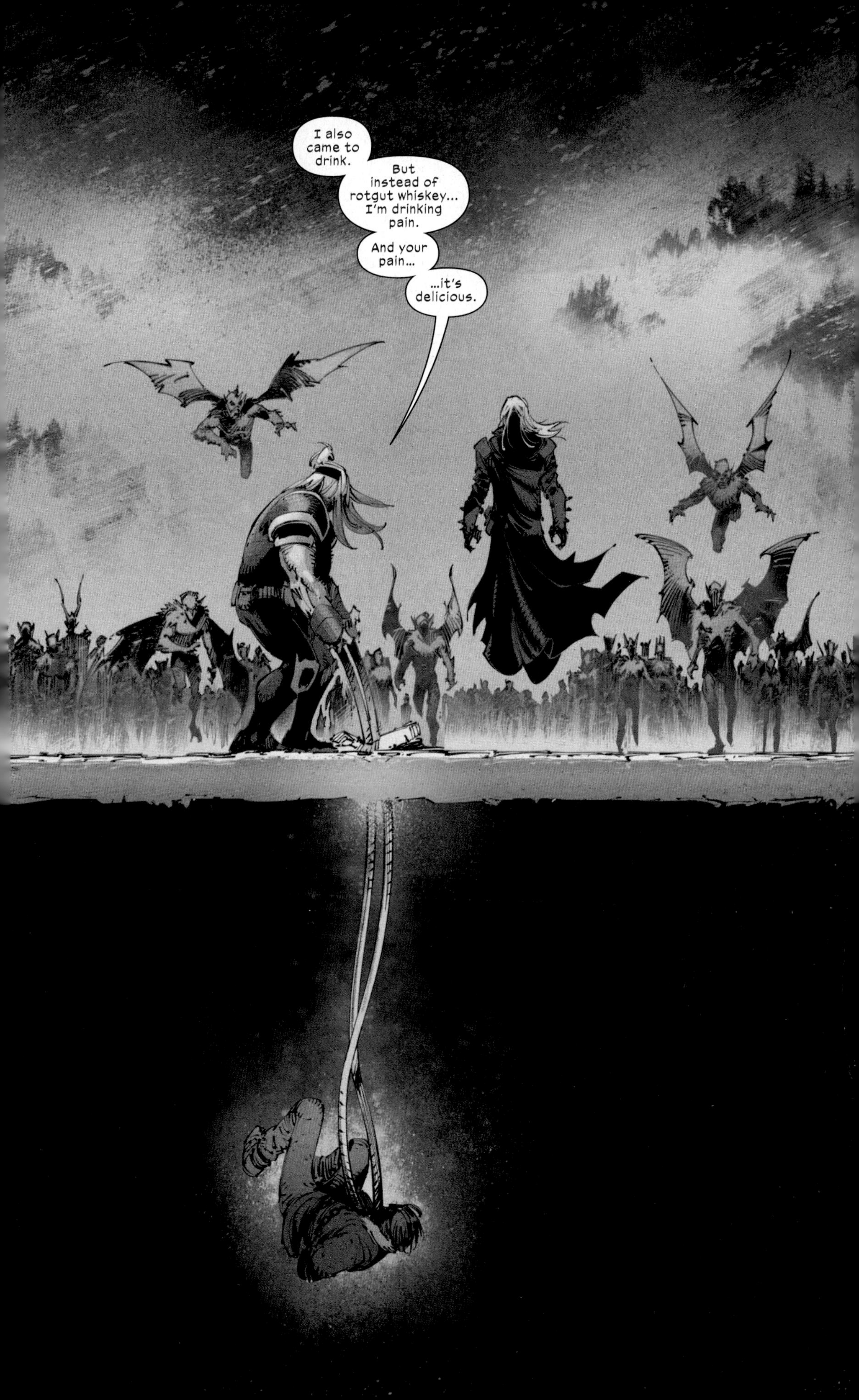
I also came to drink.
But instead of rotgut whiskey... I'm drinking pain.
And your pain...
...it's delicious.

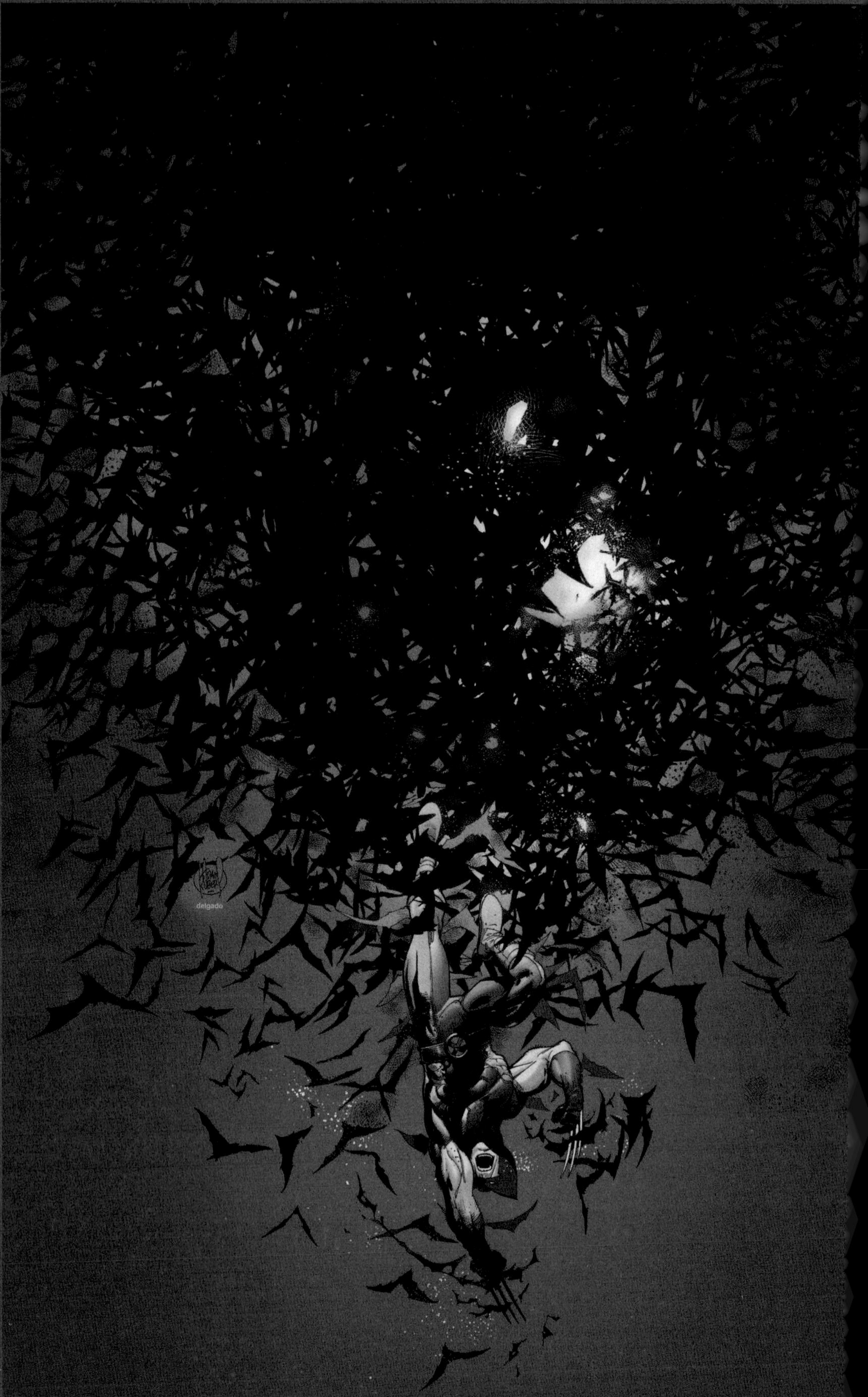
delgado

Bloodclocks

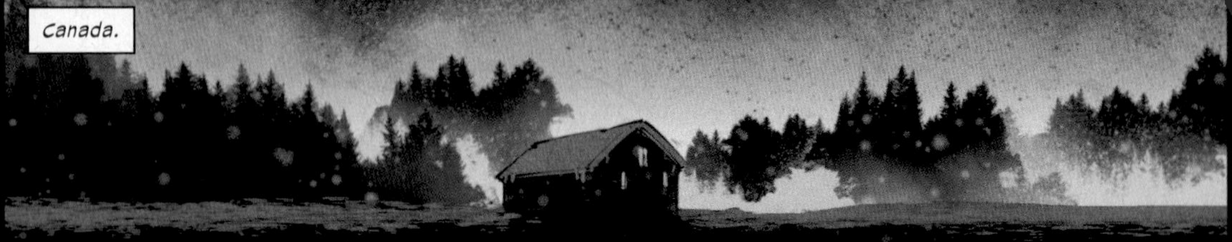
Canada.

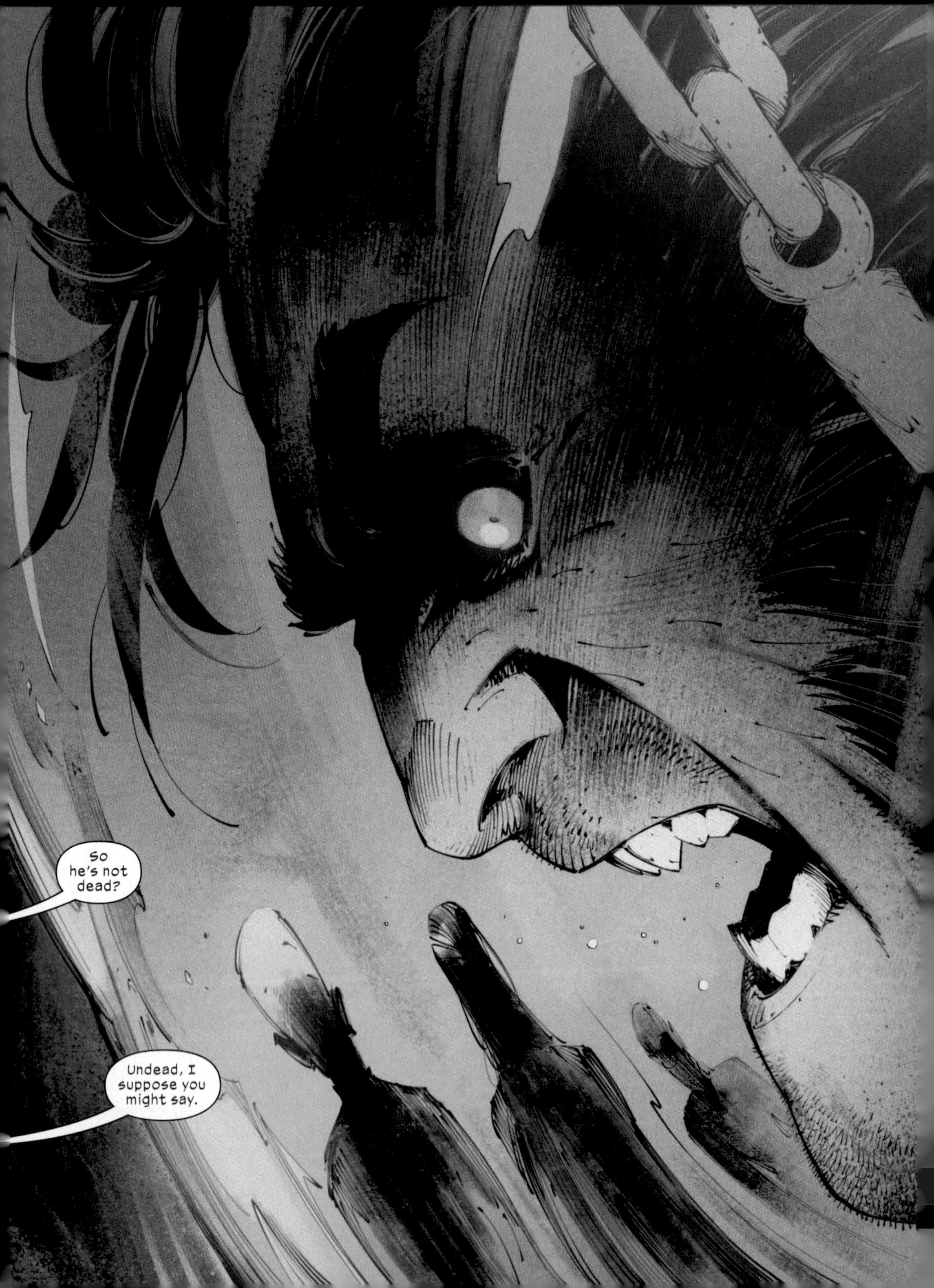
So he's not dead?
Undead, I suppose you might say.

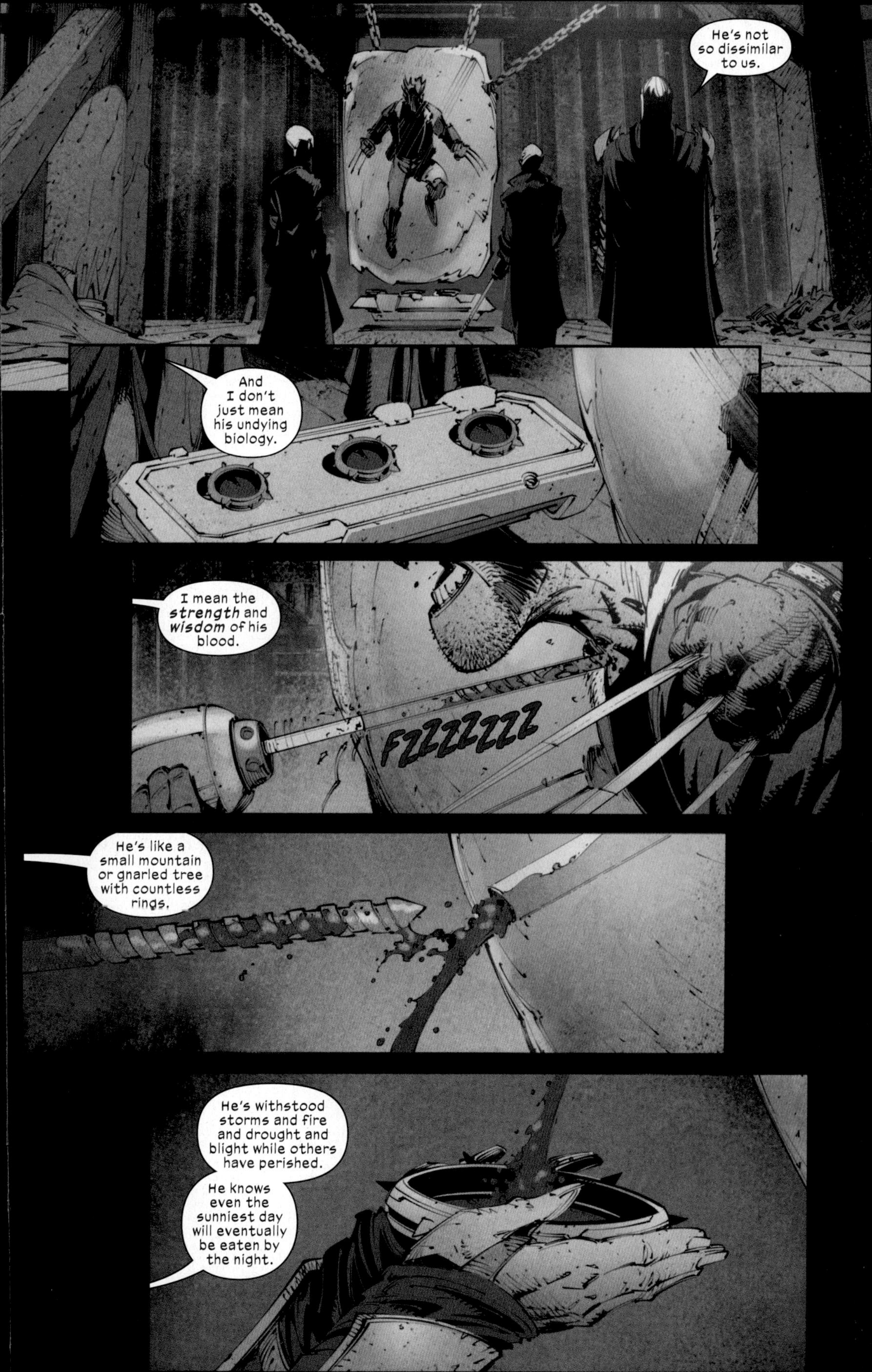

He's not so dissimilar to us.
And I don't just mean his undying biology.
I mean the *strength* and *wisdom* of his blood.
FZZZZZZZ
He's like a small mountain or gnarled tree with countless rings.
He's withstood storms and fire and drought and blight while others have perished.
He knows even the sunniest day will eventually be eaten by the night.

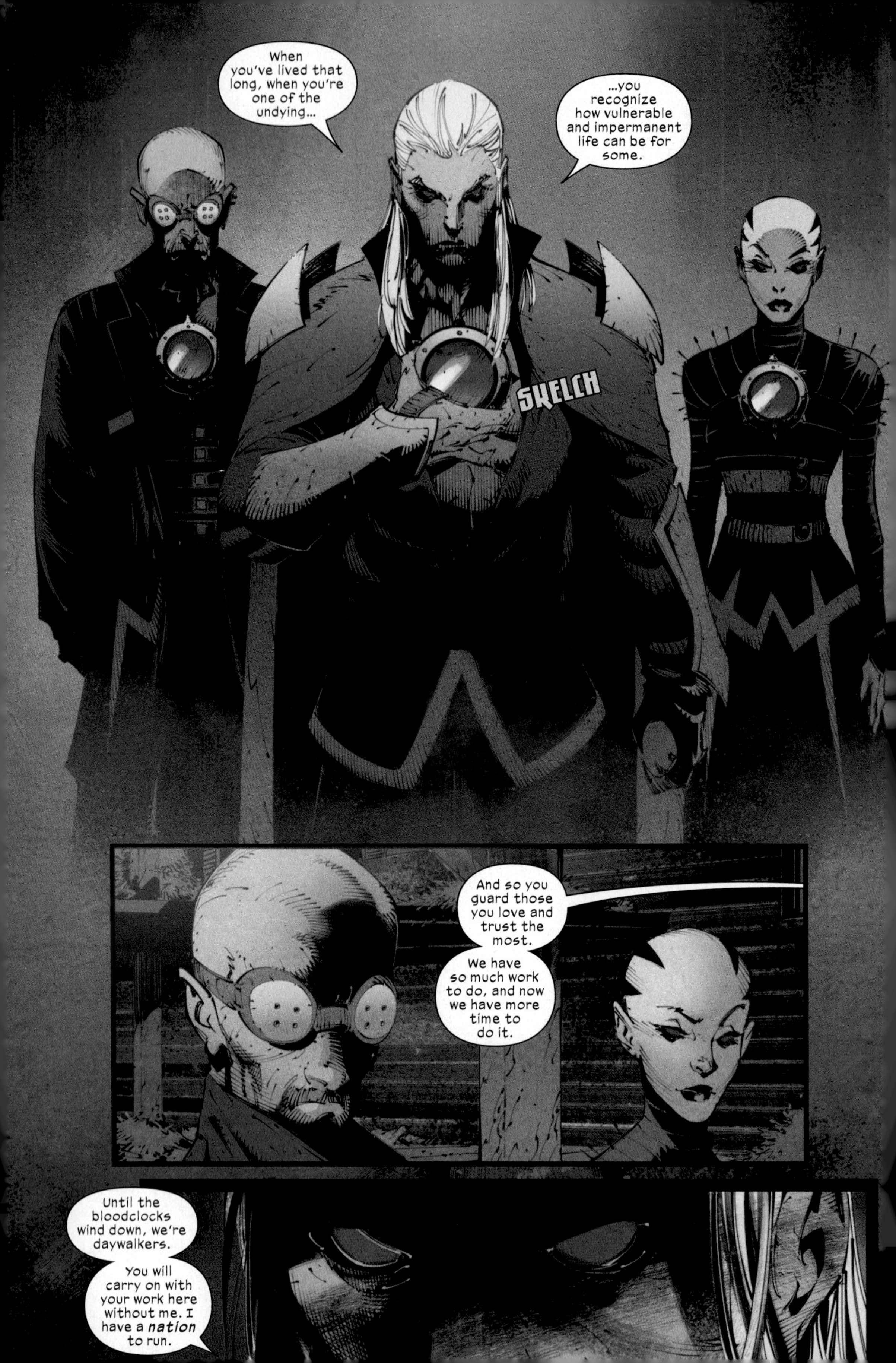
When you've lived that long, when you're one of the undying...
...you recognize how vulnerable and impermanent life can be for some.
SKELCH
And so you guard those you love and trust the most.
We have so much work to do, and now we have more time to do it.
Until the bloodclocks wind down, we're daywalkers.
You will carry on with your work here without me. I have a *nation* to run.

WOLVERINE: BLOOD GROUP SYSTEM

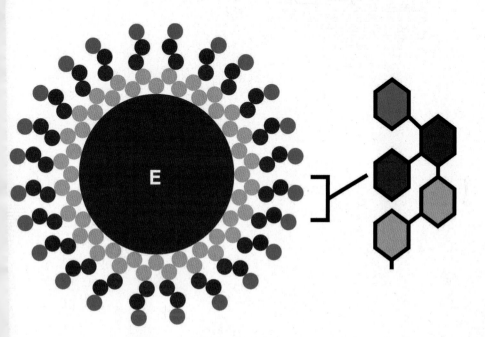

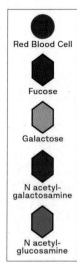

Red Blood Cell

Fucose

Galactose

N acetyl-
galactosamine

N acetyl-
glucosamine

TYPES	DISTRIBUTION	RATIOS
O +	1 PERSON IN 3	38.4 %
O -	1 PERSON IN 15	7.7 %
A +	1 PERSON IN 3	32.3 %
A -	1 PERSON IN 16	6.5 %
B +	1 PERSON IN 12	9.4 %
B -	1 PERSON IN 67	1.7 %
AB +	1 PERSON IN 29	3.2 %
AB -	1 PERSON IN 167	0.7 %
E	1 PERSON IN 8 BILLION	0.000000 %

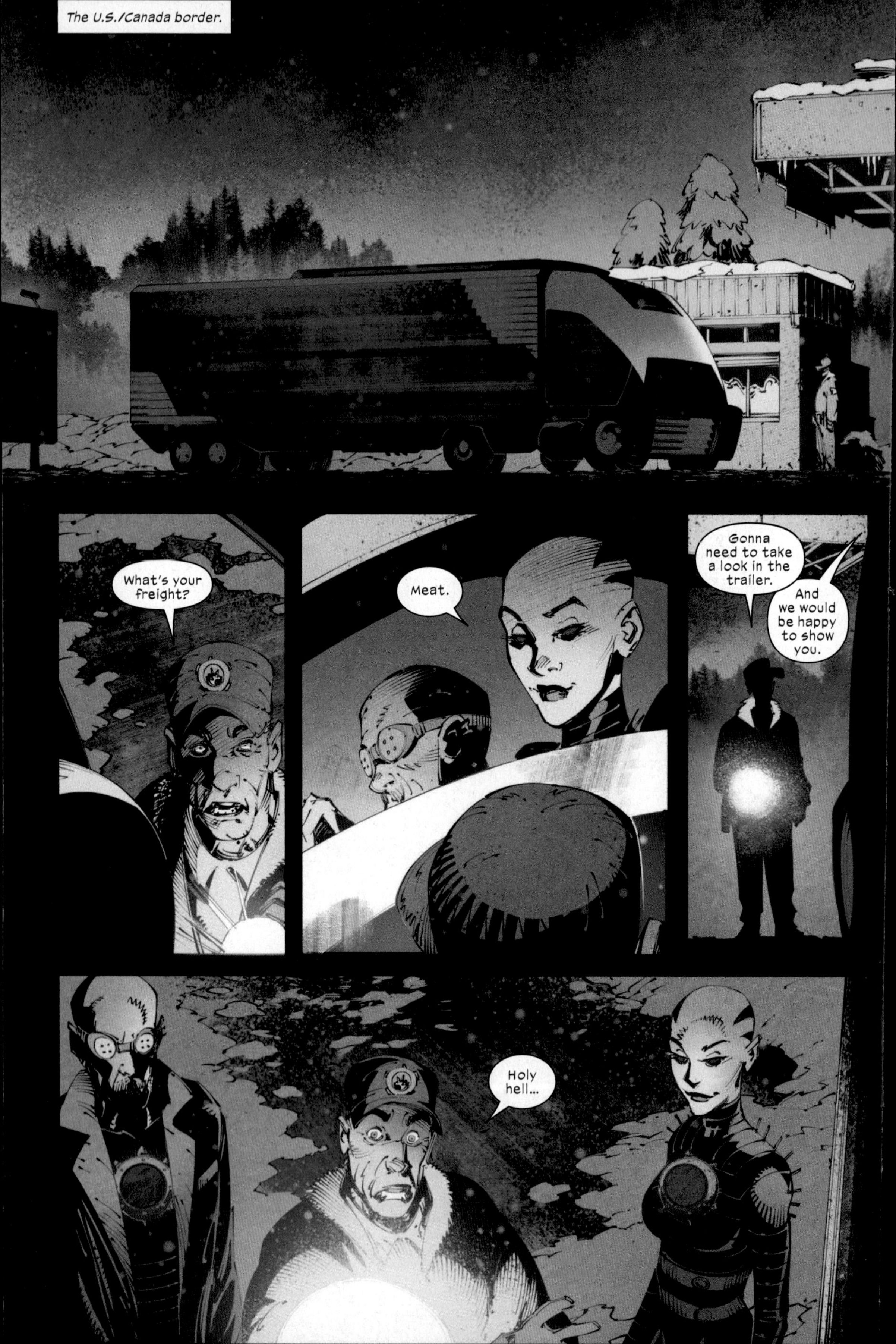
The U.S./Canada border.
What's your freight?
Meat.
Gonna need to take a look in the trailer.
And we would be happy to show you.
Holy hell...

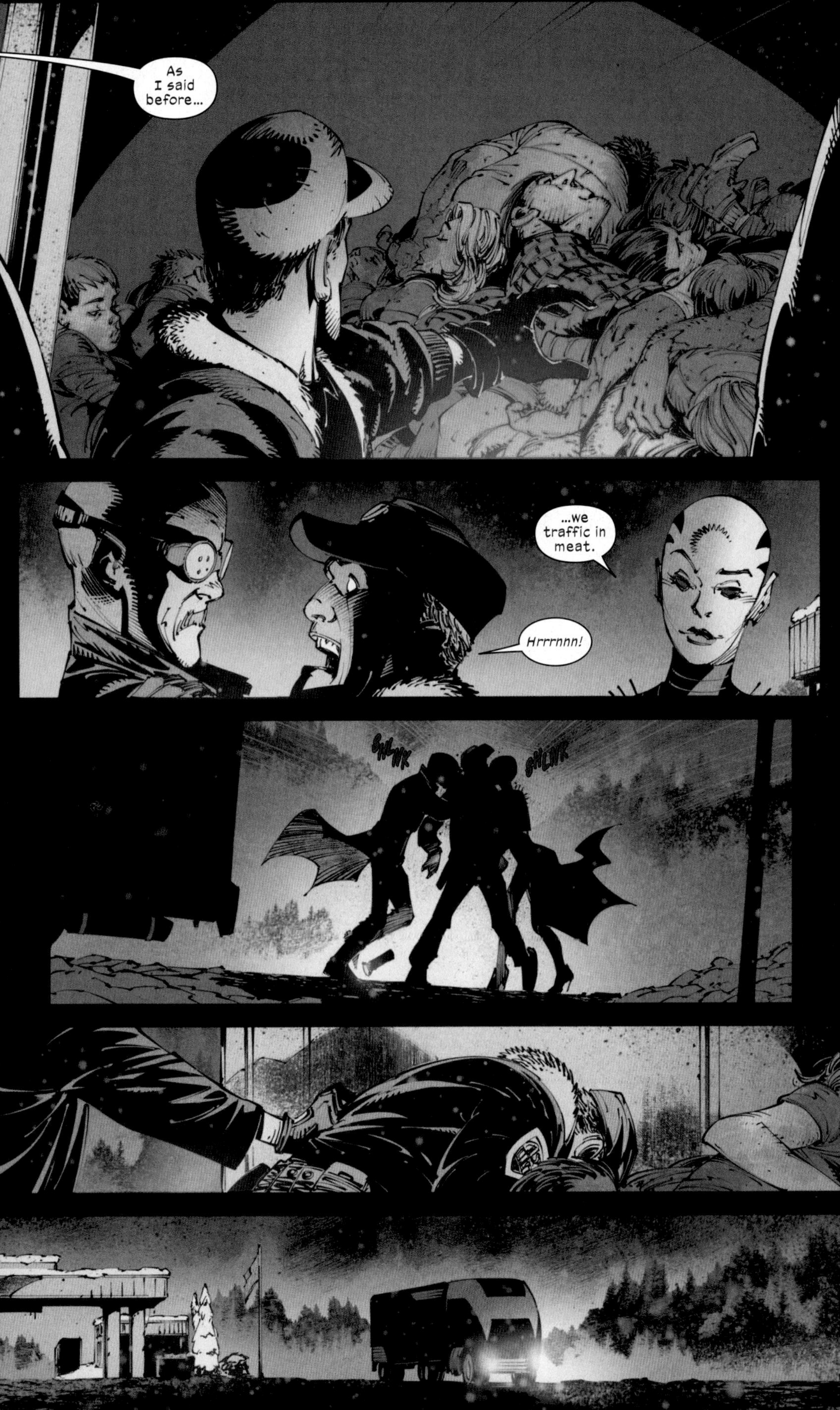
As I said before...
...we traffic in meat.
Hrrrnnn!
SHLNK
SHLNK

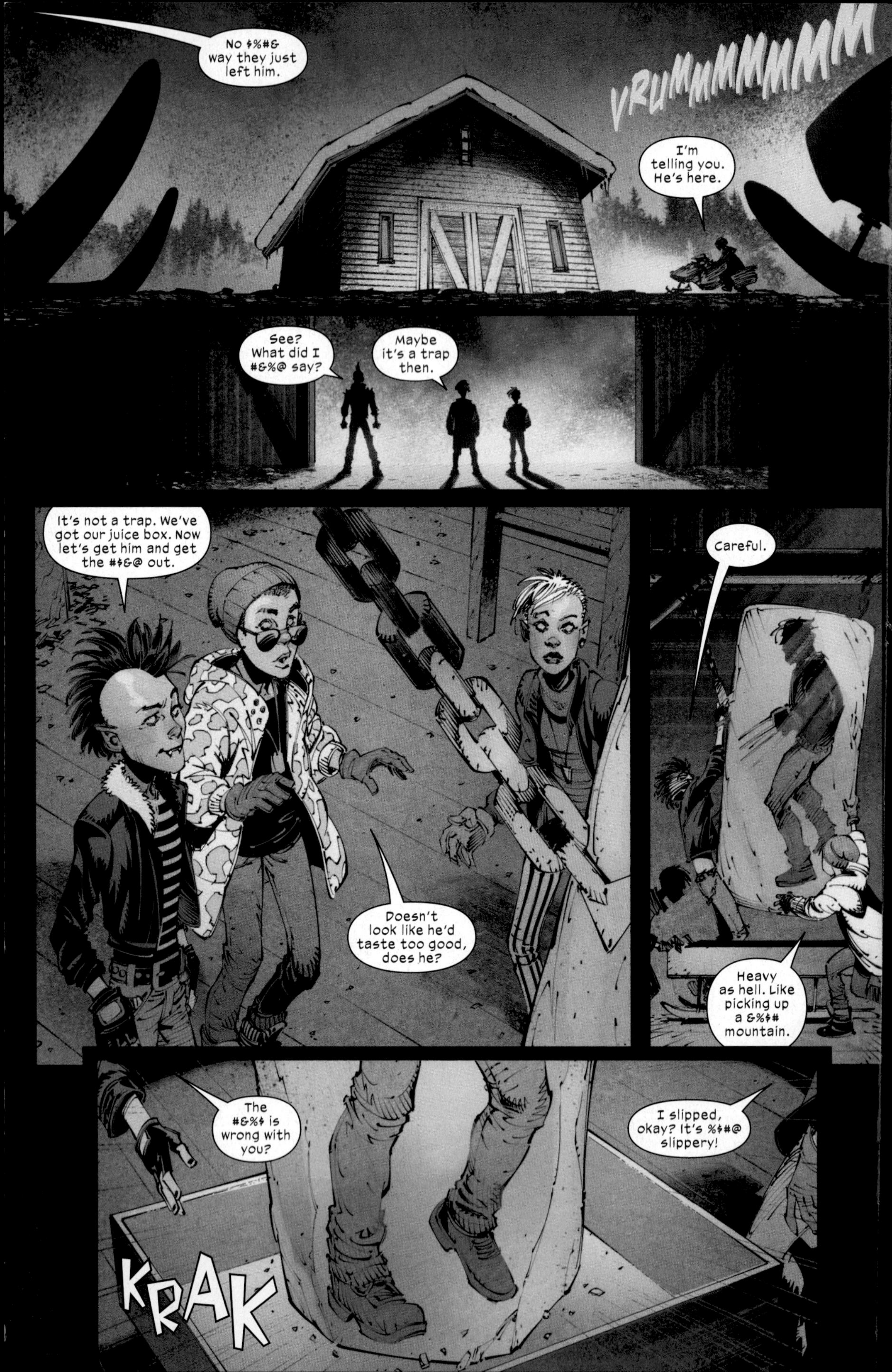
No $%#& way they just left him.
VRUMMMMMMMM
I'm telling you. He's here.
See? What did I #&%@ say?
Maybe it's a trap then.
It's not a trap. We've got our juice box. Now let's get him and get the #$&@ out.
Doesn't look like he'd taste too good, does he?
Careful.
Heavy as hell. Like picking up a &%$# mountain.
The #&%$ is wrong with you?
I slipped, okay? It's %$#@ slippery!
KRAK

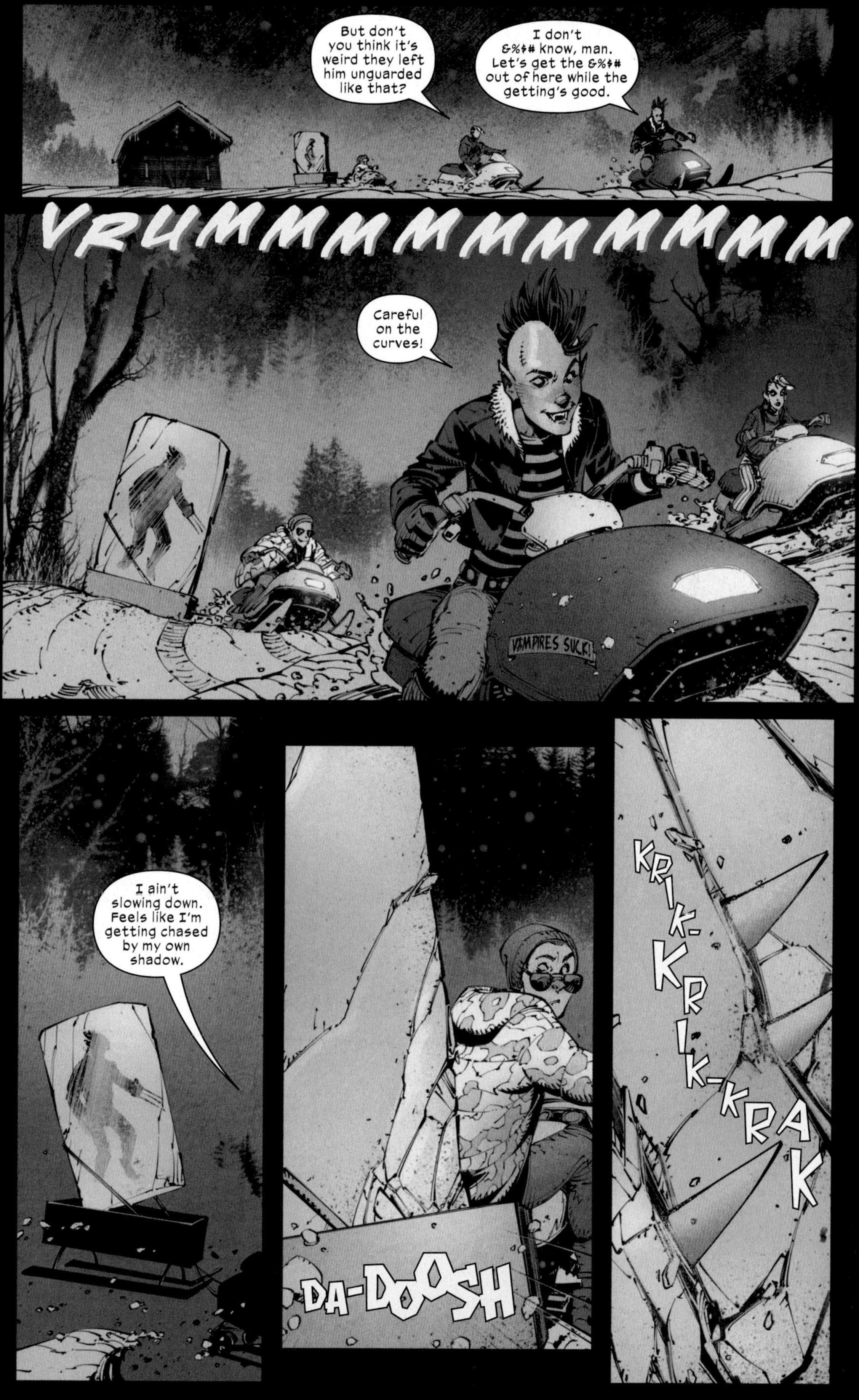
But don't you think it's weird they left him unguarded like that?
I don't &%$# know, man. Let's get the &%$# out of here while the getting's good.
VRUMMMMMMMMMMMM
Careful on the curves!
VAMPIRES SUCK!
I ain't slowing down. Feels like I'm getting chased by my own shadow.
DA-DOOSH
KRIK-KRIK-KRIK-KRAK

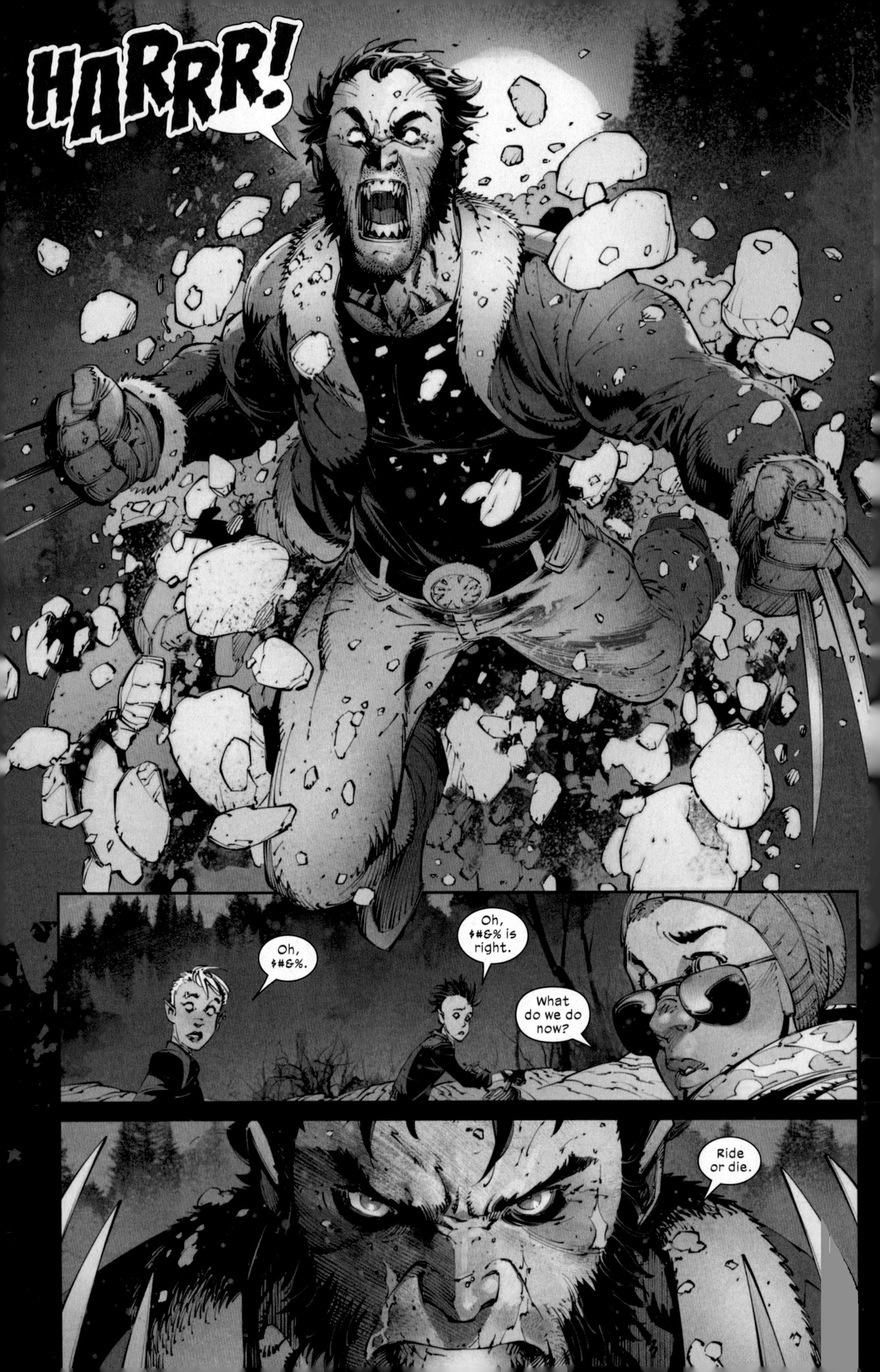

HARRR!
Oh, $#&%.
Oh, $#&% is right.
What do we do now?
Ride or die.

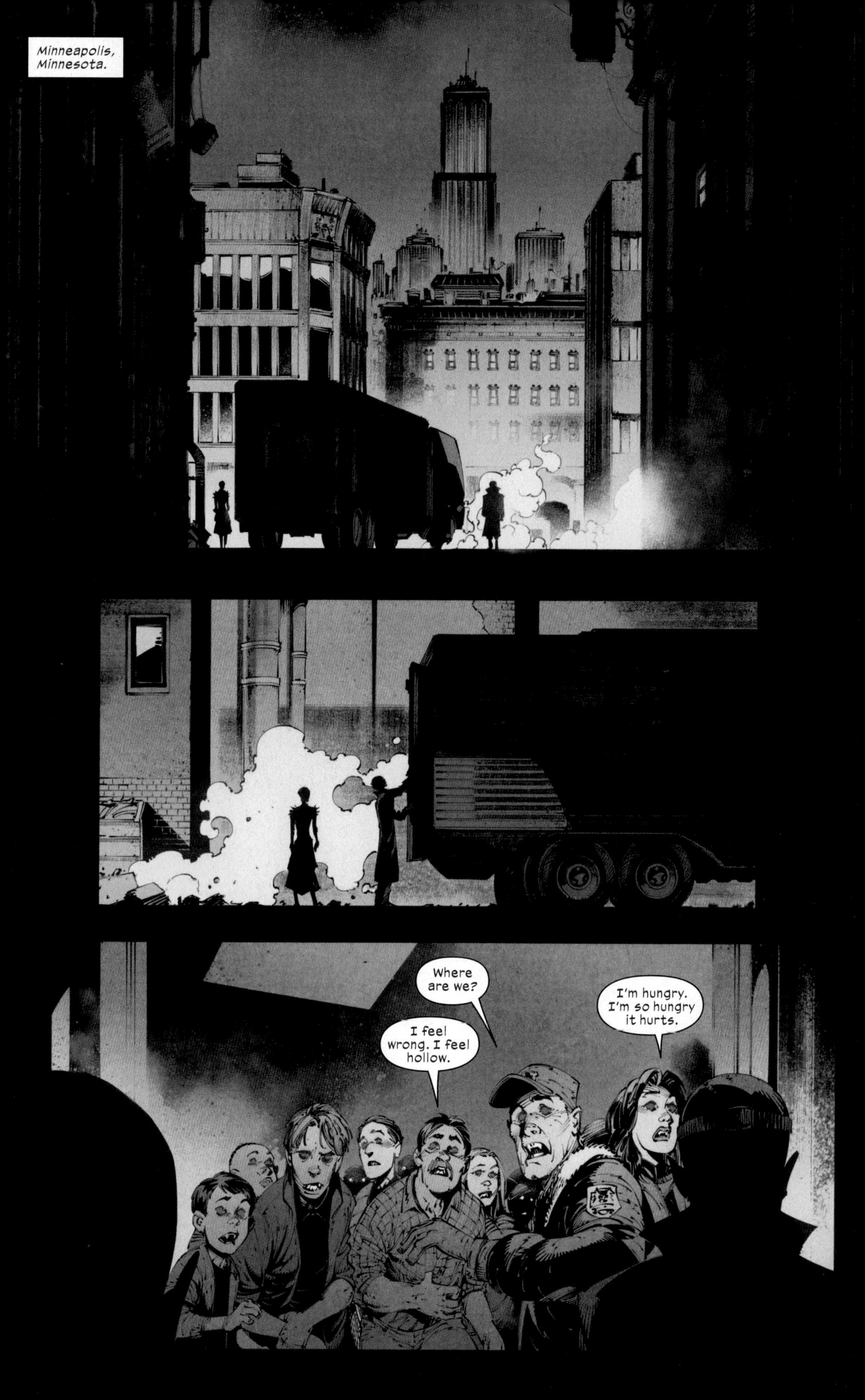
Minneapolis, Minnesota.
Where are we?
I feel wrong. I feel hollow.
I'm hungry. I'm so hungry it hurts.

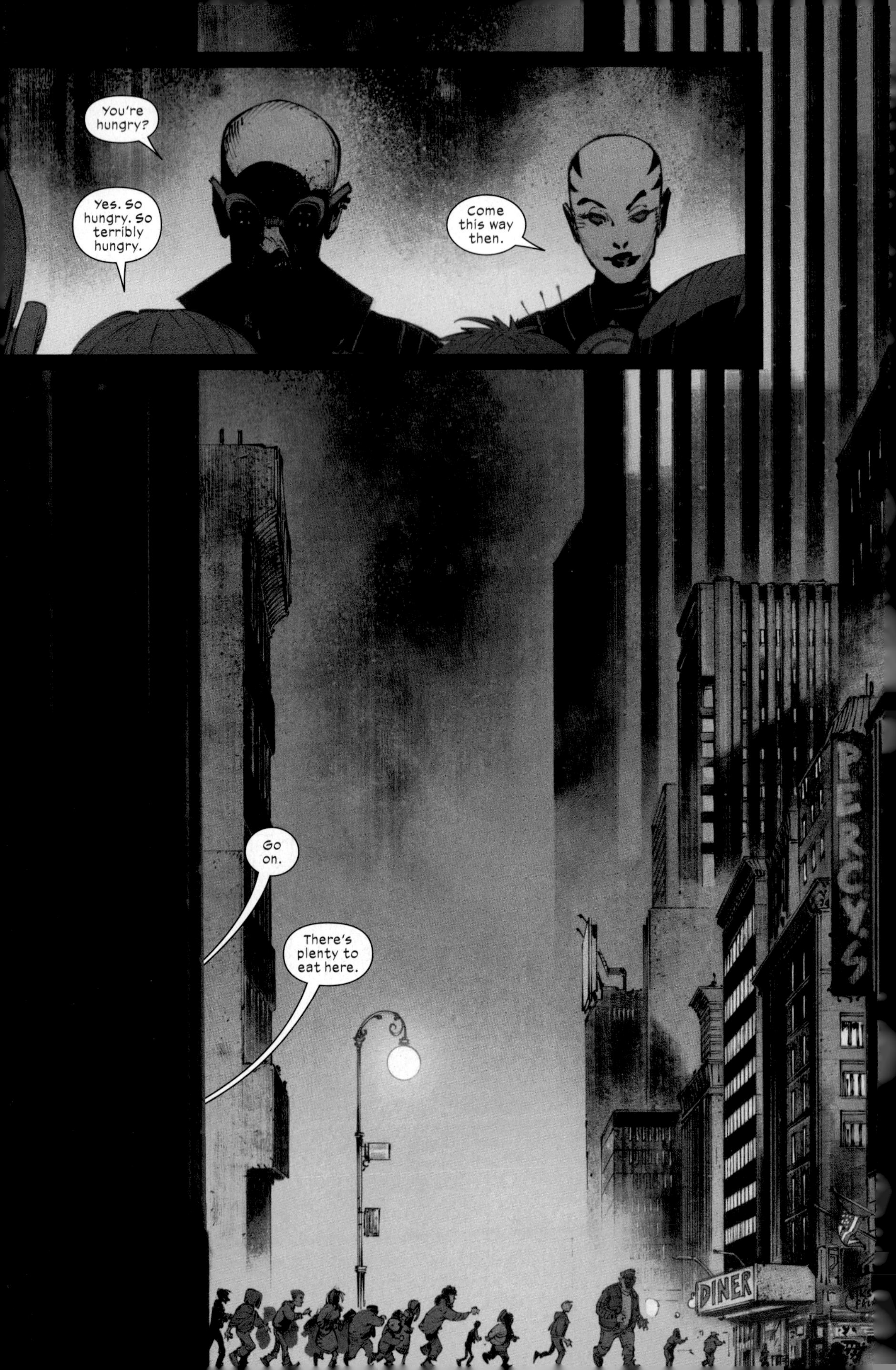
You're hungry?
Yes. So hungry. So terribly hungry.
Come this way then.
Go on.
There's plenty to eat here.
PERCY'S
DINER

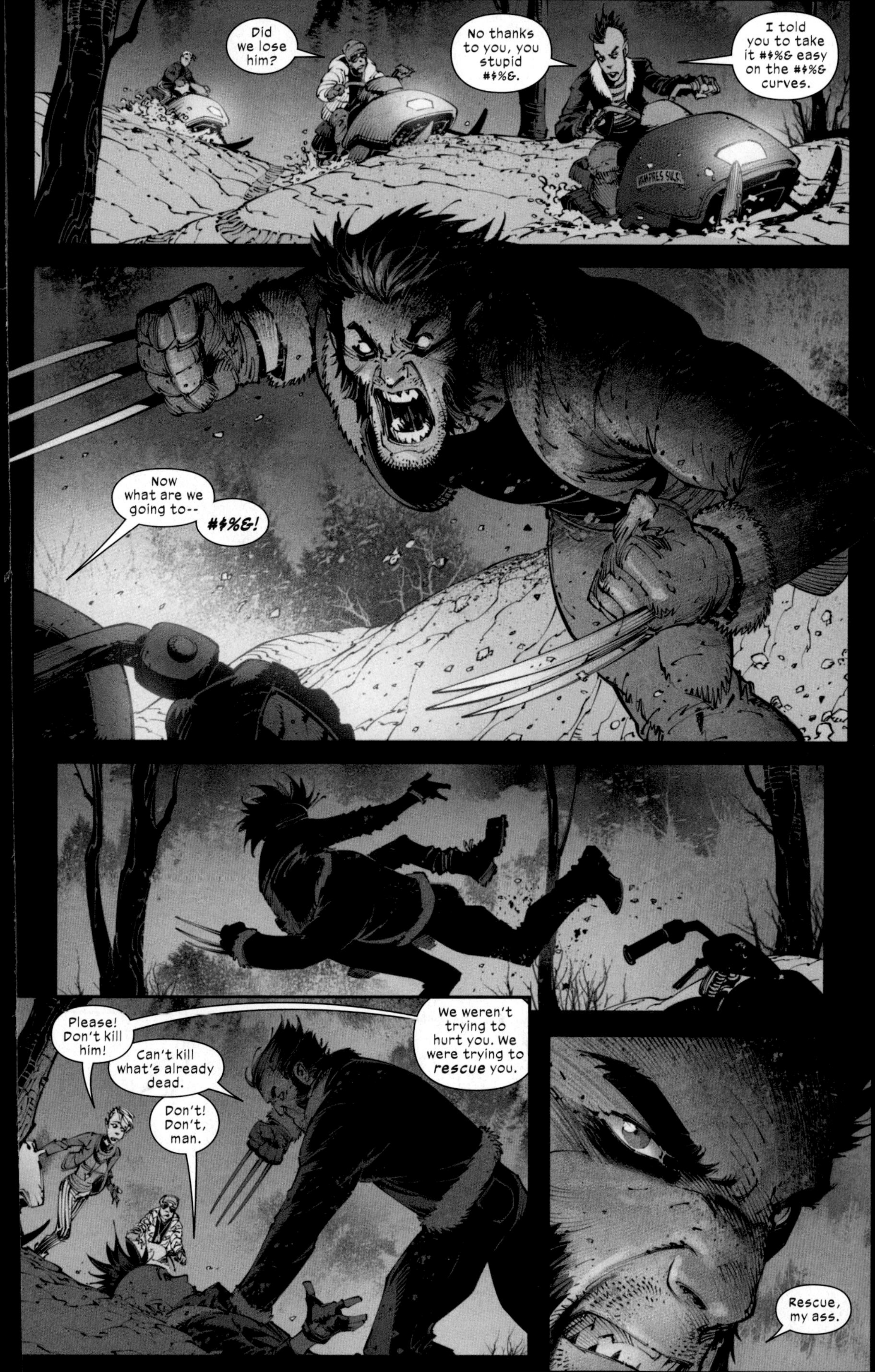

Did we lose him?
No thanks to you, you stupid #$%&.
I told you to take it #$%& easy on the #$%& curves.
Now what are we going to-- #$%&!
Please! Don't kill him!
We weren't trying to hurt you. We were trying to *rescue* you.
Can't kill what's already dead.
Don't! Don't, man.
Rescue, my ass.

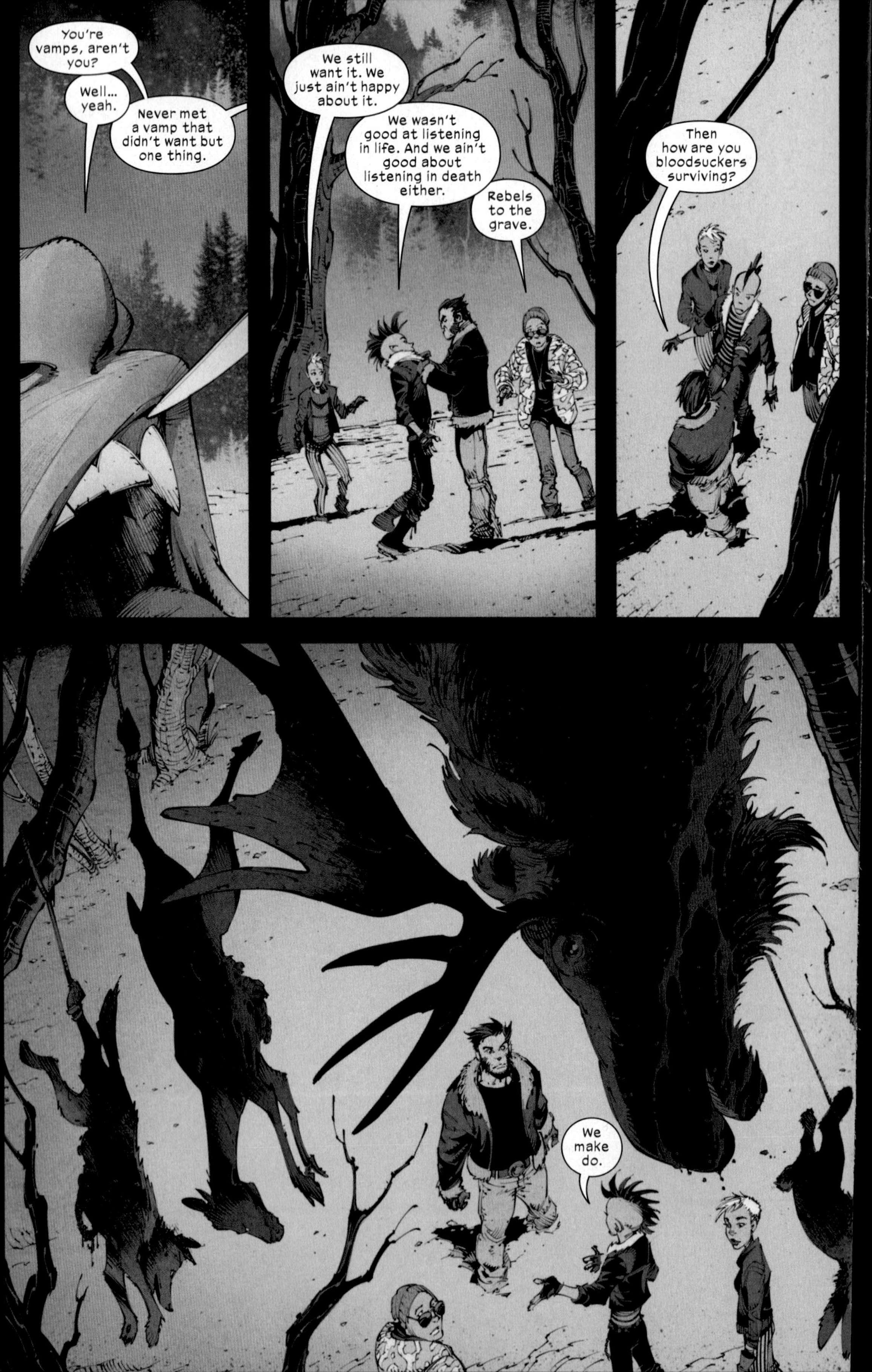
You're vamps, aren't you?
Well... yeah.
Never met a vamp that didn't want but one thing.
We still want it. We just ain't happy about it.
We wasn't good at listening in life. And we ain't good about listening in death either.
Rebels to the grave.
Then how are you bloodsuckers surviving?
We make do.

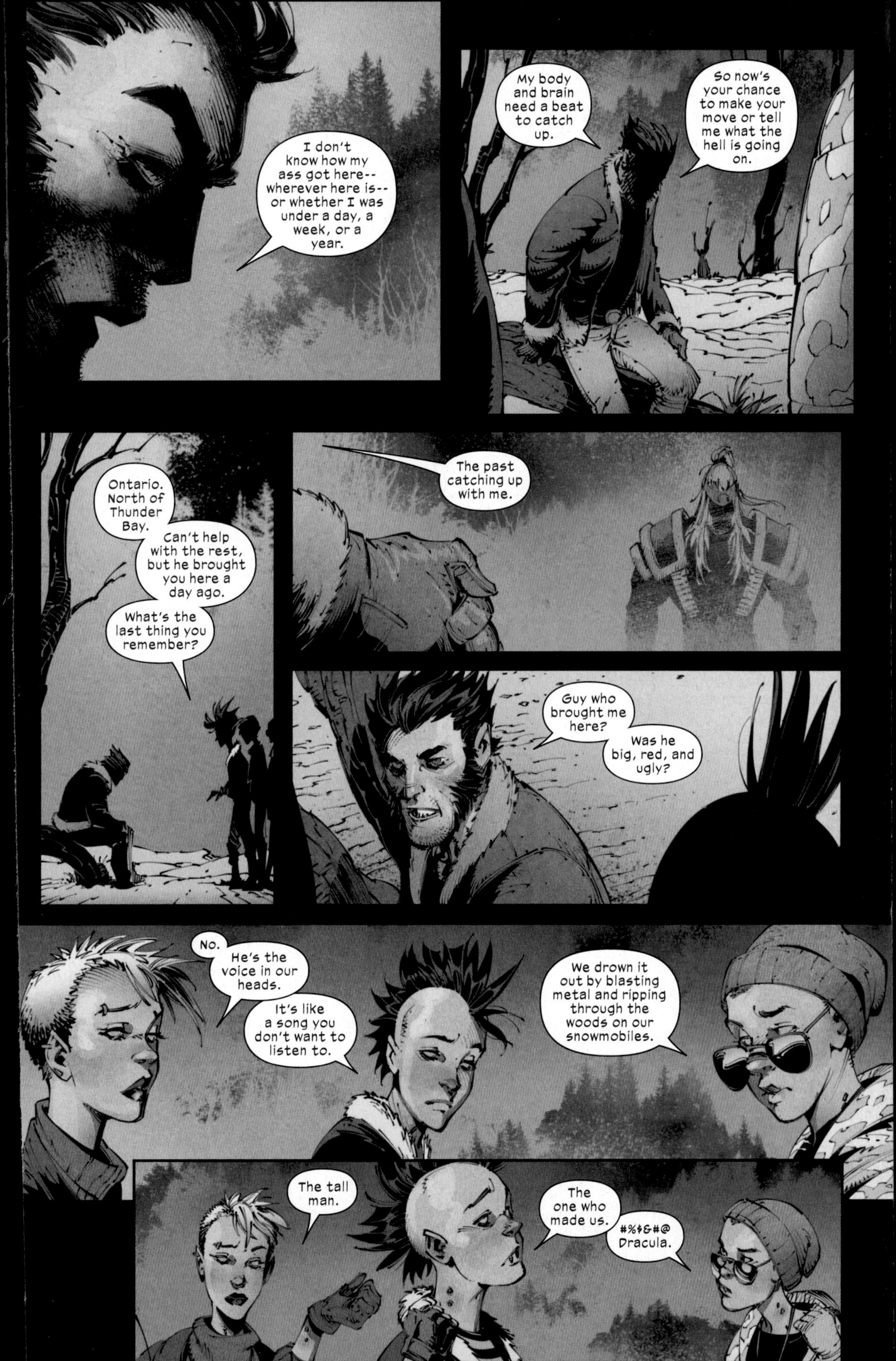

I don't know how my ass got here-- wherever here is-- or whether I was under a day, a week, or a year.
My body and brain need a beat to catch up.
So now's your chance to make your move or tell me what the hell is going on.
Ontario. North of Thunder Bay.
Can't help with the rest, but he brought you here a day ago.
What's the last thing you remember?
The past catching up with me.
Guy who brought me here?
Was he big, red, and ugly?
No.
He's the voice in our heads.
It's like a song you don't want to listen to.
We drown it out by blasting metal and ripping through the woods on our snowmobiles.
The tall man.
The one who made us.
#%$&#@ Dracula.

Louise,

I ever needed you, you said to find the loose floor tile in the Saint Julien le Pauvre. The one with the cross scratched into it. So that's what I did. And if you're reading this, it means you found my note.

Think I know what happened in the catacombs. They let us go, but they took my blood with them. Because it strengthens them. Juices them up.

Dracula walks by day now. And he ain't the only one. Because of me. So that's one more blood debt for me to settle.

You told me the Vampire Nation is growing their army. And you were right. Up north, they're taking out the small towns. Places where the mines and the sawmills have shut down. Places where the people are just scraping by. There's not as much noise when they go dark.

The vamps turn them and truck them into cities and let them swarm the human buffet. Can't imagine this is the only corner of the globe they're targeting.

I don't know what you and your Nightguard are doing to turn the tide, but I've done my part to help the vamps, so now I'm doing my part to hurt them.

Bet you'll figure out how to find me, but if not, just howl at the moon.

Logan

—

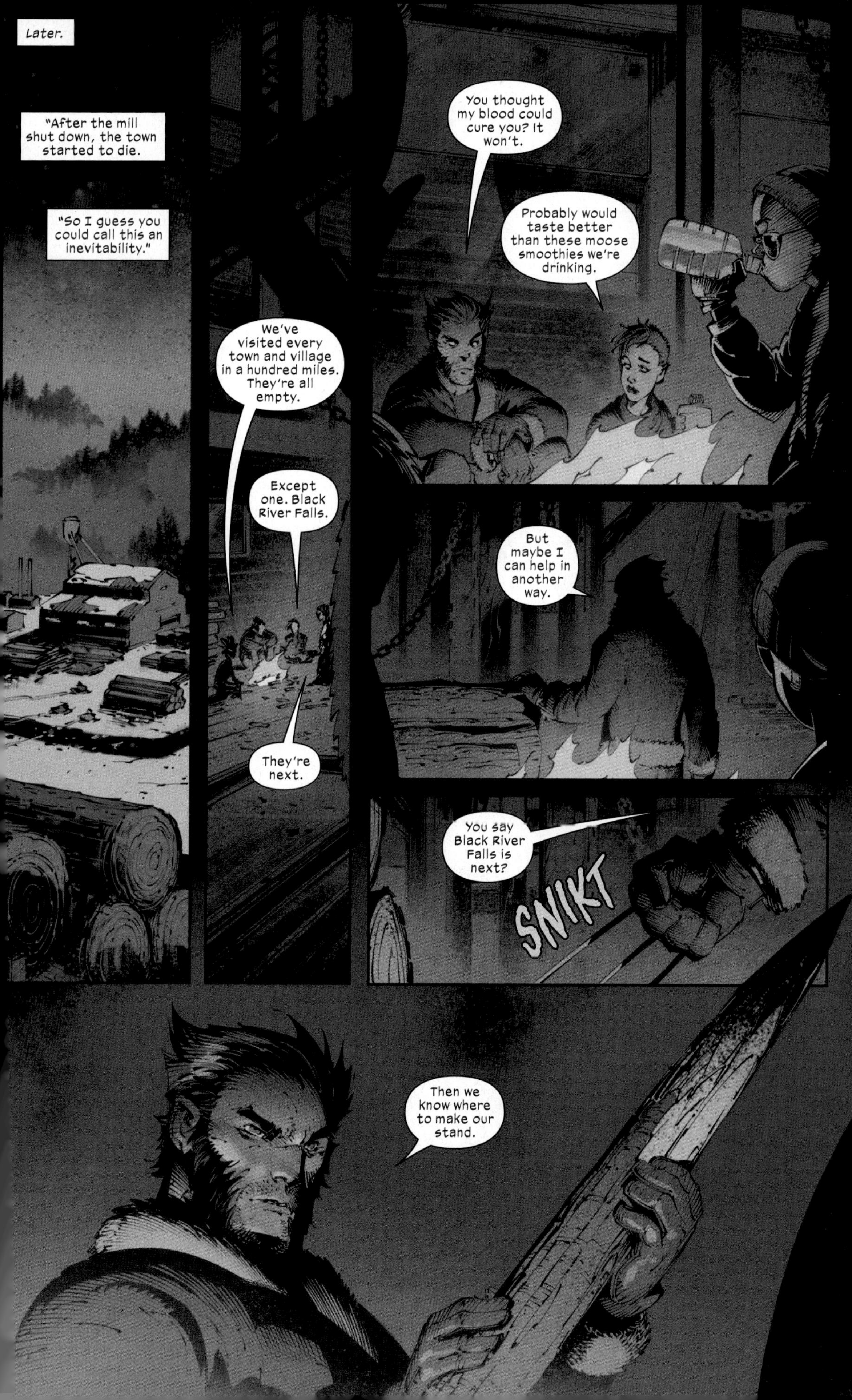
Later.
"After the mill shut down, the town started to die.
"So I guess you could call this an inevitability."
You thought my blood could cure you? It won't.
Probably would taste better than these moose smoothies we're drinking.
We've visited every town and village in a hundred miles. They're all empty.
Except one. Black River Falls.
They're next.
But maybe I can help in another way.
You say Black River Falls is next?
SNIKT
Then we know where to make our stand.

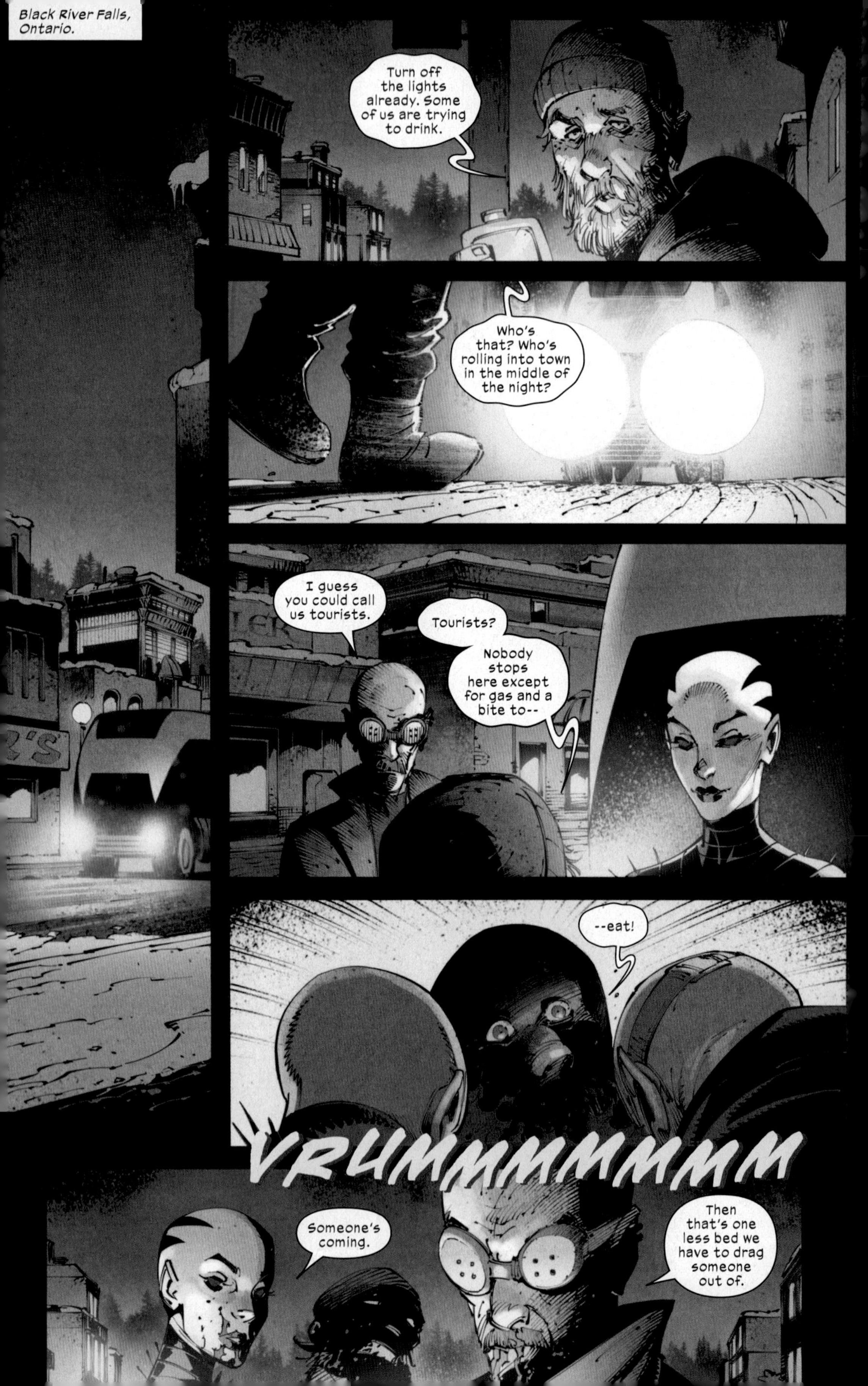

Black River Falls, Ontario.
Turn off the lights already. Some of us are trying to drink.
Who's that? Who's rolling into town in the middle of the night?
I guess you could call us tourists.
Tourists?
Nobody stops here except for gas and a bite to--
--eat!
VRUMMMMMMMM
Someone's coming.
Then that's one less bed we have to drag someone out of.

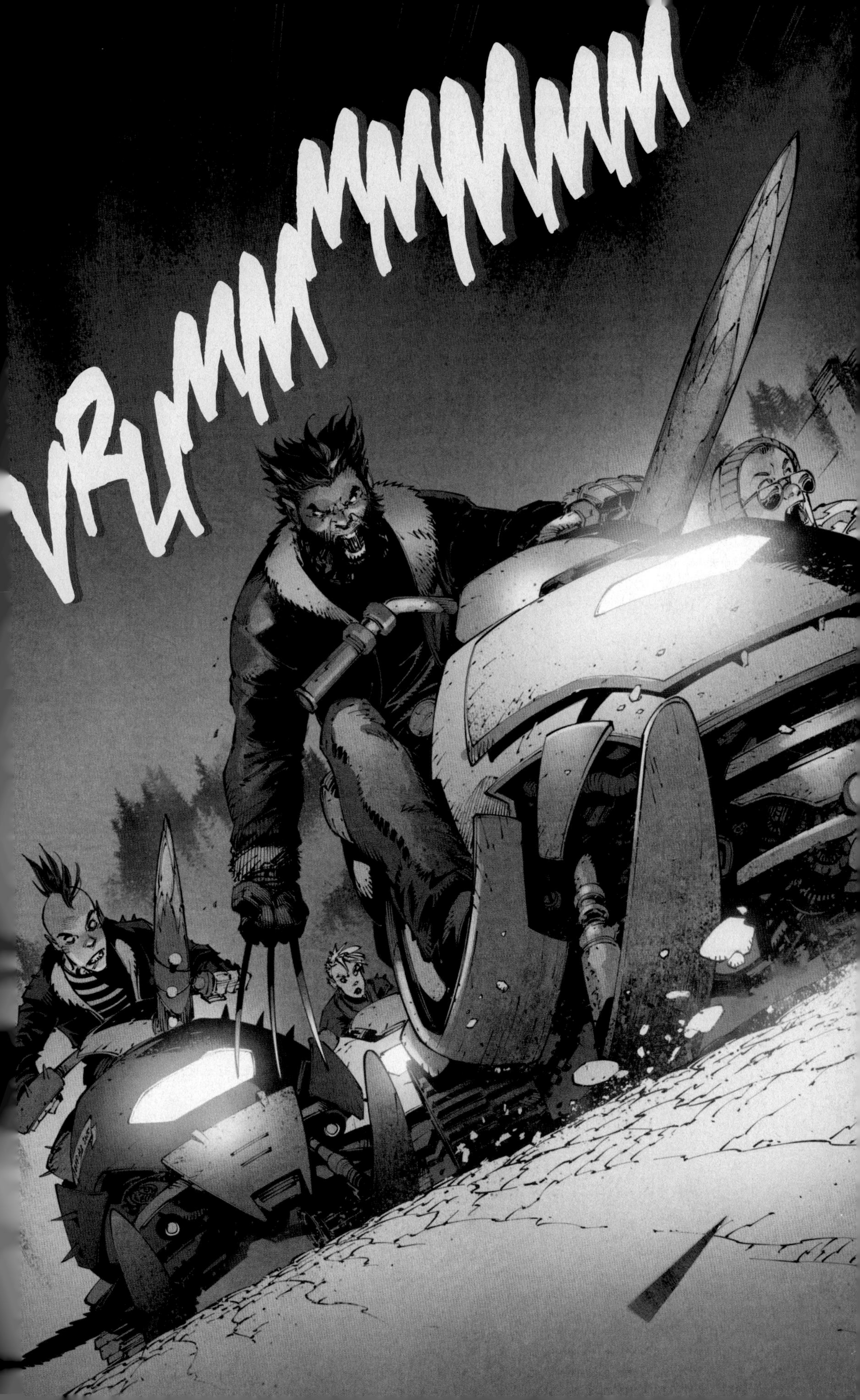
VRUMMMMMMM

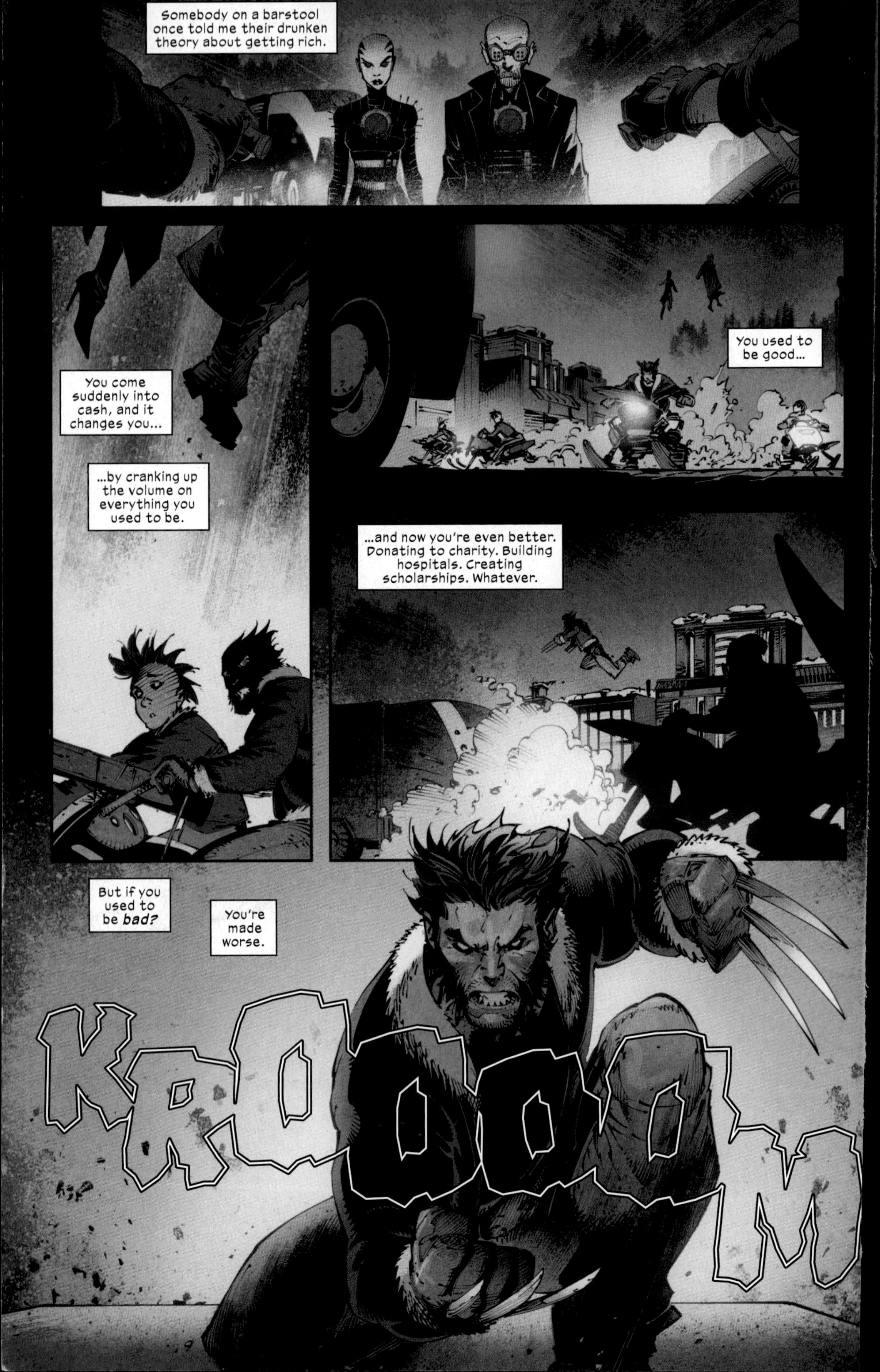
Somebody on a barstool once told me their drunken theory about getting rich.
You come suddenly into cash, and it changes you...
...by cranking up the volume on everything you used to be.
You used to be good...
...and now you're even better. Donating to charity. Building hospitals. Creating scholarships. Whatever.
But if you used to be *bad?*
You're made worse.
KROOOOM

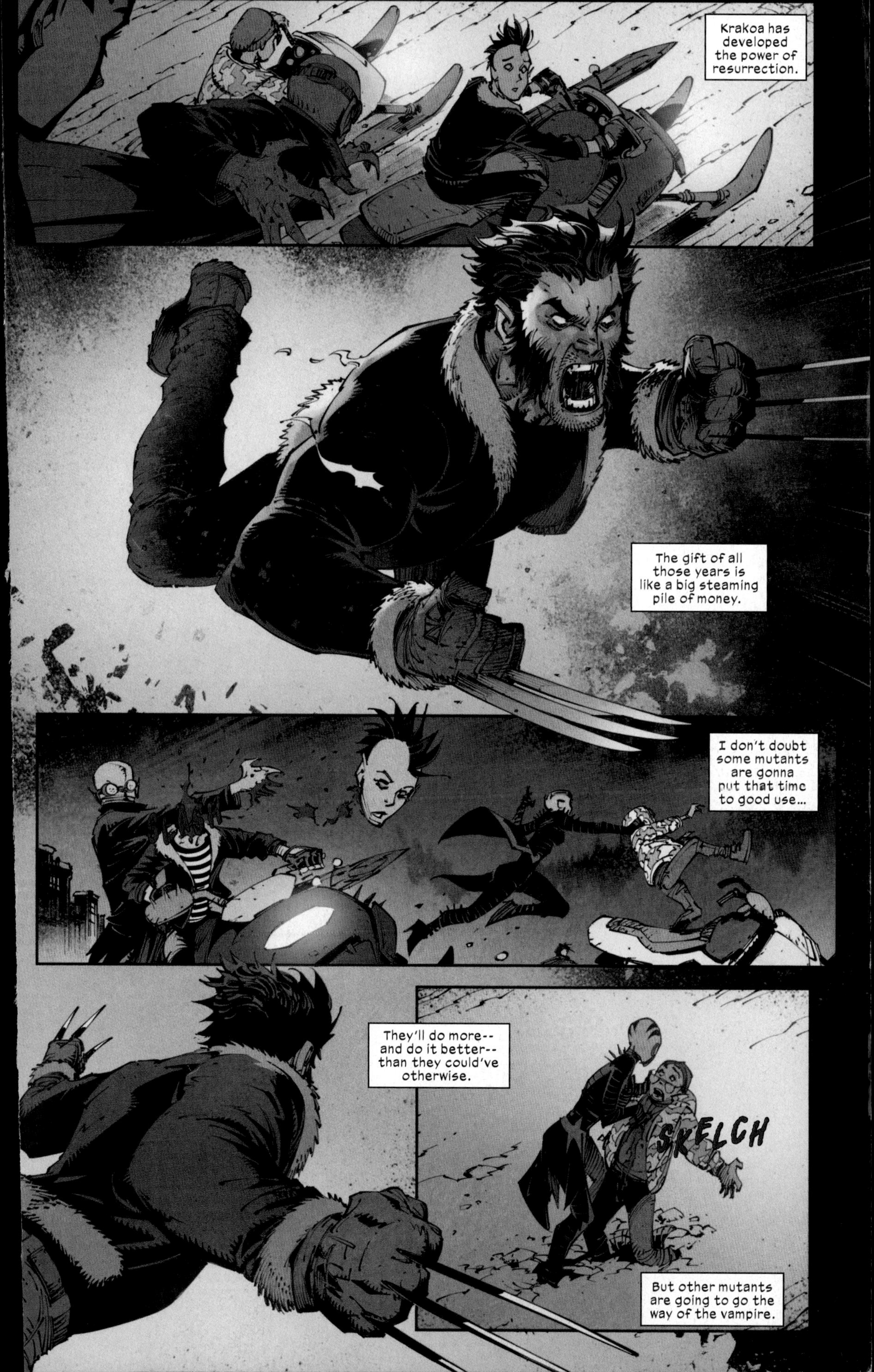
Krakoa has developed the power of resurrection.
The gift of all those years is like a big steaming pile of money.
I don't doubt some mutants are gonna put that time to good use...
They'll do more--and do it better--than they could've otherwise.
SKELCH
But other mutants are going to go the way of the vampire.

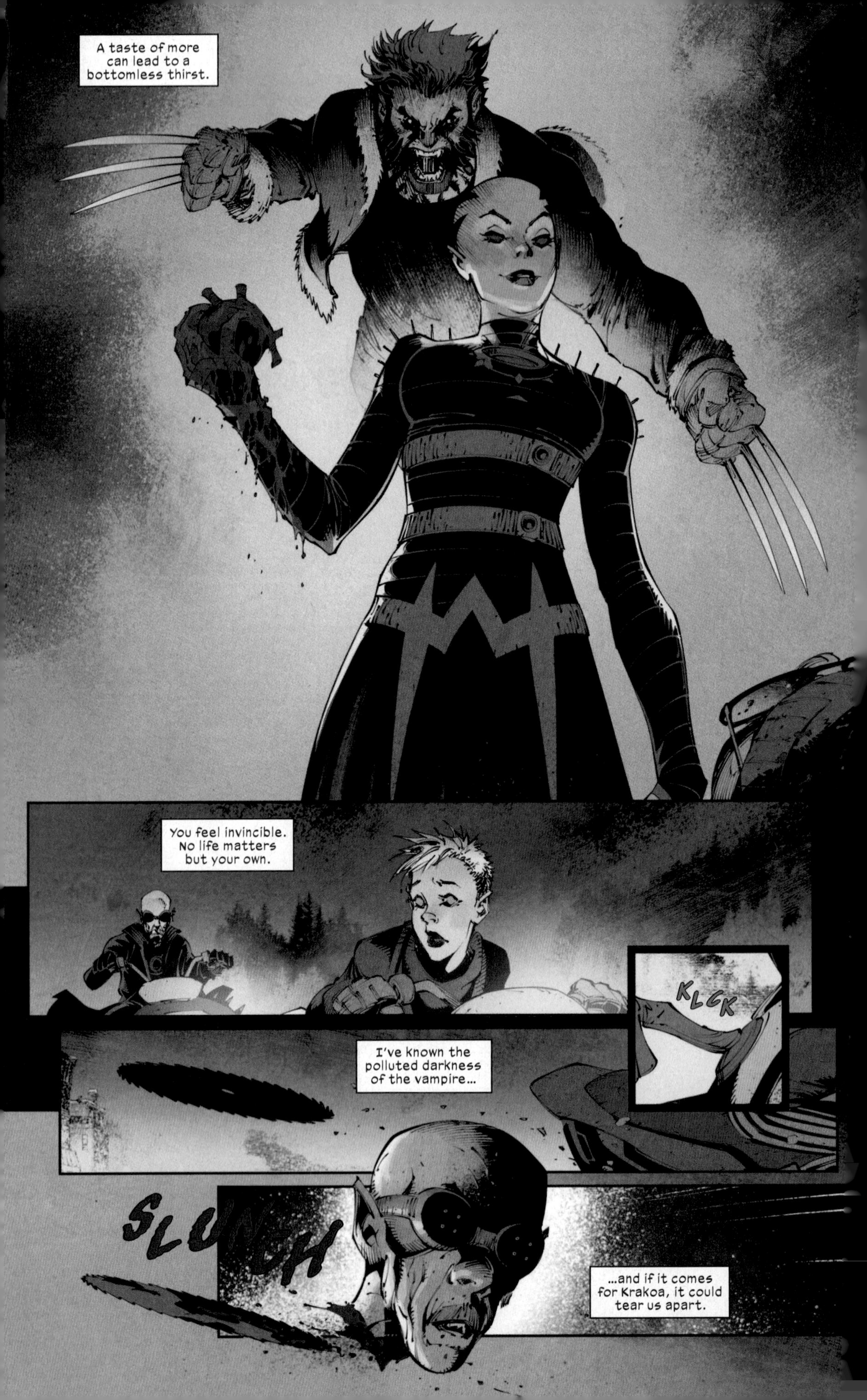
A taste of more can lead to a bottomless thirst.
You feel invincible. No life matters but your own.
KLCK
I've known the polluted darkness of the vampire...
SLUNCH
...and if it comes for Krakoa, it could tear us apart.

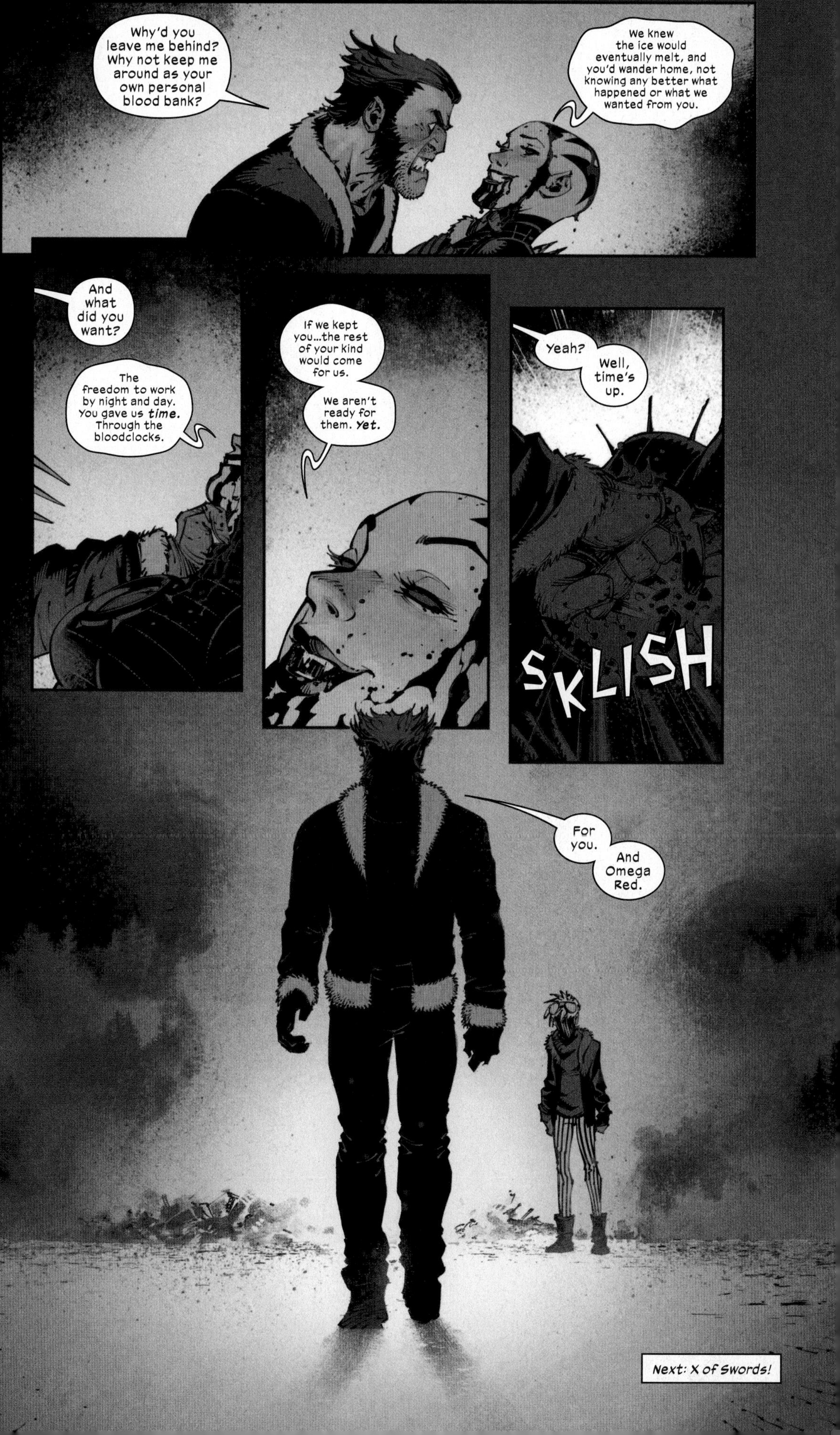
Why'd you leave me behind? Why not keep me around as your own personal blood bank?
We knew the ice would eventually melt, and you'd wander home, not knowing any better what happened or what we wanted from you.
And what did you want?
The freedom to work by night and day. You gave us *time.* Through the bloodclocks.
If we kept you...the rest of your kind would come for us.
We aren't ready for them. *Yet.*
Yeah?
Well, time's up.
SKLISH
For you.
And Omega Red.
Next: X of Swords!

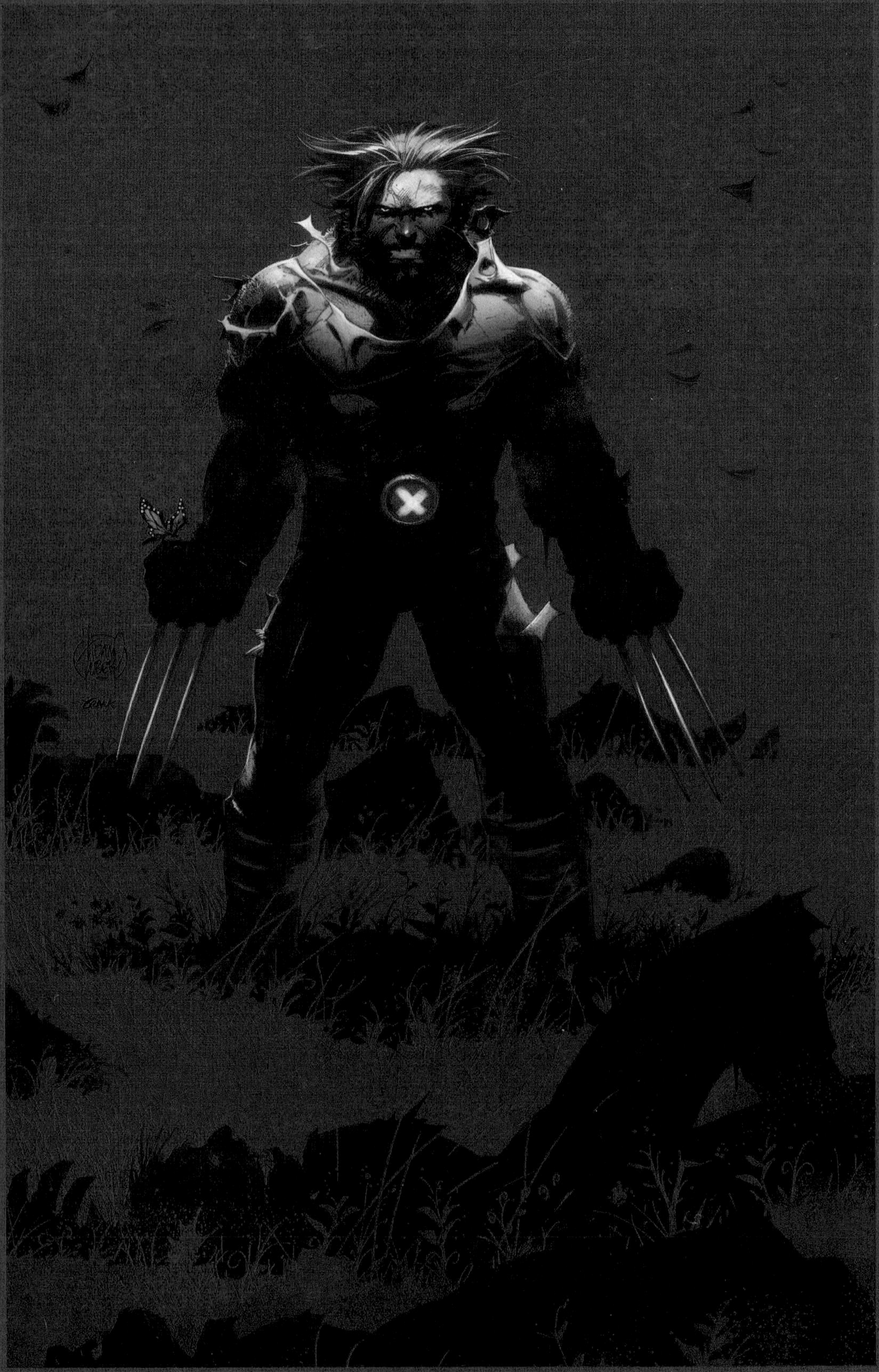

Wolverine #1

by Adam Kubert
& Frank Martin

Wolverine #2

by Adam Kubert
& Frank Martin

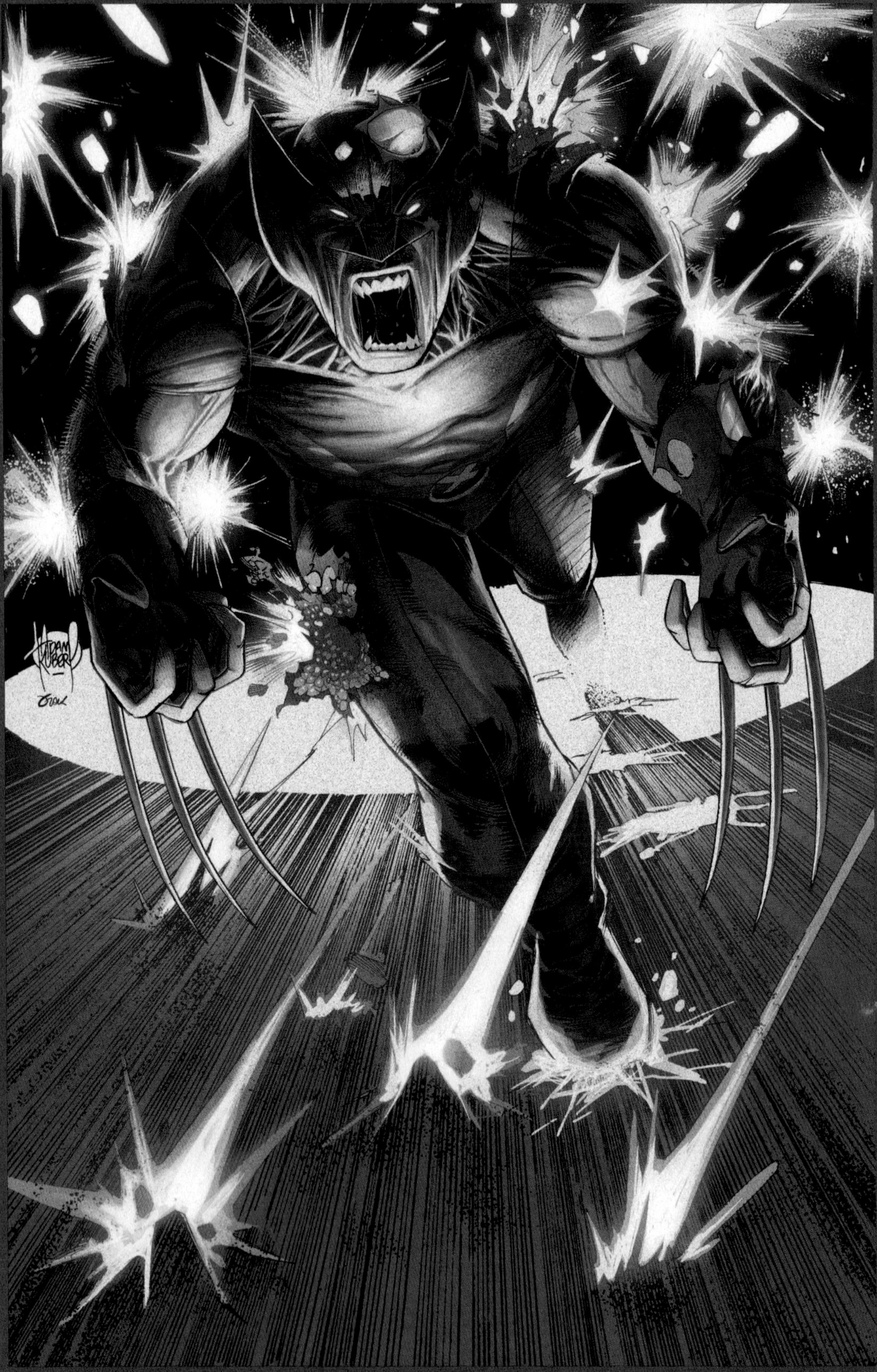

Wolverine #3

by Adam Kubert
& Frank Martin

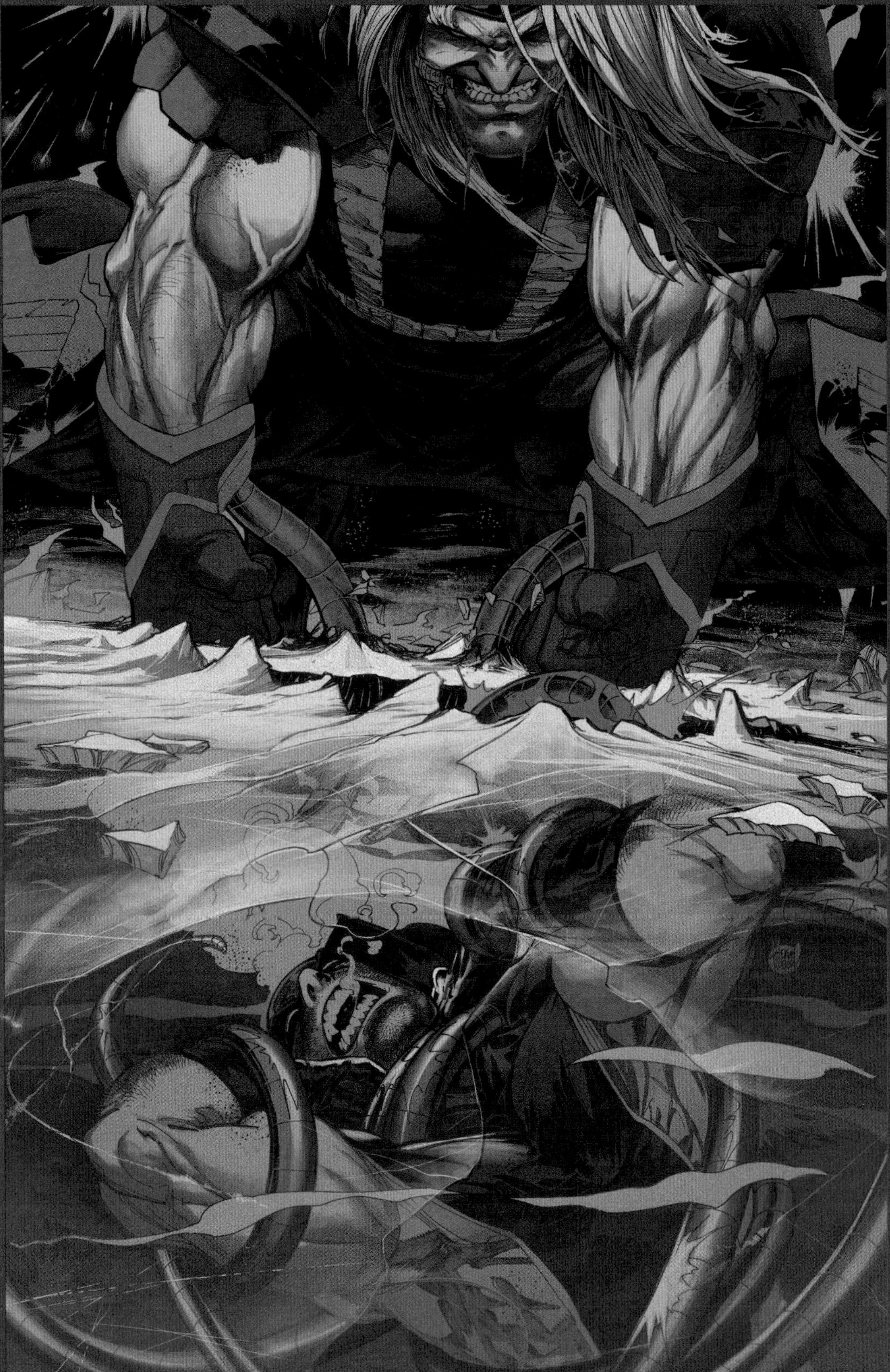

Wolverine #4

by Adam Kubert
& Frank Martin

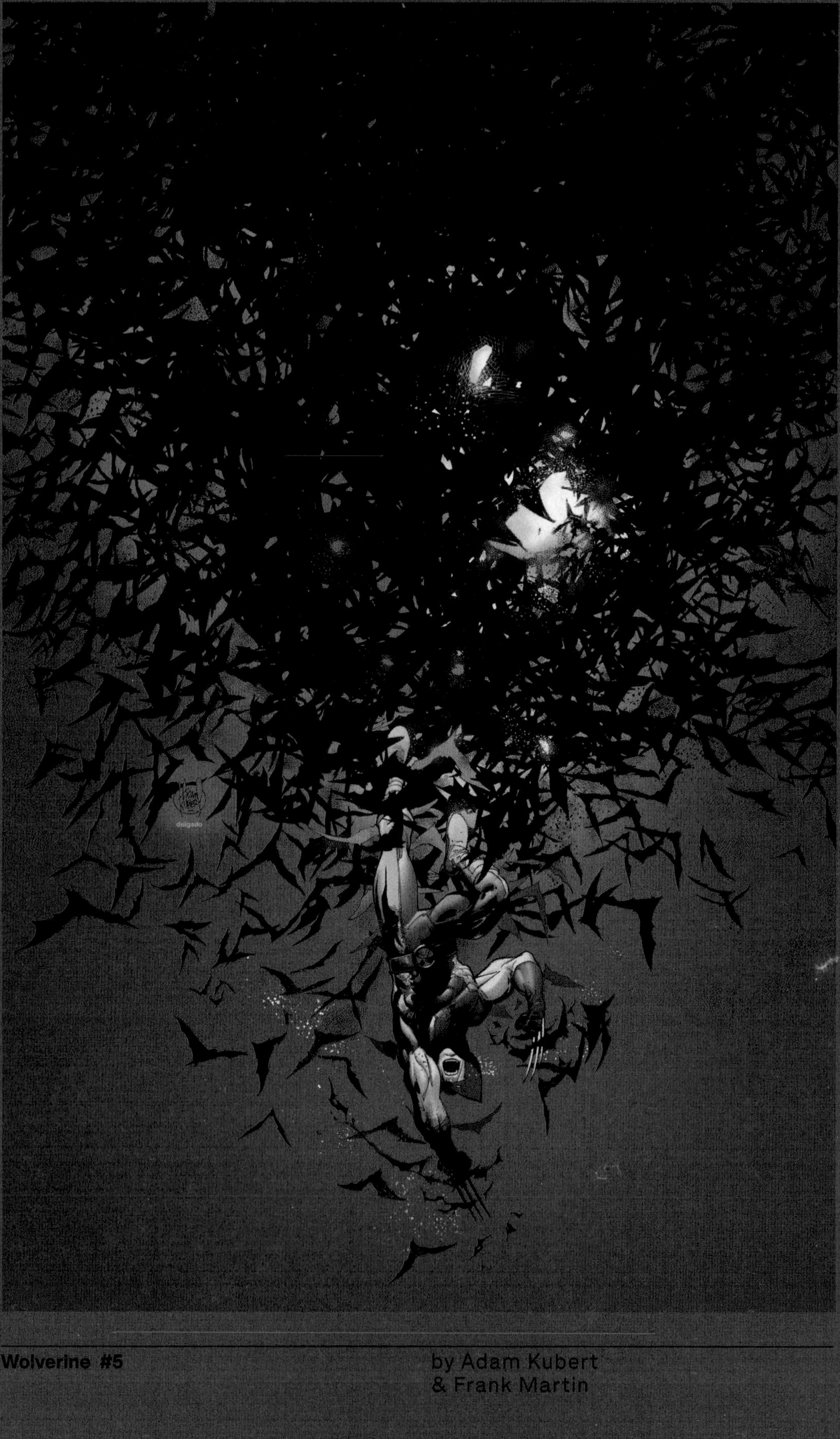

Wolverine #5

by Adam Kubert
& Frank Martin

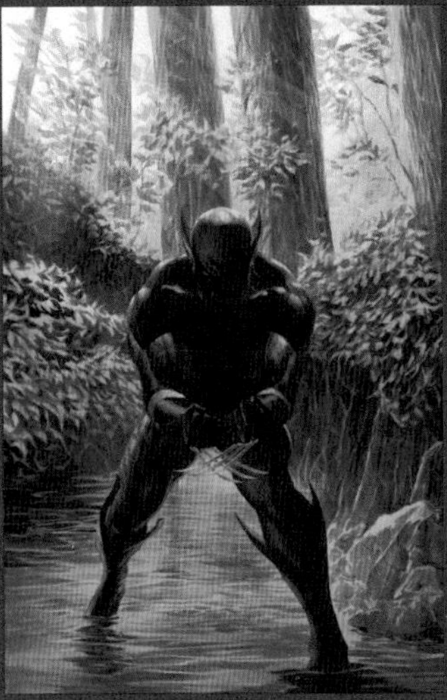

#1 Variant
by Alex Ross

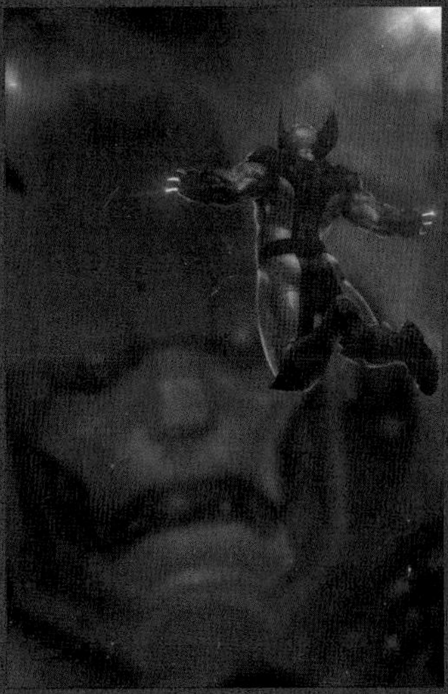

#1 Variant
by Jeehyung Lee

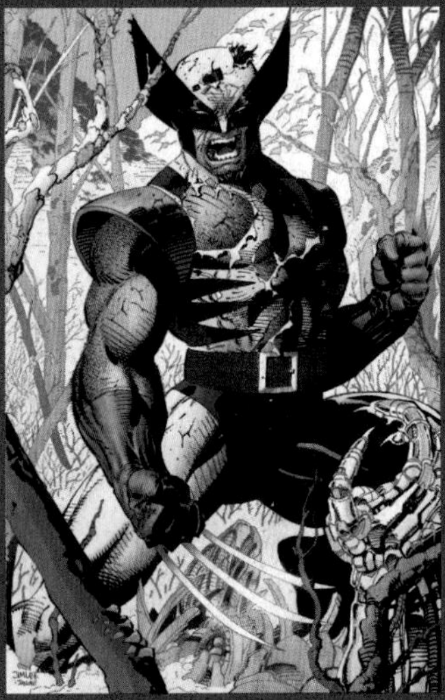

#1 Hidden Gem Variant
by Jim Lee & Jason Keith

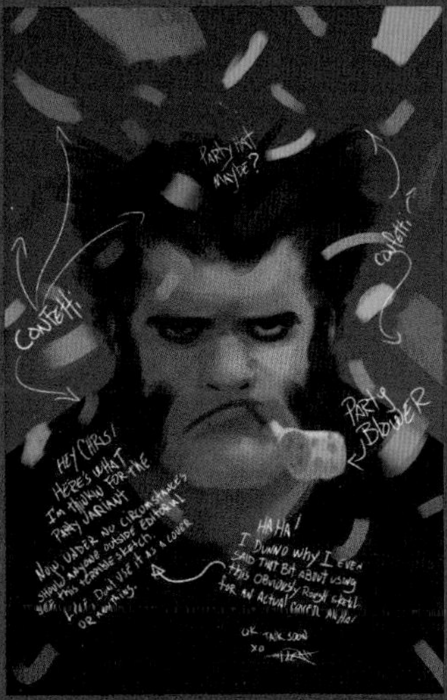
CONFETTI
confetti
PARTY BLOWER

#1 Party Sketch Variant
by Rahzzah

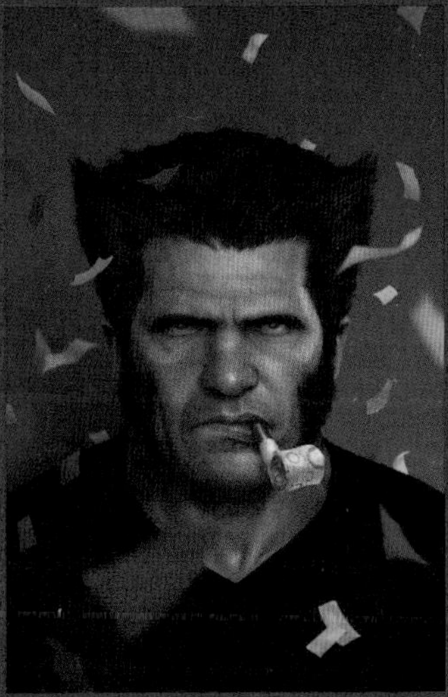

#1 Party Variant
by Rahzzah

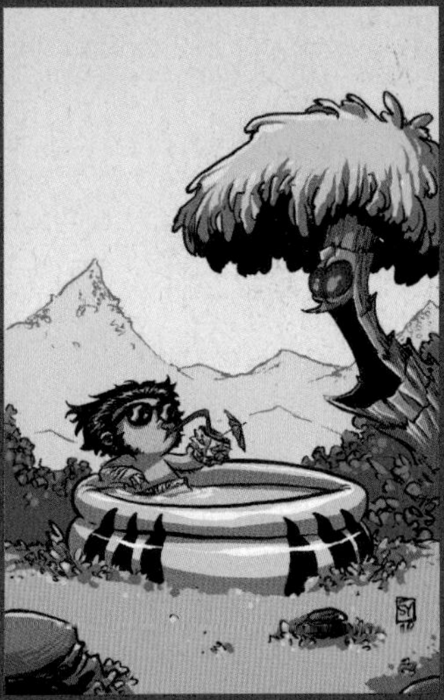

#1 Variant
by Skottie Young

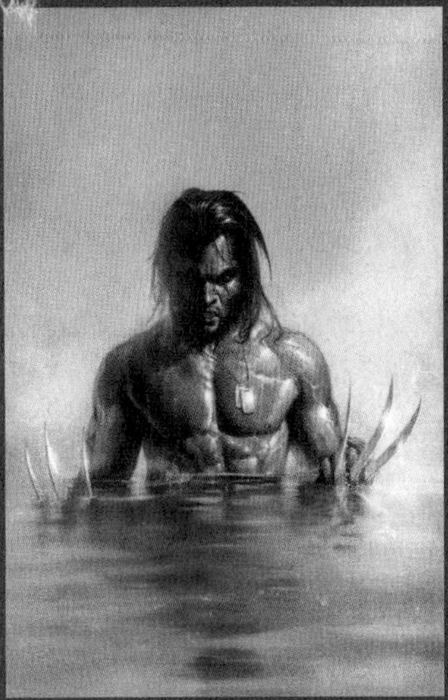

#1 Variant
by Gabriele Dell'Otto

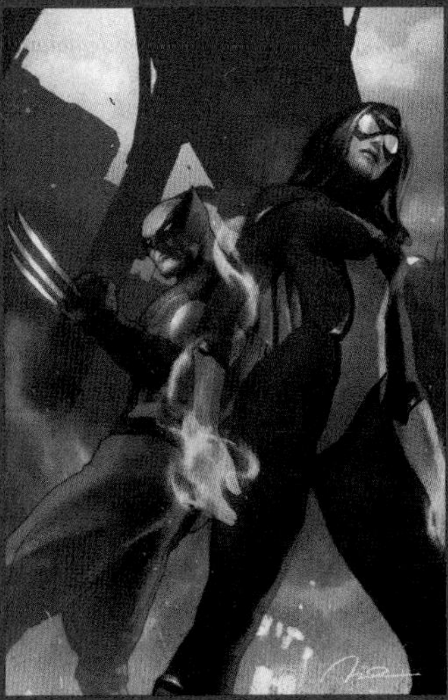

#2 Spider-Woman Variant
by Gerald Parel

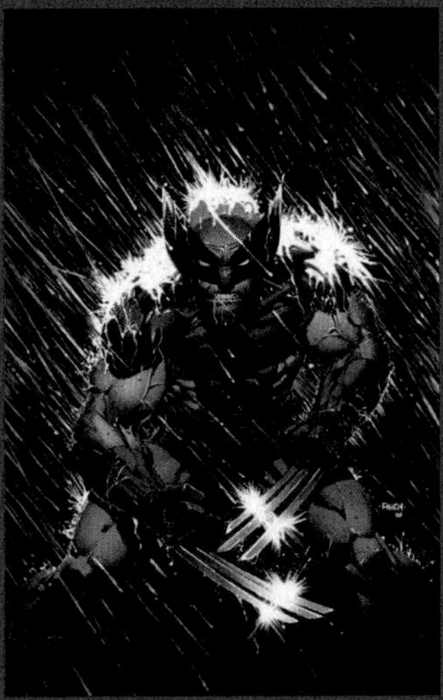

#2 Variant by David Finch & Frank D'Armata

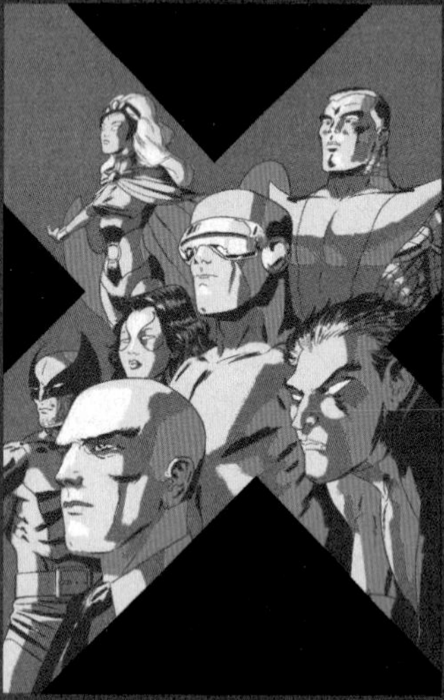

#2 God Loves, Man Kills Variant
by Marcos Martin

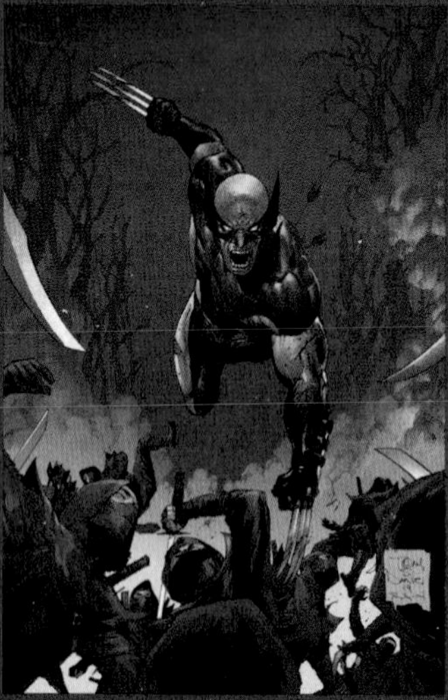

#3 Variant
by Tony Daniel & Rain Beredo

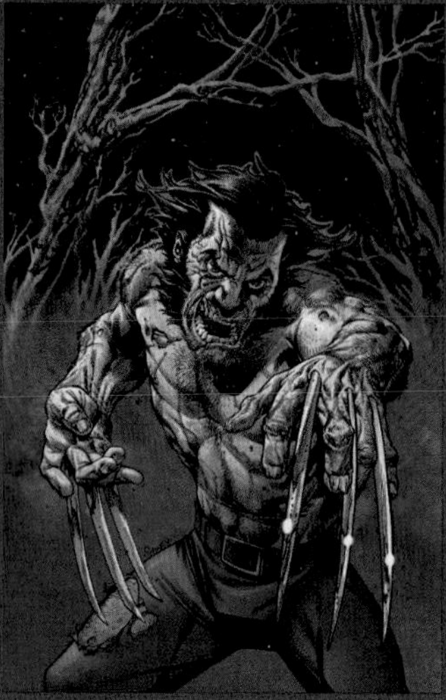

#3 Marvel Zombies Variant
by Tom Raney & Dean White

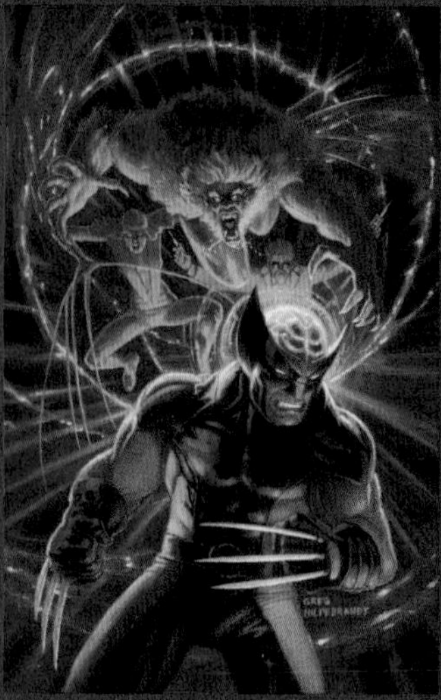

#3 Variant
by Greg Hildebrandt

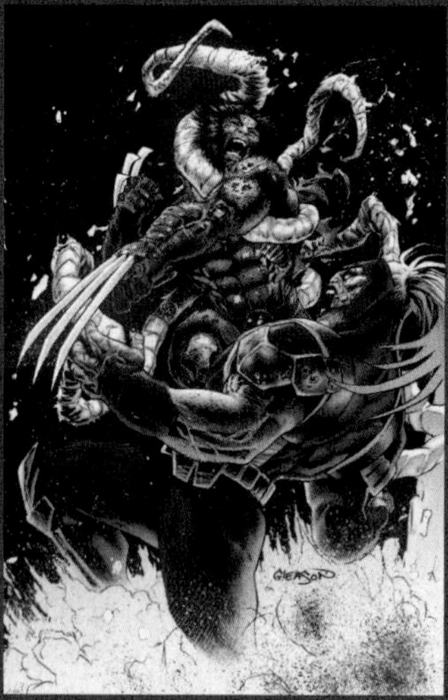

#4 Variant by Patrick Gleason & Morry Hollowell

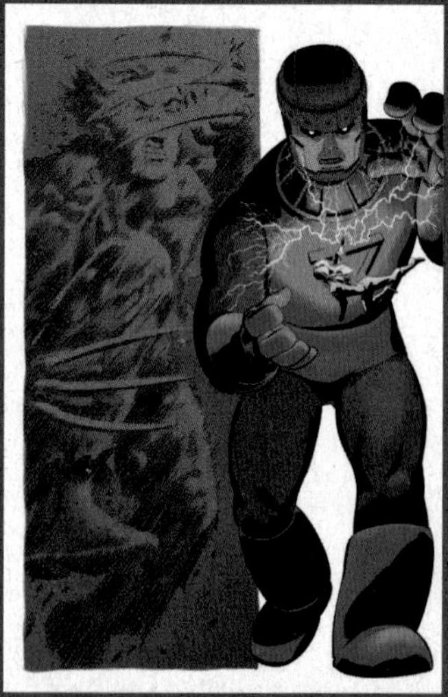

#4 Days of Future Past Variant
by Marcos Martin

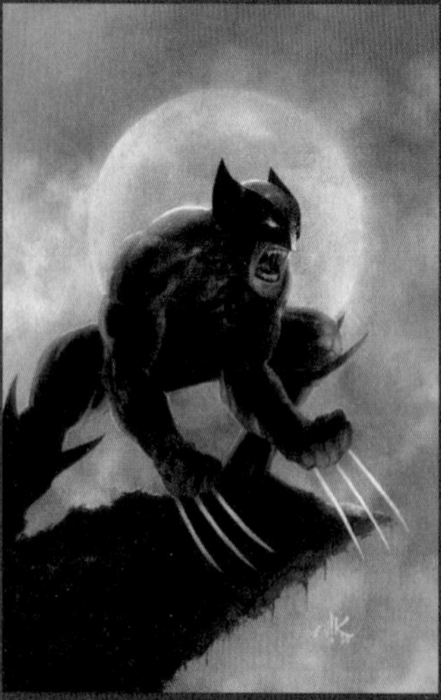

#5 Variant
by Viktor Bogdanovic

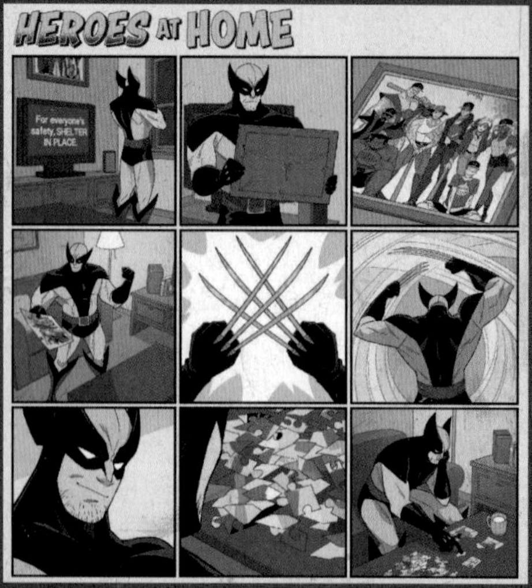
HEROES AT HOME
For everyone's safety, SHELTER IN PLACE.

#5 Heroes at Home Variant
by Gurihiru & Zeb Wells